Sarah's Star Signs

Connecting You To The Cosmos

by
Sarah Delamere Hurding

"We are all in the gutter, but some of us
are looking at the stars."
Oscar Wilde

Also by Sarah Delamere Hurding

StarScope

StarScope with Psychic to the Stars Sarah Delamere Hurding

Sarah correctly predicted the final line up of the pop band Six. Bono called
her in when he was setting up his Kitchen nightclub at
The Clarence, and according to Louis Walsh, she's
"the woman who knows everything."
Now Ireland's top psychic has decided to share her gift in probably
the only horoscope guide you will ever need to buy.
For the inside track on where your love, life, career and health
are heading, keep this by your bedside.
Which celebrity shares your birthday? What lies ahead for you this year? Are
you in the right relationship or are you and your partner
completely incompatible? Are you in the right career?
Where should you go on holiday?

Get your life in balance with Sarah and *StarScope*
Published by *Poolbeg Ireland*.

Wish upon a star!

CONTENTS

CONTENTS

ACKNOWLEDGMENTS
Mollie, Jake, Charlie, Stanley, Ralphie,
Penny, Lottie, Freddie, Harley.
#woof

1 RULING PLANETS

This chapter identifies your Ruling Planet and the various energies that influence your Sun Sign. Use this chapter for added insight on 'the face' you present to the World. Check out the forces that describe your emotional landscape and reveal the uniqueness of your nature. Keep an open mind and prepare to be surprised.

ARIES
March 21st – April 20th

RULING PLANET: MARS

Aries is ruled by the fiery uncompromising planet Mars. This glowing red explosive energy influences sex drive, our competitive streak and physical activity. Mars inspires a warrior like mentality that fires up adrenaline levels and takes no prisoners. Aries therefore possesses a determination to win at all costs. This sign is well equipped to deal with most crisis situations.

The energy of planet Mars inspires the Arian to swift action and the resolution of pressing issues. On the down side Aries struggles with temper flares and a fierce unbending will - good in some situations, but do not rush in where angels fear to tread.

PERSONALITY: Technically Aries is the first sign of the Zodiac and its symbol is The Ram. The Ram represents the beginning of the birthing process - the Zodiac Journey. It charges headlong into life with a big statement: I AM! The Arian determination to beat the pack is legendary. And because of this focus Aries makes an inspirational leader. Arians hate to lose at anything and their dynamic nature ensures that they rarely do.

Aries energy is able to adapt and cope with a great variety of stress and strain. The ability to do several things at once is also an enviable trait. However, the rot sets in when Aries starts to flounder or loses balance. If the Aries personal equilibrium is challenged, the fun begins.

Do be careful of your tendency to lash out verbally or even physically if you feel you are losing your grip, Aries. Stay calm, cool and be assured that you will win, even if it does not always look that way. You have the power and control to influence things in your favor; but only if you remain serene under pressure. Never show the opposition chinks in your armor. Patch them up and get on with the contest.

Watch that stubborn streak too. It would really benefit you to learn how to use charm, words and clever flattery to get your own way. Be careful not to kick and scream when things do not go as you wish. Aries also needs to keep busy and active. You have so much surplus exuberance that it can manifest as restlessness if you do not find an outlet.

Keep things moving and make sure that your vitality is expended on positive and constructive pursuits. Physical activity of any kind helps; be it sexual, sporty, or moving around in a busy job.
Aries has a brilliant sense of humor too. Truly a fireball of energy, activity and fun - quite a combination.

FUTURE CAREER: In work the Arian enthusiasm must be fully engaged or focus gets scattered. Find a job that keeps you on your toes, as Arians love to quite literally think on their feet. Co-ordinating a team of people really suits the leadership qualities of Aries. You must feel valued, independent and indispensable. Not too much to ask for.

When challenged, Aries can be very inventive and is expert at defending territory and interests. Aries copes well under pressure. But if you are Aries be careful not to alienate people with your need to control events and circumstances.

Being a Fire Sign, quite literally a job as fire fighter, metallurgist, or welder would suit. Aries is also brilliant at arts and crafts.

Aries energy links well to the professions of psychiatry, dentistry and psychology. As Aries does not beat about the bush, you can be guaranteed to give a fair and accurate assessment in whatever field you work in.

FUTURE HEALTH: To maintain optimum health, Aries must channel energy wisely. This fire sign is very linked to the 'fight or flight' adrenal glands. Excess restlessness should therefore find a physical outlet. Competitive sports suit Aries, so attempt anything you can go out and win. If there is a trophy to bring home, then it suits you.

Aries may occasionally be troubled by headaches. Keep an eye out for persistent mild headaches that may indicate a secondary kidney problem. Aries is very connected to the head. So it would be a rare Arian who did not experience the odd bash, bump or bruise. Guard against clumsiness. But if you are sporty you can expect sprains and strains every now and again.

Aries is an intrinsically healthy sign. As long as you pay attention with a good, sensible routine not much will go wrong. Stick to savory foods and eat plenty of protein. Be aware that spicy foods introduce too much fire to your system- you have quite enough already! Do the basics of eating, sleeping and exercising hard. Then overall you can look forward to years of good health.

FUTURE LOVE: Aries is a dynamo and falls in love very quickly; or should I say lust? Of all the signs Aries is not backwards about coming forwards. With a dynamic Arian things move quickly. They are quick to show interest when they fancy someone, but they tire just as quickly once the fun is over. Aries has a low tolerance level. And if their ferocious physical appetites are not satiated, there will be problems. Partners have to keep up - or else!

If you are Aries pay a little more attention to the finesse of romantic relationships. Some signs love to be wooed and want love to develop slowly but surely. Unless you can develop some grounding and patience, you are liable to miss out on the subtle nuances of seduction.

Also, be cautious re commitment. Make sure your feelings are going to last before you say "I do." However, if you have found someone who can match your lust, enthusiasm and appetite for life therein is a lasting connection. Hold onto it for dear life. Rarely does such intensity and reciprocity come around twice. So be willing to put in the work and effort once you are settled. Build on equality in your relationships and all will be well. Singletons however should sew their wild oats and proceed with caution. Passion is a seductive feeling of course. But more haste, less speed would not go amiss.

COMPATIBLE SIGNS: Fellow Aries understands your passionate nature. But guard against major rows when stubborn wills clash. Gemini is very suitable and compatible. And Leo is all heart. Sagittarius is a great match in the bedroom. But things could get boring quickly. Scorpio is a sexy sign but the Scorpion need to be in control could trouble Aries. Ideally, Aries should avoid Taurus 24/7. But it can work if independence is respected. Pisces is way too intense and overly romantic - the language of love is just too different.

BIRTH STONE: Diamond.
COLORS: Reds and gold.
ZODIAC NUMBER: 5
FAMOUS SEXY ARIANS: Warren Beatty, Vic Reeves, Victoria Beckham, Chris Evans, Elton John, Russell Crowe, Mariah Carey, Eddie Murphy, Joan Crawford, Celine Dion, Charlie Chaplin, Marlon Brando, Vincent Van Gogh, John Major, Quentin Tarantino, Vivienne Westwood, Colin Farrell.

TAURUS
April 21st – May 21st

RULING PLANET: VENUS

Venus is the planet that engages our feelings. This emotional energy challenges the way we relate to each other socially and financially. Venus heightens the connection between our romantic and economic relationships. She demonstrates that everything is inter-linked. According to this Ruling Planet: love, money, sex and material possessions are irretrievably married - for better or for worse.

Venus emphasises partnerships, professional and personal. If you are Taurus, notice how your attitudes concerning money reflect in your attitudes re love and romance. This may sound particularly mercenary. But remember Taurus is a practical Zodiac sign that oozes common sense. Love comes at a price with Taurus.

PERSONALITY: Taurus is the second Zodiac sign. The keynote of The Bull is "I have". This methodical creature needs to roam the pastures, assess the landscape, graze and generally plod around. Taureans are loyal and respect their own. Eternally charming, they cover their tracks in the nicest possible way. Taurus is one of the Zodiac's nifty movers.

There is definitely an emphasis on material goods with this sign. Possessions represent stability and safety for Taurus; for when surrounded with the trappings of wealth, Taurus can take on the world. Material decadence amounts to self-confidence and pride for this Earth sign.

Aside from an innate natural charm, Taurus is prone to possessiveness. With their need for security and surety, Bulls are sticklers for control. Taureans need to know where they stand, and that everything is going to be "just so," shake their financial foundation or threaten the Status Quo, and you can expect short shrift.

Never corner a Taurean, if you know what is good for you. Ever heard of the 'red rag to a Bull'? Once 'level headed' Taurus loses its temper, you can expect a stampede. So it is best to allow this fixed sign to rule the roost in a laid back, easy manner.

Taureans are not the Zodiac's chief risk takers. They will gamble only on a sure thing. And like to see proof of a return before an investment is made be it emotional, financial or romantic.

Your Taurean birth right ensures oodles of patience, beauty and charisma. You can truly charm the birds from the trees. What you say is always interesting. For you have a natural intelligence and instinctual understanding of life. You are methodical, systematic and deliberate in your gestures. Just be careful not to take advantage of that seductive ability.

If you are Taurus avoid unnecessary or prolonged stress by facing things as and when they arise. Do not buy into proverbial Ostrich behaviour. Or hide your head in the sand when the going gets rough.

FUTURE CAREER: Taurus loves a steady routine with predictable hours and no upsets. The ability to organize a wide range of people, items, and functions means that many careers are suitable. If you are Taurus, never work with someone who wants to run the show or control the proceedings. For this will drive you quite mad, as you need to feel indispensable.

With the emphasis on all things material and financial, Taurus possesses a great propensity to make money. Being great bankers, the large co-operations suit this methodical mentality.

Taureans are disciplined and anxious to succeed. For the fulfillment of ambitions provides the necessary stability which Taurus holds so dear.

Naturals in the world of beauty or luxury items, Taurus has aesthetic taste and a nose for classic items. And since Bulls are naturally linked to the Earth, suitable careers are agriculture, farming, and architecture.

Taureans are wonderfully musical. So expect chart success and major accolades when you express your creativity.

FUTURE HEALTH: Taureans have a natural grace and beauty that often inspires jealousy in others. But, your love of food makes you prone to weight gain if you are not careful. Rich foods are the bug-bear of your existence. So go easy on the sauces, chocolate and sweets. Plenty of fresh fruit and vegetables will keep your system revved up and working more efficiently – Lay off the gunk!

Exercise is crucial for Taurus, as your metabolism is rather slow. You also respond well to a regular gym routine. The repetitive movements of weight training suit you. And you can expect good results quite quickly. Taurus loves the after-glow of a sensuous massage and sauna. But the discipline of the workout must come first.

Taurus is connected to the voice and neck. So do guard against sore throats and voice problems. Also, keep an eye on thyroid function, especially if you notice weight gain you cannot account for - be honest about the cream buns whilst making your assessment.

FUTURE LOVE: Natural good looks and bucket-loads of charm enable the Bull to play the field; and have the pick of the crop. But Taurus is rarely in a hurry to connect. This earthy creature wants to be sure of a good thing first - those security issues again! Marriage brings the 'safe' feeling that loyalty and commitment provide. And once committed, Taurus tends not to stray. Well not when anyone is watching anyhow.

There is no escaping the compelling Taurean. Sounds ominous? Well it can be. For when Taurus is off balance, there are issues of possession and an obsessive tendency can ruin otherwise healthy relationships.

Taurus finds it difficult to let go, and needs to express anger and frustration vocally. For if emotions become blocked the eventual explosion is not a pretty sight. Never treat loved ones and friends as possessions. Learn to respect their freedom and independence…your loyalty will be well rewarded. A great provider, and seriously dependable; you make an ideal partner for those who want security, safety and material stability.

Romantic gestures come easy to Taurus and you are the stuff dreams are made of. No Zodiac sign is as sensual, intense and romantic all at the same time. What is your number?

COMPATIBLE SIGNS: Earth signs Virgo and Capricorn are true Soul Mates. They understand your need for reliability, grounding and sensual expression. Scorpio, your opposite provides a powerful telepathic link - sexy too! Leo is good fun and looks great. And Pisces is something of a loose cannon. Aries does is not a good idea 24/7 – it could end in tears. Aquarius is detached and missing the TLC factor. And Sagittarius is too unpredictable and flighty. Cancer and Libra are good friends, but too different. And go easy with fellow Taurus – a potential clash of the Titans.

BIRTH STONE: Emerald.
COLORS: Pale Blue and Greens, Also Pink.
ZODIAC NUMBER: 6
FAMOUS SEXY TAUREANS: Jack Nicolson, Al Pacino, Michael Palin, Shirely Maclaine, Bianca Jagger, Cher, Andrea Corr, Bono, Michelle Pfeiffer, Meryl Streep, Diana Ross, Priscilla Presley, Sigmund Freud, Pope Jean Paul II, Queen Elizabeth II, William Shakespeare, Buddah, James Brown, Barbara Streisand, George Clooney, Karl Marx, Orson Welles, Salvador Dali, David Beckham, Tony Blair, Jean Paul Gaultier, Andre Agassi, Janet Jackson, Pierce Brosnan.

GEMINI
May 22nd – June 22nd

RULING PLANET: MERCURY

Mercury's influence is cerebral and lively. This Planet's position is the best indicator of the way a person's mind works. Mercury is a small but potent planet that impacts our intelligence and thought patterns. Mental agility may be instinctive, logical, slow and deliberate, or somewhat scattered. Whether we are intuitive or excruciatingly systematic in our thinking, Mercury provides the clue.

Mercury enhances our ability to make decisions. And it also determines how we communicate. It is no wonder that Gemini's have such lively minds and original ways of thinking. Their interest in a great diversity of people, places and subjects also reflects Mercury's activity.

PERSONALITY: Gemini is the third Zodiac sign represented by The Twins. The keynote of Gemini is "I think". Consequently, the mental plane is the main domain of this cerebral sign. The Twins inhabit an 'airy' environment. So a certain amount of duality is inevitable. It goes with the territory, and makes Gemini a challenging and stimulating sign to relate to.

Gemini can do several things at once - always useful! In fact the more external 'mental' activity this sign engages in, the better; reading many books, thinking about diverse and varied subjects. And setting themselves mind-blowing tasks keeps Gemini amused. Concentration is the 'bug-bear' of Gemini existence.

An innate restlessness combined with a predisposition to boredom means that Gemini is difficult to entertain. Living with such in-built duality is a job in itself. And Gemini's need to utilize strengths and develop patience in order to retain sanity.

Gemini is likely to gloss over subjects and does not take kindly to dredging up emotive issues. This nifty avoidance inspires accusations of superficiality; and Gemini is inclined to be flippant when bored. On the plus side, Gemini is eminently entertaining and guaranteed fun. Not much will destroy this determined sensibility that looks for the good in everything.

The Gemini destiny demands a lively lifestyle. But Gemini is inclined to live on frayed nerves. This expends a lot of energy and can spread Gemini - who wants to get everything done yesterday - a bit thin. At its best the Gemini mind is constructive, optimistic and keen. However, Gemini is capable of deception, fraud and underhand behaviour in a bid to stay amused.

Gemini recognises the complexity of life and the human tendency to wriggle. So rarely does this sign trust implicitly. This of course puts the question mark permanently over their behaviour, if we are to believe the validity of projection.

FUTURE CAREER: Gemini is liable to quietly insane unless permanently stimulated. A predictable routine is virtual suicide for a sign that needs endless entertainment. Something must hold Gemini's attention, or it is not worthy of that attention.

Never settle for tedious work that makes you feel ungrounded, or tired, Gemini. You must be energized by the task in hand. Or expect copious amounts of hot air to be expended in frustration.

Many leading surgeons, counsellors and psychotherapists are Gemini. And for those who like to bounce ideas around, teaching and lecturing are perfect.

Communications, media work and publishing are tailor made...And the Internet holds endless possibilities, as does the travel industry. The ideal career involves a laptop, travel and the requirement to speak on the phone several times a day.

Film work or creative work behind the camera is OK in theory. But Gemini has to be focused and determined to make it to Hollywood.

FUTURE HEALTH: Gemini is essentially a lithe, wiry, healthy person. But the tendency to get over stressed should be tempered. Correct channeling of energy is crucial to Gemini health. And any activity that expends excess or frantic stress is to be indulged.

Gemini tends to have a high metabolism. But can become slow and sluggish if bored, listless, or unfulfilled. A happy Gemini is a slim, fit and lively individual – a stimulating mind encapsulated in an 'airy' body. The Twin with the sulky face however, can be overweight, over indulgent and very wasteful of time, food, and money.

Vigorous daily exercise keeps Gemini at the peak of fitness. For both mind and body benefit from a strict routine. Anything that enables Gemini to feel the wind in their hair is recommended. Cycling, hang gliding, parachuting, running, and racket sports offer the variety Gemini needs.

Gemini rules the lungs – So do not even think about smoking. And since Gemini influences the shoulders, arms and hands, the avoidance of broken limbs is also highly recommended.

FUTURE LOVE: It is relatively easy for Gemini to make the moves when they are attracted to someone. These great communicators of the Zodiac possess a fine imagination. Charming, witty and creative, not much stands in the way of Gemini on the prowl.

Over time however, Gemini's dual nature is a potential spanner in the works. Along with their low boredom threshold…An immature Gemini finds the battle to settle down a constant struggle. Indeed, complete faithfulness is a rare achievement for those with lashings of Gemini energy.

Partners of Gemini have to understand their need to fulfil restless urges. Or at least permit a semblance of freedom. The looser the leash, the more likely it is Gemini will stay true, so it certainly does not pay to mistrust or nag Gemini.

With Gemini, the risks are worth it. For Gemini is great at expressions of heart felt love. Gemini is not afraid to verbalise feelings, and indeed may astound many with the speed at which they fall madly in (and out) of love. Also, sexually Gemini make for lively and imaginative bedfellows. Complaints in the 'boudoir' department are unlikely.

Gemini needs to avoid the slippers and sofas syndrome at all costs.

COMPATIBLE SIGNS: Aries is a great match - these two can be best friends as well as lovers. Fellow Gemini understands; whilst Aquarius has intelligence and detachment, which keeps the interest up. Cancer is far too emotional and needy. And there is a lot of game playing and potential deceit re Pisces. Virgo and Capricorn are way too staid, organized, and predictable for flighty Gemini. But Scorpio and Sagittarius present a challenge. Scorpio is the seducer and Gemini will play along. And Sagittarius is playful, but too fiery.

BIRTH STONE: Agate.
COLORS: Bright colors, Yellow in particular.
ZODIAC NUMBER: 7.
FAMOUS SEXY GEMINIS: Julian Clary, Kylie Minogue, Nicole Kidman, Liz Hurley, Mark Walberg, Denise Van Outen, Tom Jones, Sir Paul Mc Cartney, Mel B, Bob Dylan, Clint Eastwood, Brooke Shields, Marilyn Monroe, Judy Garland, Bob Hope, William Butler Yeats, Queen Victoria, Henry Kissinger, John F Kennedy, Naomi Campbell.

CANCER
June 23rd – July 23rd

RULING PLANET: THE MOON

The Moon influences our lives at a profound level. Her powerful lunar energy has an amazing impact on our creativity. Both our psyche and energy are invariably affected. And depend upon her current phase and position.

The Moon connects us to the feminine aspect, regardless of our natal sex. The nurturing energies of The Moon define our parenting skills, and emotional impulses. Its gentle but relentless force shapes our familial and domestic arrangements.

Lunar inspiration affects intuition, instinctual reactions; and the ebb and flow of our feelings. Moon energy rules the changing tides of the sea. But she also governs the twists and turns of our behavior patterns.

PERSONALITY: Cancer is the fourth Zodiac sign represented by The Crab. The keynote of Cancer is "I feel". The personality of this Crustacean is difficult to describe. Defensive at apparently illogical times, Cancer is still one of the most loving, open Zodiac signs. The innate 'Crabby' tendency at unpredictable moments only adds to the fun.

Cancer is a receptive and highly sensitive sign, capable of huge empathy. The Crab cuts to the chase, giving oodles of love, care and reassurance when required. Moody and unfathomable, maybe...But win Cancer's trust and you ensure a lifetime of friendship and support.

It is very easy to get on the wrong side of Cancer. Even casual, cutting remarks can have a devastating effect on the sensitised Crab. Be warned! Cancer is very black and white when someone wrongs them. There is no negotiation, and no reprieve - You are history.

When off balance, Cancer can be its own worst enemy. A born worrier, The Crab can get quite worked up about silly details and arrangements. This sign is not great at going with the flow. Worries can become quite irrational, and self-defeating.

Cancer need to be nurtured, loved and treasured in order to flourish. Only when they feel secure do they reach peak form. Shake their foundation and surety? Cancer will beat a hasty retreat, ignoring you thereafter.

The contents of the Cancer brain are vivid, lively, and entertaining. Prepare to be greatly amused. The Crab possesses a wicked sense of humor; plus an uncanny ability to see through fabrication, and deception.

There is a touch of genius about Cancer; hence the temperamental nature. Cancer is creative with an incredible imagination, which often feeds unpredictable reactions. Obviously, Mr or Miss Crabby is liable to make a mountain out of a molehill, when under pressure.

If you are Cancer, learn to channel your imagination in constructive and positive ways. For, when you are inventive and focused, few can match your original, impressive demeanor.

FUTURE CAREER: Cancer should emphasize career enjoyment rather than riches and wealth. When the correct life path is found, 'filthy lucre' inevitably rolls in. But Cancer comes unstuck when overly focused upon finances and security issues.

In work, The Crab's creativity requires an outlet. However, Cancer also needs routine, and responds well to structure. Continuity is important, as well as variety and change. Cancer loves to be surprised and stimulated, but not unnerved or disarmed.

Cancer is astute with a keen nose for business. This sign is shrewd, and can turn anything into a profit-making venture.

Since Cancer has a great connection to the past, and is the traditional hoarder of the Zodiac, the Antique and Fine Art disciplines make sense too. The caring and pampering professions allow Cancer to nurture and inspire others; and Crabs are often great cooks, who love the whole foody thing.

This creature's natural habitat is the open sea. So work on cruise ships, freight carriers and ferries fulfil the need for adventure combined with security of tenure.

FUTURE HEALTH: Cancer is generally healthy with a strong constitution. But stress and rumination are the scourge of this lunar creature. Ruled by The Moon, routines with an eastern or spiritual origin are particularly beneficial. Yoga, swimming, and aerobics help Cancer channel energy constructively.

Do not panic about the connection between Zodiac Cancer and the disease of the same name - there no link. However, be responsible and keep up with routine checks of the breast and chest area.

When you are off-balance a stomach upset is the main event! So do monitor your reaction to different foods. For if your system is over stressed or sensitized you are more prone to Intolerance. Rotate foods, and keep an eye on cravings.

Cancer skin is particularly sensitive, and prone to itchiness or rashes of untraceable origin. A dietary approach plus attempts to de-stress will help you manage.

For optimum health, Crabs should listen to heart, body, and soul at all times. Never doubt those inner rumblings.

FUTURE LOVE: Cancer thrives on the nurturing possibilities of Love connections. But strong and powerful emotions should be monitored, or The Crab risks overwhelming the object of their affection.

Cancer is a true romantic who enjoys being wooed and seduced. However, domesticity may set in, if the urge to nurture and protect takes precedence. Crab's should maintain their independence. And so guarantee a lifetime of intensity and passion.

If you are Cancer, be flexible within your relationships, and allow for development and change. Protect yourself, or you may feel left behind and abandoned when love moves on. Respect freedom. There is no point drowning someone in kindness. Besides, your wonderfully warm sensuality and ability to 'tune in' will keep them coming back for more.

You are an expressive and brilliant lover. Guard your heart though, for you are quite sensitive and susceptible. Always make sure that your affections are reciprocated, before you get in too deep.

Temper the urge to be overly sentimental about the past, for this may hamper your progress in the present. Current relationships do not respond well to a persistent potted history of past encounters. For sanity's sake, discard those rose tinted spectacles.

COMPATIBLE SIGNS: Fellow Crab is a match made in heaven. Whilst Virgo is a stabilizing influence and support. Scorpio is a whirlwind in the bedroom. And Pisces is a lot of fun with a wicked sense of humor. Taurus is a compelling partner though there will be differences of opinion! Capricorn is reliable and steady. But on balance is probably too austere and cold. Leo will get distracted and not be able to give full time attention. Gemini is too flirty, though shares a sense of humor. Air signs do not measure up.

BIRTH STONE: Pearl, Moonstone.
COLORS: Pale Blue, Silver, Sea Greens and Greys.
ZODIAC NUMBER: 2.
FAMOUS SEXY CANCERIANS: Pamela Anderson, James Cagney, George Michael, Neil Morrissey, Mike Tyson, Dani Behr, Courtney Love, Richard Branson, Harrison Ford, Robin Williams, Tom Cruise, Princess Diana, Nelson Mandela, Gareth Gates, Michael Flatley, Louis Walsh.

LEO
July 24th –August 23rd

RULING PLANET: THE SUN

The Sun is the most luminous and obvious "planet" in the sky. Down the aeons The Sun has been worshipped for its Life giving Force. Without The Sun we would not exist and our lives would have no warmth, heat or sustenance. The Sun is the centre of our World, and the Universe. All the other Ruling Planets revolve around it.

The Sun enhances and emphasizes our primal instincts. It heightens a person's power, and lends them an air of ultimate authority. Ego issues go hand in hand with those ruled by The Sun - it could be no other way! But The Sun also ensures great generosity and a magnanimous attitude. Along with an open heart and sunny disposition, those ruled by The Sun are difficult to resist.

PERSONALITY: Leo is the fifth Zodiac sign represented by The Lion. The keynote of The Lion is "I Create." The Leo personality loves to be adored and is compelled to find a kingdom over which to rule. Leo is the performer of the Zodiac who needs a 'spot' in which to shine. It is inevitable that Leo will stumble into the limelight. For there is no place to run and hide once The Sun comes out.

Leo takes enormous pride in achievement. And The Lion is typically deserving of accolades and reverential treatment. Spells of depression last but a moment. For The Lion is eternally optimistic. Leo does not buy into negativity or toxic thinking; and is not prone to self-sabotage.

Natural serenity, dignity and regal grandeur identify Leo; who makes an entrance, even when incognito.

Life must be experienced to the MAX according to Leo. The Lion does not waste energy ruminating about the past, or feeding off regrets. Every moment is savored and heightened for complete sensation. Leo is prone to hedonism; and loves to luxuriate in comfortable surroundings indulging an inherent laziness.

Leo is a master at energizing a team, task or situation. For it is difficult to feel down cast in the face of such a sunny, jolly disposition. But Leo must also be very careful not to antagonize. Unruly

Leo can be quite argumentative. And there is certainly an air of natural authority that comes with the Leo buzz. Leo should watch out - Mistakes are made when bloody-minded arrogance goes to the leonine head.

If you are Leo it is advisable to develop some tolerance and flexibility. Leave things to unfold organically as much as possible, and bend others to your will with a softer approach.

A slightly understated Leo is going to go much further, than one who is in-your-face garish and bordering on the offensive. Basically, if Leo can keep the reins on over-the-top behaviour, gestures and statements, there is no competition.

FUTURE CAREER: Leo is the Zodiac showman/show-woman. Never mind the occupation, The Lion inevitably finds a way to make an impact. Leo is a creative sign with the potential for vast achievement. Leo combines beguiling maverick style with inspirational energy. Here is an ambitious sign that loves the thought of adulation, if not the experience.

Leo is prepared to put in Trojan effort to ensure success. But the lion plays fair and will not sabotage the reputation of others for personal gain. The Universe acknowledges this honesty. And victory is sweeter for a genuine display of honor.

Work linking to stage, music, theatre or film is highly desirable. Leo makes a great TV presenter, and the occasional mad chef is also Leo. For controlled, disciplined Leo, a career in the army is appropriate.

The Lion who enters the ministry makes a very effective pastor or preacher; whilst natural charm and charisma render Leo a potent politician - of the performing variety of course.

FUTURE HEALTH: Leo needs warmth, whether from a log-fire, hot water bottle, or The Sun itself. The Zodiac Lion has a strong constitution and can weather most things; but must take care of circulation above all. Leo rules the heart. So Lions must nurture this vital organ with the correct diet, exercise and emotional support.

Stretching exercises, swimming and yoga are all great exercises for The Lion who needs to guard against back problems in later life. Maintaining suppleness and flexibility will protect both the flow of energy and the posture of Leo.

Any form of movement that requires imagination and self-expression is great leonine exercise. Music and dance keeps the heart in peak condition, along with a daily constitutional in the fresh air.

Leo is well advised to stay away from formal exercise or team sports unless it is possible to avoid the natural inclination to show off! Pumping iron is not for Leo either – for the same reason.

FUTURE LOVE: Leo is all heart, and should therefore guard against being hurt. The Zodiac Lion is readily wounded, and falls in love heavily and swiftly. If intense feelings are returned in full, Leo is destined for blissful happiness. But life can be unkind. And Leo will usually experience heartache, before peace and harmony finally descends. Leo is a faithful creature, who is naturally loyal but open. The Lion loves social intercourse, and needs the stimulation of a variety of connections. Partners should understand that Leo is completely faithful when given free rein. The Leo heart is slow to heal, for Leo feels things deeply and intensely. If you are Leo be careful not to overwhelm your partner with your generous spirit. Less is definitely more when you are in love. You do need to make a heart connection, but hold back to protect yourself. Make sure that your partner is up for it and committed before you let it all hang out.

Be careful not to be too dominant in your relationships or you will scare everyone off, never mind the love interest. Accept that sometimes people will say "no". Leo needs an enthusiastic and responsive partner - Someone who can occasionally give what for.

COMPATIBLE SIGNS: Fellow Fire signs suit Leo. Passions fly, and there is understanding without tedium. Taurus is low key, but provides quality romance which Leo desires. Gemini is lively and interesting. However, loyalty issues could send it all pear-shaped. Water signs are generally too broody and intense for Leo. Pisces is liable to outwit The Lion, which will not go down well. And Scorpio is a match for any Leo - These conflicting egos will fight it out incessantly! Virgo sees through leonine traits in an instant. And Capricorn is just not up for the permanent party.

BIRTH STONE: Ruby.
COLORS: All the colors of the Sun from Sunrise to Sunset.
ZODIAC NUMBER: 19.

FAMOUS SEXY LEOS: Bill Clinton, Mick Jagger, J Lo, Arnold Schwarzenegger, Madonna, Alfred Hitchcock, Fidel Castro, Napoleaon Bonaparte, Mussolini, Jacqueline Kennedy Onassis, Robert Redford, Geri Halliwell, Neil Armstrong, Princess Anne, Roy Keane.

VIRGO
August 24th – September 23rd

RULING PLANET: MERCURY

Mercury enhances mind power, empowering both intuition and logical thought. Sun signs ruled by this energy usually have staggering intellectual capacity. Mercury enables its people to see around corners, and to cover all aspects of an argument. This planet is thorough, brilliant, and leaves no stone unturned.

Mercury facilitates the decision making progress, propelling us towards conclusions. Whether by logic or intuition, Mercury allows for optimum mind function. Those ruled by Mercury possess the inside track to swift resolution. Some situations need the clear, sharp discipline of logic, or lateral thought; whilst others cut to the chase with a searing and impressive intuition. Mercury wins either way.

PERSONALITY: Virgo is the sixth sign of the Zodiac. The keynote of this Earth Goddess is "I serve." Supposedly modest, shy and prudish, Virgo has a reputation for being the cool, aloof Zodiac Virgin. Nothing could be further from the truth. Virgo's links to harvest, fertility, and female goddess energy conjure up a suitably prolific image.

Virgo is perhaps the Zodiac's best kept secret. This sign is right about most things - Much to the infuriation of those who think they know best. Many Little Oracles are born under Virgo! The combination of intuition, logic, and grounded sensibility make Virgo a formidable opponent indeed.

Virgo has tunnel vision when focused; and is inclined to get caught up in the intricacies of an argument. Virgo is innately intelligent. But an over cautious attitude to life is a potential problem. Virgo waits for life to happen. Or rather, life happens whilst Virgo sits there, observes, takes notes, and then writes about it.

Typically, Virgo finds it difficult to engage in the fray. The Zodiac Virgin is not inclined to 'put it out there'. Consequently gets overlooked much of the time. But given a chance to shine by being *asked,* and Virgo quickly outwits the competition.

Virgo is a practical Earth sign with an answer for everything. Virgo pays attention to detail and gets results. However this little worrier is inclined to miss the bigger picture fretting about inconsequential nonsense.

Virgo is no great chatterbox. But can knock the socks off anyone in an argument. When The Virgin speaks, it means something. There is a purpose to every Virgo action, thought, word and deed. Here we have the Zodiac workaholic who makes every second count.

If you are Virgo, be mindful of your intimidating intelligence. You have the ability to 'blind with science,' and few can match you. Because you are usually right, you may inspire jealousy. So stay silent rather than alienate the world. One thing is for sure; your searing intuition ensures your impact as a weapon of massive distraction.

FUTURE CAREER: To flourish, Virgo needs a secure, safe environment. Any work that diverts negative rumination into positive output is to be encouraged. It is very difficult to pick holes in Virgo's work. For they have already spent hours doing just that. Virgo makes a great publisher, writer, secretary, or personal assistant. Anything left to Virgo will be done efficiently and brilliantly in next to no time.

Group activities and teamwork do not always suit. Virgo tends to get overlooked, or may become annoyed with everyone else's incompetence.

Virgo makes a brilliant teacher. As ruler Mercury ensures the delivery of clear, accurate, information. Investigative journalism is also suitable. For Virgo can write effectively and has an original way of putting things.

Because Virgo tends to ruminate about health issues, careers in medicine and alternative healing are ideal.

Finally any career that connects Virgo to Mother Nature is restorative and calming. Opportunities to empty and de-stress that busy mind should be welcomed.

FUTURE HEALTH: Virgo has impressive levels of physical and mental energy. But any excess is liable to find an outlet in worry and stress. Virgo needs to sublimate wayward energies and enhance connections to Mother Earth.

Virgo rules the nervous system and stomach. So when things go wrong, stomach complaints and frayed nerves surface. Whole foods and simple recipes form the best fodder for Virgo. And the avoidance of additives is advisable.

Alternative approaches to healing suit Virgo's disposition. Treatments like Reiki, Yoga, Crystals, and homeopathy knock niggles on the head.

An aerobic exercise such as Yoga is much better for Virgo than a rigorous gym workout. But a regular routine is crucial to ongoing health. Variation will nip the scourge of boredom in the bud.

FUTURE LOVE: Virgo finds it difficult to believe that anyone would fall for them. Highly self-critical, Virgo likes to offer perfection only. So if they feel inadequate in any area – not slim, tall or cute enough – they will take some persuading. The irony is that Virgo is often quite stunning; and others fail to understand where the reluctance to engage comes from.

Virgo often gets called, aloof, snobby, or unattainable. But a smug Virgo is a rare creature indeed. If you want to woo and win a Virgo plenty of reassurance about your genuine intentions will be needed.

Virgo modesty can be a problem in the bedroom. But what is rarely reported is that when The Virgin gets into gear, he/she is earthy and passionate, once committed Virgo is loyal and faithful. Even if the physical aspect of a relationship has diminished, Virgo will not stray.

If you are a Virgo, be careful not to project your issues onto your partners and loved ones. Modify your expectations of people, places and things for sanity's sake. Learn to accept others on their own merit and appreciate the positive aspect of doing things differently. You cannot expect to realistically control the proceedings from dawn to dusk, so chill.

COMPATIBLE SIGNS: Taurus and Virgo fulfil each other's wildest dreams! And Cancer has the full-on sensuality Virgo needs. Virgo and Virgo are liable to drive each other wild with desire, but mad with frustration. Pisces is highly charged with oodles of sex appeal; whilst Scorpio is suitably sexy, minus the control issues. Aries is a loose cannon, without stability. Similarly, Gemini is exciting company. But as for life-long commitment, forget it! Aquarius understands, but gets exasperated when Virgo is right. Libra is funny, irresistible and hard work. Leo and Sagittarius are okay for a fling.

BIRTH STONE: Sardonyx.
COLORS: Browns, Dark Grey and Navy Blue.
ZODIAC NUMBER: 7
FAMOUS SEXY VIRGOS: Hugh Grant, Michael Jackson, Pink, Claudia Schiffer, Cameron Diaz, Liam Gallagher, Keanu Reeves, Harry Connick Jnr, Guy Ritchie, Stella McCartney, Barry Gibb, Sophia Loren, Gloria Estafan, D.H. Lawrence, Leo Tolstoy, H. G. Wells, Queen Elizabeth I, Lauren Bacall, Ingrid Bergman, Beyonce Knowles.

LIBRA
September 24th – October 23rd

RULING PLANET: VENUS

Venus heightens our feelings. This emotional energy challenges the way we relate to each other socially and financially. Venus points out the connection between our romantic and economic relationships. According to this Ruling Planet love, money, sex and material possessions are irretrievably married - for better or for worse.

Venus' activity in Libra emphasises the importance of equilibrium and balance. Libra needs and thrives on positive partnerships. This sign flourishes when there are impartial judgements and merciful decisions to be made. Libra is characterised by the gracious and fair demeanour that Venus bestows. Merciful and magnanimous when in balance, Venus heightens Libra's ability to live compassionately and considerately.

PERSONALITY: Libra is the seventh Zodiac sign, which is symbolized by the karmic weighing scales. The keynote of these Libran Scales of Justice is "I balance". Libra needs to relate. For this sign feels incomplete and inferior when not making meaningful connections. Establishing harmony is the raison d'etre of Libra.

Music expands Libran consciousness. It is both inspirational and healing for this sign to expose its psyche to a wall of sound.

Libra is elegant from the inside out. Along with a great image and eye for what looks right, Libra always makes an impression.

Librans are not happy unless they are sharing something. They need to express their souls interdependently. Equilibrium holds the key to success; for when off balance, Libra is prone to getting caught up in relationships that are too cloying or claustrophobic.

Gregarious Libra desires nurturing company. These souls thrive wherever they are valued and appreciated. With a wicked sense of humor, Libra is invaluable socially. The Scales do not actively interfere, but they do need to feel indispensable. This sign loves to define status and boundaries, and gets mightily distressed when disorder descends.

Libra incarnates with inherent wisdom, and is well able to offer impartial judgements which help others. However, Libra is not so skilled at unravelling personal dilemmas. Indecisiveness is the traditional Libran challenge. If you are Libra, discern what will work for you, and discard what has no hope of coming to fruition. Any decision is a good one when you feel stuck.

Be sure not to sit on the fence too often. Or you will miss out on many of life's golden opportunities. It is actually better to take a leap of faith and go for something, rather than sit back and see what happens. Begin to notice that when you do this generally nothing happens. Life will not fall into your lap Libra. So learn to go after things and do not be afraid to take the initiative.

FUTURE CAREER: Getting to the top of the career ladder is a potentially isolating experience for Libra. Libra requires company and needs a team situation as a foil for self- expression. Working as the proverbial lone ranger or lighthouse keeper does not suit.

Libra loves glamour. So careers in hairdressing, styling, makeup and costume fit the bill. Many creative artists and musicians are born under the sign of Libra. Glitzy professions like theatre, media and television bring the injection buzz Libra needs.

This sign is tailor made for a small fashion boutique, or design house. Libra is skilled at one-to-one encounters, and makes a good sales person. Careers in the army, police or even a secret agency are all suitable for Librans who respond well to discipline and structure.

With their natural gregarious and humorous disposition, Libra has a nose for PR. They also make good personal assistants, and may satiate their taste for the limelight by steering others towards fame and fortune.

FUTURE HEALTH: Balance holds the key to optimum health for Libra. Librans have good energy, but can be a bit frantic if not manic at times! Exercise is an important 'grounding' experience. And energy should be expended in a measured way. Gentle but determined long haul exercise that tests stamina and durability is ideal.

The Planet Venus ensures the beauty and desirability of Libra. But Libra is inclined to put on weight if the sweet tooth is indulged. Balance and moderation in diet will ensure that alluring looks are maintained.

Libra rules the kidneys. So it is important to boost hydration levels by drinking lots of water. Venus presides over the parathyroid gland, which also indicates that bodily fluids must be balanced for optimum health. Headaches should be checked out if they are persistent.

Libra is inclined to have a slow metabolism. Aerobic exercise keeps everything ticking over. But discipline is not usually a Libran strong point. Efforts will be visible and worthwhile: persist.

FUTURE LOVE: Librans love the thought of being in love. They thrive on the anticipation as much as the event itself. Libra tends to fall in love very easily, and should make a concerted effort to choose wisely. A trail of broken hearts does not a pretty picture make. Librans must be careful with their emotions.; being aware that they may be more vulnerable than they realize. It is imperative for Libra to exercise discrimination and protect their interests.

If you are Libra learn to accept people on their own merit. And try to watch what you expect from them in return. Honor the freedom and independence of partners and family members. Then your expectations will be repaid tenfold…The looser the grip, the more you will receive. Unconditional love, painful though it may be, also guarantees big rewards.

Libra is a born romantic. So needs to keep its feet on the ground. Start to be realistic about love. Don't just plan the wedding ceremony. Work out first what a lifetime together actually means.

Romantic thoughts are all very well. Indeed they will feed your imagination for hours on end. But do remember you have to relate to human beings not knights in shining armor, or princesses from the fairy tales.

COMPATIBLE SIGNS: Aries, Libra's polar opposite, is highly compatible. Gemini is a master of delivery. And the Aquarian's sense of humor wins every time. Taurus is a great provider. Libra wants for nothing, until the boredom sets in. Cancer is highly seductive and permanently interesting. Leo has instant appeal - the fireworks fly when these two hit the sack. Libra with Libra makes a good team. But expect a clash eventually. Pisces is too emotionally clever, and tends to manipulate to get a reaction. Capricorn is too tame and tedious. While Scorpio is totally unfathomable.

BIRTH STONE: Sapphire, Diamond, Opal.
COLOURS: Indigo, Pale Blue, Green, Pink.
ZODIAC NUMBER: 3
FAMOUS SEXY LIBRANS: Brigitte Bardot, Will Smith, Gwenyth Paltrow, Sting, Luciano Pavarotti, Eminem, Danii Minogue, Sir Bob Geldof, Simon Cowell, Sarah Keating (SIX), Kate Winslet, Donna Karan, Mahatma Ghandi, John Lennon, Heather Locklear, Groucho Marx, Pele, Michael Douglas, Catherine Zeta Jones, Julie Andrews, Bruce Springsteen.

SCORPIO
October 24th – November 22nd

RULING PLANET: PLUTO
(and Mars- see Aries)

Pluto highlights personal obstacles and our ability to overcome them. This planet has a strong influence on our hidden secrets. Life's mystery and dark side loves Pluto energy. Its terrain is the skeleton in the closet, and the subterranean depths of the unconscious.

Pluto is the ancient god of the Underworld. This energy dances in the shadows, and is not afraid to stare death in the face. An intrepid fearlessness attaches to this Planet's vibration. Pluto is resilient, determined and will not take defeat lying down. Therefore, Pluto inspires transformation. But Pluto can be dark, dangerous and cruel. When off balance resist and avoid this energy at all costs.

PERSONALITY: Scorpio is the eighth sign of the Zodiac, signified by The Scorpion. The key phrase for this sign is "I Transform". Scorpio can turn negative situations around and thrives on a challenge. When determined and focused this energy has the power to succeed.

Scorpio is a deep and passionate soul that dislikes laziness. This intense nature is inclined to feel the blues. And personal storms are an important part of the Scorpio legacy. Difficult times enable a deep understanding of life. Superficiality is not an option.

Privacy is very important for Scorpio who needs to feel in control of people and situations. Personal space is at a premium for this profound Water sign. This energy hates to feel crowded and anyone who invades the Scorpion's nest had better beware! The Scorpio 'Sting in the tail' has real ouch factor.

Scorpio is a reserved but abundantly blessed Sun sign with tremendous energy, commitment and resolve. Mental, emotional and physical excess needs to be channeled constructively, as the capacity for disaster is quite high. And a wrong turn can send this Sun sign into quick decline. But with transformation as the main drive of Scorpio. It is inevitable that The Scorpion comes back for more. Like the proverbial Phoenix rising from the ashes.

Because Scorpio rules the reproductive system and genital organs, many people assume this Sun sign is sexually driven. This is of course the case, but it is certainly not the sole motivation of Scorpio. Scorpio is actually quite straight-laced, cautious, and old-fashioned about commitment, and is very loyal even when temptation strikes.

If you are Scorpio find positive ways to express yourself and engage in activities that sublimate your energy. The negative traits of jealousy, suspicion and obsessive ruminating are by no means ingrained. You have an incredible energy that is able to experience life in all its glory (and all its depravity as well!). With Scorpio around, there is certainly no shortage of drama, passion and intensity.

FUTURE CAREER: Scorpio is very ambitious and has great energy to bring to their chosen career. All that sexual excess and drive is very readily channeled into public pursuits. Work and personal development are crucial to the survival of Scorpio. For if boredom, listlessness or disappointment kick-in, the dark side comes out to play.

Whatever life path Scorpio chooses, there is an accompanying ability to make money. This sign knows about financial management and how to transform small amounts into major investments. The imaginative skills of Scorpio may be applied to any tedious task with staggering results.

With an eye for detail and acquired patience Scorpio makes a good surgeon. And with their grip on the human psyche, many specialist psychiatrists are Scorpions.

Careers in the army or policing suit the Scorpio ability to get to the bottom of things, and exercises those control issues. In the reverse, Scorpio makes a brilliant criminal. But I am not about to recommend a life of crime.

FUTURE HEALTH: Scorpio has boundless excess energy; so physical exercise is crucial to The Scorpion's health. Sports that expend a lot of effort and have a high aggressive factor are ideal. Also any link with Water based activities puts Scorpio right in their element. Scorpio should choose any exercise that stretches endurance and channels energy.

Scorpio rules the reproductive system. So Scorpio must take care of sexual organs with regular checks. There is no cause for alarm. However, it is better to be safe than sorry. The Scorpion is prone to constipation, but should be careful not to become obsessed with assimilation problems.

Scorpio can be prone to ill-health when feeling blocked. So it is important for Scorpio to clear emotional issues with plain talking. Psychological issues are part of Scorpio's legacy. At times The Scorpion may be challenged by depression or obsessive problems. Exercise de-stresses the mind, of course. But psychotherapy or the occasional heart-to-heart will knock most things on the head.

FUTURE LOVE: Scorpio is both plagued and blessed by deep emotion. This renders The Scorpion a great catch indeed. But it also signifies that there are deep-seated issues to be processed in matters of the heart. Scorpio rises to the challenge; but needs to temper obsessive and possessive tendencies in relationships. Scorpio loves to control the proceedings and feels uncomfortable when out of its depth.

It takes The Scorpion time to trust and feel comfortable one-on-one. Indeed, it is this fear of commitment and heartache that is responsible for the Scorpion's rampant reputation. Scorpio would rather have a string of affairs than commit to anticipated heartbreak.

Love needs to find its feet before Scorpio relaxes enough to enjoy deep connections. The Scorpion needs to guard against jealousy, suspicion, and resentfulness. When insecure, Scorpio is aggressive and prone to picking fights. There is inevitably intense drama when Scorpio does not feel loved.

If you are Scorpio, learn to cope with your deep feelings and be patient with yourself. When you find your Soul Mate, you will realize what a gift these emotions really are. You are loyal and committed once in love. So recognize that mischievous secret grin which manifests when Scorpio loves someone.

COMPATIBLE SIGNS: Fellow Scorpio is a true Soul Mate; while Taurus and Virgo really suit. These seductive Earth signs provide the missing link. Cancer and Pisces connect emotionally. But there maybe game playing and blackmail when things get intense. Leo and Scorpio are powerfully attracted - A very physical relationship. Aries connects well with Scorpio. But this is more friendship than intense passion. Sagittarius has to be willing to compromise. Or forget it over the long term. Avoid dominant Capricorn and flighty Gemini. Libra is a bit bland. Whilst Aquarius is too busy and distracted.

BIRTH STONE: Opal.
COLORS: Maroon and Dark Reds.
ZODIAC NUMBER: 11.
FAMOUS SEXY SCORPIOS: Joaquim Phoenix, Larry Mullen Jnr, Liam Mc Kenna of SIX, Jodie Foster, Prince Charles, Katherine Hepburn, Winona Ryder, Theodore Roosevelt, Marie Antoinette, Marie Curie, Bill Gates, Vivian Leigh, Piablo Picasso, Julia Roberts, Hillary Rodham Clinton, Sam Sheppard, Louis Nurding, Mickey

Mouse, Johnathan Ross, Leonardo Di Caprio, Demi Moore, Meg Ryan.

SAGITTARIUS
November 23rd – December 21st

RULING PLANET: JUPITER

Jupiter is the largest planet in the solar system. It is associated with expansiveness and development, both intellectual and physical. Jupiter was the king of all the gods, akin to the Roman god Zeus. This regal energy of kingship blesses those born under Jupiter dignity and composure. Along with inherent spirituality and the ability to philosophize, Jupiter bestows abundance and wealth, whilst the inherent cosmic link to ancient gods ensures great luck.. Positive mental energies direct those born under this sign. Knowledge, vision and optimism are all gifts from Jupiter. However, caution is needed for Jupiter can inspire over confidence and stubborn behavior. Watch out for extravagance and histrionic, 'Drama Queen' behavior.

PERSONALITY: Sagittarius is the ninth sign of the Zodiac. This Fire sign is symbolized by The Archer who shoots his arrow heavenwards. The keynote of Sagittarius is "I believe". Predictably, the fiery, assertive energy of Sagittarius is not easily confined. This Sun sign is identified by a great enthusiasm for life, along with a sense that anything is possible.

Sagittarius is hugely self-confident, which is all very well until this exuberant fireball goes too far, and trips itself up. No task is too lofty, and no ambition too mighty for Jupiter energy. Commendable indeed! But Sagittarius does need to temper enthusiasm with caution and common sense once in a while. To avoid major frustration and defeat, The Archer needs to inject some realism into the proceedings. Although well able to cope with challenging situations, Sagittarius should be mindful of human frailty once in a while. Even while cooking up grandiose plans. This dynamo character would do well to have plan B and C in place.

The ability to think expansively makes Sagittarius an extraordinary visionary. Dreams have a habit of coming true, simply because the wish fulfillment factor is so heightened. When grounded, Sagittarius is destined to achieve great things. So long as flexibility amidst adversity is maintained.

Freedom is so important to Sagittarius. This natural philosopher needs the option on possibilities. The grass is always greener for Sagittarius, when stifled or restricted The Archer can be difficult company indeed. Sagittarius loves to be kept guessing, and lives life close to the edge. Security, comfort and predictability bore The Archer rigid.

Sagittarius is a brave and heroic sign that is both eccentric and exasperating. The Archer aims true. And his flaming arrow hits the spot more often than not.

With a delicious sense of humor, Sagittarius is invaluable socially. This joker is guaranteed to be center stage in any prank. Here is a live wire determined to get its way. Attempt to capture one if you dare.

FUTURE CAREER: Tedious, routine jobs are anathema to Sagittarius. This free spirit needs to be permanently stimulated. Or it shrivels up and crumples in a heap! The Archer must find ample opportunity for self-expression. And strive to be challenged at every turn. Work that tests skills of anticipation or predictive ability is ideal.

Sagittarius has a healthy competitive streak. So needs an environment that gives just enough containment and discipline, without being threatening. Any job that embraces The Archer's gift of vision is desirable. For the creativity of this Fire sign must be respected.

Employment that requires attention to fine detail is not right for Sagittarius; but having said that The Archer can turn its hand to most things for a limited stretch of time. Travel, sports and languages are natural talents, so should be developed where possible.. Gifts of charm, humor, and a winning demeanor, make Sagittarius a great sales person. The inevitable high Jinx ensures endless fun, and a whistle while we work.

FUTURE HEALTH: Sagittarius needs to get sufficient exercise in as many and varied ways as possible. The Archer has a lot of nervous energy, and is quite susceptible to bouts of depression and sluggishness when unfit. Attention must therefore be paid to physical activity that both entertains and maintains fitness.

Sagittarius should to avoid becoming fired up by stress, so eastern methods of channeling surplus energy are recommended. Tai Chi, Yoga, and Martial Arts fulfil The Archer's philosophical bent, even whilst calming the system.

A sensible diet is crucial to Sagittarian equilibrium. The hips and the thighs are The Archer's domain. So the consumption of junk will inevitably show in these areas. Fresh fruit is good for this Fire sign that needs to watch the waist- line. Plus extra vitamins and minerals are often necessary to avoid the high likelihood of burn out. Sagittarius should avoid sugar. And aim to eat high protein energy foods.

Sagittarius can be clumsy, so do guard against tears and sprains during any kind of physical activity.

FUTURE LOVE: Sagittarius has boundless energy for love and life. This free-wheeling nature needs variety and diversity; which can of course herald trouble when it comes to commitment. Sagittarius has wild oats to sow, and is not ashamed to say so. Strong passionate feelings and natural urges often get the better of The Archer. Who is not intentionally unfaithful, but simply finds that things happen, now and again.

Sagittarius is never backwards about coming forwards. But as the mature Sagittarian values companionship and conversation. There is an option on the mellow route. So long as The Archer is free to roam and consider endless possibilities, fidelity is not a problem. This may be unnerving for loved ones. But if Sagittarius is respected and unconfined, no harm is done. One whiff of possessiveness and this fire sign will find ways to wander, come-what-may.

If you are Sagittarius, you may at times be too casual about love and sex. Jealousy is not in your vocabulary, which can be both liberating and disconcerting for loved ones. However, once you connect with your Soul Mate, nothing will persuade you to stray. When you truly fall for someone you will know all about it; and so will everyone else.

COMPATIBLE SIGNS: Aries has a lot of passion to share with Sagittarius; whilst Leo is ideal mentally and physically - a fulfilling connection. Libra is up for it – just about anywhere! And Aquarius is quirky but adventurous. Gemini fills in the gaps, with endless chatter guaranteed. Cancer is an intriguing and mysterious partner, who keeps Sagittarius guessing. Virgo is interesting and captivates for a certain amount of time. Where Pisces is very compelling and drives Sagittarius to distraction, for good or bad! Possessive Scorpio and the plodding earth signs Taurus and Capricorn should be avoided.

BIRTH STONE: Topaz.
COLORS: Dark Blue and Purple, Regal colors.
ZODIAC NUMBER: 27.
FAMOUS SEXY SAGITTARIUS: Brad Pitt, Ralph Fiennes, Warren Beatty, Eddie Murphy, Joan Crawford, Celine Dion, Charlie Chaplin, Marlon Brando, Winston Churchill, Frank Sinatra, Tina Turner, Mark Twain, Walt Disney, Jane Fonda, Bette Midler, Andrew Carnegie, Jane Fonda, Zoe Ball, Uri Geller, Steven Spielberg, John Galliano, Mel Smith, Lorraine Kelly.

CAPRICORN
December 22nd – January 20th

RULING PLANET: SATURN

Saturn's authority puts a restraining order on excess. This Planet holds The Universe in check. Not an easy energy, Saturn challenges recklessness. Saturn is our conscience warning against foolhardiness. Intimidating to the free spirited. Saturn may undermine weak self-esteem, heightening self-doubt and confusion.

Saturn's buzzword is do not, which may repress, depress, or comfort, according to disposition. Like an autocratic parent, this Ruling Planet is good to have around in a crisis; but debilitating when we need to muster self-confidence. Balance is crucial in the face of Saturn's warning flag. It is advisable to take the hint and put the brakes on questionable behavior. But equally important to resist Saturn's bullying.

PERSONALITY: Capricorn is the tenth sign of the Zodiac, represented by the Goat with the fishy tail. Capricorn's keynote is "I USE". The sure-footed Goat is able to traverse treacherous mountains, whilst keeping its feet firmly on Terra Firma. The fishy tail represents the ocean emphasizing the ability to swim free without constraint – the spiritual nature of being.

Traditionally Capricorn is depicted as a rigid, unbending and inflexible sign. And very stubborn with it. This is not the complete picture of course. But Capricorn's do love to get their way. And are expert at finding the chinks in people's armor. The Goat is brilliant at subtle manipulation; and well able to 'plant the seed' months in advance to ensure a specific outcome.

The Capricorn legacy combines material savvy and survival skills with spiritual expression. Practical, financial and business ventures provide The Goat with the opportunity to express their true essence. For this sign has the potential to integrate life's material and spiritual dimensions – powerful indeed.

Focus gets Capricorn absolutely everywhere. And a fully integrated Goat may achieve great things. The development of self-confidence is crucial to Capricorn's success. But it is important that The Goat does not abuse their natural authority. Or things could get ugly. If Capricorn maintains spiritual balance all will be well. However, many of the World's control freaks are Capricorn, who sacrifices kindness to serve their ambitions.

If you are Capricorn learn to adapt and survive. Rather than seek to control at all costs. Maintaining devious levels of manipulation is very self-defeating, as you will no doubt realize. So never use a string of lies to get you to where you want to be. Your stories may captivate an audience, but in time your exposure as a fraud may be too much too bear.

Your brilliant mind brings many temptations. Ambition is very important to Capricorn. Learn to delegate and ask for favors on your way to the top. Remember that with enough determination you can conquer any mountain you wish to climb.

FUTURE CAREER: Capricorn is very skilled and reliable. The Goat has a great head for facts and figures; so all business ventures suit this ambitious energy. Capricorn is guaranteed to cope well with routine, and thrives on structure and discipline. This Saturn influenced sign loves security and seeks to control the proceedings wherever possible.

The Goat has an instinct for the route to the top. So any chance to stay ahead of the game is closely monitored. The concept of failure does not exist in Capricorn's rarefied environment. And whatever this Earth sign attempts is sure to make an impact.

By definition Capricorn is a winner. There is little The Goat is not capable of. However, avoidance of equal partnerships is advisable; for Capricorn needs to stand-alone. This sign makes an ideal company director, principle, or business representative.

Many self-made people are Capricornian. The Goat is willing to tolerate 'spartan' conditions. And will do what it takes to be a success.

FUTURE HEALTH: Mobility is crucial for Capricorns. Goats need to keep active and on-the-move. So that those creaking joints work well into old age! Knees and shins are vulnerable to scrapes and sprains and must be protected at all times. Running and swift walking are good exercise for Capricorn, who should maintain supple limbs.

Capricorn skin has to be looked after. For it is prone to dehydration, never mind the weather. This organ can dry out wind, rain, or shine. So skin care should be a permanent part of The Goat's routine.

Since Capricorn rules the teeth and bones, a healthy Calcium intake is important; as well as regular visits to the dentist.

Tedious Gym visits are best avoided. But it is important for Capricorn to keep warm at all times to boost flexibility; even though The Goat may prefer to feel cool. Warmth is crucial for the prevention of rheumatic pain later in life. Capricorn can expect to trot effortlessly into the twilight years. So long as these basic rules are adhered to.

FUTURE LOVE: Capricorn is cautious in matters of the heart. The Goat needs to find its feet, and tends to warm up slowly. Once committed, Capricorn remains steadfast and true. Since few can match The Goat's devotion and loyalty. It is advisable for Capricorn to ditch the control issues. For when Capricorn develops an open attitude to feelings and emotions, anything can happen.

Capricorn often holds back for fear of rejection. Trust is the key. Plus a willingness to make mistakes occasionally. When The Goat falls in love it is usually for keeps. For, when this Earth sign surrenders, their amour is already smitten. Capricorn is not a great risk taker, and does not act on impulse; which is good protection of course. But can mean that Capricorn misses out on all the fun.

The Goat is a sure thing, who expects as much in return. Fair enough! But if you are Capricorn do unwind. Also, watch that tendency to penny pinch. You do not wish to come across mean spirited. It is not a crime to spend money. But missing out on romantic dinners, presents and gestures of affection is. Down to earth as you are, let go. Loosen purse and heart strings, just a little.

COMPATIBLE SIGNS: Fellow Earth signs Taurus and Virgo bring passion and practicality...the ideal mix for Capricorn. Pisces is adoring and malleable – very useful. But Cancer may be overly emotional. Aries is simply too hot to handle – great for a fling, if you dare have one. Scorpio likes to be in control; as does fellow Capricorn - An inevitable clash waiting to happen. Libra is simply too different. And Aquarius has to get its way – a recipe for disaster...Gemini is way too wild and challenging for Capricorn. And Sagittarius is dangerously impulsive. Opportunistic signs need not apply.

BIRTH STONE: Amethyst and Turquoise.
COLORS: Black, Dark Greys, Greens and Browns.
ZODIAC NUMBER: 33.
FAMOUS SEXY CAPRICORNS: Mel Gibson, Pete Waterman, Jim Carrey, Rod Stewart, Nicholas Cage, Kate Moss, Christie Turlington, Helena Christiansen, David Bowie, Benjamin Franklin, Elvis Presley, Joan of Arc, Richard Nixon, Edgar Allen Poe, Martin Luther King, Joseph Stalin, Mel Gibson, Henri Matisse, Paul Cezanne, Mao Tse-Tung, Noel Edmunds, Denzel Washington, Rowan Atkinson, Mel C.

AQUARIUS
January 21st – February 19th

RULING PLANET: URANUS
(and Saturn - see Capricorn)

Uranus is the planet of personal transformation. Inspirational for the individual, this Ruling Planet also blesses generations. Uranus challenges the Status Quo, and constitutes a challenging, difficult energy. Independent and radical, this planet moves slowly heralding profound drawn out change.

To be born under Uranus is an honor indeed, which needs to be treated with healthy respect. This planet inspires altruism. But also signifies self-importance and eccentricity. Uranus allows for detachment, as well as the ability to be all things to all people. This mode of being is a law unto itself. In true maverick style Aquarius knows best. A perverted rebellious streak gives Uranus the edge.

PERSONALITY: Aquarius is the eleventh sign of the Zodiac, symbolized by the Water Carrier, and described by key phrase "All for one and one for all". This mind-set connects to group consciousness. Altruistic and humanitarian, Aquarius looks outwards.

With the buzzword "I know". Aquarius is invaluable when the going gets rough. On a deep inner level Aquarius carries the full knowledge of the Universe. The Water Carrier who learns to access the unconscious is truly a walking oracle.

Aquarius is the true philanthropist of the Zodiac, with the Wisdom of Ages resting on its shoulders. This sign imparts logical and objective advice. Second to none in a crisis, Aquarius keeps a cool head. This Air sign has sympathy, wisdom, and practical help to share. Aquarius is someone the whole world can turn to in an emergency.

Glamorous, cool and aloof, Aquarius knows how to present an elegant face to the world. At times unapproachable and distant, the Water Carrier is intensely private. Far from being deliberately unfriendly, Aquarius is simply guarded.

With an inherent understanding of human nature this sign is no fool. Rarely one to let down defenses, Aquarius values loyalty. Whilst honesty and integrity are extremely important; Aquarius is kind hearted and will not judge too quickly.

As a great visionary, the Aquarian intellect takes some beating. But the Water Carrier can be quite inflexible. Once Aquarius has made up its mind, this sign is fixed and rigid with plenty to prove. The Water Carrier acquires a unique way of being. And precious little will budge this. Aquarius should guard against appearing old fashioned, by being open to the changing times. However, Aquarian quirkiness is always charming. Never mind out-of-touch.

If you are Aquarian, always follow your eccentric heart. But learn some adaptability too. Keep up with current trends. And be prepared to modify the game plan. Be aware that although you are usually right, you are NOT always so. So reserve judgement on issues you are unsure about. Pride comes before a fall.

FUTURE CAREER: There is a touch of brilliance about Aquarius. This original mind, which borders on kookiness, means that Aquarius gets the best results when left alone. Aquarius does not like to be dictated to. And needs to find a unique way through life's challenges.

With a natural affinity for science and detail the Water Carrier borders on genius. Being a natural humanitarian, Aquarius is tailor made for caring professions with substance - The medical and healing professions beckon.

Aquarius is liable to feel stifled in a noisy office situation. Although the Water Carrier is able to work as part of a team, much leeway is important. Aquarius loves to take responsibility and express creativity. This Air sign thrives on rescuing others, whatever the context. So any career that combines communications with altruistic gestures is ideal.

Aquarius loves to fly and spread their wings. The Mile High brigade is full of Aquarians who like to get their feet off the ground.

FUTURE HEALTH: Both Aquarius and Uranus are associated with the circulatory system; which makes Aquarius susceptible to varicose veins, pulmonary problems, and hardened arteries. This potential can be avoided with sensible diet and a regular fitness routine. Forewarned is forearmed.

The polar opposite of Aquarius is Leo ruler of the heart. The link between circulation and heart is immediately obvious. So Aquarians must adopt a healthy heart regime and stick to it.

Aquarians should not even think about smoking, and must take regular cardiovascular exercise. Sports like swimming, tennis, and squash allow Aquarius to shine whilst providing that crucial work out.

A low fat diet high in fruit and vegetables is fundamentally important. Be aware that porridge is brilliant for lowering cholesterol and boosting general health.

Also, Aquarius must watch their back. The spine and muscles are vulnerable to aches, pains and sprains. So, even though Aquarius likes to be cool. This Air sign needs to stay warm.

FUTURE LOVE: Aquarius is a private person who does not readily make deep, intense connections. The Water Carrier acts similarly to cautious Capricorn, but for different reasons. Aquarius is alluring, charismatic, and rarely spoiled for choice. However, Aquarius does not fall in love easily, interested in a whole range of options. Aquarius flits in and out of possibilities until surety descends.

Aquarius has a magnetic pull, which may attract and repel in equal measure. On the one hand enticing and curious, Aquarius disconnects quickly when uneasy. Of course there is nothing wrong with being careful. But Aquarius should guard against missing out on the love of their life. Too much detachment and preservation of privacy can render the Water Carrier isolated and alone. It is important that Aquarius opens up from the heart to make lasting links.

If you are Aquarius, learn to show your emotions more fully and be honest with love's expression. Once you fall for someone you fall heavily. Your choice of partner may be unusual. But your loyalty ensures that they have you for life.

Find a partner who respects your maverick nature and unique disposition. Prepare for an exciting and fulfilling relationship. And certainly don't allow anyone to sway your choices; as if.

COMPATIBLE SIGNS: Fellow Aquarius is compatible and entertaining. While Gemini offers everything, and has a great sense of humor to boot. Libra brings a lasting and lustful connection. Aries is a great idea when the balance is right. And Leo is fun for a moment or two. Virgo annoys Aquarius by being right once too often! But Sagittarius is unusually devoted. Expect a clash of the Titans with Capricorn. And watch Pisces who will get under your skin and invade your space. Taurus is too cozy and home orientated for Aquarius who wants to party.

BIRTH STONE: Amethyst and Aquamarine.

COLORS: Electric Blues and Turquoise.
ZODIAC NUMBER: 22
SEXY AQUARIANS: Robbie Williams, John Travolta, Frank Skinner, Elijah Woods, Oprah Winfrey, Ronald Reagan, Vanessa Redgrave, Virginia Woolf, James Joyce, Charles Dickens, Garth Brooks, Charles Darwin, Wolfgang Amadeus Mozart, Galileo, Prince Naseem Hamed, Cindy Crawford, Eddie Izzard, Jennifer Jason Leigh, Jennifer Aniston Pitt.

PISCES
February 20ᵗʰ – March 20ᵗʰ

RULING PLANET: NEPTUNE
(and Jupiter – see Sagittarius)

Neptune, ruler of the oceans has energy enough to transform the masses. The processes inspired by Neptune are laborious but profound. Ideologies, beliefs and social norms come under the jurisdiction of Neptune. But commendable spiritual tendencies may become off-the-wall fanaticism. The down side of Neptune involves escapism, indecisiveness, and elaboration of the truth.

Neptune off balance muddles the vision. So discernment is important. Those ruled by Neptune should guard against self-deception. For wild fantasy and wish fulfilment tendencies need to be monitored.

With Neptune in the frame, dreams and visions are loaded with significance. This depth, wisdom and imagination may be expressed as a great gift.

PERSONALITY: Pisces is the twelfth and final Zodiac Sign. The keynote of Pisces is "I understand". This sentiment signifies the end of the Zodiac Journey, represented by two fish swimming in opposite directions, but connected by a cord. The Pisces habitat is the deep oceans, seas and waterways of the Spirit world.

Pisces possesses inner knowing and profound vision, making them the most psychic of all our Star Scope signs. Life is expansive and exciting for the Zodiac Fishes. So to swim free must be the Pisces goal, bar none.

To fully embrace their birthright, Fishes are advised to dive into a voyage of self-discovery. This is nothing to be alarmed about. But is certainly a challenge as it unfolds. Pisces should embrace the leaps of faith along the way. And always pay attention to hopes, dreams, and wishes.

Pisces must learn to discern the truth of their visions. And not be afraid of a profound ability to read situations and people. Boundaries are an issue for Pisces. This Water sign needs to preserve privacy and personal space at all times. But must also be mindful of a tendency to invade the lives of others uninvited.

Pisces is a courageous and insightful friend. But should realize it is impossible to sort everyone out. The Fish needs to look after itself first and foremost.

If you are Pisces make the most of your creativity, cleverness and poetic vision. Stay awake, and keep your feet (fins) on the ground! Your tendency to dream and think profound thoughts is second to none. But be sure not to traipse down elaborate scenic routes in your imagination, which really have no bearing on reality.

Do not beat yourself up over your inherent indecisiveness. It is part of your Piscean legacy. So learn to 'go with the flow' of your changing emotions. And remember that any decision is a good one if you follow it through. Discipline the changeable dreamer. And you will always be a truthful incisive force to be reckoned with.

FUTURE CAREER: Pisces works well as part of a team, plugging away discretely in the background. Fishes are not comfortable center stage. But they greatly dislike being overlooked, reflecting the myriad of fish in the sea. The Pisces personality is diverse! Many careers are suitable, depending entirely on personal choice. When Pisces feels valued and finds a niche – anything goes.

Any career that allows Pisces room to breathe, function and express creativity is valid. Pisces likes to hide behind masks and deflect attention. So comedy and humor suit the fishy disposition.

Pisces is instinctively caring. Work that combines the expression of feeling and intuition is ideal. Nursing, counselling, social work and psychic work fit the bill.

A flexible routine containing a wide variety of tasks is best for Pisces. Versatility is a gift received at birth, but when the boredom sets in. It is off to the next challenge fairly lively. Discipline is needed for Pisces to stay around long enough to make an impression.

FUTURE HEALTH: Pisceans have an extremely sensitive constitution. Alternative medicine is often a gentler more effective approach for delicate Fish. Pisces should always liaise closely with health professionals, since they can react quite badly to prescription drugs.

Neptune connects to the nervous system, which renders Pisces highly suggestible. Someone innocently asking the Fish if they feel OK can send them off to the doctor in a mild panic. Like Virgo, Pisces gets overly stressed by worry and health matters.

Pisces has a tendency towards addiction, which acts as a buffer for suppressed issues. The development of healing and psychic ability helps Pisces manage this uncomfortable disposition. Spiritual understanding allows Pisces to arm against attack from the environment, toxic people, and dubious energies.

Pisces rules the feet. So Fish must wear shoes that fit properly. Or in time they can expect an interesting range of foot ailments. Reflexology (which massages the feet and supports a sensitive system) is an absolute 'God Send.'

FUTURE LOVE: Pisces loves to display a whole range of emotions with passion and gusto! Love delights in The Fishes' openness. But is also embarrassed by that tendency to be over eager in public places. Pisces must learn to define boundaries; and should be careful not to chase love away in an eagerness to please.

Pisces is liable to be overly intense, a little sentimental, and highly idealistic. These honest qualities echo the naïve child attempting to make a dream come true! So, Pisces must be mindful that adult relationships inspire a mixed bag of emotions. Requiring adjustment and compromise along the way.

It is all very well holding onto romantic notions of happiness for as long as possible. But life has a way of delivering harsh and insightful lessons to help us grow up. Pisces is quite vulnerable to heartache whilst this 'education' takes place.

If you are Pisces, enjoy the intensity of your passions. But learn to curb your enthusiasm. There is no one to match you romantically. And your performance is always honest. Do access the lighter side of love, life, and happiness. And do not take things quite so seriously.

You may always find refuge in the fantasies revolving around your head. But will this substitute for an experience of the real thing? I think not!

COMPATIBLE SIGNS: Cancer and Scorpio speak the Pisces language of love. Virgo is highly compelling. But once attraction fades the arguments could be interesting! Fellow Pisces either repels or attracts - Follow your instincts. Avoid Sagittarius except for an exciting fling. Taurus is up for it. But will tire of Piscean mutability. Leo goes along for the ride – up to a point. And Capricorn is too staid and not impulsive enough. Gemini is untrustworthy – Surprise! And Libra is a nitpicker! Aquarius gets down and dirty. But this is potential war, not fun at all.

BIRTH STONE: Moonstone. Chrysolite.
COLORS: Sea Greens and shades of Blue, Lilac.
ZODIAC NUMBER: 11
FAMOUS SEXY PISCEANS: Jon Bon Jovi, Billy Crystal, Michael Caine, Rachel Weisz, Patsy Kensit, Sharon Stone, Melinda Messinger, Zane Bowers, Chelsea Clinton, Liza Minelli, Sidney Poittier, John Steinbeck, Johnny Cash, Jerry Lewis, George Washington, Elizabeth Taylor, Nat King Cole, Mikail Gorbachev, Caroline Corr, Ronan Keating, Eva Herzigova, Ja Rule, Thora Birch, Tea Leoni, Kristin Davis.

2 DECANS

The subject of Decans tends to be glossed over in Esoteric books. Here is an added insight into the specific week of your birth. There are subdivisions (Decans) within each Sun sign, which reflect the great diversity inherent within each of the Zodiac signs. Check the chapter on Ruling Planets for more detail about the planets that energize your personal Decan.

ARIES
March 21st – April 20th
Ruled by Mars

FIRST DECAN: March 21st – March 30th
Planetary Influence: Mars

You are a natural leader who can be forceful and convincing. Others find you annoying but inspiring. So curb that determination to get your own way. You have boundless energy and get things done. But there is no need to be too pushy when you want victory. Simply stating your case in no uncertain terms should do it. With focus, you can achieve great things. For you are destined to win or else go down fighting. Watch that tendency to be overly stubborn though. Feisty as you are, a mellow demeanour will usually be more potent and effective than a confrontational one. You are a Zodiac Crusader: a Pioneer. With a head full of ideas, you are ever ready to spring into action.

SECOND DECAN: March 31st – April 9th
Planetary Influence: The Sun

Being influenced by the Sun your charisma is formidable. You are guaranteed to turn heads and get people's attention. And your mere presence in a room is enough to convince us of your magnetism and power. You do not even have to open your mouth to make an impact. For you have Star quality. If you have aspirations of fame, there is every chance you will be successful. A potent mix of drive and energy gives you staying power when focused. And your instant appeal will bring inevitable recognition. You are magnificent! Who would dare to turn you down? Persistence and a big smile are about all you need to clinch a deal.

THIRD DECAN: April 10th – April 20th
Planetary Influence: Jupiter

You are truly unique individual. And possess dynamic Arian traits combined with strong moral fiber. Respectful of people and responsibilities you do not give into temptation easily. Your fiery energy inspires and motivates. A strong sense of right and wrong makes you a great politician, preacher or healer. However, when it all goes pear shaped, you are one of the world's worst hell raisers! Your ability to stir emotions is intense and somewhat scary, so deal with bitterness or frustration in a level headed way. Loved ones should respect your privacy. For you cannot abide to be stifled or dictated to. Personal freedom gives you leeway to love and support those you choose.

TAURUS
April 21st – May 21st
Ruled by Venus

FIRST DECAN: April 21st – April 30th
Planetary Influence: Venus

The ruler ship of Venus renders you rock solid and dependable with a romantic sensibility. Rarely will you risk or jeopardize a sure thing. Patient, methodical, and persevering, your slow steady energy may not win the race. But you are sure to finish with a commendation. You are a force to be reckoned with, for nothing fazes you. Your grounded character ensures that you are the most loyal and loving friend or lover. Being an earthy creature, you delight in sensual pleasures of the flesh. Or indeed anything that affirms your Life Force. Nature nurtures you, whilst beauty and serenity inspire your Soul. You are centered and focused, with unshakeable foundations.

SECOND DECAN: May 1st - May 10th
Planetary Influence: Mercury

Highly creative, you possess a rare artistic sensibility. Your intuition is sensitized which ensures that you do not miss a trick. With refined taste and high expectations, you can be unexpectedly shy. Even though you are easily wounded, you have an unbending, unswerving Will which triumphs at every turn. As a born survivor, you feel things deeply but can move on when required. Your complex character is both earthy and perfectionist. But you are inclined to bury your head in the sand rather than deal with something tricky. Stay real and monitor unrealistic expectations. Your high ideals and sense of purpose guarantee that you will find what you are looking for – eventually.

THIRD DECAN: May 11th – May 21st
Planetary Influence: Saturn

Your staying power is impressive. Slow moving you may be, but you always find your way through a maze of difficulty. Life's challenges inspire you, as well as test your patience. Logical, grounded and practical, you have an answer for everything. Flights of fancy are not an option. So do not be seduced by those who sell dreams. You are pragmatic and eminently sensible. Let common sense prevail - however mysterious life gets. Your innate resilience ensures that you bounce back from the brink every time. But watch out for that lazy streak. Walk permanently in a well-defined groove, and not much will veer you off track. You attract loving friends and family connections that last a lifetime.

GEMINI
May 22nd – June 22nd
Ruled by Mercury

FIRST DECAN: May 22nd – May 31st
Planetary Influence: Mercury

Mercury bestows you with a quick wit and lively mind. Your thought processes change like the wind, and it is impossible to pin you down. This makes for an edgy exciting personality that keeps us both interested and exasperated. You are versatile and multitalented. Little is beyond your remit. Your willingness to tackle most things ensures results, so remain focused. Well able to keep the rest of us guessing, you are a resourceful character who lives by wit alone. You love to keep your options open and play the field, or at least appear to be so doing. Success is a surety for your ambidextrous disposition. You are eminently loveable, mischievous and forgiven a lot.

SECOND DECAN: June 1st – June 10th
Planetary Influence: Venus

You are blessed with a rapier wit, and lively mind. Venus and Mercury help you to seduce whomever you set your sights on. Whether for business or pleasure, you are a dab hand at getting your own way. Gentle charm ensures your success. And your cutting sense of humor makes you irresistible. You are popular and shrewd with great focus. So whatever you set your heart upon can be yours, as long as concentration is maintained. You do not have it in you to be actively devious in a damaging way. But you can be pretty nifty, when push comes to shove. Expect a fun-filled life of humor, joy, love and understanding.

THIRD DECAN: June 11th – June 22nd
Planetary Influence: Uranus

You are quite 'Out There' and always on the lookout for new experiences. For you, reality is one big joy ride that occasionally becomes the ghost train. As an eternal optimist, you have visions and dream dreams, each one more magnificent than the last. Your natural intensity means that you experience life by the minute. You are a law unto yourself in true maverick style. Your upbeat groove does not have to indicate immaturity. But there is a part of you that will never grow up. Uncompromising as ever, you will stick your neck out, rather than damage your personal integrity. You are a powerful figure with the Midas touch, who can quite literally run the show without being there.

CANCER
June 23rd – July 23rd
Ruled by The Moon

FIRST DECAN: June 23rd – July 1st
Planetary Influence: The Moon

You are highly intuitive and emotional: a lunar creature who is responsive, empathetic, and sensitized. Nothing passes you by, for you are profoundly psychic. Relationships come easy and you are tailor made for human interaction. Always engage in the full flight of your emotions. Never mind the climb up the career ladder. Home is where the heart is, and you will not rest until you find your Soul Mate. Your dedication and like-ability ensure your success. You are not the most 'pushy' sign, but you are inherently lucky. It is impossible not to love you. You have a unique perception, and view the world in a matter of fact but astute way. There are no flies on you.

SECOND DECAN: July 2nd – July 12th
Planetary Influence: Pluto

You are a mysterious and enigmatic personality: a passionate and deep individual who feels everything on an intense level. Life is exhausting but exhilarating for those connected to you. Certainly, there is never a dull moment. At times you feel like an alien in a strange land. You are highly psychic with many overwhelming perceptions and intuitions. For sanity's sake, find an outlet so that your incredible imagination can express itself. You are liable to implode and beat yourself up when things go wrong. But to an extent you thrive on hardship and respond well to a challenge. Resilient and defiant, you are fiercely independent and treasure your privacy.

THIRD DECAN: July 13th – July 23rd
Planetary Influence: Neptune

You are very sensitive with a lovely gentle energy. As you have an innate ability to understand and empathize, you make a great confidant. With your personal, intimate relationships you can be clingy. You love to be loved, and need to be needed! Reassurance is important, but displays of affection are always repaid in kind. You can be intense and demanding, but you also have a lot to offer. Watch out for irrational reactions and guard against moodiness. You are artistic, creative, with a definite eye for beauty. Expend your energy positively for maximum fulfilment. Let your intuition be your guide, and you will end up better off than those who follow the logical route.

LEO
July 24th – August 23rd
Ruled by The Sun

FIRST DECAN: July 24th – August 1st
Planetary Influence: The Sun

You are a powerful compelling character, possessing great charisma and appeal. With incredible magnetism, you know how to command attention, and you are skilled at getting your own way. You are never likely to be ignored, even when incognito. Ego is an issue. But you automatically instill respect in both loved ones and opponents. Using humor and witty rhetoric you maneuver situations to maximum effect. Loyalty, generosity, and restraint make you a regal creature that never stints on affection and support. Your warmth of character and skills of performance attract the limelight. Express yourself on the stage of life. And expect the spotlight to shine upon you.

SECOND DECAN: August 2nd – August 12th
Planetary Influence: Jupiter

You have extra determination and expansive vision: truly, a Master who can see the bigger picture. Somewhat idealistic, you are a pioneer who wants to save the World. Never mind laziness, you need to maintain a sense of purpose. You have a wicked humor and know where to find the fun. Jupiter's influence renders you brave and optimistic, very little demoralizes or defeats you. You are kind, open hearted, and destined to be successful- without even trying. You inspire friendship and treasure your intimate relationships. It is very difficult to dislike or begrudge you anything. Your Midas touch makes you perhaps the luckiest sign in the Zodiac. It is your destiny to win big, in some respect.

THIRD DECAN: August 13th – August 23rd
Planetary Influence: Mars

As one of life's true survivors, adversity brings out the best in you. You are a dynamic character, who is willing and able to take on challenges. Indeed you are powerful. Whatever you set your heart on, can be yours. But stay on track and avoid confrontation. You possess rare grace and charm. So there is no need for masterstrokes or manipulation. Acknowledge your gifts, and develop self-confidence.

You are able to achieve great things through faith and belief alone. As a true entrepreneur, you can seal the deal with the full force of your personality. Few distrust or doubt you. Your reassuring presence instills confidence in the rest of the World. You understand life and the people therein.

VIRGO
August 24th – September 23rd
Ruled by Mercury

FIRST DECAN: August 24th – September 3rd
Planetary Influence: Mercury

Failure is not in your vocabulary. You set very high standards and are extremely self-critical. As someone who can objectify and assess situations at the drop of a hat, you are flexible and adaptable. A born survivor, you can turn disappointing events into a real gift. You are a cerebral Sign, adept at both logical and intuitive thinking. A natural student, you transport the Wisdom of Ages into the present. Hard working and studious very few subjects are beyond the remit of your lively mind. You can tackle most things standing on your head. But your creativity needs to be permanently stimulated or you get bored. Love has to be heart, soul and passion, or you will not bother.

SECOND DECAN: September 4th – September 13th
Planetary Influence: Saturn

You are a veritable force to be reckoned with. There is no point trying to pull the wool over your eyes...you can see around corners. With your exacting standards and strong ambition, you are inclined to take life quite seriously. As well as being determined and focused, your organizational skills are second to none. It is virtually impossible to fault you! You are a master of discernment, with an innate understanding of human nature. And since you never take 'no' for an answer, your success is guaranteed. You are reliable, honest, and not in the least bit ruthless. There is an on-going sense that anything can happen in your life, and probably will…You carry infinite possibilities.

THIRD DECAN: September 14th – September 23rd
Planetary Influence: Venus

Venus introduces a warm, loving and tolerant quality to your personality. You are content with simple pleasures and do not aspire to the giddy heights. You are warm, affectionate, and respond to plenty of TLC. Because you are all heart, you give freely with no strings attached. But you are no push over. Your natural intelligence renders you canny, witty and wise. And you are so self-assured that you feel no need to control people. In love you are earthy, sensuous, and 'in it for keeps'; but with no tedium or boredom factor. And you make an exceptionally caring and considerate lover. Loving and patient, you forgive and tolerate a lot without damaging your self-esteem. Are you human?

LIBRA
September 24th – October 23rd
Ruled by Venus

FIRST DECAN: September 24th – October 3rd
Planetary Influence: Venus

The very core of your being yearns for harmony. Finding peace is the sole motivation of your body and soul. You are gentle and companionable, making a genuine and reliable friend. Beautiful from the inside out, you are pure with oodles of integrity. Even though you are stoic and determined, you will usually put others first, for your loyalty and generosity are beyond question. What you may lack in terms of ambition and determination, you make up for with charm and skills of diplomacy. You have enviable social talents! With skillful self-expression you will 'tell it like it is' is the nicest possible way; your imagination, astounding creativity, and your gift of the gab guarantees success.

SECOND DECAN: October 4th – October 13th
Planetary Influence: Uranus

As a cool customer, you are willing to calculate your moves. You are nobody's fool. Independent and candid, you are not afraid to tackle things head-on. Not much is beyond you. You keep a cool head in a crisis, and know when to act for maximum impact. Logically minded, you are not liable to get carried away. You are free spirited. But, you do not compromise readily. Things have to be on your terms, or they tend not to happen. Outgoing, popular and approachable, you never want for company. And your in-built protection is that inherent like-ability. Your originality holds the key to wealth and riches. Whilst honed instincts will propel you to the level of success you choose.

THIRD DECAN: October 14th – October 23rd
Planetary Influence: Mercury

Lively, witty, versatile, with an imagination second to none, you are an enthusiastic chatterbox! And great company to boot. Boredom is not a word in your vocabulary. You are the Zodiac "wild child" who guarantees eternal high jinx and endless fun! There is the touch of the Maverick about you. For you will not be dictated to, or 'told'. Entertaining, mad and hilarious company, the rest of us cannot expect to get a word in edgeways. Communications and conversation stimulate you and your social calendar is always busy. You are attractive to many, and boy don't you just know it. You love to be in love, and feel less than complete without it. Get the next round in.

SCORPIO
October 24th – November 22nd
Ruled by Pluto and Mars

FIRST DECAN: October 24th – November 2nd
Planetary Influence: Pluto

Your dynamo personality is captivating and compelling. And your powers of persuasion are irresistible. Not one to give up easily. You are the Master seducer/seductress of the Zodiac. Nothing will defeat you, whilst your heart is open and compassionate. You bring warmth, discipline and passion to your relationships. Whilst your magnetic charisma means there is no need for words – one look from those soulful eyes does the trick. Insightful, but non-judgmental, you get straight to the point; and are great to have around in a crisis. Your level head and sensible demeanor sorts things out. And you are able to wriggle out of compromising situations in a most charming way. Complex, but utterly adorable, nothing escapes your Eagle Eye.

SECOND DECAN: November 3rd – November 12th
Planetary Influence: Neptune

Laid back Neptune makes you less intense and driven than fellow Scorpio. You are charitable, giving, and maintaining the status quo is a priority. Being family orientated you make sacrifices for the sake of peace and quiet. Getting ahead is not so important. Job satisfaction is crucial, but prestige and status are not. You are stimulating, interesting company; somewhat offbeat, but eminently charming. Mystery emanates from your very pores. And you have a unique way of looking at the world. It is difficult to fathom your thinking and perceptions. But wherever you go, quirky fun and intrigue surely follow. You are intense and meaningful without being intrusive - delicious company, altogether.

THIRD DECAN: November 13th – November 22nd
Planetary Influence: The Moon

The Moon enhances your mystery and powers of seduction. You are guaranteed to be compelling and alluring, even first thing in the morning. Truly magical, you have the ability to captivate anyone you care to mention. All things to all people, you are very feminine and powerful, never mind your gender. Enticing in the extreme, you are also very domesticated. Tender, loving, and caring, you give priority to security and comfort in the home. Silence is golden when you are around. For your presence is simply enchanting. Your allure is transmitted with a gaze, touch or meaningful gesture. You are subtle, canny and adaptable. If any person is capable of casting a spell it is you.

SAGITTARIUS
November 23rd – December 21st
Ruled by Jupiter

FIRST DECAN: November 23rd – December 2nd
Planetary Influence: Jupiter

Jupiter guarantees you eternal optimism and an indomitable spirit. You are endless fun with a serious side that surfaces intermittently. Love of life and the acquirement of knowledge are your strong motivations; for you are an intelligent philosopher who likes to get to the bottom of things. You crave freedom and cannot stand any form of restriction. Restless as you are, you can be exhausting but stimulating company. Life must be a continual exploration and journey; as you do not respond well to the idea of arriving somewhere. Books, literature and philosophy expand your horizons if you cannot literally travel. But you are destined to go far, one way or another.

SECOND DECAN: December 3rd – December 12th
Planetary Influence: Mars

Oh Boy, you are a handful! With more than your fair share of energy and zest, you are entertaining but tiring. Once you have decided something, there is no stopping you. You possess an indomitable will. And you will make things happen, come what may. Quite compulsive, your determination to succeed is a wonder to behold. But you are generous spirited, and will not intentionally tread on toes. Truly you are a force to be reckoned with. You like to be stimulated, unsettled, and amused – all at the same time. But you are endlessly entertaining and rarely cause offence. With your sense of fun, stamina levels and passion power. You should come with a government health warning.

THIRD DECAN: December 13th – December 21st
Planetary Influence: The Sun

What a regular dynamo! With clarity of purpose and extra energy, you get things done. The Sun bestows you with an open, generous spirit. And not much stands in your way. You are inherently lucky; for even when challenged, something will surely happen to save-the-day. Optimism is a way of life. Rarely does your will get crushed beyond repair. You look for the good in everything and everybody. And often the leap of faith is repaid in full. People love your off-the-wall madness and wicked sense of humor. Variety is the spice of life, and you thrive on a bit of scandal or gossip. You need endless stimulation, and were not created to be ignored. The Craic sure is mighty.

CAPRICORN
December 22nd – January 20th
Ruled by Saturn

FIRST DECAN: December 22nd – December 31st
Planetary Influence: Saturn

Determination will see you through – But life is hard work. So expect character-forming challenges to occur regularly. A true survivor, your achievements are precious indeed. Stoic qualities serve you well. And much effort goes into the attainment of your dreams. With grounded equilibrium, you are a formidable force when focused. Your tenacity and discipline win every time. When up against it, keep your head down. Expect to reach the dizzy heights of success. But first prove your durability. Fame awaits you if you are patient and do not give up. You are sensual and practical: a skillful, considerate friend and lover. Appreciate the view along the way, and learn to value the 'little things' in life.

SECOND DECAN: January 1st – January 10th
Planetary Influence: Venus

Your artistic temperament and diverse talents ensure that you do not miss a trick. Less the drama queen, more the queen bee, you are compelling and seductive. A photographic style memory serves you well. But, watch you do not lose perspective. Even Super humans need to keep a grip on reality. That high intelligence may tempt you to take advantage - Lesser mortals beware. An aesthetically appealing environment is very important to you. And you do have impeccable taste. Domestic and material bliss travel hand in hand. You make a reliable and committed partner, but only when you have reached a respectable position. First things first; you *are* romantic; just not before it is "appropriate" to be so.

THIRD DECAN: January 11ᵗʰ – January 20ᵗʰ
Planetary Influence: Mercury

Mercury gives you the edge. You are highly motivated and disciplined. Nothing blocks your route to the top of the tree. And you possess a ruthless streak that comes into play if someone attempts to sabotage or undo your good work- understandable. You do not respond kindly to competition – you have to be the best – or else. A true perfectionist, you have a brilliant mind. There is indeed a touch of genius when you are in full flow. An exceptionally creative and powerful personality, you cast a spell. And who can say no? With a computer's memory for detail, you take some beating. Facts and figures trip off your tongue. When you want to impress, you surely will.

AQUARIUS
January 21ˢᵗ – February 19ᵗʰ
Ruled by Uranus

FIRST DECAN: January 21ˢᵗ – January 29ᵗʰ
Planetary Influence: Uranus

A truly free spirited being, you are not afraid to follow your heart. One of life's philanthropists; there is not a selfish bone in your body when you are balanced and stable. Your destiny is to serve humanity with discernment and wisdom. Speak the truth as you see it, and always be willing to help. Life is a trip! There is always something to think about, and to be getting on with. No problem is insurmountable. Your great instincts and innate wisdom mean that you are a walking oracle, with enviable skills of detachment. You know how to isolate and intercept dilemmas even as they arise. Pearls of wisdom trip from your tongue. So, focus on what counts.

SECOND DECAN: January 30th – February 8th
Planetary Influence: Mercury

Lively and quick-witted, your mental agility is impressive. Liable to be academic and highly intelligent, you happily grapple with most topics. With great eloquence, you are rarely lost for words. You hate to admit mistakes so will store up excuses just in case. But that perfectionist streak makes you your own worst critic. A true Renaissance man or woman, you need a lot of stimulation or boredom sets in. Very sociable but intensely private, you are complex. Adaptable and willing to work in unusual conditions and in unusual ways, you will try anything once. Flexibility is your middle name whilst you amuse and amaze. You respect life, humanity and see the best in everyone, without being wet.

THIRD DECAN: February 9th – February 19th
Planetary Influence: Venus

You house an interesting blend of energies. Less cerebral and intellectually driven than the previous two Decans, objectivity is not the strong point of your feeling-based personality. Compassionate in the extreme, and beautiful with it, you do not possess the ability to detach and consider. With a tendency to get in too deep, you get involved with other people's problems far too readily. Out of the goodness of your heart, you want the World and its Auntie to 'be OK!' Altruistic in the extreme, you must guard against a tendency towards self-sacrifice for the benefit of loved ones. Toughen-up a bit...Your creativity is second to none. So channel positive energy into yourself, and do not disperse your life force.

PISCES
February 20th – March 20th
Ruled by Neptune

FIRST DECAN: February 19th – February 29th
Planetary Influence: Neptune

Neptune governs transcendence, spirituality, illusion, and suffering. So you are one interesting, compelling human being. Inspirational and creative, it is nigh on impossible to fathom your murky depths. Even your silence is loaded and fascinating. Quiet and unassuming, no one is bored in your company. For your mere presence ensures an element of mystery. Generous spirited you are willing to give without guarantee of a return. A true romantic with a poetic soul, you are naturally psychic, wise, and profound. Your sensitivity and compassion makes you highly desirable. But your spirituality ensures that you are not impressed by anything superficial. Natural ease combined with a romantic, dreamy, and sexy spirit, makes you a great catch indeed.

SECOND DECAN: March 1st - March 10th
Planetary Influence: The Moon

The feminine energy of the Moon heightens your sensibilities. You are a gentle, nurturing soul. Above all you are caring, sharing and kind. A beautiful person indeed, the finer feelings of love, romance and perception encapsulate your *raison d'etre*. There is no active deception or nastiness hidden away. In fact the very idea you having hidden secrets is quite a joke. Okay, so everyone has a shadow side. But it is difficult to find it in your case. With a talented and unusual disposition, you possess a refined, artistic nature. You are a creative and poetic personality, skilled enough to make a fortune by not doing very much at all! The art of living excites you.

THIRD DECAN: March 11th – March 20th
Planetary Influence: Pluto

You are positively spooky! The energy of Pluto ensures that you miss nothing. Being very psychic and intuitive, it is impossible to lie to you. And with your great intensity and heightened sensitivity you are exceptionally powerful. Not much stand in your way, once you are committed to a plan of action. Your great intelligence identifies you. With a lively mind and definite vision there is no stopping your Pluto driven character. Natural flexibility and versatility make you a winner every time...You are not held back by negative or corrupt ideas and thoughts. Life flows for you. And you are truly blessed with access to phenomenal opportunities. Live and let live.

3 MERCURY RISING

Most people have heard of the lively little planet Mercury. But what does it mean to us on a daily basis, if anything? Well, if you believe that astrology has some bearing on our lives, you will be well aware of the chaotic influence which retrograde Mercury can have from time to time.

Mercury retrograde is somewhat infamous for causing havoc with all things mechanical and with written communications in particular. E mails, texts, faxes, documents need special attention, and extra vigilance is important on the roads. Mercury retrograde is potentially a time of delays, frustrations and mix ups. But there is an upside, and I do believe if we are aware of when these phases are, a lot can be done to make them very productive indeed.

It is most definitely *not* a good idea to sign important documentation during the three week stretches of Mercury retrograde, unless you really know what you are letting yourself in for. If you keep a vigilant eye out for the warning signs, Mercury retrograde can be a time of introspection and deep thought. Links back to the past can be especially fortuitous and indeed may hold clues as to how we might progress once things get moving again.

Out-with the retrograde phases, Mercury's influence is cerebral and lively. This planet's position is the best indicator of the way a person's mind works. Mercury is a small but potent planet that impacts our intelligence and thought patterns. Mental agility may be instinctive, logical, slow and deliberate, or somewhat scattered. Whether we are intuitive or excruciatingly systematic in our thinking, Mercury provides the clue. Mercury enhances our ability to make decisions, and it also determines how we communicate. Mercury enhances mind power, empowering both intuition and logical thought.

Sun signs Gemini and Virgo are ruled by this energy and usually have staggering intellectual capacity. Mercury enables its people to see around corners, and to cover all aspects of an argument. This planet is thorough, brilliant, and leaves no stone unturned.

So where was Mercury residing at your time of birth and how does its position in your chart facilitate your decision making processes and your ability to communicate in love, friendship and in the work place? If you are near a computer, you can find the information even more quickly on-line, by googling "Mercury position in natal chart." Find Your Mercury Sign in the tables at the back of this book. You may already know the positioning of Mercury in your natal chart, in which case read on.

Mercury in ARIES

With Mercury in Aries: You are upfront, direct and impetuous. Impulsive with your assertions, there is no messing about and no doubt, what you are all about. Blunt and to the point, you are open and quite fierce with the way you put things across. Your competitive streak leaves rivals quaking in their boots. They realize there is not much point in taking you on. For you fight to the death and always defend what you feel is yours. To your credit you do not play games, nor do you trifle with people's affections. Loved ones and enemies alike always know where they stand with you. Okay you are hotheaded in a row, but just as quickly the calm descends.

Sometimes you come across as quite self-serving. But it is usually because you wish to make the best of things. You do not always consider the consequences of your actions and tend to act first and think later. Some may assume you are superficial, but actually you feel things deeply and mean every word you say. It is just that what you feel, mean and say can change overnight.

You are loud, proud and dangerous to know. Unfortunately you are prone to jealousy and when you are angry what happens next is not particularly pretty. For the most part you are lively, congenial company. You just need to learn how to relax.

How to Handle Mercury in ARIES

In Yourself: Focus on one thing at a time if possible and aim to complete it. You are easily distracted and must be more disciplined and productive. Don't try to do everything at once and do count to TEN before you jump in and express your controversial opinions.

In your Lover: Keep a lover with Aries energy keen. Aries-heads are easily distracted and easily bored, so you will have to keep them on their toes. Do not "treat them mean, to keep them keen." But do have a few tricks up your sleeve and makes dates as varied as possible. Expect action packed shenanigans. Match the odd put-down with a witty response.

In your Friends: Aries type friends are young at heart and will keep you free and spirited if you allow them to influence you in positive ways. Adventurous and up-for-it, life is never dull with a person who has Mercury in Aries. Expect them to be provocative and argumentative at times though. Stay cool and do not rise to the bait.

In your Boss: Keep your communication short and sweet. Make your point; then listen for clues. They *will* get their own way, so you might as well make it easy on yourself and do not fight your corner too much. Make the Mercurial Aries boss think everything is their idea. Then you won't go far wrong.

Mercury in TAURUS

With Mercury in Taurus: When you are emotionally comfortable you are tactile, flirty and romantic with your words and responses. But put the wind up you and you switch quickly into merciless, defensive mode. You fight like a cornered rat with cutting remarks and hurtful quips when someone upsets your personal equilibrium. Plus you have no tolerance for disloyalty or phoney gestures.

Your mental stability and the general Status Quo is of supreme importance and you cannot function properly without balance. As a result you can be quite controlling and tend to over invest in the preservation of your interests. People become your possessions and when you feel uneasy you often test their intentions. Try to chill and not be such a control freak.

You are quite conservative in the way you put things across and your traditionalism sometimes gets in the way of a good time. Let your hair down once in a while and do not try to keep tabs on everyone and everything. You are an expert at commanding the stage of life, and not many people would disagree that you have great natural authority.

You command situations with steadiness and surety. But you have a wicked stubborn streak and hate to be dictated to. Perhaps your worst weakness is that you automatically assume that you are in the right. You are not very open to other's opinions or ways of being. You may listen, but when push comes to shove, you just know that you are right.

How to Handle Mercury in TAURUS

In Yourself: Do try to be more flexible with your ideas and slightly less staid and fixed in your approach to life. Definitely recognise when a way of thinking, living and being has passed its sell by date. You must accept when it is time to move on with your ideas, creativity and thinking. Do not get "stuck in a moment."

In your Lover: This lover is easily wooed with romantic words, poetry and music. The way to this love's heart is through good quality merchandise too. Mercurial Taurus loves luxury and sensuous items.

"Touchy-feely" is an understatement for this tactile persona. Be gentle and verbally cute to win this heart and mind. Good food and clever spending keep links strong.

In your Friends: This friend takes their time to deliberate and may really try your patience when there are important decisions to make. Once their mind is made up you will not budge it. Stubborn is not the word. Be accepting and tolerant to keep this one on board. There is no point in locking horns. You will never change this friend; don't even try.

In your Boss: A boss with Mercury in Taurus wants to make money, and if you can sell an idea based on performance and profit margins, you are in the good books! The only way to impress this boss is by being productive and financially viable. Always look good and be convincing even when you are quaking in your boots.

Mercury in GEMINI

With Mercury in Gemini: You are playful, flirtatious and communicative. Your lively mind is captivating and you thrive in varied company and situations. Displays of verbal affection and flirtation come naturally and perhaps a little too easily to you. Like a child who flits from person to person, you can come across as superficial and fickle. Actually, you feel things deeply, just not in the way everyone else does. Always on the hunt for new experiences, it is difficult to keep up with you.

Colleagues, friends and partners may feel they do not get the input they deserve; but you are great fun, and never boring. Lively, intelligent and extrovert, you are a restless spirit, always on the look-out for new amusements and mad entertainment. Your need for permanent stimulation is an exhausting prospect for lovers and family alike. Open minded as you are, your attentions are easily diverted, which is not great for the commitment factor.

Gemini energy feels a divine entitlement to two of everything. So you are capable of several things at once as well as playing both ends against the middle. Life is never dull with you in the room. You provide hours of entertainment and like to keep things sweet with your gregarious nature.

You are a nifty character, who thrives on impromptu, off-the-cuff comments and situations. Your responses are quick and you are at your best in mad, hectic situations.

How to Handle Mercury in GEMINI

In Yourself: Do be a bit less ready to share your secrets with all and sundry. Yes you like a good old gossip and heart to heart. But you DO need to develop a modicum of discretion; right? Also guard against expending too much nervous energy. You burn out easily and sometimes have *too* much fun. Calm down just a tad.

In your Lover: Do *not* be possessive with this lover. They need to develop a whole range of friends and contacts. But they are probably not up to half as much as you think they are. So live and let live. Be sharp and witty and make sure you know about the latest films, books and media events. Listen up and let your lover talk: *a lot!*

In your Friends: This friend is great for a good old gossip, but please do not tell them your secrets unless you want the world to know. Your latest thoughts will do the rounds very quickly, so be careful. Easily distracted, this mate is fun, exhausting, and more than a little nosy.

In your Boss: This boss is impressed by your creativity and ability to put ideas across. Apparently quite scatty, you can scribble down what they and take the credit for it later. They will have forgotten they said it in the first place. Boost the old ego and point out their genius qualities; they will love you.

Mercury in CANCER

With Mercury in Cancer: Strongly influenced by the Moon, you can be anxious and moody, if not a little temperamental. Your reactions, words and intensions are acute and you are highly intuitive.

If something or someone does not feel right, you will steer clear. You should never doubt your hunches. But your sensitive nature is a mixed blessing. Not much escapes your notice; but you are prone to cutting off your nose to spite your face. Very black and white with your responses, no one crosses you and gets away with it. Protective of your interests, you are also quite controlling. You like to know what's going on and to whom. People confide in you; which keeps you ahead of the game. You have learned the hard way and can be quite defensive when you feel threatened. You know how to keep people guessing, which is great when you want to keep people interested. Your best quality is a talent for nurturing those you love, or in whom you have a vested interest. Watch you do not get too manipulative with these undercurrents of control. You are powerful, so use your gifts wisely. Remember that privacy and personal space are crucial to your sanity. Too often you have a melt-down for no good reason and no one understands the tantrum; least of all yourself. You need an outlet for these complex emotions; but try to keep it positive and retreat privately when you feel an irrational storm brewing.

How to Handle Mercury in CANCER

In Yourself: You are prone to bleak moods and thoughts because of your sensitive nature. Nurture the skill of positive thinking and develop your intuition. Balance emotional responses with a dose of logic and keep those feet on the ground. Your psychic ability if developed will give you the edge.

In your Lover: This lover is nostalgic and loves to reminisce. Mementos and memories turn this person on, so do make an effort to preserve your personal history together. It is the best way to keep this sensitive soul hanging on; for ever and a day. Be aware you may never shake them off if you impress them too much.

In your Friends: This friend is a great listening ear and gives good advice with those sharp intuitive responses. They will rarely be wrong and they are something of an oracle, so ignore them at your peril. Of course it could get tedious if you feel *you* are right. But do keep listening; you will not regret it.

In your Boss: Security issues are important to this boss, so always have a back-up plan for risky ideas and moments. Think contingency plan at every step and you will not go far wrong. Also keep copies of everything and make sure your tracks are covered. This boss will be sensitive to your needs, so do ask for that pay rise.

Mercury in LEO

With Mercury in Leo: You are warm and kind hearted to those who light your fire; but you can be catty and controlling when up against it. For the most part your verbal responses and thought processes are fair and you give others the benefit of the doubt. However, you can be a bit of a show off and become quite bossy when you are on a roll. Be careful you do not railroad people into particular ways of behaving and watch your expectancy levels. You are certainly powerful enough to get your way in most things, so use this power wisely.

Your open-hearted nature and generosity of spirit will always generate the quality connections you need in order to thrive. So err on the bright side and ditch those with whom you clash; you are better off without them. It is no secret that you are a bit of a performer. In fact you are the original drama queen. You know how to keep the rest of us entertained. But when you kick up a fuss, it really is no laughing matter. Your temper tantrums are legendary. Indeed, you can be quite childlike when you do not get your own way.

Passionate and dynamic, you are indeed quite a handful. Learn to ease off the gas and give others a chance to give you something in return. Your creativity is enviable and you have good energy reserves for the things that grab your imagination. But routine stuff bores the pants off you.

How to Handle Mercury in LEO

In Yourself: Try to step off the gas and give others a look in from time to time. You will make greater progress if you become just a tinge self-absorbed. Ironically you will get your own way more readily if you use reverse psychology and let others have more say. Learn to handle criticism more graciously too. You just might learn something.

In your Lover: This lover needs to be adored and complimented. Egocentric but in a rather cute way, you will need to be patient as well as very tolerant. Be firm and fair when the ego loses the run of itself. But apart from that, this lover is hot, and will provide hours of endless action and entertainment.

In your Friends: This mate is a drama queen of the highest order, but is very funny and entertaining with it. You will have to be patient and possess an ever-listening ear to keep this friend on side. Expect to get a bit drained as things can get a bit one-sided when Leo energy is prominent in someone's chart. Fight to be heard

In your Boss: This boss will need to think they have come up with all the good ideas, so you will have to be low key and magnanimous in order to succeed. You may get overlooked on occasion. But so long as the boss is happy, you will be rewarded generously for your efforts. Take note of their likes and dislikes and act accordingly.

Mercury in VIRGO

With Mercury in Virgo: You are a sensitive individual with unique responses. A law unto yourself; you will not be dictated to. You do things in your own way, or not at all. Even though you are a stickler for truth, you will still bend the rules when it suits you. Often you run on an excess of nervous energy and tend to push yourself to the max.

When you are in light and bright mode, your wit and humour are deadly and you actually have more control over what happens than when you are stressed and fraught. You are a perfectionist with high standards who must try not to judge so harshly.

With your high intelligence and verbal superiority you beat the best. Your way with words is legendary. You can out-smart the best of them. Make good use of these tools, for you have the power to cut like a knife or sow the seeds of good will.

When you are stressed and wound up, you can fall victim to high levels of anxiety. Take a chill pill and put things into perspective. It does not do you any favours to ruminate endlessly about the past, present and future. Simply be in the moment for your sanity's sake. Avoid your tendency to pick things apart. You have an analytical streak that's enviable, but it can also be your downfall. You are inclined to be overlooked by the Zodiac's more assertive types; but you make your voice heard in subtle ways, which ultimately works to your advantage. With your systematic, methodical streak, you work your way into hearts and minds.

How to Handle Mercury in VIRGO

In Yourself: Learn to lighten up and laugh a whole lot more. You can get over anxious and very bogged down in other people's concerns as well as your own. Remember, life is too short for too much grief. Find ways to calm down your over-active mind and so soothe its effect on your nervous system. Be much less hard on yourself.

In your Lover: Take an interest in this lover's interests. You will need to keep their mind as well their body and spirit entertained. The way to this lover's heart is through their mind power and finding common ground. So do your homework and prepare to talk 'til the cows come home.

In your Friends: This mate is a walking oracle. Matter of fact and good company this friend does not beat about the bush. You will feel safe and comfortable in their company and you can always rely on their support and good advice. The down side is the nagging which will kick in if your mate gets over stressed and anxious. Make him/her laugh and all will be well.

In your Boss: This boss respects attention to detail and does not tolerate silly slip ups. Be efficient and thorough in your work to impress and do not shout about it. If you do a good job it will not go unnoticed, and you will be fairly rewarded for your efforts. This boss will point out your mistakes; so pay attention or ship out.

Mercury in LIBRA

With Mercury in Libra: You are a cool customer with an impartial measured way of putting things across. This does not mean that stuff does not get to you; but you usually manage to be quite dignified and mature in your delivery. Somewhat idealistic, you hate confrontation and always make a concerted effort to keep the peace. You are a stickler for a harmonious atmosphere and will bend over backwards to avoid a row. This too can sometimes work against you, and you would do well to speak your truth more often. The rest of the world will not disrespect you if you stand your ground.

Do not allow your indecisiveness to make you prey to more ruthless types. With a tougher exterior, you can protect your interests with a clear conscience. If all else fails, use your gifts of flirtation to make a point. You are well able to wrap anyone around your little finger with your effervescent wit and charm. But, because you are so good at empathizing with others, you often sacrifice your own beliefs, desires and ideas to help the along.

You may also find it difficult to process resentment and frustration. Stop being quite so nice all the time. Buried anger can be poisonous and will not ultimately do you any favours. In typical Libra style, you are sometimes assertive; sometimes shy. You blow hot and cold, which always keeps things interesting. But your dithering can sometimes be quite exasperating, so discern when to go for it!

How to Handle Mercury in LIBRA

In Yourself: Remember, a good old humdinger can clear the air and facilitate the process of moving on. Sometimes in your desire for permanent harmony, you miss the rectitude of righteous anger. Learn to identify problems, and more importantly do not assume you can always gloss over them. Do be willing express anger as part of your verbal repertoire. Your care for others will then be more effective.

In your Lover: Keep things full of fun and humour when you are around this lover. They don't like confrontation or too much angst. So keep the soul searching and aggravation, for your mates or the punch bag. This lover responds to major flirtation. Just keep it fairly clean and uphold their interest. Do not try to stir up jealousy; it is pointless.

In your Friends: This mate is charming and very good at keeping everyone sweet. They will calm you down and diffuse a row, even while they dither about anything and everything. Reassure your mate and help them with good advice to reason through their decisions. They probably will not be able to make them without you.

In your Boss: This boss is sound and has good judgement, as well as a fair approach to everyone and everything. Calm, logic and diplomacy are skills that will take you far under the watchful eye of a boss like this. Demonstrate balance and sound judgement yourself and you will be laden with well-paid responsibility.

Mercury in SCORPIO

With Mercury in Scorpio: You are passionate and intense with unfathomable depths. Often you do not needs words for your eyes do the talking much of the time. Your responses are often loaded and you give deep and meaningful a sexy frisson. You are a delightful mystery to more simple souls who hang on your every word.

Your complexity is truly captivating and your depth of expression and sheer presence enable you to cast many a spell on the unwitting. Often you are not aware of your charisma and power; which is of course what appeals to and charms those who find you so compelling. The danger is, when you wake up to your personal power, you are quite inclined to use it skilfully to get your own way. So, be respectful of those you reel into your delightful but sticky web.

No one messes with you; that is for sure. When you get a bee in your bonnet about something, nothing will persuade you to back down.

Passionate and intense, you are a veritable volcano in a verbal set-to. You do not believe in half measures and when you are committed to an opinion, you make sure that everyone knows where you stand. Passionate responses come easy to you; people get the measure of you quite quickly; mainly because you let them know what is what. In a whirlwind of intensity you make your links, only to find that all too often they just as quickly fade away.

Get the balance right and learn to hold back until you are sure of your staying power in particular situations.

How to Handle Mercury in SCORPIO

In Yourself: You have a powerful mind and will need to learn a lot of self-control to make the most of what this finely honed instrument has to offer. Know yourself. Watch that you do not fall foul of too much power play or mind games. You are hypnotic and charismatic and must use these skills responsibly and wisely. Think karmically.

In your Lover: Do not be an open book to this lover. You need to keep them guessing and keep an air of mystery in everything you do. Reel this love in with intrigue and allure. Your sexiness must be hypnotic and irresistible, if not a little risqué! Mind games, illicit shenanigans and erotic encounters keep the home fires burning.

In your Friends: Remember the sting in the tail with this mate. They will automatically know your business, yet will hold out on you with a whole lot. This friend will keep their secrets and will expect you to do the same. You do not betray this mate and get away with it. They like to control things and can be very stubborn.

In your Boss: This boss values loyalty and discretion. There will be a lot of gossip and whispering around the office for this boss inspires such a reaction. Just do not get caught on the hop. You must be seen to be doing things by the book or the reprimands will be immense. To impress, use your investigative skills to unravel a mystery or solve a problem.

Mercury in SAGITTARIUS

With Mercury in Sagittarius: Open and responsive; you are a livewire who follows up every scintillating opportunity and conversation with lots of fun and high Jinx! You are verbal dynamo and your sense of humour is legendary. But you come across as a bit reckless; which does not instil much trust in those who want to invest in you.

Ever the adventurer, you view every encounter as an exciting exploration. Situations have to hold your interest, for your mind wanders very readily. Once you get the measure of the current landscape, you are anxious to move on to greener pastures. It goes without saying that you get bored easily. If someone or something does not hold your attention, you are off unceremoniously looking for new distractions.

You do not respond well to pressure, and you do not like to fight. This means that you walk away from things too readily and often live to regret such hasty reactions. Your optimism is infectious though and you have a natural zest for life. Straightforward and adventurous, you are up for anything that tickles your fancy.

You are quite a rowdy soul, liable to be boisterous even in the wee small hours when the rest of the world is asleep. With endless reserves of nervous energy, you are a motor mouth at risk from burn out if you don't learn to unwind, occasionally.

How to Handle Mercury in SAGITTARIUS

In Yourself: You need to focus and be efficient in all things. You have a lot to offer, but can be too scattered as you try to do everything at once. Take life one step at a time. Harness your creativity and personal power by realising that you cannot know everything. Do not be a jack of all trades, master of none. You are worth more than that; so prioritize.

In your Lover: Keep this lover's interest up with lots of scooting about and travel plans. Be as informed as possible on as many subjects as possible and take special note to read up on this love's hobbies. You will need to have lots of energy and be willing to share a whole lot. Keep your sense of humour and prepare to have some serious fun.

In your Friends: This mate is a great craic! You will be in stitches most of the time, so let's hope there is not work to be done when you are in each other's company. Sometimes this friend is overly blunt and can be a bit of a know-it-all. Be patient, as their company is definitely worth holding on to. There is no point in falling out.

In your Boss: If you catch this boss's imagination with your vision and creativity, you are in the good books right away. Think expansively and make your points with humour and originality. Keep the bigger picture in mind and always put things in context. Prioritize your work and pay attention to detail as this boss is hopeless on that score.

Mercury in CAPRICORN

With Mercury in Capricorn: You are very determined, focused and quite deliberate in your conversation and delivery of an opinion. You do not suffer fools gladly and you hate people without decorum and dignity.

Quite traditional, you know when it is best to stay silent. Slow and steady wins the race as far as you are concerned. But your caution and control can also be a bit intimidating to those who are perhaps more trusting and naïve. This gives you the edge in competitive situations but can be a bit of a drawback personally.

Articulate and charming in a subtle understated way, you can also be cool and unapproachable. I guess you are quite fussy and protective about who you spend you precious time with; for you do not like to expend energy on people who do not matter. This could be called ruthless, but equally it could be called discerning. Just get the balance right or you may alienate important contacts without intending to do so.

When things are not going your way you tend to moan and complain, sometimes even resorting to devious measures to make a point. You are an earthy, matter of fact soul, who can be quite calculating. This means that you carefully guard your interests and always keep your boundaries in check, but you are eminently nice with it. Perhaps develop your acting abilities, since it is better to keep your moodiness at bay.

You are a bit unadventurous and staid at times. So tap into your fun side and develop your humour as your best lethal weapon.

How to Handle Mercury in CAPRICORN

In Yourself: You are reliability personified, though would benefit from a flexible, more relaxed approach. Life is messy: "things happen," and you cannot always be there to sort it all out. Free yourself up a bit, by accepting the flow of events and the challenge of new circumstances. Try to trust people and life a little more; not everyone is out to get you.

In your Lover: This lover is sensual but shy, so be calm, considerate and low key as you get to know them. Let them organise you and run the show, for this love needs to feel in control. Expect understated affection and the soft touch. Just remember understated passion is often heartfelt and genuine. Romance is practical, but commitment is a given.

In your Friends: This mate is down to earth and offers good advice. An old head on young shoulders; this mate is rather traditional and straight-laced. But with their unquestionable reliability and loyalty at your disposal, you would be mad not to treasure them. A wicked dry sense of humour makes this mate invaluable. Their trust is not in question for a second.

In your Boss: Impress this boss by being as perfectionist as possible. The only problem is you will never be as impressive as this authoritarian. But this Boss is a good mentor and if you assist them with their goals and priorities, you will be duly rewarded. Work hard and display loyalty and all will be well.

Mercury in AQUARIUS

With Mercury in Aquarius: Eccentric and a law unto yourself, you make things up as you go along. You have a wicked turn of phrase and a unique way of putting things. Fresh approaches and unusual ideas turn you on. You can cope with most forms of weirdness and precious little offends you. You are an old soul, so life is not one big quest for excitement; but you are equal to it all when the madness sets in.

Your rebellious streak comes through with your wry sense of humour which usually manages to find expression even in the most serious circumstance. Work, friendships and partnerships must stimulate your mind, and you make mental connections very readily.

You are altruistic, but also intensely private, which makes you very giving one minute, then quite inaccessible the next. You have a talent for detachment, and a way of putting things which hits the spot every time. You give objective, wise advice and appropriate support.

With your wicked sense of humour, you have a novel way of looking at the world which keeps people amused. Quick off the mark; nothing gets past your extreme powers of perception. With your altruistic tendencies, you are full of empathy and understanding. But you know your limits too.

You do not suffer fools gladly and anyone who takes advantage of your good nature gets short shrift. Experimental, adventurous, and a skilful flirt; new ideas and experiences grab your imagination, and you are willing to give most things a try.

How to Handle Mercury in AQUARIUS

In Yourself: Keep those feet on the ground. Your fantastical notions and ideas sometimes go a bit too far; but weirdly you are often proven right. You are quite the visionary, so do learn how to handle your eccentricity and wisdom which is as old as the hills. Sometimes your reactions are a bit extreme; stay calm and measured in your responses.

In your Lover: This lover is unconventional and probably quite kinky. Do not expect the traditional romantic gestures though. You will have to be imaginative and unusual as well as informed on every subject under the sun. This love likes to talk; but equally likes privacy. Make a mind connection and the rest will follow.

In your Friends: This mate will keep you entertained with their weird and wonderful ways. They will keep you amused; but may occasionally go off on one. Be patient and laugh along, even though you may feel concerned. Do not worry; it will not last long. This mate is an inspiration and you will never follow the crowd ever again. Express yourself.

In your Boss: If you justify your creativity and good ideas to this boss you will get a listening ear. This unconventional leader is altruistic and open to most things. You cannot really lose here as you will be able to at least get a shot at putting your ideas into action. Be unusual and effective, you will not be overlooked.

Mercury in PISCES

With Mercury in Pisces: Highly sensitive and intuitive, you are very in touch with your feelings, and you know how to express yourself from the heart. Often though, you get overwhelmed by your strong psychic intuition and you stay quiet. You are also quite changeable and likely to flip your opinions and perceptions without warning. This can be bewildering for those who think they have the measure of you.

You are unpredictable, hate confrontation and are liable to be evasive when put on the spot. Kind and giving, you are also likely to tell the odd white lie to keep the peace. You are very susceptible to the ebb and flow of what is going on around you. Like a psychic sponge, you soak it all up.

It is important to protect yourself and not get too hooked into what everyone else is thinking and feeling. Your mind does not miss a trick which is a mixed blessing. You have great powers of empathy and perception, which makes you nice to know. But you do have a nosy streak, and love to be at the heart of other people's business.

Your natural psychic ability and sensitivity give you the edge in many situations. However, you can be a bit vague and you will not be pinned down when you are unsure. Evasive and deceptive when cornered, you are a subtle mover with wily ways. No you are not actively dishonest, but you do not like confrontation and will do anything to wriggle away from it. You are good at reading people and quite skilful at nipping problems in the bud.

How to Handle Mercury in PISCES

In Yourself: Do learn to discern what is important and what is not. Focus holds the key to your best decisions, and a slow deliberate chat can sort out most things. Do not be evasive when this is required. Sometimes you get disillusioned that things do not happen as you deem they should. But you are not a control freak, merely an idealist. Always guard against confusion and use your common sense!

In your Lover: This lover will read you like a book. You can run but you definitely can't hide. Indeed, why would you want to? This lover is usually gorgeousness personified. Romantic and really intense, this lover will not let you go. When they are with you, they are with you. Enjoy, and breathe easy, when you can come up for air.

In your Friends: This mate is really emotional and psychically in tune. Listen to the insights and visions of this friend and you won't go far wrong. There is another worldly quality about this one and you will have to acquire a taste for the fantastical and magical. Prepare to share emotions and do lots of soul searching. You will sort the world out.

In your Boss: This boss has some fantastic ideas, but probably no sense of how to make them happen. This is where you can come in. If you can grasp the gist of what your boss wants and put your own spin on it in a practical, achievable way, you will really make an impression. You will have to pin down that pay rise though. Make sure this boss delivers on a promise.

4 MOON SIGNS

The Moon influences our lives at a profound level. Her powerful lunar energy has an amazing impact on our creativity. Both our psyche and energy are invariably affected, and are more dependent upon The Moon's current phase and position than we would perhaps care to admit.

The Moon connects us to universal mother energy, regardless of our natal sex. The nurturing energies of The Moon define our parenting skills, and emotional impulses. Its gentle but relentless force shapes our familial and domestic arrangements. Our home lives, relationships and responses are all profoundly influenced by The Moon's Cycles.

Lunar inspiration affects intuition, instinctual reactions; and the ebb and flow of our feelings. As we all know, the Moon rules the changing tides of the sea. But she also governs the twists and turns of our behavior patterns; our feelings, our needs, and our reactions. In Astrology The Moon represents our emotions, and has a profound impact upon our imagination and intuition. The lunar energy also links to our inherited traits, maternal instincts, and the feminine aspect of our natures.

My belief is that The Moon often reveals even more about our natures than our Sun Sign. This lunar magic is especially revealing of our humanness in all its hidden glory. With the ebb and flow of our lives and experiences, there is no doubt that a correct interpretation of The Moon in your chart can be pretty crucial.

So where was The Moon residing at your time of birth and how does its position in your chart facilitate your decision making processes and your ability to communicate in love, friendship and in the work place? Find Your Moon Sign in the tables at the back of this book. If you are near a computer, you can find the information even more quickly on-line, by googling "Moon position in natal chart." You may already know the positioning of The Moon in your natal chart, in which case read on.

Moon in ARIES

You are upfront, direct and impetuous. Generally up for it, you are not one to sit on your laurels. Your sense of adventure is lively and impulsive. But perhaps you need to learn patience and more tolerance of those who lag behind. Not everyone is as ever ready, willing and able as you are. Sometimes you come across as quite self-serving. But it is usually because you wish to make the best of things. You do not always consider the consequences of your actions and tend to act first and think later. Along the way you are quite likely to receive some unsettling lessons that will not dampen your spirits; but which will make you more careful and wise.

Learn to tread lightly through things, rather than rush headlong in where angels fear to tread. Life contains many lessons and adventures that you are more than able for. Just do not let jealous types contain you. Your ego is legendary and you have a fiercely competitive will, but you are generally likeable and cute with it.

You are provocative, compelling and a great rival to those who would dare take you on. Failure is not an option you even consider, which is all very well; but do learn not to be quite so unbending. Remember that others are entitled to a look in and that possibly you do not have *all* the answers. Independent though you are; do try to accommodate loved ones and their need to give you a helping hand. You are a passionate soul who cannot resist a challenge.

Moon in TAURUS

When you are emotionally comfortable you are tactile and romantic with your responses. But put the wind up you and you switch quickly into merciless, defensive mode. You fight like a cornered rat when someone upsets your personal equilibrium. Plus you have no tolerance for disloyalty or phony gestures. Your status quo is of supreme importance and you cannot function properly without stability and balance. As a result you can be quite controlling and tend to over invest in the preservation of your territory. People become your possessions and when you feel uneasy you often test their intentions.

Try to chill and not be such a control freak. People are human and of course their failings are ever present. So there is no point isolating yourself out of fear or intolerance. Access your altruistic self and trust life a little more.

You are quite conservative in your expectations and your traditionalism sometimes gets in the way of a good time. But your practical self gets things done and you are more than a match for those who take you on. Watch that stubborn streak though; it could be your down fall. Let your hair down once in a while and don't try to keep tabs on everyone and everything. Okay your intuition is a major tracking device. But sometimes you get things wrong. Try to be big enough to admit your mistakes and do not think you can lord it over people who ask for your advice.

Moon in GEMINI

You are a nifty character, who thrives on impromptu, off-the-cuff actions. Your emotional responses are quick and you are at your best in mad, hectic situations. Freedom is your buzz word and you feel stifled when others expect you to behave in a certain way. You love lively scenarios that allow you to think on your feet. But you are sometimes accused of superficiality and duality. The truth is you just *love* variety. You are the original social butterfly who flits around until you find a profitable and comfortable place to land. When you stumble upon your personal nirvana you are capable of commitment, but only on your own terms. If you feel the pressure; you are off pretty fast. A myriad of options is the nectar which gives your life meaning. You can quite happily handle two of everything and if this makes you superficial; you do not really give a damn.

Of course you are capable of meaningful connections; but you are also great at playing the field and exploring the full range of people, places and relationships available to you. If this life is about being true to yourself, then you have a big "self" to be true to.

Your heart is a mansion with many rooms to fill. Understandably it is difficult for you to trust your emotions and frequently your heart and mind disagree. This produces an interesting internal dialogue that not many would be able to follow. You justify your actions in the strangest ways.

Moon in CANCER

Strongly influenced by The Moon, you can be anxious and moody, if not a little temperamental. Your emotions are intense and you are highly intuitive. If something or someone does not *feel* right, you will steer clear. Rightly so. You should never doubt your hunches. But your sensitive nature is a mixed blessing. Not much escapes your notice; but you are prone to cutting off your nose to spite your face.

Very black and white with your responses, no one crosses you and gets away with it. Protective of your interests, you are also quite controlling. You like to know what is going on and to whom. People confide in you; which keeps you ahead of the game. But perhaps you would do well to soften up a bit and trust life a little more. You have learned the hard way and can be quite defensive when you feel threatened. On the plus side, you are sensual and unpredictable.

You know how to keep people guessing, which is great when you want to attract the opposite sex. Just do not resort to devious tactics in a bid to keep them. When your heart is open you are brilliant at making people feel comfortable. Your best quality is a talent for nurturing those you love, or in whom you have a vested interest. Watch you do not get too manipulative with these undercurrents of love and control. You are powerful, so use your gifts wisely. Remember that privacy and personal space are crucial to your sanity.

Moon in LEO

You are warm and kind hearted to those who light your fire. But you're not always the proverbial pussy cat. For the most part your emotional responses are fair and you give others the benefit of the doubt. However, you can be a bit of a show off and become quite bossy when you are on a roll. Be careful you do not railroad loved ones into particular ways of behaving and watch your expectancy levels in relationships. Live and let live!

You put a lot of love, light and effort into your closest relationships, and get quite wounded when someone short-changes you in return. Just do not resort to blackmail; it is *very* undignified, and there is absolutely no need. Besides, your open hearted nature and generosity of spirit will always generate the quality connections you need in order to thrive. Simply, ditch those who take advantage of your better nature: you're better off without them. It is no secret that you are a bit of a performer. In fact you *are* the original drama queen. You know how to keep the rest of us entertained. But when you kick up a fuss, it really is no laughing matter. Sometimes your need to be adored, stoked and cajoled gets the better of you; certainly, you will not take "no" for an answer.

Passionate and dynamic, you are indeed quite a handful. Learn to ease off the gas and give others a chance to give you something in return. You really do not have to demand it.

Moon in VIRGO

You are a sensitive individual with unique responses. A law unto yourself; you will not be dictated to. You do things in your own way, or not at all. Even though you are a stickler for truth, you will still bend the rules when it suits you. Often you run on an excess of nervous energy and tend to push yourself to the max in emotional situations.

Learn to be kinder to yourself; less critical and more forgiving. Be careful not to take on the role of teacher in your close connections.

Have some fun and learn to access your ready wit and humor. You are a perfectionist with high standards who must try not to judge so harshly. Relax and do not be so hard on yourself and your loved ones. Notice that relationships have a natural free flow of energy and that you do not need to control that flow.

Your way with words is legendary. You can out-smart the best of them. Make good use of these tools, for you have the power to cut like a knife or sow the seeds of good will. When you are stressed and wound up, you can fall victim to high levels of anxiety. Take a chill pill and put things into perspective with good mates as often as possible. It does not do you any favors to ruminate endlessly about the past, present and future. Simply be in the moment for your sanity's sake. Avoid your tendency to pick things apart. You have an analytical streak that's enviable, but it can also be your downfall.

Moon in LIBRA

You are a cool customer with impartial emotional responses. This does not mean that things do not bother you. But it does make you very dignified and mature in the way you handle difficult situations. Somewhat idealistic, you make a huge effort to keep the peace. You are a stickler for a harmonious atmosphere and will bend over backwards to avoid confrontation. This can work for and against you. You would do well to speak your truth more often. Okay, you are very discerning and tend to sit quiet rather than offend. But do learn to risk the odd reality check, even if it makes you feel uncomfortable. The rest of the world will *not* disrespect you if you stand your ground.

Generally, you can be a bit of a push over, and your indecisiveness makes you ready prey for ruthless types. Develop a tougher exterior and protect your interests with a clear conscience. Use your gifts of flirtation to make a point if all else fails! You are well able to wrap anyone around your little finger with your effervescent wit and charm. Because you are so good at empathizing with others, you often sacrifice your own beliefs, desires and ideas. This has no doubt led to some expensive or regrettable mistakes. You may also find it difficult to process resentment and frustration. Stop being quite so nice all the time. Buried anger can be poisonous and will not ultimately do you any favors.

Moon in SCORPIO

You are passionate and intense with unfathomable depths. With deep and meaningful responses, you are a delightful mystery to more simple souls who hang on your every word. Your complexity is truly captivating and your depth of emotion enables you to cast many a spell on the unwitting. Often you are not aware of your charisma and power; which is of course what appeals to and charms those who find you so compelling. The danger is, when you wake up to your personal power, you are quite inclined to use it skillfully to get your own way. So, be respectful of those you reel into your delightful but sticky web. No one messes with you; that is for sure.

When you get a bee in your bonnet about something, nothing will persuade you to back down. It just is not going to happen. Try to be a bit more gracious and trust that life will bring you what you signed up for, no more, no less. You cannot out-wit, or by-pass destiny, though you may sometimes try to do just that. When you begin to sense the full scope of your capabilities, is also when your personal responsibility kicks in.

Learn to be less obsessive and possessive about the objects and people you desire. You can channel your turbulent emotions by using positive focus and determined effort. Just make sure it is all good, for what you project into the ether is bound to bounce back, such is your personal magnetism and power.

Moon in SAGITTARIUS

Open and responsive, you are a livewire who follows up every scintillating opportunity. Luckily your energy levels are good; though you do risk emotional burn out when you get extra hyper. Try to be more measured in your approach. For you can come across as a bit reckless; which does not instill much trust in those who want to invest in you. Ever the adventurer, you even view your relationships as an exciting exploration. The problem with this is that once you get the measure of the current landscape, you are anxious to move on to greener pastures. Loved ones need to keep you interested, or you are off looking for new distractions. Yes, you get bored easily. But generally there is no harm done, so long as others respect your freedom to roam and explore.

You do not respond well to emotional pressure, so your requirements of trust are high. When you are fully loved and appreciated you always return to that base called home. But until you find what you *think* you are looking for, anything is possible. Try to learn more caution and restraint; for chances are you have kissed goodbye to many a situation and lived to regret it.

Do not be so restless or hasty. Your optimism is infectious and you have a natural zest for life. However, you will come unstuck unless you take your most difficult risk ever and start to put down roots. Continue to take things as you find them. Just learn to appreciate what you already *have*.

Moon in CAPRICORN

You are very determined to maintain good relationships. But this can make you a bit overbearing at times, especially when loved ones need personal space. When your infectious sensuality is in full swing, people tend to stay around. Just watch for the times when you feel a bit insecure or frantic and be careful you do not alienate others with your distrust.

You are prone to getting wound up and anxious when you don't feel properly appreciated. But remember that until you love and appreciate yourself, no one else is going to grant you that kind of respect. Often when things are not going your way you moan and complain, sometimes even resorting to devious measures to make a point.

Watch that need you have to control people's responses. Your key to good vibes and lasting emotions is to retreat when you feel the bad moods descend. Learn to go away into a quiet place and get through your stuff alone. Loved ones will not thank you for any projected anger and frustration. Only use your touchy, sensitivity in positive ways. Then you can turn bad moments around and keep everyone happy. Perhaps develop your acting abilities, since it is better to keep your moodiness at bay in company. Find an outlet for its expression that will not do any harm: a punch-bag perhaps? You can be a bit unadventurous and staid at times. So tap into your fun side and develop your humor as your best lethal weapon.

Moon in AQUARIUS

You are altruistic in your emotional responses, but also intensely private. This makes you very giving one minute, then quite inaccessible the next. No, you are not quite *that* inconsistent or changeable, but loved ones do need to read your moods in order to get the best out of you.

Generous hearted and empathetic, you have great gifts of understanding. However, you can also be quite eccentric and a law unto yourself. When you need to be alone, nothing will tug at your heart strings and distract you. Actually this is a blessing, for it means you have a talent for detachment.

You are skilled at sensing when to back off, which preserves both your sanity and independence. Also, you give objective, wise advice and appropriate emotional support without others then feeling they owe you for life. In short you are great at unconditional love; but with oodles of self-respect you know your limits too. With your wicked sense of humor, you have a novel way of looking at the world which keeps people amused.

You will always have support when you need it; but could gain brownie points by leading loved ones to believe you are needier than you actually *are*. Accept their input and gestures more readily and you're all laughing. You are brilliant at surprising people with your unpredictable ideas, which is great for romance and friendship. Use that vivid imagination and access your unusual spirit.

Moon in PISCES

Highly sensitive and intuitive, you are very in touch with your feelings. But you are also quite changeable and likely to flip your perceptions without warning. This can be bewildering for loved ones who think they have the measure of you. Indeed you are likely to drive those with an interest in you quite crazy. You are unpredictable, hate confrontation and are liable to be evasive when put on the spot. You are kind and giving, but likely to tell the odd white lie to keep the peace. Fair enough, but do stay as grounded as possible.

There is a need for consistency and stability with the Moon in Pisces. Learn to stick to decisions which felt good at the time and recall your reasons for making them. You are very susceptible to the ebb and flow of emotions around you, so it is important to protect yourself and not get so hooked into what everyone else is thinking and feeling.

Put up your boundaries and know when to stop tuning-in to life, the universe and everything! Your sensitivity is a mixed blessing. Not much passes you by. But you are inclined to get overly paranoid and give inconsequential details too much thought.

Learn to filter important messages and visions through a major reality check. There is no point getting lost with your head in the clouds. Easily moved to great happiness or sadness, it is quite difficult to keep track of the rollercoaster ride of emotion when you're in full flow.

5 VENUS LOVE WAYS

Venus the planet of love influences both our visual and romantic responses. If we like what we see, our heart will surely follow. This planet heightens our feelings and thereby challenges the way we relate to each other socially and financially. Venus makes the link between our romantic and economic relationships. According to this Ruling Planet love, money, sex and material possessions are irretrievably married - For better or for worse. Kind of makes sense does it not?

Venus assists our partnerships, professional and personal. Particularly if you are a Taurus or Libran ruled by Venus notice how your attitudes about money reflect in your approach to love and romance. This may sound particularly mercenary. But Venus also links to our integrity and choices, so we can always choose to take the high road.

Venus' activity emphasises the importance of equilibrium and balance in our relationships. She enhances our need for positive partnerships and bestows beauty on all those willing to make an effort. Also this planet assists us when there are impartial judgements and merciful decisions to be made. Venus bestows a fair demeanour and blessings on those who choose to live compassionately and considerately. But best of all, she assists our love choices and offers us guidance, urging us to follow our heart.

So where was Venus residing at your time of birth and how does its position in your chart facilitate your love life, and your ability to communicate in love, friendship and partnership? Find Your Venus Sign in the tables at the back of this book. If you are near a computer, you can find the information even more quickly on-line, by googling "Venus position in natal chart." You may already know the positioning of Venus in your natal chart, in which case read on.

Venus in ARIES

You are enthusiastic and demonstrative with your affections. Passionate and impulsive, you love the thrill of the chase. In typical Aries style, you dive headlong into intense connections, and often live to regret your haste. Some may assume you are superficial, but actually you feel things deeply and mean every word you say. It is just that what you feel, mean and say can change overnight.

When you are committed, your demanding nature can put quite a strain on things. You need constant love and affection, not because you are insecure, but because you are full on. Okay you are adorable and loving too, but at points you can be a bit too full-on.

You love life in all its glory and expect loved ones to keep up with your pitch of excitement. As a result you can be quite tiring company. For you, life is an endless stream of possibilities; and you move quickly on from those who do not share your joy of constant partying. Anything which brings the adrenaline rush you crave gets your vote.

You are loud, proud and dangerous to know. Unfortunately you are prone to jealousy and when you are angry what happens next is not particularly pretty. For the most part you are lively, congenial company. You just need to learn when to sit in silence. Balance your approach to your loved ones, and you will keep interest, and prevent hurt.

Venus in TAURUS

You are physical and sensual with your affections. Loved ones feel appreciated, valued and strengthened by your attentive ways. A cute face always sparks your imagination, for you love beauty in all its forms. Touchy and feely as you are others often get the wrong idea. You do not really intend to give the wrong impression; but you invariably do.

Many people respond to your charisma and presence, and you are never short of admirers. But you are something of a social chameleon and tend to hide the extent of your emotions. It is very easy for you to make connections; just not that easy to own up to your feelings. For you actions speak louder than words. Sometimes though, even your actions can not be easily read.

You are cautious and a tad distrustful, especially when you have been hurt in the past. Loved ones tend to be possessions, and you can get quite jealous when someone threatens to steal them. You are loyal, steadfast and true when committed; and you expect the same respect in return. This makes you a bit of a control freak if you are in any way uneasy or unsure of love.

Somewhat passive, you are slow to get started. Your passions sizzle until you are ready. Then you make your lasting ties, and there is no getting away from you.

Venus in GEMINI

You are playful, flirtatious and communicative. Your lively mind is captivating and you thrive in varied company and situations. Displays of affection come naturally and perhaps a little too easily to you. Like a child who flits from person to person, you can come across as superficial and fickle. In reality nothing could be further from the truth.

You feel things deeply, just not in the way everyone else does. This of course leads to misunderstandings; especially when you *know* you are trustworthy. Appreciate that you give the impression that you are anything but; then you might be more empathetic towards loved ones who remain baffled by your behavior. The irony is, left to your own devices, you will not stray. It is only when your freedom is threatened and you feel stifled, that you will play away from home.

Sadly loved ones will never really know where they stand, for you are not the most deep and meaningful person.

You are expressive, lighthearted and charming; just not particularly profound. Always on the lookout for new experiences, it is difficult to keep up with you. Partners may feel they do not get the input they deserve. But you are great fun, and never boring. Your curiosity is insatiable.

Venus in CANCER

You are sensitive and protective with displays of affection. Those you love get your undivided attention; but your intensity can be overwhelming. Temper your good intentions with a healthy dose of independence for the sake of sanity and balance. Inclined to be temperamental when out of sorts, you snap at the silliest things. Just make sure your grumpiness does not alienate people. Too often you react, getting petulant for no good reason, and no one understands the tantrum; least of all yourself. You need an outlet for these complex emotions; but try to keep it positive and retreat privately when you feel an irrational storm brewing.

Your shyness is surprising and you get insecure about the strangest things. But intimacy is important to your well-being; as is sharing and caring in a close knit environment. Family life suits you and provides ample opportunity for the connections you crave. Just learn to distance yourself from other's issues and problems. You have more than enough to cope with as it is.

You cannot sort everyone out; nor should you feel obliged to do so. When things are running smoothly you give unconditionally; but you can be put off by demands from others and like to run the show on your own terms.

Venus in LEO

You are loyal and generous hearted; and loved ones never feel shortchanged by you. Attentive and kind, you can be quite in-your-face with your gestures. You are the proverbial drama queen, and your emotions are bizarrely over the top when you become unbalanced. When you are appreciated, this does not really happen; but when you are abused or taken for granted the claws come out. Not afraid or ashamed to fight your corner, you can be quite haughty about correct behavior. Okay, you do not keep tabs; but you do notice when things are not quite right.

Your temper tantrums are legendary. Indeed, you can be quite childlike when you do not get your own way. Too often you demand to be the center of attention and feel quite uncomfortable when there is a more interesting diversion. For this reason you are a consummate performer, excellent at bringing the conversation back to your favorite topic: *you*! Be careful not to alienate people with your natural flamboyance. You can be wonderfully entertaining; but also exceptionally tedious.

Learn to discern when things have moved on and do not labor the point. You are a born showoff and lovable with it. But your open heart always wins out and saves the day.

Venus in VIRGO

You are loyal, kind and modest; but a stickler for perfection. Your standards are high and you cannot be demonstrative when things do not feel right. You show your love and affection in practical ways; so even your tidiness and organization indicates your level of involvement. When you cannot be bothered, things get left undone (dishes in the sink syndrome). But when you are wholeheartedly up-for-it, you are the chirpiest homemaker in the kingdom.

Because of your analytical ability you are quite a cool customer. You express yourself dispassionately, so can come across as fairly aloof to those who do not know you very well. You seek perfection in many things and can get held back by your need to have everything just right. Remember relationships *are* messy and learn to get stuck in more readily. Life is too short to hold back after all. You might as well give it a whirl and see where you get to. Your emotional reserve does not do you any favors really; so learn to ditch it and access another aspect of your complex nature.

Steer clear of being overly critical of yourself and others and do not resort to pettiness in a row; as you are inclined to do. You are a sensitive, intelligent soul; who is perhaps easily offended: Do, not be.

Venus in LIBRA

You are idealistic and lots of fun. On the one hand you expect the world from your relationships; on the other you can be refreshingly lighthearted and even flippant! You express your affections sometimes extravagantly, sometimes hesitantly. Your varied responses reflect typical Libran dithering; yet they serve a purpose by keeping your loved ones entertained. That wicked sense of humor and natural charisma attracts all sorts of people. But you do have a tendency to stifle intimacy in your avoidance of conflict.

You may feel you are being usefully magnanimous when you bite your tongue and avoid a row; but really is it that wise to always steer clear of confrontation? Remember, a good old humdinger clears the air and facilitates the process of moving on.

Sometimes in your desire for permanent harmony, you miss the nuances of simmering resentment. Learn to identify problems, and more importantly don't assume you can always gloss over them. Issues come along in many shapes and sizes, and you are right; harmony and peace are desirable commodities. But do be willing to identify anger as part of your emotional repertoire. Then your provision of pleasure, comfort and caring will be all the more effective.

Venus in SCORPIO

You are compulsive and passionate, which is great for intense connections. On the down side though, you get overly suspicious and are a tad obsessive. Try to be more measured in your responses, for as it stands you have a tendency to overwhelm loved ones and stifle their self-expression. Your great gifts of passion and mystery can also be a burden. On the one hand no one can fathom your intriguing depths; on the other you can be overly secretive and protective.

It is important to the sanity of your loved ones that you learn to open up; to give and take. Perhaps you are not fully aware of the extent to which you control your reactions. But because you are a natural detective, psychologist and psychic; there are no flies on you. Indeed you can be quite intimidating, disconcerting company. You know how to unnerve your prey, and get your own way, time and time again.

There is no point advising you to lighten-up, for you take everything so damned seriously. You are nothing if not profound. So long as your exacting standards are met in relationships, things go well; but if someone dares question your natural authority? Where you are concerned, 'common ground' is a concept akin to a peat bog: There is *no* compromise.

Venus in SAGITTARIUS

You are open with your affections and somewhat idealistic too. Over-the-top is not the word! When you feel love, the whole world knows about it; and you can be quite excessive with its expression. This is great if the object of your affections likes you to make a fuss. But not so good if you are with someone more discrete and private than your exuberant self. Learn to read the mood and do try to enjoy low key subtle moments from time to time.

There is no doubt; you are a regular gal or guy who gives freely and whole-heartedly. Watch that you do not get taken advantage of by unscrupulous types. You wear your heart on your sleeve, so are likely to learn a few lessons the hard way. Apart from that, precious little dampens your lively spirit.

You are tolerant and broadminded. Most misdemeanors go unnoticed when you are in the room. It takes a lot to get you riled; and even then you are one of the most forgiving souls on the planet. You are not exactly gentle, but you are faultlessly kind. Your wicked sense of humor and adventurous out-look make you difficult to keep up with, but always good fun. The only problem is; you assume everyone else is feels it the way you do. Unfortunately this is not the case.

Venus in CAPRICORN

You are faithful and dutiful with your affections and your relationships are somewhat sanitized. Indeed you are so meticulous about doing things the right way; that you often create a joyless, edgy atmosphere, without meaning to.

In trying to do things by the book, you sometimes lose your spontaneity and sense of humor. Loved ones potentially feel stifled, by always having to be on their best behavior. Not that you force such loyalty or respect; but you do command it *somehow*!

You take relationships seriously, which is commendable. Whilst you are sensual, faithful and down to earth; you are rather exacting too! Your reserve sometimes comes across as snobbish. But your loved ones know they can trust you. You are reliability personified, though would benefit from a flexible, more relaxed approach. Life is messy; things happen, and you cannot always be there to sort it all out! Free yourself up a bit, by accepting the flow of events and the challenge of new circumstances.

Your conscientiousness and caring nature mean that you are not afraid to commit. But it does take you a long time to trust and open up within new relationships. At least your loved ones know you mean it: there is no funny business when you are around.

Venus in AQUARIUS

Your displays of affection are unconventional and experimental; if not rather odd! You are eccentric and a law unto yourself. Anything goes and you are offended by precious little. So long as you are free to express your feelings you are happy. Privacy is crucial to your sanity; but you are also sociable and lively of wit and mind. Your unusual sense of humor takes some beating and you are a match for most people.

Quick off the mark; nothing gets past your extreme powers of perception. With your altruistic tendencies, you are full of empathy and understanding. But you know your limits too. You do not suffer fools gladly and anyone who takes advantage of your good nature gets short shrift! Loved ones have to get used to your unusual, slightly weird habits.

You are not about to change for anyone; for you are quite set in your ways. Things get done as you ordain them, or not at all! On the plus side, you make a lively, interesting lover. Experimental, adventurous, and a skillful flirt; new ideas and experiences grab your imagination, and you are willing to give most things a try. However, you are quite the fantasist, who must make a concerted effort to stay grounded. Sometimes your reactions are extreme and you go just a bit too far.

Venus in PISCES

You are romantic and compassionate, if not a little wet with your displays of affection. Some may say that you get over sentimental about inconsequential details, but at least you care. No one could ever accuse you of neglect or flippancy. But you are a soft touch. Watch out for ruthless or self-indulgent types who are likely to take advantage of your amenable nature.

Try to toughen up, and use discernment re what or who to say "yes" to. Your perceptions are acute and your powers of sympathy heightened; but you must learn to protect yourself better. Sensitized to many emotions, feelings and reactions, you experience everything to the full, which is of course very tiring. Idealistic and overly sensitive, you are likely to become a tad unhinged if life serves you up a blow or a lesson. Also you are inclined to be economical with the truth to spare people's feelings and to preserve your own interests. Quite capable of devious behavior, you do not deliberately double-deal; but, you do sift information and keep track of every little detail. Sometimes you get disillusioned that things do not happen as you deem they should. But you are not a control freak, merely an idealist. Always guard against confusion and use your commonsense.

6 DEEP-FRIED MARS SIGNS

Mars is a fiery and uncompromising planet. This glowing red explosive energy influences sex drive, our competitive streak and physical activity. Mars inspires a warrior like mentality that fires up adrenaline levels and takes no prisoners.

Aries is the Zodiac sign ruled by Mars and this energy possesses a determination to win at all costs. Mars enables us to deal effectively with most crisis situations. This planet supports us as we think on our feet. But sometimes it may take us too far and we rush headlong into things. Certainly Mars plays things to the max. The up side is prolific energy and a dynamic nature, the down side is inherent clumsiness and foolhardiness too.

The energy of planet Mars inspires us to swift action and the resolution of pressing issues. But may also stir up temper flares, a fierce unbending will and mad flashes of passion. Sounds like fun? Well quite often it is, but do treat this planet with a healthy respect and do not rush in where angels fear to tread.

So where was Mars residing at your time of birth and how does its position in your chart facilitate your love life, and your ability to communicate in love, friendship and partnership? Find Your Mars Sign in the tables at the back of this book. If you are near a computer, you can find the information even more quickly on-line, by googling "Mars position in natal chart." You may already know the positioning of Mars in your natal chart, in which case read on.

Mars in ARIES

You are impulsive with your assertions. There is no messing around, and no doubt, what you are all about! Blunt and to the point, you are open and quite fierce with your affections. Your competitive streak leaves rivals quaking in their boots. They realize there is not much point in taking you on. For you fight to the death and always defend what you feel is yours.

To your credit you do not play games, nor do you trifle with people's affections. Loved ones and enemies alike always know where they stand with you. Okay, you are hotheaded in a row, but just as quickly the calm descends. You are very good at leaving things behind. Moving on is your special skill. So when someone or something is past the sell-by date, you do not waste time or beat about the bush. Somewhat direct and reckless, you go straight for what you want. What is more, you do not let up until it is all yours.

Needless to say you are a dynamo between the sheets. Lovers have nothing to complain about, and you would win prizes for your intense, possibly short lived, passions. You are not particularly good at commitment though. You give your heart and soul to the moment; and of course there are many moments to speak of. Be very careful and respectful of your impatience; it can get you into trouble.

Mars in TAURUS

Earthy and affectionate, you are a full-on sexual being. You delight in your senses and experience every aspect of life completely. The moment is yours to savor; cos you make it so. You are an expert at commanding the stage of life, and not many people would disagree that you have great natural authority.

You command situations with steadiness and surety. But you have a wicked stubborn streak and hate to be dictated to. Somewhat conservative in your approach to life, you need to control what is happening. It makes you very uncomfortable to know (or think) that someone else has the upper hand.

You are self-assured and confident, but you have to be the best. Perhaps your worst weakness is that you automatically assume that you are in the right. You are not very open to other's opinions or ways of being. You may listen, but when push comes to shove, you just know that you are right. Okay, you often are; but it is crucial to your well-being and adjustments in life that you appreciate that sometimes you are not. Your energy levels are second to none and you have great stamina. Lovers are not complaining any time soon. But you have a big potential problem with jealousy. Always remember, loved ones are not possessions.

Mars in GEMINI

You are lively, intelligent and extrovert. A restless spirit, you are always on the lookout for new amusements and mad entertainment. Your need for permanent stimulation is an exhausting prospect for lovers and family alike. Variety is the spice of life and boredom will not be tolerated.

Open minded as you are, your attentions are easily diverted, which is not great for the commitment factor. Gemini energy feels a divine entitlement to two of everything. So you are capable of several things at once as well as playing both ends against the middle. Skilled at deception as you are, it may not be deliberate, but it is pretty much inevitable.

Loved ones need to understand your needs, or else ship out fairly lively. You do not demand loyalty, as you cannot give it. But your definition of loyalty is quite different to the norm anyhow. As long as you are there when someone really needs you that's what counts. Life is never dull with you in the room. You provide hours of entertainment and like to keep things sweet with your gregarious nature. Youthfulness is your key trait and in many ways, you will never grow up. Life is to be relished in all its glory. Needless to say, you run on nervous energy. But do unwind enough to sleep now and again.

Mars in CANCER

You are a great believer in taking things easy. It is anything for the quiet life, as far as you're concerned. As a result, you can be quite indirect and understated. You do not spell things out and you expect people to read your mind, in the same way you can intuit what is going on in theirs. Very self-protective and cagey about your deepest feelings, you can be quite moody and petulant. You are good at ducking and diving and you know how to keep people guessing.

When you are committed though, you nurture and care to a fault. Often, you are plagued with insecurities and inner wobbles. But you are pushy and tenacious when you have to be. Anxiety is your inner demon; and it tends to dictate your attempts to control life.

You thrive in a safe environment and are great at nurturing those who will be useful to you. Okay this makes you a bit of a user, but you generally do mean it when you offer your support. When the person or circumstance has served its purpose however, you can be quite ruthless at shutting down and moving on.

You are deep and emotional, but tend to spend too much time analyzing how you are doing. If you expend too much energy fretting, learn to chill for the sake of your sanity, equilibrium and relationships.

Mars in LEO

You are dramatic and flamboyant. No one would dismiss you as a wallflower that is for sure. Definitely a drama queen; you are madly vibrant, but good fun to be with. Your creativity is enviable and you have good energy reserves for the things that grab your imagination. But routine stuff bores the pants off you! There is a definite lazy streak that kicks in when you have made up your mind something just is not going to happen. You will not be persuaded against your inclinations, yet you manage to be fairly charming when you say "no."

Linked to the Zodiac Lion, you are a proud creature who will not be told what to do. Although you are dutiful, it is not in a meek way.

You take pride in looking after your own, but can get quite fierce amidst injustice and abuse. When the claws come out, it is not a pretty sight.

Your need to be adored is a key aspect of your sexual drive and prowess. When you are not appreciated to the point of ridiculousness, you will find your solace elsewhere. Your need for compliments and ego massage is legendary. But you are not nasty when everything is in place; just as you like it.

It is a different story when you feel uncomfortable though: you are controlling, pushy and not particularly nice to be with.

Mars in VIRGO

You are modest, dutiful, and possibly a bit of a wall-flower, on first impressions. Of course once people get to know you, the real personality comes out to play. But until then, you are inclined to be overlooked by the Zodiac's more assertive types. You make your voice heard in more subtle ways, which ultimately works to your advantage.

With your systematic, methodical streak, you work your way into hearts and minds. Incredibly picky, you take a long time to warm up in relationships. You are critical of others and yourself and don't believe in making things easy. Quite fussy, you have exacting standards that must be met.

In your search for perfection, you block yourself off from all kinds of interesting connections and liaisons. But casual links and superficial people are just not your style. Certainly not the most easygoing person on the planet, you come across as quite aloof, vain and unapproachable. Self-contained and independent, you do not really need others, except in their vaguely useful kind of way. Your main problem is that you over analyze everyone and everything, instead of engaging fully in life's rich tapestry. You handle things in your own way; but must learn to give life more than half a chance.

Mars in LIBRA

You are romantic and full of good will and co-operation. Undeniably in love-with-love, you sometimes make ill-informed choices. You are a sucker for candle-lit dinners and romantic gestures, so you are easily seduced by traditional expressions of feeling. Be aware that sentimentality and a bunch of roses does not always equate to undying love. Of course such attention is always nice to receive. But when push comes to shove, you need hard evidence of someone's staying power before you commit

In typical Libra style, you are sometimes assertive; sometimes shy. You blow hot and cold, which always keeps relationships interesting, though don't overdo it. Your dithering can sometimes be quite exasperating, so discern when to go-for-it!

Even when committed, you flirt for Ireland and are very sociable, something partners and loved ones would do well to understand. You are not likely to act on impulse however; for your sexual wiles are measured, fair and tactful.

Your whole being strives for harmonious connections, so you hate confrontation and unnecessary rowing. Casual liaisons and one night stands repulse you. You have to set the scene and make sure everything is just perfect before you get intimate.

Mars in SCORPIO

Passionate and intense, you are a veritable volcano between the sheets! You do not believe in half measures with the love stuff; and when you are committed to a course of action, you go for it. To make a connection let your eyes do the talking.

Your natural mystery and allure does the rest. There is no need to be overt or in-your-face; you have all the skills of attraction in place when you step out the door. Passionate responses come easy to you; people know where they stand and that is that. What you cannot guarantee is how long things will last. In a whirlwind of intensity you make your links, only to find that all too often they just as quickly fade away. This is not deliberate maliciousness on your part. In fact it is as much a riddle to you as it is to your trail of spurned lovers. Of course you *can* commit, and when you actually *do* fall in love; you know all about it. That knowing smile is a dead give-away.

Driven to deep emotional intimacy, you do need to protect yourself a little better. Get the balance right and learn to hold back until you are sure of your staying power in particular situations. You do have great energy levels and powers of endurance; but these need to be channeled in the right direction: or else.

Mars in SAGITTARIUS

Straightforward and adventurous, you are up for anything that tickles your fancy. You are quite a rowdy soul, liable to be boisterous even in the wee small hours when the rest of the world is asleep. With endless reserves of nervous energy, you are at risk from burn out if you do not learn to unwind, occasionally.

In love you are idealistic; but this does not mean you are on the lookout for perfection. Born optimist that you are, you have embarked on a continual quest to improve your lot. You strive for the good things in life and your restless spirit demands that this search is continuous; even when you have already got a quite a good deal. In love ties you can take it or leave it a lot of the time. Especially before you commit, you are a soul who experiments and experiences a whole range of connections.

Even after tying the knot the urge to stray is often overwhelming. But you are not devious. You simply enjoy other people's company; and of course, the grass is always greener over the hill! On the plus side, your sense of humor is wicked. You will find that throughout life, you are forgiven most things, for one particular reason only: you are extremely huggable and loveable. Just do not take advantage of your strong position.

Mars in CAPRICORN

You are an earthy, matter of fact soul, who can be quite calculating. This means that you carefully guard your interests and always keep your boundaries in check, but you are eminently nice with it. One night stands are anathema to you; you rarely go there, except with the long term in view. If something feels right, you *will* follow through, but you certainly will not connect for the sake of yet another experience.

You are not the most curious person on the planet. Quite a traditionalist; before you commit, you are on the hunt for a soul mate to settle down with. Once you have found them, you are a faithful soul, who is hardly mad, bad and dangerous to know. No, you are not boring, but you *are* an acquired taste.

In the bedroom you shine; in a conservative, safe kind of way. But your sexual drives are strong, relentless, and your stamina is good. You have commendable self -control, and will not make your move until the time is right. You are cautious with the love stuff and not afraid of commitment. However, sometimes this works against you and you may come across as a sure thing to someone unscrupulous. Get over it. Once you find your feelings reciprocated, you have it made. You are humorful and offer great affection.

Mars in AQUARIUS

You are a truly unique humanoid! Eccentric and a law unto yourself, you make things up as you go along. Anything goes, so long as it feels okay. Convention and tradition be damned: you do things in your own way, or not at all. Anyone who dares dictate to you gets short shrift.

You have a strong altruistic streak, but you will not suffer fools. Your humanitarian, caring gestures are from the heart; but you do not allow others to take advantage. In the bedroom, you are imaginative and free spirited. Anything goes and your lovers are invariably in for a treat once you get going.

Fresh approaches and unusual ideas turn you on. You can cope with most forms of weirdness and precious little offends you. Life is not one big quest for excitement; but you do not say "no" when the madness sets in. You are wide open to suggestion!

During your single years, you do not have a problem sacrificing intimacy for the sake of a superficial connection. But once you make a commitment you honor it to the hilt; on your own terms of course. Someone has to bend to your will, though this is usually easy enough to do.

Your rebellious streak is certainly a cause of amusement for those who can handle it. Just steer clear of conventional types who are easily offended. You need a partner who stimulates your mind: the rest then naturally follows.

Mars in PISCES

You have great powers of empathy and perception, which makes you nice to know. But you do have a nosy streak, and love to be at the heart of other people's business. Your natural psychic ability and sensitivity give you the edge in many situations. However, you can be a bit vague; you will not be pinned down when you are unsure.

Evasive and deceptive when cornered, you are a subtle mover with wily ways. No you are not actively dishonest, but you don't like confrontation and will do anything to wriggle away from it. You are good at reading people and quite skillful at nipping problems in the bud. In intimate situations you bring it all together with an intriguing mix of confidence and sensitivity.

Hardly a tough nut, you do have an unbreakable strength that sometimes passes for weakness. Others assume you don't know what's what; but your intuition and perceptions give you the edge. Idealistic with the love stuff, you are a bit vulnerable to disappointment. Perhaps you hope for too much too quickly?

Once committed, the main problem is your irrational moodiness. Learn to steer clear of loved ones when the black cloud descends. Try to be less of a soft touch; you are sometimes too obliging for your own good.

7 JUPITER ASCENDING

Jupiter is the largest planet in the solar system. It is associated with expansiveness and development, both intellectual and physical. Jupiter was the king of all the gods, akin to the Roman god Zeus. This regal energy of kingship blesses those born with a strong Jupiter component to their chart with dignity and composure.

Along with inherent spirituality and the ability to philosophize, Jupiter bestows abundance and wealth; whilst the inherent cosmic link to ancient gods ensures great luck. Positive mental energies direct those influenced by Jupiter. Knowledge, vision and optimism are all gifts from this generous spirited planet. However, caution is needed for Jupiter can also inspire over-confidence and stubborn, if not bloody-minded behavior. Do watch out for extravagance and histrionic, drama queen behavior, when Jupiter traits get out-of-control.

So where was Jupiter residing at your time of birth and how does its position in your chart facilitate your love life, and your ability to communicate in love, friendship and partnership? Find Your Jupiter Sign in the tables at the back of this book. If you are near a computer, you can find the information even more quickly on-line, by googling "Jupiter position in natal chart." You may already know the positioning of Jupiter in your natal chart, in which case read on. Find your Jupiter sign influences your luck in life. What does Jupiter reveal about your personality and how can this generous planet ensure your success and happiness?

Jupiter in ARIES

You are a fiery, dynamic character. Generally up-for-it, you like to do things for kicks and enjoy the rush of adrenaline which comes from taking a big risk. Your energy levels are good and you love a challenge. Not much is beyond your expansive abilities. But you can be head strong and overbearing. Do try to be a bit more sensitive to others, and learn to bend a little when it counts. Spiritually, you have a simple faith and innocence akin to that of a child, which stands you in good stead. You really *can* trust your intuitions and creative know-how.

Jupiter expands your assertiveness and leadership qualities. You are dominant, confident and generally lucky. As the eternal optimist you know how to find the good within even the direst dilemma. Unafraid to use your initiative, you seize opportunities readily and when they are not available, you create your own.

Fortune Cookie: Travel, adventure and exploration are very lucky for you. Tap into your upbeat side for great results. Big projects and expansive ideas suit you down to the ground. Nothing is beyond you, so never limit yourself or doubt what you can achieve. Simply go for it.

Luck Factor: Jupiter encourages you to network to full-effect. Your best opportunities will come from chance meetings in the pub; obscure phone calls you simply were not expecting; and a huge dose of courage which inspires you to follow your hunches to the hilt. Do not miss a trick.

Jupiter in TAURUS

You are generous and open hearted. Your company is delightful and you have a witty turn of phrase which "knocks-the-socks" off the best of them! Never far away from a good time, no party is complete without you. Often the center of attention, you hate to be overlooked. But you expect the same show of loyalty from loved ones and colleagues that you unquestioningly give to them. Watch out for the expectations and conditions that you project onto those who captivate your heart and soul. Try to be as unconditional as possible with your affections.

Jupiter sometimes overwhelms you emotionally, so you tend to bury your head in the sand when difficult feelings surface; do *not!* This all-encompassing planet expands your earthiness, stability and creativity too. You definitely possess the Midas touch, and your ability to spot a money-spinning moment never fails.

Fortune Cookie: You are a veritable cash-magnet. Nifty moves in the world of banking, property and finance serve you well. You are likely to be musical and creative with a love of the great outdoors. But, hearth and home are where true wealth lies. Generosity of spirit also brings huge luck. Remain practical.

Luck Factor: You have solid values and are as reliable as they come. But with your Jupiter influence, you need to get real. Relationships should not be maintained just because you have made a promise. Your heart and soul must be fully engaged too; otherwise, you are simply being dishonest.

Jupiter in GEMINI

Your searing wit and mental agility make you a force to contend with. You have many talents and not much is beyond the grasp of your intelligent mind. Up-to-the-minute, you are always aware of the latest trends and ideas. Facts and figures do not faze you either, so you offer prospective employers the full package. You are well able to talk or think your way out of trouble; which is just as well as you are not the most discreet person on the planet. You like to take risks and you are easily bored. But life is fun with you around, and you are truly an inspiration.

Jupiter expands your mind and you are able to embrace obscure ideas and out-there philosophies. Your versatility and flexibility benefits too. You can transform mundane circumstances, routines and assignments into a mad adventure. Mental tasks bend your mind and bring you good luck.

Fortune Cookie: Your hunger for knowledge helps you to prosper. Media, communications, travel and personal quests all lead to great developments. Writing, speaking and in-depth investigations take you far. Fortune comes with learning and link-ups. You can never know too many people.

Luck Factor: Use your turn of phrase to great effect whenever possible. Do not miss a beat and be ever ready to pipe up. Say yes to all travel opportunities and be open to swift developments you had not planned on. Unpredictable elements and events hold the best fortune. So, go along with even the weirdest options.

Jupiter in CANCER

You are a sensitive soul, who needs the warmth, protection and support of friends and family. Your intuition is highly a-tuned and you can see through anyone fake. Imaginative and creative, you also reserve the right to change your mind. It is your prerogative. A highly developed motherly instinct makes you inclined to collect life's waifs and strays along-the-way. Not exactly a push over; you can be quite easily persuaded by those who grab your interest. You act with sincerity, but have no tolerance for disloyalty. If someone crosses you; that is it.

Jupiter expands your emotional capacity, so you have great empathy and understanding. You are flawlessly caring and sympathetic to those who need it most. But if someone abuses your good nature, you can cut to the quick. Luck and happiness links you closely to the family unit, and home is your haven.

Fortune Cookie: Great benefits come to you through parents, siblings and extended family. Your compassion for others and caring nature ensures that the universe will reward you in great ways. Even so, you have an appreciation for small pleasures, which means when the big stuff hits; you are reeling.

Luck Factor: Any home based business plan or pleasure is bound to flourish. Writing, artistry and creativity produced under your own roof has the magical touch. Use your intuition to guide you forward. Just make sure others do not drain your sensitive energies. Do reserve your oomph, for *you*.

Jupiter in LEO

You are a veritable dynamo. Optimistic and brave in all you do. Your heart and mind are truly magnificent, and you possess great generosity of spirit. You embrace life in all its glory and when you are around, there are no half measures. Huge self-belief means that you get results. Yet despite your expansive ambition, you do not tread on too many toes. You are a born extrovert, who loves to shine by being the center of attention. In fact, you are quite full of it once you get going. Because you are so well loved though; it does not matter a bit. Play on.

Jupiter gives you a huge drive to find the nearest party. And, you can be quite restless if you feel you're missing out on all the fun. Life for you is one big pleasure cruise; you really are a bundle of laughs. On a bad day though, you are the proverbial drama Queen from hell. Ostentatious, demanding but loveable; that is you.

Fortune Cookie: Your convictions and beliefs are compelling. Listen to whatever drives you from within, for this is your key to fame and fortune. The power of what you put across is formidable. Personally and professionally, you are very difficult to turn down. Be careful what you wish for, so.

Luck Factor: Take pride in everything you do. Your success is guaranteed, so long as you can develop your sensitivity quotient. Reverse psychology always serves you well, so be a bit cute and use it. You are going to get your own way anyhow, so you might as well be nice about it. Your luck is in.

Jupiter in VIRGO

Jupiter gives you an eye for detail and the mental ability to ground all sorts of wonderful ideas. You are meticulous and exacting. Nothing escapes your notice. Anyone trying to pull the wool over your eyes is doomed to failure. A compassionate soul, you often put the needs of others before your own. This is of course commendable, but you do need to define your personal boundaries more efficiently. Karma will serve you well because you are so nice. But remember, destiny is not something you can side-step with a full quota of good works. Be more confident.

Jupiter expands your social consciousness and you work tirelessly for the good of all. But, you are inclined to get bogged down in details. Do learn to put things into perspective and appreciate the bigger picture. With this placing, you may have workaholic tendencies. Go easy on yourself.

Fortune Cookie: Your innate ability to make something out of nothing is enviable indeed. You are born with a natural genius and it is difficult to keep up with your creativity. You will always land on your feet, so must not doubt what you can achieve. Look at your track record of success any time your confidence needs a boost.

Luck Factor: Use your practicality and logic to great effect. But do not scrimp on your sensuality. Your charm will open doors; never mind your ability to outwit the competition. Well-chosen words at the right moment will totally transform your world. Good communication reels in what you want.

Jupiter in LIBRA

You are an easy going, social bunny who loves good company and revels in luxurious surroundings. When you feel comfortable you automatically prosper; so your living and work environments are crucial to your success. With natural charm and charisma, others are drawn to you. But thankfully, they are not in the least bit tempted to take advantage. Your natural antennae for bullshit sees to that. Justice is supremely important to you, and you cannot abide anything unfair or off-balance. The only problem is; you do not always muster the oomph to act on what you feel.

Jupiter expands your popularity, which is just as well as you do not like to be on your own for long. Your charms and talents inevitably lead to great success. Your great belief in fair play ensures good relationships personally and professionally. Sometimes though, you sacrifice your own interests for the greater good. Fair enough.

Fortune Cookie: Partnerships benefit you and you would do well to treasure them. Your success lies with a give and take approach to life. Selfishness definitely does not suit you; so for an easy life, your ego often goes walkabout. Just be careful that you do not dissipate your focus and energies when it really counts. Do not be afraid of decisions.

Luck Factor: Always focus and pin things down. Negotiate to full effect and do not be afraid to push for resolutions to your dilemmas. Decisive action brings definite results. Jupiter potentially boosts your finances and luck big time. Good partnerships always maximize your luck, enabling you to move forward.

Jupiter in SCORPIO

You are a full-on master of life. Your energy knows no bounds and you frequently tire out those who try to keep up with you. Do learn to preserve your oomph for what really matters. Your self-belief is beyond question and you certainly make a formidable opponent. It pays to be nice to you, let us put it that way. When you are focused, you will not let up until you have achieved your objective. But your charisma and intensity part the waves in your favor more often than not. You are very uncompromising, but your passion brings you every good thing.

Jupiter expands your depth of feeling and ability to get to the bottom of things. Naturally psychic and probably quite spiritual too, you understand life. With you, there are no half measures. Great endurance and perception allows you to reel in whatever you set your heart on. It is only a matter of time, once you have made up your mind.

Fortune Cookie: You are very shrewd in money matters, and possess the savvy to make a lot of money once you find your niche. Just be patient and wait for the universe to signal the correct direction. Do not worry you will know when to act and when to keep silent. Sexual liaisons serve you well and add to your innate mystery.

Luck Factor: Your determination and will power are the great keys to your success. Do not bother with what anyone else is up to. Even though you have the personal power and ability to control others; you will actually do better if you concentrate on your own agenda. Leave others to make their own mistakes.

Jupiter in SAGITTARIUS

You are apparently optimistic, generous spirited and generally up-for-it. Yes it is all true, but only you are aware of your other side; which you keep well-hidden. Intelligent, with a wicked sense of humor, you really are very good at putting things into perspective. It is just that you really must learn not to gloss over important issues that need your attention. Ditch procrastination and see what a difference it makes to your productivity. Sometimes you expect too much from people, and often set yourself up for disappointment. But, the good news is, your natural joie-de-vivre gets you through most things. Life is good to you.

Jupiter expands your bizarre sense of humor and ability to find the fun in even the direst situation. Be careful not to be insensitive.

Watch out for too much flippancy at inappropriate moments. Your sense of adventure is tireless and you are always on the look-out for the next person, event, or hobby to capture your attention.

Fortune Cookie: Jupiter is your ruler, so you are naturally luckier than most. Your generosity of spirit draws abundance, fortune, and many blessings towards you. Travel is always a good idea, so keep on the move and expand your horizons whenever you get a chance. Study and debate catch your attention and serve you well.

Luck Factor: Fitness levels can peak, and boost your life in so many ways. But only if you make the effort. Your ruler Jupiter enables you to unravel many a mystery. Your intuition will be jumping, so do not ignore those hunches. Pay heed to your dreams and visions; and take steps to pin things down.

Jupiter in CAPRICORN

You are resourceful and pretty relentless, so you are naturally very good at creating your own luck. Not one to wait for things to happen; you *make* them happen. In all things you are conscientious and generally you have good levels of integrity; which is just as well for you are capable of bending many people to your will if you so choose. Use your power wisely. Sometimes you get bogged down with things and come across as quite serious minded. Often you possess tunnel vision and will get lost in something you are trying to manifest. Lighten up a little.

Jupiter expands your focus, dedication and moral standards. Just do not become too inert and stuck-in-a-must-do-the-right-thing-rut. Have some fun as you go about your business. Your levels of success are going to be phenomenal come-what-may, so you might as well enjoy the ride.

Fortune Cookie: You are a wise soul, who is primed for success and longevity. Diligent and reliable, career commendations will be coming out of your ears once you find your niche. All set to make oodles of money for both yourself and your employer, you are destined to be a star on the corporate ladder.

Luck Factor: Unafraid to put the work in, you are not a great believer in the quick-fix. But the beauty of it all is that you will find the required turnaround much more quickly than you expect. Your instincts will be honed to perfection, and this will land you great choices and deals in next to no time. Just say yes!

Jupiter in AQUARIUS

You are a philanthropic soul who wants the best for the world, and you have a magnanimous, generous nature. An independent spirit, you are the true maverick. You do your own thing in your own way and that is that. Because you are interested in others, fair minded and free from prejudice, you expect the same respect in return. Injustice gets under your skin, and you are the pioneer of freedom and original thought. Even though you are quite private, you love your family and friends to the maximum, and would do anything to protect them.

Jupiter expands your leadership skills and sense of fair play. You are great at delegation and detachment. Your emotions do not rule your decisions or influence you adversely. But you are not cold; simply calm and collected. Intellectually superior, your mind is agile and you love to be stimulated in strange ways.

Fortune Cookie: Your popularity and ability to put your point of view across guarantees your success. There is a touch of genius about you, and you rarely fail at what you set out to achieve. Though you are sometimes tempted to control things, generally you concede to let things unfold organically. Good choice!

Luck Factor: Friendships are fortuitous for you, so develop those that really matter. Keep a cool head as you strive to get ahead. Your luck comes in strange ways, so do remain open minded and open hearted. That life changing moment will happen in the blink of an eye; do not miss it.

Jupiter in PISCES

You are sympathetic and well liked. A compassionate soul, you are sensitive and kind to all. Do guard against psychic vampires who would take advantage of your better nature. Spot the blood suckers with your spot-on intuition and give them a wide berth. This will strengthen you; your aura and life will benefit. Spiritual and highly imaginative, you love mysterious people, events and places. Do protect yourself though. It really is the difference between success and failure for you. You can be taken in by the unscrupulous, and are prone to weak decisions.

Jupiter expands your sensitivity, creativity and intuition. You need a huge measure of freedom, so the possessive need not apply. In love you are true and hugely romantic. But you need to know you can explore other options, even if it is just in your imagination. You love a healthy dose of fantasy; and why not?

Fortune Cookie: A great deal of your good fortune derives from your generosity to others. Always give freely of your time, money and favors. Just steer clear of those who are taking advantage of you. Religious and spiritual concerns develop you, body, mind and spirit. But avoid fakes, phonies, and anyone ungrounded like the plague.

Luck Factor: Your emotional sensitivity and imagination hold the key to your success. But people may well be jealous of your spookiness and try to undermine you. Be strong and believe you are right; do not doubt it. Do not be afraid to tackle two things at once. It could just be the recipe for success you need.

8 SATURNINE MOVES

Saturn's authority puts a restraining order on excess. This Planet holds The Universe in check. Not an easy energy, Saturn challenges recklessness. Saturn is our conscience warning against foolhardiness. Intimidating to the free spirited. Saturn may undermine weak self-esteem, heightening self-doubt and confusion.

Saturn's buzzword is "don't," which may repress, depress, or comfort, according to disposition. Like an autocratic parent, this Ruling Planet is good to have around in a crisis. But debilitating when we need to muster self-confidence. Balance is crucial in the face of Saturn's warning flag. It is advisable to take the hint and put the brakes on questionable behavior. But, it is equally important to resist Saturn's bullying.

Some of you may have heard of the scourge of The Saturn Return, but not really have a clue what it means to your life in detail. Generally people know that something happens when we hit the phase of our lives between the ages of twenty-seven and thirty, because they observe big adjustments, shifts and changes in circumstances that are most definitely beyond their control. So how is this sometimes uncomfortable experience explained astrologically?

Saturn, the planet symbolically associated with time, challenges, fear, doubt, confusion, difficulty, heaviness and hard lessons is also more positively linked with structure, accomplishment, power, maturity, reflection, order and prestige.

Saturn takes approximately twenty-nine, and a half years to orbit The Sun when it then returns to exactly the degree which it occupied at the time of your birth. When this happens in your natal chart, you are going to feel the tremors of Saturn's power like it or not. Our thirtieth birthday is for this reason a major rite of passage, and in Astrological terms it is even more important than your twenty-first, coming of age.

At the tail end of our twenties we all begin the build up to our Saturn Return which is going to force us to restructure our lives and grow up a little. This phenomenon purges what is not good for us and it is generally a case of "do or die" during this rite of passage.

There are always definite moves we can make to give ourselves some structure in the midst of The Saturn Return. It is possible to give it some shape and meaning despite the turmoil and confusion which goes on at the time. If you remember that the goals to aim for are independence, maturity, responsibility, ambition, and self-evaluation, you will come through it with your dignity intact.

Okay we are not all going to be Hollywood Stars. But we do all need to make the most of our lives and get through its challenges in one piece. Our rewards the other side of this process called The Saturn Return will reflect how we handled it. As we get stuck into this final test which paves the way for adulthood, we need to stay calm, trust and focus on our life goals. Yes, some people cannot cope and go off the rails, others become somewhat introverted for a time. But those who shine through it all are those who access their personal power, truth and stick-ability.

To make the most of The Saturn Return phase of your life you need Determination with a capital D. Even if you do not know what you want before it begins, the process itself will show you and by the end of it all you will be as clear as the cold light of day.

Should you envy those who are already ambitious and focused? No! For even the best of us cannot escape The Saturn Return. With those who are already sorted and established it is more likely to be quite a traumatic process emotionally. So no one escapes the scourge of Saturn completely, it is an important part of our lives, and without this tricky planet which throws up interesting challenges, life would probably be rather dull.

The energy stirred up by the planet Saturn teaches us a whole lot and especially helps us to find balance and maturity if we work with it and do not baulk at what is happening. The Saturn Return teaches us to be brave and face up to whole lot. It is definitely not a good idea to brush things under the carpet during this phase. If you do that the damage in the long term could be pretty hideous. Embrace your fears and confusion during this time and the rewards will be great indeed. Remember, life does not serve you up with more than you are able to cope with and Saturn that seven-ringed planet in the sky certainly will not either. In fact, to end on a positive note, The Saturn Return can help you to find and express yourself more fully and authentically. By teaching us how to be real and truly ourselves if we listen and observe its lessons Saturn can serve us well.

Saturn returns to each Zodiac sign every twenty-nine or thirty years for approximately three years. So where was Saturn when you were born and how does its placing distinguish you from your fellow Star signs? Find out here below, or check on-line with your Natal Chart information by googling "find Saturn position in Natal Chart." There are no tables necessary in the back of the book for this one.

Saturn in ARIES:

April 1937 to March 1940
March 1967 to April 1969
April 1996 to February 1999

Saturn in Aries makes you less impulsive than other fire signs. This placing controls your impulsive streak and general assertiveness by keeping you in check. You definitely have more patience than other Arians too, which cannot be a bad thing. Saturn in Aries teaches you more composure, patience and tolerance.

Saturn in TAURUS:

July 1939 to May 1942
May 1969 to February 1972
June 1998 to April 2001

Saturn in Taurus affects your materialistic concerns making you less acquisitive and ambitious than other zodiac bulls. It perhaps makes you more cautious, and less touchy feely too when it comes to sensual match ups. Saturn in Taurus teaches you to be practical and realistic about your expectations and material well-being.

Saturn in GEMINI:

May 1942 to June 1944
June 1971 to August 1974
April 2001 to June 2003

Saturn has the effect of keeping you grounded and sensible; enabling you to use your communication skills very effectively. You are more logical than your Gemini counterparts and tend to get results with cute practical decisions. You are much less susceptible to illusion and crazy ungrounded notions. Plus your restless streak is well controlled.

Saturn in CANCER:

August 1914 to June 1917
June 1944 to July 1946
August 1972 to June 1976
June 2003 to July 2005

This is a good placing for Cancer, for Saturn acts as a protective barrier. Emotions and responses tend to be more controlled and measured. The exterior outer shell is hardened and acts as a foil to those things which normally defeat your much more sensitive fellow Cancerians. You learn quickly how to deal with feeling inferior and para-noid.

Saturn in LEO:

June 1917 to August 1919
August 1946 to September 1948
September 1975 to July 1978
July 2005 to August 2007

Saturn calms you down in comparison to your more gregarious fellow Zodiac lions. You are still fun, but you tend to be more measured and less reckless with love, money and decisions. Saturn also teaches you to take responsibility. You are a natural leader who is able to shoulder many issues. It is all water off the duck's back.

Saturn in VIRGO:

August 1918 to October 1921
September 1948 to August 1951
July 1978 to September 1980
August 2007 to October 2009
April 7th 2010 to July 21st 2010

Saturn puts your analytical and practical nature within firm boundaries. Your restless, neurotic streak is kept in check and you usually have the means to argue your way out of a corner. Saturn helps you concentrate on one thing at a time and makes you even more systematic than your fellow Virgoans. You also complete things.

Saturn in LIBRA:

October 1921 to September 1924
November 1950 to October 1953
September 1980 to August 1983

October 29th 2009 to April 7th 2010
July 21st 2010 to 2012

Your charm and politeness is low key which is no bad thing. It means you can come across as more genuine and deep than your fellow Librans. You still have a serious perfectionist streak. But you are trained by Saturn to be aware that actions speak louder than words. Your discipline and integrity is commendable. You deliver on a promise.

Saturn in SCORPIO:

December 1923 to November 1926
October 1953 to October 1956
December 1982 to November 1985
October 2012 to December 2014
June 2015 to September 2015

Saturn in this placing limits and controls your deep turbulent emotions making you more balanced than natal sun sign Scorpions. You also possess more tolerance and understanding than usual. Under Saturn's direction learn that perseverance is the key to success in most things. You are able to channel your deep responses to help others

Saturn in SAGITTARIUS:

December 1926 to November 1929
January 1956 to January 1959
November 1985 to November 1988
September 2015 to December 2017

You are more realistic and have less of a mad sense of adventure than your fellow Sagittarians. Freedom you appreciate; but you know how to monitor your selfish desires and demands. Saturn bestows on you a more understanding and empathetic quality. You are mature and know how to be content with what you have. Appreciation is everything.

Saturn in CAPRICORN:

December 1929 to November 1932
January 1959 to January 1962
February 1988 to February 1991
December 2017 to December 2020

The harsh and ruthless qualities of typical Capricorns are dampened down with Saturn in this position.` You have a quiet cool confidence and know how to progress slowly but surely. Success is a given and you never panic about what might go wrong, because of course things rarely do. You are in control in a good way.

Saturn in AQUARIUS:

February 1932 to February 1935
January 1962 to December 1964
February 1991 to January 1994
December 2020 to 2023

Aquarians tend to be overtly friendly and altruistic But Saturn in this position makes you more cautious and private. Under this planet's direction you learn how to absorb and apply information to your benefit. You are thorough and possess great leadership qualities. In short, you do not miss a trick. Just watch for a tendency to be overly controlling.

Saturn in PISCES:

February 1935 to January 1938
March 1964 to March 1967
May 1993 to April 1996

This is a great placing and you have the edge on fellow Pisceans. You are less gullible and get better protection. Your sensitive emotions and responses are under control and you know your boundaries well; which is unusual for a Piscean. Your ability to put on a brave face to the world is formidable and you give the illusion of being steely: no bad thing.

9 URANUS PLUTO NEPTUNE

The "out-there" planets Uranus, Neptune and Pluto are the three slow moving outer planets which influence our natal charts and daily lives. Because they take so long to amble through the heavens these are planets which influence generations. Each generation has markedly different placements of these planets. This logically then distinguishes how each decade or so we have such unique changes to our culture.

When one of these three slow movers shifts into a new sign in the Heavens above, we see marked changes in our external environment. Everything from hairstyles to car design to social structures undergo through radical change.

A most significant shift of this nature was when Pluto moved from Libra to Scorpio in 1984, until the end of 1995. Through this whole phase Plutonic activity lead to the development of nuclear weaponry, destruction via landmines, an increase of crimes of sex and violence and huge increase in the development of the porn industry.

Pluto moving through Scorpio brought much of this to light, preparing for the shift of Pluto into Sagittarius during 1996. Did we then see an increase in comedy, philosophical ideas and discussion and increased emphasis on religious issues? Probably we did.

The three outermost planets of the solar system take 84, 65, and 248 years respectively to orbit the Sun. They therefore stay 7, 14, and 28 years in a Zodiac sign, with slight variations whilst retrograde.

Find out where these three planets were at the time of your birth and what their placements mean for you. There are no tables at the back of the book for these planets, as their movement is so slow, huge tables are not required.

URANUS

Uranus is the planet of personal transformation. Inspirational for the individual, this Ruling Planet also blesses generations. Uranus challenges the Status Quo, and constitutes a challenging, difficult energy. Independent and radical, this planet moves slowly heralding profound drawn out change.

To be born under Uranus, which all Aquarians are, is an honor indeed, which needs to be treated with healthy respect. This planet inspires altruism. But also signifies self-importance and eccentricity. Uranus allows for detachment, as well as the ability to be all things to all people. This mode of being is a law unto itself. In true maverick style Aquarius knows best. A perverted rebellious streak gives Uranus the edge.

Uranus returns to each sign once every 84 years, and remains in the same sign for usually seven years. Its influence is general. But this sign certainly dictates your urge for freedom, and the way your individuality is expressed.

Where was URANUS at the time of your birth?

Uranus in ARIES

Uranus has been in Aries for only 9 years since the 1800's from April 1927 to March 1935. It returns to Aries in March 2011, until May 2018.

Characteristics/identifiers:
Dynamism, assertiveness, self-absorption, fires.

With Uranus in Aries, your spirit of adventure is pronounced, and you seek freedom at any price. In the extreme this urge for freedom can cause alienation, estrangement and frequent departures from what has gone before. You are blunt and outspoken. Watch that fiery temper. You would do well to develop more empathy and understanding.

Uranus in TAURUS

June to October 1934, and April 1935 to May 1942. Uranus returns to Taurus in March 2018, until 2026.

Characteristics/identifiers:
Strength, dictatorship, structural damage.

Often with this placing you are looking for new and practical ideas re money and material gain. You love to change the old way of doing things at every given opportunity. You have great determination and courage. Full of purpose you always get things done. Watch that stubborn streak though; it can definitely hold you back. Practice free expression.

Uranus in GEMINI

May 1942 to June 1949.

Characteristics/identifiers:
Intellect, versatility, educational changes.

You are a genius and intuitively brilliant. You have the ability to pioneer new concepts in the work place, and have great passion for what grabs your interest. But you can be deeply restless and often lose patience with your best ideas far too quickly. More self-discipline will enable you to bring things to fruition. Self-belief is everything

Uranus in CANCER

June 1949 to August 1955, and February to June 1956.

Characteristics/identifiers:
Detached emotions, unique family heritage.

You really need freedom of emotional expression and simply hate to be stifled. Authority figures make you baulk. As your tastes develop you love unusual décor and surroundings. You are quite the eccentric. You are highly likely to be psychic and need to stay grounded. There is a risk of instability at times. You need to be nurtured and understood.

Uranus in LEO

June 1956 to August 1962.

Characteristics/identifiers:
Great achievements, royal births, egomania.

Your need for independence means that in love and romance you like to lead the way. You are a born leader who needs to dictate how things are going to be. You are artistic with certain standards and you redefine set standards asap. Watch out for egotism with this placement. Your chance to make the best impact comes when you consider others. Become altruistic!

Uranus in VIRGO

August 1962 to September 1968.

Characteristics/identifiers:
Neurotic behavior, Health Changes, Mental restlessness.

You have original and unique ideas regarding health and well-being. You are very innovative with science and technology also. Meticulous intellectual research comes naturally and you get to the bottom of whatever you undertake to understand. You may feel you have health niggles; but these inspire you to get busy. You always find solutions.

Uranus in LIBRA

October 1968 to November 1974, and May to September 1975.

Characteristics/identifiers:
Unique talent, coldness, superficiality

Ironically you find your independence through relationships and partnerships. You set yourself up for stress and disharmony if you hook up with someone too demanding. Choose partners carefully. You have an unusual legal brain and often find ways to reform rules and structures in your environment. You are unconventional, inspirational and probably musical.

Uranus in SCORPIO

September 1975 to November 1981, and October 1974, and April 1975.

Characteristics/identifiers:
Sexual deviations, emotional coldness, cruelty.

You find that independence comes through radical and inspirational change. Bound to be over emotional with this placement; you also have unique psychic insights and pick up far more than is humanly useful. Your sensitivity is certainly heightened, and you need to find ways to protect yourself. Watch that temper. Sometimes you insist on change in dictatorial fashion.

Uranus in SAGITTARIUS

1904 and November 1981 to November 1988.

Characteristics/identifiers:
Exploration, unique records, new discoveries.

You have very unique individualistic ideas about religion, philosophy, spirituality and education. You are eccentric and have a bizarre way of coming up with pertinent perspectives. No doubt you are interested in anything hidden and mysterious. But be careful in your exploration of things which may be more powerful than you. Beware natural forces.

Uranus in CAPRICORN

1905 to 1911, and December 1988, and January 1996.

Characteristics/identifiers:
Ruthless power, insensitivity, new regulations.

This generation brings about powerful changes in government and business power structures. You know how to keep the best of the old traditions, whilst making radical plans for significant grass roots reform. Doubtless your ambitions are strong. Your desire to succeed is formidable and you have ways of making people walk and talk. Be kind.

Uranus in AQUARIUS

February 1912 to March 1919, and January 1996 to March 2003.

Characteristics/identifiers:
Inventions, rebellion, advanced space travel.

Old outmoded ideas do not cut the mustard for you. You have to have the freedom to make your own decisions. No one is going to tell you what to do anytime soon. You use intuition more than logic; but you get some serious results by trusting your visions. You set the trends and the rest of us follow. You are no sheep that is for sure.

Uranus in PISCES

April 1919 to March 1927, and March 2003 to 2011.

Characteristics/identifiers:
Unique talent, emotionally chaos, tidal waves.

You seek to bring about change and assert your independence with the use of your heightened intuition. You dig deep and have a good understanding of the universal unconscious as well as formidable self-awareness. You can be idealistic though and expect the best of people. You get disappointed; but not much perturbs you.

PLUTO

Pluto highlights personal obstacles and our ability to overcome them. This planet has a strong influence on our hidden secrets. Life's mystery and dark side loves Pluto energy. Its terrain is the skeleton in the closet, and the subterranean depths of the unconscious.

Pluto is the ancient god of the Underworld. This energy dances in the shadows, and is not afraid to stare death in the face. An intrepid fearlessness attaches to this Planet's vibration. Pluto is resilient, determined and will not take defeat lying down. Therefore, Pluto inspires transformation. But Pluto can be dark, dangerous and cruel. When off balance resist and avoid this energy at all costs.

Pluto entered Sagittarius in late 1995 and this significant shift brought about significant pressure for all of us, depending on what issue it hit.

Where was PLUTO at the time of your birth?
Pluto in ARIES

Characteristics/identifiers:
Sudden eruptions, nuclear wars.

This is a reforming placement; but without the staying power to complete the good ideas. This transit begins in 2082 and ends in 2101. Maybe Aries pioneers in the future will be exploring the outer reaches of the Universe and finding everything we never could.

Pluto in TAURUS

Characteristics/identifiers:
Dedication, underground activity.

A resistance to initial changes but then acceptance and long term results once the new regime in place. The long haul produces major change. Pluto moves into Taurus in 2101 and stays there for 31 years.

Pluto in GEMINI

Characteristics/identifiers:
Advanced changes in communications, verbosity.

Regeneration manifests through the dissemination of ideas and good communication. Pluto moves into Gemini in 2132 for 30 years. It is perhaps hard to imagine but there will be new forms of communication and new ways to distribute information developed under this influence.

Pluto in CANCER

Characteristics/identifiers:
Family traumas, obsessions, ultra-sensitivity.

July 1913 to June 1939, for the first time since the 1600's.
Regeneration of society will come through the deep emotional involvement in the home and homeland. Pluto in this position will domesticate new worlds, new environments and new emotional attachments.

Pluto in LEO

Characteristics/identifiers:
Changes in power and authority.

1939 and 1956, and January to August 1957, for the first time since the 1700's.

Regeneration manifests dramatically through power struggles internationally. Potentially a dangerous time. The last time Pluto was in Leo saw the power struggles which led to the Second World War. Hopefully the proceeding reign of Pluto in Cancer establishes a peace which cannot be threatened by such shenanigans.

Pluto in VIRGO

Characteristics/identifiers:
Minor obsessions, earthquakes, ingenuity.

October 1956 to October 1971, and April to July 1972, for the first time since 1720.

Purging of society and life occurs through the analysis of what is or is not essential. This is a practical time. Under the last reign of Pluto in Virgo great advances were made in surgery and medicine. Perhaps by this time science will have the capacity to defrost all those frozen cryogenically.

Pluto in LIBRA

Characteristics/identifiers:
Transforming legal change, intense charm

October 1971 to Nov 1983, and May to August 1984 for the first time since 1735.
Regeneration of society comes through revamped partnerships, relationships and marriages. By the time this reign occurs it will be interesting to see if it will see a return to the traditional values we just

about still hold dear. Or will there be harems, and multi-dimensional marriages galore?

Pluto in SCORPIO

Characteristics/identifiers:
Sexually transmitted diseases, alternative therapies

November 1983 to January 1995, and April to November 1995 for the first time since before the Revolution in Europe.

This is the eleventh hour placement of Pluto in Scorpio, which last occurred from 1983 to 1995. This is the time when Global Warming became established in our hearts and minds as a serious issue.

AIDS surfaced as a serious threat and alternative medicine developed its influence significantly. Will we all still be here by the time Pluto hits Scorpio again?

Pluto in SAGITTARIUS

Characteristics/identifiers:
Prophetic powers, extrasensory perception, extensive travel.

November 1995 to February 2008, and June to November 2008 for the first time since the American Revolution.

In this sign Pluto leads to the success or failure of the transformation which has gone before. Perhaps by this time we will all be more enlightened spiritually and bound by our beliefs and common humanity. Preoccupation with materialism, profit, and loss do not work. It is make or break time.

Pluto in CAPRICORN

Characteristics/identifiers:
Return to law and justice, earthly restrictions

January 25th 2008 to June 14th 2008, and November 26th 2008 to January 21st 2024, for the first time since 1762 to 1778 during the American Revolution.

This is a practical time where the debris and loose ends of the Pluto in Sagittarius reign get tied up and sorted. The Aquarian age gets reconstructed and new rules are put in place.

The last time Pluto was in Capricorn the French Revolution brought serious reform and change across Europe, and the United States was founded.

Pluto in AQUARIUS

Characteristics/identifiers:
Development of the new world, uniqueness, spiritual science.

In 2041 a New Order will be established and structures in place which will benefit from Aquarian altruistic reforms. A more altruistic phase begins.

Pluto in PISCES

Characteristics/identifiers:
Self-destruction, enlightenment, strengthening of the emotions.

This regime next begins in 2061, more than 50 years from now. By this time we should have a much deeper understanding of who we are and what our priorities should be. Here is hoping. Why can we not get there sooner?

NEPTUNE

Neptune ruler of the oceans has energy enough to transform the masses. The processes inspired by Neptune are laborious but profound. Ideologies, beliefs and social norms come under the jurisdiction of Neptune. But commendable spiritual tendencies may become off-the-wall fanaticism. The down side of Neptune involves escapism, indecisiveness, and elaboration of the truth.

Neptune off balance muddles the vision. So discernment is important. Those ruled by Neptune should guard against self-deception. For wild fantasy and wish fulfilment tendencies need to be monitored. With Neptune in the frame, dreams and visions are loaded with significance. This depth, wisdom and imagination may be expressed as a great gift.

Neptune spends twice as long in a sign as Uranus, usually about 14 years. This is most definitely a generational planet. But it has an important influence in your natal chart depending on which zodiac house resides in. Neptune links to your spiritual and intuitive talents.

Where was NEPTUNE at the time of your birth?

NEPTUNE in ARIES

Characteristics/identifiers:
Dissolution of leadership, spiritual evolution.

This placing fires your imagination big time. It also allows you to act on your psychic impulses with the full force of trust and faith. Ego needs to be watched for this can be a dangerous combination when off balance. Powerful indeed.

NEPTUNE in TAURUS

Characteristics/identifiers:
Financial losses, gothic architecture,

Neptune next in Taurus in 2052.

Imagination and spiritual energies are channeled into concrete practical expression. This is a handy grounded placing. The danger lies in your tendency to put too much emphasis on material well-being. The illusory seduction can be that you are too rooted in reality! Work that one out.

NEPTUNE in GEMINI

Characteristics/identifiers:
Instability, openness to spiritual awareness.

Your heightened intuition bridges the gap. A great combination where left and right brain function tend to be well balanced. Imagination and spiritual issues are channeled through logic and reasoning. You are formidable and must guard against burn out and thinking you can conquer everyone and everything.

NEPTUNE in CANCER

Characteristics/identifiers:
Psychic development, oceanic changes.

July 1901 to July 1915 for the first time since before the American Revolution.

This placement ensures heightened psychic ability. But also makes you quite impressionable if you are not aware of your own ability. There is a need for grounding; and an acute need to be aware of the difference between reality and illusion.

NEPTUNE in LEO

Characteristics/identifiers:
Theatrical talent, dissolution of royalty.

July 1915 to July 1929, for the first time since the American Revolution.

This is a bold, creative and imaginative placing. You are bound to be extremely expressive and imaginative. Watch that your ego does not alienate people or hold you back. Yes you can conquer the world; but do not advertise the fact.

NEPTUNE in VIRGO

Characteristics/identifiers:
Floods, mental instability, agricultural booms.

August 1929 to September 1942, and April to July 1943.

You are cute and know how to handle your productive imagination and spirituality. You carefully analyze and understand what is what. Just do not over analyze as you need to trust a greater freedom of expression. You cannot always fit your spirituality into a box.

NEPTUNE in LIBRA

Characteristics/identifiers:
Flower power, hallucinations, peace, beauty.

October 1942 to October 1956, for the first time in 200 years.

You use beauty and harmony to express your spirituality and your essence. Watch for misplaced idealism and do not assume you can save the world. You perhaps can; but would do well to be practical and channel your good energies wisely.

NEPTUNE in SCORPIO

Characteristics/identifiers:
Lack of control, addictions, healing power.
October 1956 to November 1970, and previously in 1806.

Your great imagination serves you well and allows you to understand deep spiritual matters if you are so inclined. Watch for the temptation or pull of drug and substance abuse. You may be prone to sex issues. Just keep your deep dark side in check and talk things through when needs be.

NEPTUNE in SAGITTARIUS

Characteristics/identifiers:
Restlessness, visions, religious fervor.

November 1971 to January 1984, and June to November 1984 for the first time since 1820.

You may not yet appreciate the psychic ability you have and you would probably want to try to understand it intellectually first before using it. Um, it does not work like that: *Use* it. You really need creative freedom and self-expression is your most valued asset. In the exploration of all things spiritual you may be drawn into the cult/guru thing; be careful.

NEPTUNE in CAPRICORN

Characteristics/identifiers:
Dissolution of laws, clouded principles.

January 1984 to January 1998, and August to November 1998 for the first time since the Civil War.

You have a practical side which allows your spiritual ideas and impulses to be expressed sensibly. Watch that the voice of reason does not completely stifle your imagination and psychic impulses. You always double check your messages and tend to doubt things unless they are staring you in the face.

NEPTUNE in AQUARIUS

Characteristics/identifiers:
Intellectual depreciation, great visionaries.

February 1998 to February 2012 for the first time since the Civil War.

Great spiritual changes and developments are linked to this placing. You have the capacity to be quite the innovator. Not much passes you by and you have a unique perception which can really help others. You may not appreciate that your talents can be grounded to help you in practical ways.

NEPTUNE in PISCES

Characteristics/identifiers:
Compassion, surrealism, spiritual awareness

2012. 2018

You have a vivid imagination and might as well see where it can take you. But you need to stay grounded and not get lost in a world of illusion. Learn how to balance your psychic insights with practical application. You can help many with your messages but need to test that you are getting it right before you can be fully confident.

10 WOMEN VENUS: MEN MARS

WOMEN are from Venus; MEN are from Mars. Look for your friend or partner's Star Sign and Gender here below for clues to their love, friendship and relating style. Find out if they can be trusted. Are you destined for a life-time of bliss, contentment, fun and laughter; or are you "barking up the wrong tree?"

ARIES:

MEN: Men with strong Aries energy are spontaneous and exciting. These are the ambitious, uncompromising Alpha males of the Zodiac. Assertive, and focused, Aries man does not take no for an answer. This chap is driven by his passions and is well able to segregate physical activity from emotional engagement, if you get my drift! Ruled by Mars, Aries man is dynamic and energetic between the sheets; but empathy is not his strong point. You may not get wined and dined ad infinitum, though you will get a good romp between the sheets for sure. Not the most refined sensibility, this man is capable of curbing his desires in order to learn some finesse. But this only happens when he has fallen deeply in love. Apart from that, this guy is hormonally driven and is quite happy to undertake a new connection based solely on a person's appearance.

WOMEN: This feisty lady needs no seducing. Aries female is fully in touch with her carnal desires, and needs very little coaxing to get busy between the sheets. This little lady suits herself and she is not likely to suppress her hormonal responses once she has set her sights on you. Even if she is spoken for, she is quite capable of the odd liaison along the way. I am not saying that she inevitably will; but she sure as hell *might*, if the fancy takes her. This woman is very masculine and dynamic with her love making. Not afraid to take the lead, Aries woman is as good at the love them, and leave them game as the next man. With strong sexual drives as her defining quality, Aries woman is not big on emotional drama. She is independent and does not need too much input. Some men may mistrust this and find their hearts' challenged in the face of such self-sufficiency. Hurts does it not?

TAURUS:

MEN: Taurus man is a supremely gorgeous lover who will seduce you in subtle ways. But be warned! The Zodiac Bull is a flirt, who will invariably test the water with many of the females in his domain. Taurus man is intrinsically loyal and hates to risk his comfort zone. But, he is not beyond indulging those sensual desires if he feels he can get away with it. If Taurus is not free to act, he is likely to leave you dangling, having fired up your hormones to a torturous level. Taurus is useless at failure and rejection and is likely to play the field in these circumstances. But keep him satiated with lots of sex, intimacy and understanding, and the Zodiac Bull is loyal, fully relishing the status quo you provide. Taurus man is a passive creature who likes a dominant, independent mate. He is not particularly predatory, but boy, will he respond if you make the moves. Well, may be.

WOMEN: Taurus woman does not ask for much; she wants it all! Wit, charm, sexual prowess, personality and a mischievous boyish outlook are all part of the package she requires. Think, you are in the running? Well to woo this little minx, you must also have a huge wad and be more than happy to indulge her every whim. She loves to leave you hanging on, and will play a merry devious game which leaves you eternally wrapped around that doll-like finger. Miss Taurus is the marrying kind, but she also likes the bohemian groove until she has the man of her dreams finally pinned down. She will not marry for the sake of it. This female requires loyalty and devotion without the boredom factor. Watch for the little girl coquettishness and the public displays of affection which are extremely manipulative, however beguiling. She casts her spell with girlish charm.

GEMINI:

MEN: Gemini male is a smoothie who loves to dip his finger in as many pies as possible. He is what he is; which is not the most trustworthy dude on the planet. But you are bound to forgive him most things, as he is as loveable and cute as they come. Turn a blind eye and enjoy the good stuff, for Gemini man is witty, entertaining and a bundle of laughs. Okay, he is easily distracted, somewhat two-faced, and masterful at covering his tracks. It is all true. But the upside is you get to spend time with a cultured, refined, intelligent individual who loves to talk and bounce ideas around; amongst other things! Close to his family and friends, the Gemini fella *does* have a loyal streak and he does not mess with his deepest emotions. It is just that he loves sex and can segregate his feelings into interchangeable compartments. His heart is a mansion with many rooms, you might say.

WOMEN: Gemini female is a funny mixture. She loves her independence and privacy, but she does have a vulnerable streak and likes to role-play the little-girl-lost, when the situation requires it. You will doubtless enjoy rescuing her from whatever it is that plays upon her mind; for she is beguiling, playful and childlike on a good day. Just steer clear when the thunder clouds are a-forming, and be prepared for the odd bit of nifty deception when she is trying to get ahead. The Gemini chick is competitive and likes to excel in her chosen field. But this prowess, luckily for you, extends to the bedroom. You can expect hours of fun, so long as you do not become boring and predictable. If Gemini woman does demand one thing; it is a vivid imagination between the sheets. She is dangerous in manipulative mode, but strangely innocent as she indulges her desires. Enjoy!

CANCER:

MEN: The Cancer male is a great believer in taking things easy. It's anything for the quiet life, as far as he is concerned. The Zodiac Crab can be quite indirect and understated, even a little cold. Not the best communicator in the world, this fella expects you to read his mind in the same way he can read yours. Very self-protective and cagey about his deepest feelings, he can be quite moody and petulant. He is also good at ducking and diving and knows how to keep you guessing. Plagued with insecurities and anxiety, he can still be pushy when he has to be. If a person or circumstance has served its purpose he can be quite ruthless at shutting down and moving on. When committed though the scuttling Crab can be coaxed into nurturing and caring. Deep and emotional, this man tends to spend too much time analyzing how *he* is doing. What about you?

WOMEN: This woman is sensitive and protective with her displays of affection. Those she loves get her undivided attention; but her intensity can at times be overwhelming. Inclined to be temperamental, the female Crab can snap at the silliest things. Too often she loses her cool, for no good reason. This sensitive lady needs an outlet for her complex emotions; if you know what I mean. Get busy between the sheets and most things can be readily forgiven. Remember, her shyness is surprising and she gets insecure about the strangest things. But intimacy is important to her well-being; as is sharing and caring in a close knit environment. She really is very unlikely to stray as family life suits her, providing ample opportunity for the connections she craves. When things are running smoothly this lady gives unconditionally; but she can be turned off by other's demands.

LEO:

MEN: The Zodiac Lion is a dramatic and flamboyant lover. No one would dismiss this beast as a wallflower that's for sure. Definitely inclined towards dramatic gestures, the regal male is madly colorful and good fun to be with. This man's creativity is enviable and he has good energy reserves for the things which grab his imagination. Let's hope one of them is you! Remember, routine stuff bores the pants off him; but he does have a lazy streak which allows him to snooze off at the drop of a hat when there is nothing better to do. Keep him stimulated and interested and the loving will intensify. Give up too readily, and he will go out on the prowl to peruse his domain. The Lion will not be seduced for the sake of it; yet of course he manages to be intrinsically charming when he says no. But his need to be adored is a key aspect of his sexual drive and general prowess.

WOMEN: The Zodiac Lioness is loyal and generous hearted. Attentive and kind, she loves to dominate her terrain and takes tremendous pride in her brood. But she can also be quite controlling and in-your-face with her gestures. The Leo female is the proverbial Drama Queen, and her emotions are bizarrely and entertainingly over the top when she becomes unbalanced. However when she is fully appreciated, this does not really happen. Just watch out for the claws if you ever take her for granted. Her temper tantrums are legendary, and she can be quite childlike when she does not get her own way. If she's going to stray, this would be the time, so it kind of pays to keep her happy. Indulge her and she will repay you with more loving than you know what to do with. Scary really! On the plus side, this female is wonderfully engaging and magically open hearted.

VIRGO:

MEN: The Virgo man is usually low-key, modest, dutiful, and possibly a bit 'mousy' on first impressions. But don't be fooled, this earthy sign warms up eventually and there are few who could beat him for overall performance. This man makes his voice and presence felt in subtle ways and he is intrinsically loyal. He really *is* worth your time and attention if you are looking for lasting love, fun and commitment. But watch out for his systematic, methodical streak, as he works his way into hearts and minds. He does have a controlling streak and of course that tendency to worry too much can be a bit of a pain. The Virgo man is incredibly picky and perfectionist. Likely to be critical of himself and others he does not believe in making things easy. On the plus side, casual links and superficial people are just not his style. What you see is what you get with this reliable fella.

WOMEN: This female is loyal, kind and modest; but a stickler for perfection. Her standards are high and she finds it difficult to be demonstrative when something does not feel right. The Zodiac Goddess shows her love and affection in practical ways. Even her tidiness and organization indicate her level of involvement. When she is wholeheartedly up-for-it, she is the chirpiest homemaker in the kingdom. But this lady has a cool analytical side and can express herself dispassionately. She may come across as aloof and fussy to those who don't know her very well. Virgo woman seeks perfection and sometimes gets held back by her need to have everything 'just so'. But she is unlikely to stray even if things get dire. Not great at revenge, you will probably be forgiven if you are unfaithful to her. Remember though, she will be tortured by it and will never forget.

LIBRA:

MEN: Libra Man is romantic, full of good will and happy thoughts. Well, in theory. In love-with-love, Libra will make uninformed choices until they hook up with their Soul Mate. A sucker for candle lit dinners and romantic gestures; this male is easily seduced by traditional expressions of feeling. It takes him a while to realize that sentimentality and a bunch of roses do not equate to undying love. When the situation gets serious, the harmonious Libran ups his game and pursues hard evidence of his chosen amour's staying power before he fully commits. In typical Libra style, he is sometimes assertive; sometimes shy; blowing hot and cold, often to your eternal frustration if you have already fallen for him. Yes, his dithering can indeed be quite exasperating, and even when he is committed, you will have to remember that he will flirt for Ireland whenever possible.

WOMEN: Libra Female is idealistic, dreamy and good calming company. She expects a lot from her relationships. But she can also be refreshingly lighthearted and even flippant. She expresses her affections sometimes extravagantly, sometimes hesitantly and her varied responses reflect typical Libran dithering. Unlikely to stray once she has fallen in love, this Zodiac female is reliable and unusually beautiful. Others may try to seduce her and you may feel insecure when she is out and about. But rest assured; this little lady does not look elsewhere so long as she is not stifled or pushed into a corner by you! Okay, that wicked sense of humor and natural charisma attracts all sorts of people. It's just the way she is and you will have to appreciate this sociable aspect of her nature if you are going to keep her happy and buoyant. She hates conflict and will walk not talk.

SCORPIO:

MEN: This passionate Zodiac Sign is surprisingly reticent about casual connections. The one-night-stand circuit is not the first choice of behavior for the Scorpion. Of course this is a habit that is easy to fall into if there is an underlying fear of being hurt by love which there often is. But contrary to most Zodiac Scorpio myths, this man does not tumble into bed at the drop of a proverbial hat. Intense and deep, commitment is important to Scorpio male. One thing is for sure, this man does not believe in half measures with the love stuff. When committed to a course of action, which hopefully involves you, this man will follow through to the maximum. If you are unsure of his advances, watch his brooding eyes for clues. The truth is in there if you care to see it. This man certainly is a catch with great energy levels and spectacular powers of endurance. Passionate responses come easy.

WOMEN: This hot Zodiac female is compulsive and passionate, which is great for intense connections. Yes, she may be likely to stray if the notion takes her. But there is no point getting het up about it. You may pick up the vibes and be completely wrong, so if you love a Scorpio female, give her lots of space. She is much more likely to wonder what you are up to, which will keep her on the straight and narrow like nothing else. Be aware that her mystery, privacy and charisma are all part of her allure. If you breathe down her neck in a less than seductive way she may turn against you, becoming overly suspicious and a tad obsessive. Her great gifts of passion and intensity can also be a burden. You will have to be a self-contained, self-assured and charismatic fella to attract and keep this lovely lady. She quickly casts a spell that will keep you hooked. Enjoy!

SAGITTARIUS:

MEN: Sagittarius male is straightforward and adventurous. If you are up for an experience that will tickle your fancy, do hook up with a Sagittarian. Yes, they are hyper, busy and sporty, and you will sometimes wonder where you fit in. But apart from that, you are signed up for a rollercoaster ride with never a dull moment. If you enjoy peace and quiet; do not bother. But if you like to be entertained, and never bored; go right ahead. This fiery soul is idealistic in his quest for true love. He is a born optimist who in this life has embarked on a continual quest to improve his lot. Sagittarius male is a restless spirit who keeps up the pressure, even when he has already got quite a good deal. Yes, the grass is always greener and he loves to spend time with the lads. Here is a free spirit who will experiment ad infinitum with a whole range of connections; like it or not!

WOMEN: The Sagittarian female is open with her affections and somewhat idealistic too. When she feels love, the whole world invariably hears about it. This is fine if you like the object of your affections to make a fuss; but not so good if you are the discrete, private type. This female wears her heart on her sleeve and she can be quite easily led, which is great if you want to seduce her; but may unnerve you if you want to keep a hold of her. A firm, loving approach should do the trick and a busy schedule too (for her). Be strong and self-contained to keep her interest. Apart from that, precious little dampens her lively spirit, which is great for intimate shenanigans, but not the best if you need a night's sleep. It takes a lot to get this lady riled; and even then she is one of the most forgiving souls on the planet. She is difficult to pin down, but hours of endless fun.

CAPRICORN:

MEN: This fella is an earthy, matter of fact soul, who can also be quite calculating. If you are with him, you need to guard your interests and keep your boundaries in check. One night stands are anathema to this man, so that is a comfort. But the down side is you will not often get a let-up from his intensity and need to control things. Can you handle it? Of course love covers a multitude of sins, and you can have full confidence in your relationship if you have adjusted through the tricky times. Once the deeper levels of love have kicked in, this man is full of romance, love and tolerance too; a great mixture for the archetypal family man, really. The Capricorn male is quite a traditionalist even before commitment sets in. But as a singleton he is not beyond the quick fling. Still, he makes his selection carefully, and then usually ends up marrying her anyway.

WOMEN: This woman is faithful and dutiful with her affections; but her relationships can be somewhat boring and sanitized. Meticulous about doing things the right way; she is prone to creating a joyless, edgy atmosphere, unwittingly. In trying to do things right this lady is in danger of losing her spontaneity and sense of humor. Loved ones potentially feel stifled, so be warned if you start to feel like you always have to be on your best behavior. This earthy lady takes relationships seriously, which is commendable. But whilst she is sensual, faithful and down to earth, she is also rather exacting too. Her natural reserve may come across as snobbish. But she is not dull and you will quickly know you can trust her with your life, heart and just about everything else too. Be patient with her when you first meet. She needs time to warm up and trust you.

AQUARIUS:

MEN: This man is unique. Eccentric and a law unto himself, he makes it all up as he goes along. What is expected, be damned. Aquarian man does things as he wishes, or not at all. If you are involved with him, be aware that he can be controlling. Anyone who dares to influence him adversely gets short shrift. On the up side this man is a real catch as he has a strong altruistic streak. He does not tolerate idiots; but he is wise, with a knowing air. His caring gestures are from the heart. In the boudoir he is imaginative and free spirited too. Anything goes and lovers are invariably in for a treat. Fresh approaches and unusual ideas turn him on, and he can cope with most forms of weirdness. This man is a good mix as he is loyal too; until he gets bored. Brush up on your intellect and knowledge to keep him hooked and things will flow in a longstanding, blissful way.

WOMEN: This lady is affectionate but unconventional and experimental. She can be a little kooky and odd and her fashion sense is certainly individual. But she is interesting and humorful. Little fazes her and she is offended by precious little. As long as she is free to express her feelings she is easily pleased. Privacy is crucial to her equilibrium; but she is also sociable and lively of wit and mind. Do not expect an easy ride with this Zodiac Queen. You have met your match in her that is for sure. Quick off the mark, nothing gets past her extreme powers of perception. She makes a great mother too, for with her altruistic tendencies, she is full of empathy and understanding. You will have to get used to her quirky habits and unusual ways.

But she will keep you entertained and ready for anything. She makes a lively lover; she is experimental, adventurous, and a skillful flirt.

PISCES:

MEN: This man has great powers of empathy and perception, which makes him nice to know. But he is not beyond deceptive activity if it is required. He goes through phases where he likes to be unavailable and mysterious. He also has a nosey streak, and loves to be at center of other people's business. Pisces man has a natural intuition and sensitivity, which gives him the edge in many situations. However, he can be a bit indecisive and vague when does not understand his deepest emotions. Do not doubt his feelings. But do be prepared for frustration at his non-verbal communication and reticence just when you want to get busy. Be warned, he can be evasive and deceptive when cornered; he is capable of subtle moves and wily ways. But when in love he falls deep and is idealistic in his expectations. Prone to depression, you will have to be patient to keep him.

WOMEN: This lady is romantic and compassionate, if not a little over sentimental with her displays of affection. No one could ever accuse her of neglect or flippancy. But she is a soft touch, so don't take advantage of her in a ruthless way. She will fall for you. You have been warned. Protect her from ruthless, self-indulgent types who are likely to take advantage of her amenable nature. Yes, she needs to toughen up, and use more discernment. But her perceptions are acute and powers of sympathy heightened. You will not get away with anything underhand yourself as she is extremely psychic. But she is capable of deception herself, and may stray if you have wronged her first. Pisces lady is good at walking into situations that don't reflect her in the best light. So, it is best to trust her and let her make some mistakes. She will listen the next time. Well, maybe.

11 COMPATIBILITY INDICATOR

Look for your magic combinations here below. This simple scale of compatibility will give you an indicator of how your relationships will roll. It is a more detailed way of assessing if you are going to get along, or if you should run for the hills quickly. Look for your Star Sign first and then match yourself with the correct gender of your partner. All permutations are covered here below.

Scale of Compatibility

@@@@...Hot to trot: can you handle it?

@@@..... Gets better & better: practice hard!

@@........ Friendship, slippers & Hot chocolate!

@……….. Don't go there: potentially messy!

ARIES

Aries Woman/Aries Man

There might be fireworks at dawn with this combination. Lots of fun. But the down side is the power struggle. Who will be the center of attention? A competitive but entertaining coupling. A shared fitness regime keeps it sweet.

@@@

Aries Woman/Taurus Man

This is to be avoided 24/7. But it can work if independence is maintained and respected. Mutual support has to be a given. Whilst good communication is fundamental. Things fall apart where one or the other is taken for granted. Aries is a hothead.

@@

Aries Woman/Gemini Man

A stimulating combination, providing hours of endless fun. Time alone is important and keeps passion alive. Flirting with others can lead to fun and games. Whilst playing away from home is quite likely from time to time. Not a relaxing situation.

@

Aries Woman/Cancer Man

An odd combination: Cancer is an old softie who likes to know what is going down. Whilst Aries is demanding and up for anything. It can work with good communication and mutual understanding. These two are tantalizingly different.

@@

Aries Woman/Leo Man

A dynamic duo! This sizzling combination is too hot to handle. But it is lots of fun. Never mind the burn out factor. It gets heated very quickly. But may subside if the intensity cannot be replaced with warmth, tolerance and forgiveness.

@@@@

Aries Woman/Virgo Man

This is a bit of a clash waiting to happen. Would you even bother? Of course love covers a multitude of sins. But Virgo's obsessive nit-picking can get a bit much. Aries is a live wire that Virgo may never control or get to grips with.

@

Aries Woman/Libra Man

A sexy, coupling! Libra is a scream who provides hours of entertainment. Game for a laugh and generally up for it, Libra has to be patient with Arian impatience. Aries finds Libra's inability to make a decision exasperating.

@@@@

Aries Woman/Scorpio Man

Scorpio is probably too intense and deep. Aries may not be able to keep up and is quite superficial at times. Scorpio likes to run the show and is not at all flexible. Whilst Aries is dynamic and full-on. If Scorpio falls in love, Aries may scarper!

@@

Aries Woman/Sagittarius Man

This is great fun. Frolics galore and lots of laughs keep these two interested and interesting. The social whirl provides hours of entertainment. But Aries and Sagittarius may find it difficult to sit still for more than five mins: exhausting!

@@@@

Aries Woman/Capricorn Man

Capricorn likes watching Aries act on impulse. But the Zodiac Goat is quite staid and predictable. Aries may get bored in the long term. Capricorn has to let go a little. Whilst Aries makes compromises and enjoys that earthy sensuality.

@@

Aries Woman/Aquarius Man

These two need to complement each other by blowing hot and cold at the same time. Intense passion at the hot moments is worth hanging around for. But healthy respect and independence are important when Aquarius needs privacy.

@@@

Aries Woman/Pisces Man

If these magnets attract rather than repel, all is well. Pisces is a hopeless romantic. But may not be able to handle the volatile Aries temperament full time. Small doses work wonders and keep the interest alive. A mutual decision!

@@@

TAURUS

Taurus Woman/Aries Man

Instant magnetism has to develop into lasting love or this fizzles out. Aries may have second thoughts re commitment and has to be kept on a short but loose lead. Taurus loves to control so may not manage the balancing act for long.

@

Taurus Woman/Taurus Man

A hot steamy combination initially which can deteriorate into a power struggle. These two poetic souls should give each other a chance. Mutual support and friendship work along with sensual moments and heartfelt communication: bless.

@@

Taurus Woman/Gemini Man

Put the brakes on this. Or at least proceed with caution. Gemini is flirtatious and may drive Taurus nuts by going after friends, neighbors, and strangers. It works if Taurus has the patience of a saint and can turn a blind eye. Romance factor may make it all worthwhile though.

@@@

Taurus Woman/Cancer Man

This provides warmth and companionship: great for mutual understanding and support. Good friends at least and when passion fades, these two are lifelong mates. Taurus must not play the martyr or sulk when Cancer is moody or grim.

@@@

Taurus Woman/Leo Man

Leo is flamboyant and not comfortable with Taurus' caution. Leo unnerves predictable Taurus who hates to be challenged. It 'happens' so long as notable differences are accepted. Powerful if it works: dismally depressing otherwise

@ or @@@!

Taurus Woman/Virgo Man

Great rapport: a quite magical, earthy combination. Definite soul mates these two! Sexy goddess meets Mr loyal and reliable: what can go wrong? Virgo's attention to detail suits Taurus' ability to organize. Great compliments abound.

@@@@

Taurus Woman/Libra Man

Libra is full of ideas. So practical Taurus must be careful not to bring the 'air head' down to earth with a bang. Tongues will have to be bitten for this potential clash to work. Libra humor tickles the fancy lightening up the mood.

@@@

Taurus Woman/Scorpio Man

A love: hate relationship that can swing between the two extremes. A bit of a head wreck when it is a bad day. But intensely passionate when the sun is shining. A roller-coaster ride that is tumultuous and unpredictable: not boring!
@@@

Taurus Woman/Sagittarius Man

Sagittarius needs a permanent option on freedom. Whilst Taurus loves to feel safe, stable and secure on the home front: not an easy combination. If Taurus lets go whilst Sagittarius goes off on one, it can work. But it's not an obvious pair.

@

Taurus Woman/Capricorn Man

This is the stuff of friendship certainly: an earthy connection. But stubborn wills and tempers can kill off the passion fairly lively as a grim stalemate sets in. Someone has to bend or peace will never be restored. Sensual links hit the spot.

@@

Taurus Woman/Aquarius Man

Aquarius is everyone's friend and stays on good terms with the ex-factor. This is difficult for Taurus, but not impossible. Grownup discussion sorts out most problems. But an air of silent resistance can make things awkward. A bit cool!

@@@

Taurus Woman/Pisces Man

Pisces leans heavily on sensible Taurus and should not give in so readily. Taurus invades space in the nicest possible way and Pisces is not complaining. But this can be intense, if not a little possessive. It is for keeps, but care is needed.

@@

GEMINI

Gemini Woman/Aries Man

Great natural rapport between these two: they both flirt for a living! But Aries man is somewhat self-absorbed and hot headed. Gemini may tire of fanning the flames.

@@@@

Gemini Woman/Taurus Man

He is all man, very physical and sensual. She has no problem staying interested. Gemini has a lively, mind and keeps Taurus amused for hours: a delicious combination altogether.

@@@

Gemini Woman/Gemini Man

These two have the measure of each other. They can both play games and change like the wind. Surprisingly there is little tension as they have an innate understanding: anything goes. A childlike union.

@@@@

Gemini Woman/Cancer Man

Cancer man is caring, kind and possibly too clingy for carefree Gemini. This could get a little cloying and claustrophobic. Cute, but restrictive, and his moods may be too much to bear!.

@@

Gemini Woman/Leo Man

He is a drama Queen, but Gemini loves his antics. He is warm, generous and loads of fun. However, Gemini is required to play the glamour role until the cows come home: could get tedious over time.
@@@@

Gemini Woman/Virgo Man

This will be instant attraction, or instant dislike. The love/hate thing is liable to play out in a roller-coaster ride. She is funny and witty, but he is intellectually superior and loves to prove it: yawn!

@

Gemini Woman/Libra Man

A sexy combination that will spend a lot of time in the boudoir! He has a mischievous mind and will keep her amused for hours: do not ask! This one is romantic and sweaty.

@@@@

Gemini Woman/Scorpio Man

Great for commitment this one if they can get past the love/hate stuff and control issues. It can be quite dramatic, but never boring. These two stay interested: she is fun, he is brooding.

@@@@

Gemini Woman/Sagittarius Man

This is a powerful physical attraction that rarely fades, even once they have split! These two are a great match: better stay together to avoid the annoying ex factor.

@@@

Gemini Woman/Capricorn Man

She is indecisive and he is a professional quiz-master: not likely to be much fun. She hates being cornered and he turns into her father.
@

Gemini Woman/Aquarius Man

A meeting of minds: these two keep each other hooked for hours on end. He does not give much away, which drives Gemini nuts, but keeps her in place.

@@@

Gemini Woman/Pisces Man

He is adaptable and changeable and so is she. They are very different, but also very similar! He indulges her fantasies, but she may need more definite signs in time.

@@@

CANCER

Cancer Woman/Aries Man

He is passionate and full of it, which she finds thrilling but uncomfortable. She is more discreet and intense. She needs security and safety in time: commitment sends him packing: oops!

@

Cancer Woman/Taurus Man

An easy-going combination, which is heaven sent. These two understand each other. There is mutual acceptance & admiration. He loves security, she is cute and homely and they both love food.

@@

Cancer Woman/Gemini Man

He loves variety and needs his mind stimulated, whereas she is the queen of emotion who gets intense. He may not be able to handle her cloying nature and she will not know where she stands.

@@@

Cancer Woman/Cancer Man

Both have an innate fear of rejection, so this takes a while to warm up. It can become rather intense. But the magic is there, especially once commitment sets in.

@@

Cancer Woman/Leo Man

He knows everything and is extremely flamboyant at times. But once he calms down he is the purring pussycat. She simply has to stroke him frequently!

@@

Cancer Woman/Virgo Man

He is sensible and pragmatic, whilst she loves the hidden mystery of life. These two are different, but she may need his grounded nature. He loves her tenderness.

@@@

Cancer Woman/Libra Man

He is idealistic and visionary, which suits her mysterious nature. He has the fantasies and she makes sure they happen. It is an up and down thing that works!

@@@

Cancer Woman/Scorpio Man

He is a control freak, but she loves being tied up and controlled (up to a point). She is feminine and he is passionate: a great combination emotionally and physically!

@@@@

Cancer Woman/Sagittarius Man

These two are magnets drawn together by their differences. She is secretive and sensitive and he is 'out there' and always ready. He is the eternal optimist keeping her buoyant and happy.

@@@

Cancer Woman/Capricorn Man

He needs to control his life and the lives of those around him. She needs to keep her emotions under wraps. It could be a bit repressed without good communication. But it can work.

@@@

Cancer Woman/Aquarius Man

He needs to move on when he gets the measure of what is going on. So she has to stay mysterious and not too clingy to keep him. This involves game playing, but it can 'find its feet.'

@@@

Cancer Woman/Pisces Man

Both these two are sensitive and intuitive: a psychic combination, so there will be few secrets and endless chats about the Universe. He cannot make decisions which suits her: she can run the show!

@@

LEO

Leo Woman/Aries Man

A fiery, passionate meeting, that can burn out quick. A very physical connection, but these two are very self-absorbed which is tedious: they need to look at each other!

@@@@

Leo Woman/Taurus Man

She is a drama queen, whilst he is a behind the scenes kind of guy. He likes to take it easy. But Leo has to be in the thick of it, stirring things up. He may tire of her attention seeking.

@

Leo Woman/Gemini Man

Leo is all heart, whilst Gemini does the head stuff. These two live differently and think 'out of sync'. He is witty and fun and she is sociable: good friends, but commitment sucks!

@

Leo Woman/Cancer Man

He is moody and silent, whilst Leo never shuts up! She is fiery, needs attention, but loves his air of mystery. Cancer is passionate but in a discreet way. He may dampen her ardor if he cannot handle it!
@@@@

Leo Woman/Leo Man

Two lions are intense, fiery and competitive. They vie for power and only one can reign supreme. It is a challenge that could get tedious. Both are proud and will not admit mistakes.

@@@@

Leo Woman/Virgo Man

She is always on a mission with too much on her plate. He is down to earth and fairly laid back. She is demanding and he may tire of her need for drama. He hates hassle.

@@@

Leo Woman/Libra Man

These two love the social buzz. Both take pride in their appearance and have 101 friends. But she is very definite and may hate his dithering nature. It is okay if he lets her make the moves...

@@@

Leo Woman/Scorpio Man

She is a showy tease who is dramatic and insatiable. He is difficult to satisfy and likes to control things. A powerful attraction with a lot of kissing and making up going down.

@@@@

Leo Woman/Sagittarius Man

A hugely physical connection, that is passionate and playful. Commitment issues do not usually surface. So long as these two are having fun, all is well. To be taken at face value!

@@@

Leo Woman/Capricorn Man

She is exciting, dramatic and fiery: he is earthy sensual and dynamic. Both understand control issues differently. So this can work and these two are quite complimentary!

@@@

Leo Woman/Aquarius Man

These two opposites definitely attract. There is a sense of destiny hanging in the air: a magical, mystical rapport. It comes unstuck when he wants to wander and she needs to settle.

@@@

Leo Woman/Pisces Man

A warm, spicy combination: she is intense and he is dreamy! It is all quite passionate and romantic, until he starts to dither. Let Leo run the show and all will be well.

@@

VIRGO

Virgo Woman/Aries Man

Opposites attract! She is private and he is 'out there'. But this can work as a passionate, intense combination. He will be delighted at her bedroom antics: it is his secret.

@@@

Virgo Woman/Taurus Man

These two earth signs connect in an earthy, passionate, intense way: there is no need for words. Natural connections mean this union makes so much sense. There is little in the way.

@@

Virgo Woman/Gemini Man

He is mischievous, which keeps her amused. Both ruled by Mercury, these two are sufficiently different to stay interested. Lots of chats and mad times. He is likely to challenge her patience and loyalty though.

@@@

Virgo Woman/Cancer Man

He is needy and emotional once he has let his guard down. But Virgo is sensible and pragmatic. She can be cool when it gets too intense. If the work is done, these two can make it.

@@

Virgo Woman/Leo Man

A potential clash here, for Virgo is always right, but Leo thinks he is. Oops! Leo is too proud to admit a mistake. So Virgo has to be kind and forgiving of rather a lot!

@@@

Virgo Woman/Virgo Man

A mutual understanding society that may lack intensity and passion. Great friends who have long chats and sort the world out. Ok if they do not need to 'walk on the wild side.'

@@

Virgo Woman/Libra Man

A sweet combination that comes close to perfect at times. He is idealistic and considerate, but wants to get it right all the time. Admirable, but Virgo may need outside interests.

@@@

Virgo Woman/Scorpio Man

He is passion personified and is hungry for more. She loves this and her secret sexy side can come out to play. He can be assured that it is all for him, so he feels comfortable and accepted.

@@@@

Virgo Woman/Sagittarius Man

Great for romance, but Virgo must be up for it! She needs a sense of adventure and crazy streak. Sagittarius loves Virgo and will go to the ends of the earth: she must too! Give and take.

@@@

Virgo Woman/Capricorn Man

There is a great and sexual rapport between these two. It is passionate, accepting, intense, and can stand the test of time. Good levels of companionship and understanding.

@@

Virgo Woman/Aquarius Man

This is an intellectual meeting of minds, an unusual combination. She loves his detached cool view of life, but may miss intense passion. He loves her sensible streak and up-front nature.

@@@

Virgo Woman/Pisces Man

He is intuitive and romantic: she is earthy and sexy. The sexual rapport and mutual understanding is great. These two get the balance right. It is not too intense and not too cool.

@@

LIBRA

Libra Woman/Aries Man

This is an intense, immediate attraction. He takes the reigns and runs the show. But Libra loves it! A compatible match indeed: she is witty and funny and he can do his own thing.

@@

Libra Woman/Taurus Man

He is down to earth and sensible, so she may feel short-changed romantically. If she can leave aside her expectations and take him as he comes this can work. A good double act!

@@@

Libra Woman/Gemini Man

He is sexy and hilarious and so is she! These two are not too intense and simply enjoy each other's company. There is lots of fun to be had, until the commitment issues surface.

@@@

Libra Woman/Cancer Man

An exotic combination. He is emotional and mystical, whilst she loves romance and jovial fun. She will not get much of this when he hides under his shell, so she might get frustrated!

@@@

Libra Woman/Leo Man

It is a hedonistic match between these two. With a mutual love of material goods and an appreciation of beauty, both love life itself. Works when there is glamour, sex, and lots of money.

@@@@

Libra Woman/Virgo Man

Virgo is ideal for Libra romantically and in the long term. But there will be adjustments to make along the way. He may get 'picky' and critical which could kill patience.

@@@

Libra Woman/Libra Man

Instant understanding and rapport between these two airheads! Lots of chats and fun times, but will they ever decide on anything? Now there is the rub. A sexy combination: love actually.

@@@

Libra Woman/Scorpio Man

It is a deep, intense, sexy connection between these two. They are very different and spend lots of time exploring why. There is little conflict, if Scorpio makes the decisions.

@@

Libra Woman/ Sagittarius Man

This is a fun duo! She must keep up with his spirited nature and he can make the decisions. If she can accept him for who he is this works. It is full of life but not lovey-dovey.

@@@

Libra Woman/Capricorn Man

He is no nonsense, earthy and sensible, but she loves to be wined and dined. She must ditch her expectations and work out if she loves him!. Different approaches to life cause a clash.

@@@

Libra Woman/Aquarius Man

Very sexy mind games go on between these two. There is great attraction and it starts in the head! His independence may frustrate her and she may not feel 'connected' over time.

@@@

Libra Woman/Pisces Man

It is fantasy heaven when these two get together. Shared dreams, visions and magic mean these two may never leave the bedroom. Work needs to be done when the rot sets in.

@@@@

SCORPIO

Scorpio Woman/Aries Man

These two definitely get stuck in! There is a great spark between them and a whole lot of mischief. He is a party animal, but eventually she will want something more.
@@@@

Scorpio Woman/Taurus Man

There is magnetic attraction between these two zodiac opposites. It is a love/hate thing that can run on and on and on. It is erotic, tantalizing and down-right infuriating too.

@@@@

Scorpio Woman/Gemini Man

He needs to be kept on his toes. But finds compelling Scorpio sufficiently interesting to stay around. She can beguile him, hypnotize him, and wrap him around her finger.

@@@@

Scorpio Woman/Cancer Man

These two water signs love each other's deep brooding intensity. They keep each other amused for hours: even silences are golden and loaded. Good for the long haul.

@@

Scorpio Woman/Leo Man

He is full of ideas and adventure, but she wants to run the show. Commitment issues maybe a spanner in the works if she gets too pushy. Jealousy can spoil things: he loves company.

@

Scorpio Woman/Virgo Man

She is passionate and chaotic in her emotional displays. He will not take the bait and is coolness personified. This may drive her nuts if she is looking for a reaction. Unfulfilling probably.
@

Scorpio Woman/Libra Man

He craves perfect love and romance and she is intoxicating. Her mystery and allure keeps him interested and as he is not pushy, she gets her own way. Let us hope he does not catch on.

@@

Scorpio Woman/Scorpio Man

This sexual, emotional heaven and the power struggles add to the fun. However, once the physical side wears off, this can get messy. These two vie for control and outwit each other.

@@@@

Scorpio Woman/Sagittarius Man

He is a free spirit, who likes to come and go. Unless she has some diversion or secret she will hate this! A great fling and buzz of sexual energy lies here. But wedding rings? Mm!

@

Scorpio Woman/Capricorn Man

Sexual dominance and power make this a heady combination. Mind games and sensual rewards are inevitable. She is intensely passionate; he is pragmatic and will not suffer fools.

@@@

Scorpio Woman/Aquarius Man

This is an erotic, sensual combination. Aquarius keeps Scorpio guessing and is detached, which drives her nuts in the nicest possible way! He is unconventional and kooky.

@@@

Scorpio Woman/Pisces Man

He is social, romantic and likes to go with the flow. There is an intense emotional connection if they can get past the dithering. She is more definite and needs answers he will not have.

@@@

SAGITTARIUS

Sagittarius Woman/Aries Man

This is an intense fiery combination: hot stuff indeed! But as for long term delights? I think not; unless there is a huge willingness to compromise and make it work.

@

Sagittarius Woman/Taurus Man

Taurus can be possessive and Sagittarius is a free spirit. There could be a clash over what is important. But essentially this is good stuff: dynamic and satisfying. Grows over time.

@@@

Sagittarius Woman/Gemini Man

These two are Zodiac opposites. This is a magnetic attraction with lots of fun and sociability. A zesty, dramatic relationship with a lot going down. Both can expect to be kept on their toes.

@@@@

Sagittarius Woman/Cancer Man

He loves home, domesticity, and security. But she is a free agent with a lot to be getting on with. Okay, if he is willing to play house-husband. But there could be a clash over priorities.
@@@

Sagittarius Woman/Leo Man

Lots of glamour, flirting and messing goes on between these two. It is an exciting combination, than can weather a few storms. There is mutual understanding and respect. Watch out re jealousy.

@@@

Sagittarius Woman/Virgo Man

He is captivated by her sense of humor and fun: he has not had it so good in a long time! But she may find him a bit ordinary and stuffy at times. She is late and he is always on time: oops!

@@

Sagittarius Woman/Libra Man

He is inclined to be too keen. She needs to think she can walk away at a moment's notice and come back when she feels like it. She will get under his skin, but he likes that.

@@@@

Sagittarius Woman/Scorpio Man

He is liable to get intensely jealous of her friends, flirtations and commitments. She makes him feel dispensable, which of course he is! It is exciting though if he is cool enough to handle it!

@@@@

Sagittarius Woman/Sagittarius Man

Mutual understanding here makes this a match made in heaven. They must allow each other room to breathe. But there is trust, compassion and a hot connection. Magic!

@@

Sagittarius Woman/Capricorn Man

He is liable to look on her as a trophy or piece of property! She is rebellious when confined and constricted. So this will only work if he stays calm and taps into his earthy side.

@@@

Sagittarius Woman/Aquarius Man

A great combination that works if there is personal freedom, and space, room to breathe is essential. There is a mutual fascination. This can work for years if it does not get heavy.

@@

Sagittarius Woman/Pisces Man

A sexy duo: the attraction is intense. But he is a slippery fish and she is equally unreliable. The fun begins when the arguments start. Making up is passionate: it is worth the fight.

@@@@

CAPRICORN

Capricorn Woman/Aries Man

He is full of himself and she is not far behind! This can turn into a battleground. Who has the upper hand in this domestic drama? Lots of sexy antics when it gets hot and heavy.

@@@@

Capricorn Woman/Taurus Man

This is a great combination. These two are very earthy and sensual. But there is competition for control of the purse strings and it can get autocratic! Who runs the show: does it matter?

@@@

Capricorn Woman/Gemini Man

This is a sexy duo, but he needs constant stimulation. She may be too matter of fact for his tastes. He likes to be kept on his toes and she can be a no-nonsense control freak!

@@@@

Capricorn Woman/Cancer Man

This is sexy, serious and emotionally intense. She makes him feel secure and grounded: but she will never replace his mother! But this lasts for the long haul, God willing.

@@

Capricorn Woman/Leo Man

He is a poser and she loves status, so these two will be quite 'out there' socially. The best of everything is what counts, but they could get bogged down with material concerns.

@@@

Capricorn Woman/Virgo Man

An earthy, fulfilling connection, which becomes the stuff of long-term contentment. These two enjoy the same pleasures, tastes and preferences. Harmony reigns supreme.

@@

Capricorn Woman/Libra Man

These two are very different which makes it interesting at first! However, her stubborn nature and his flippancy can become annoying. He needs perfection, she thinks she is perfect: oops!

@

Capricorn Woman/Scorpio Man

Both understand the constructs of power. So this is an ambitious pairing who can take on the world. They make good business partners and great lovers too! It can go sour though.

@@@

Capricorn Woman/Sagittarius Man

He loves the trappings of status and she is hungry for material comfort and credibility. Appearances count for a lot. Things have to be 'just so': watch that white carpet.

@@@

Capricorn Woman/Capricorn Man

This is a sexy combination, but these two are very similar. The novelty could wear off. They are more like brother and sister after a time, but make great companions.

@@

Capricorn Woman/Aquarius Man

These two are different and keep each other interested. But there is no chance of agreement once a difference of opinion is established. It is live and let live; or else move on.

@@@

Capricorn Woman/Pisces Man

This is not easy! She is very definite and knows what is what (or so she likes to think). Whilst he is changeable and likes to go with the flow. A clash of personalities!

@

AQUARIUS

Aquarius Woman/Aries Man

This is a passionate and intense emotional connection. He likes to do his own thing and she must be careful not to dominate. But there is mutual understanding and great love.

@@

Aquarius Woman/Taurus Man

He likes to possess things and she is fiercely private and at times independent. She will not explain herself at every turn, which may drive him nuts. He is passionate and sensual. Nice!

@@@@

Aquarius Woman/Gemini Man

He is great fun, but also a pain in the proverbial backside! He is liable to go off on one. She will not be able to handle him for more than five minutes, unless she turns a blind eye.

@

Aquarius Woman/Cancer Man

He may get jealous of her mates and the ex- factor is a problem. She is liable to stay friends with previous lives and he will find this difficult. He needs her heart and soul. It is all a bit intense.

@@@

Aquarius Woman/Leo Man

He is sexiness personified. These two are Polar opposites, so complement each other well. This is a great heart connection. But loyalty is supremely important. Love stuff works well.

@@

Aquarius Woman/Virgo Man

These two have a lot to share and talk about. They are different but complimentary. With each other, they have everything they need. A healthy match indeed.

@@

Aquarius Woman/Libra Man

This can be a lot of fun. But it is liable to get a bit silly and out of hand! He is a live wire and she may tire of endless laughter! It really can work so long as it avoids intensity.

@@@

Aquarius Woman/Scorpio Man

He is heavy and intense, which she detests! A battle of wills as he pursues her heart and soul and she runs quickly in the opposite direction! He will have to play games to keep her.

@

Aquarius Woman/Sagittarius Man

He needs lots of freedom and space, which suits her down to the ground. A great combination devoid of possessiveness (well it has to be!). She likes her privacy and he is often away!

@@

Aquarius Woman/Capricorn Man

He is conventional and traditional, whilst she is kooky and eccentric. This is a clash of temperaments. Aquarius likes to do things differently and Capricorn follows the rules.

@

Aquarius Woman/Aquarius Man

A meeting of minds this. Hours of intellectual conversation means the bedroom antics may never happen! Mutual honesty and integrity make this run and run. Heavenly love.

@@

Aquarius Woman/Pisces Man

He is charming and seductive with love skills to make her quake in her boots! He can get intense and falls heavily, which she may find tedious over time. He will have to stay cool!.

@@@

PISCES

Pisces Woman/Aries Man

He is passionate and confident and she loves to be invaded. He loves her sensual reactions, but she may get a bit too intense at times. She must keep him interested and stay cool.

@@@@

Pisces Woman/Taurus Man

She is sensitive and he is easily seduced by her feminine wiles. He melts when she walks by, and she loves his warm responsive touch. Finances may cause grief though.

@@

Pisces Woman/Gemini Man

He is funny, light and bright, but may get up to things she does not need to know about! If she can turn a blind eye and take him at face value all will be well. Not easy.

@

Pisces Woman/Cancer Man

He is passionate, broody and moody which keeps her interested. She needs to be kept on her toes, so long as he is loyal. Great sexual connection this and her fantasies have a field day.

@@@@

Pisces Woman/Leo Man

She is a dreamer, but he keeps it real. They may not be able to meet half way for long. He finds her kooky and intense, but may be waylaid by warmer natures and fiery temperaments.

@@@

Pisces Woman/Virgo Man

There is a great sexual connection between these two Polar opposites. She can read him like a book and they are intuitively in harmony: words need not be spoken. Great long-term

@@

Pisces Woman/Libra Man

Romantic indeed, but he is an intellectual who needs constant mental stimulation. She likes to float along in dreamland & he is not the most grounded company!

@@@

Pisces Woman/Scorpio Man

Great stuff this: an intensely deep watery connection. But these two may drown in each other's company! He may get possessive as she floats along regardless, not paying attention!

@@@

Pisces Woman/Sagittarius Man

He loves to roam the green fields and she needs intense love and romance. These two seduce each other very easily: great for a fling. But it could end in tears. She must ignore too much to be able to cope or justify this long term.

@

Pisces Woman/Capricorn Man

He is reserved and not the most communicative man on the planet. She needs to feel wooed and romanced at every turn. She may not feel fulfilled and he may get frustrated as he does his best!

@

Pisces Woman/Aquarius Man

He is proud and intellectually superior. Whilst she has a different emotional agenda. It is sexy, but she will have to stay cool and develop outside interests. Anything can happen!

@@@

Pisces Woman/Pisces Man

This is fantasy heaven and very romantic. Will these two ever leave the bedroom and get on with life? They are liable to become co-dependent and may not do things separately: puppy love!

@@

12 SEXTROLOGY

Find how to seduce the different Star Signs in this chapter. How to cope with being single depending upon your Sign, and what love clues to use which will lead to perfect happiness and harmony with another. Use the Zodiac to seduce, and answer your love dilemmas in grand style. Follow the pointers, they just might work! Spice up your love life with the Sextro-logical erogenous zones.

ARIES

Love Clue: Love is always within reach. Focus on your assets and be your charming self to reel them in Your innate charisma will get you everywhere and take you places. Do not ever doubt yourself.

Singletons Consider: The friend of a friend perhaps. Explore all your options fully. Earthy signs are good company.

Charm ARIES: Attend the gym, look after your appearance, and make them think they have competition.

ARIES turn on: Hot sex, more hot sex! Oh, and did I mention; endless hot sex? Be impulsive and spontaneous. This lover is not for prudes. Aries wants to be your best ever, so be very open. Prepare to experiment.

Erogenous Zone: THE HEAD. Stroke the hair, kiss the eyes and massage the back of the neck.

TAURUS:

Love Clue: Concentrate on the good times. Let them roll and forget the rest. Fret not, for stress-free vibes will rev up your love life. Remember: you are the catch!

Singletons Consider: Fire signs Sagittarius and Leo have a lot to offer for the fun times. Pisces is great company and highly romantic.

Charm TAURUS: Romantic meals do it every time. Taurus loves to be wined and dined. The natural look attracts Taurus, as do earthy, sensual colours and fabrics.

TAURUS Turn on: Laze around in bed, for grand seduction style. Massages both given and received engage Taurus attention. This earth sign is hands-on and sensual. Set the scene with music and fine food. Get out the aromatherapy oils, and bingo!

Erogenous Zone: The NECK. No, strangulation is not everyone's cup of tea and it is dangerous, sometimes fatal. So do not even think about it. Kiss and bite the neck; but leave the rough stuff to the bondage parlours. The throat is Taurus' weak spot: kiss it and they melt!

GEMINI:

Love Clue: Open your mind and the rest will follow. Love strikes when you least expect it. Let cupid engage your attention! Second time around can work.

Singletons Consider: Leo and Sagittarius are all action and lots of fun. They will show you a new love style. Pisces is emotional and romantic.

Charm GEMINI: Gemini has a lively mind and needs to experience your wit and humour. Be lively, chatty and witty. Gossip is good, but do not go too far too quickly. If you look great you are more than half way there.

GEMINI Turn on: Texting, e-mailing and phone calls float the Gemini boat! Anything technological catches Gemini's attention. Secret notes and flirting and that sense of not being quite sure are important to keep up the interest.

Erogenous Zone: SHOULDERS/ARMS. Highlight this part of the body and dress to full effect. Kiss the neck, shoulders and forearms for easy seduction. Arms can be tied if there is enough trust.

CANCER:

Love Clue: Take a risk or two and do not be afraid to stick your neck out. Speak up! Now is not the time to hide under your shell: embrace love.

Singletons Consider: Water Signs Scorpio and Pisces are great emotionally and physically. Capricorn is seriously sexy and full of good intentions. Get thee to the cinema!

Charm CANCER: Gentle, easy lines work. Give Cancer the option to run for cover now and again. Listen and be kind. Cancer needs to open up and may be slow to trust. Family ties bind, so respect commitments.

CANCER Turn on: Cancer is smouldering sexy, but it is not immediately obvious. If things get off to a slow start, panic not, for the best is yet to come. Soothing watery locations and hassle free environments do the trick.

Erogenous Zone: BREAST/CHEST area. Try different techniques and focus on the torso, Cancer will be eternally grateful. Take it slow (or not) and you might get away with tweaking and some rough stuff! (Ouch!)

LEO:

Love Clue: Do not try so hard. Let love come a-knocking of its own accord. Sit back and smile broadly. Be your good self and the right person will notice.

Singletons Consider: Reunions hold a lot of promise. Cancer and Scorpio have a lot to offer. Taurus looks interested.

Charm LEO: Dress up and turn it on to reel in Leo. You have to be well kitted out and look a million dollars, even if you do not have a bean. To your name!

LEO Turn on: Leo loves to luxuriate in sumptuous surroundings. Mirrors and the chance to watch catch the Leo imagination. Weekends away and living it up in style satisfies the regal Lion. Leo likes to be showy.

Erogenous Zone: BACK AND SPINE. Massage the pressure points of the spine to spark up the Lion!

VIRGO:

Love Clue: Do not get wound up or stressed about the slightest thing. You are blocking the love stuff. Relax and party. Be eternally positive and optimistic. Love awaits.

Singletons Consider: Water signs Scorpio and Pisces bring deep love and sexy encounters. Leo is exciting and offers something different: be daring. Stay alert at work.

Charm VIRGO: Virgos like clever, sophisticated people, who are interesting, funny and unusual. Do not be loud or crude with Virgo. But do remember they hold sensual surprises beneath a cool exterior. Be sure you can handle it.

VIRGO Turn on: Virgos are apparently shy. But in private, they come alive. They are the Zodiac's best kept secret. Sensual, earthy and up for it, you would be hard pushed to find a better lover. The turn on is *you!*

Erogenous Zone: STOMACH. Food from the fridge can be served up on this. But if that is all a bit messy, concentrate your attention on the Virgo stomach with touch and tenderness. Champagne in the belly button works.

LIBRA:

Love Clue: Friendships and deep bonds develop your love style. Love reaches new heights and peace reigns supreme. Get past the rough stuff. Party!

Singletons Consider: Fellow Airheads Aquarius and Gemini will always amuse you. Enjoy fun times. Aries is a challenge and responsive. Get to the gym.

Charm LIBRA: Make sure you are well groomed and take good care of your appearance. Libra notices the little things. Your clothes, style and colour choices speak volumes. Oh and laugh a lot at Libra's jokes!

LIBRA Turn on: Romance, soft lighting and mood music hit the spot for Libra. Flowers, chocolates and all the traditional gestures are expected. Spontaneous gifts and love notes inspire Libra to perform to the max.

Erogenous Zone: KIDNEYS. Difficult to get this internal with the love stuff. But gently rub the lower back and pay special attention to drinks. This is a sexy part of the back, make the most of corsets and intimate hugs.

SCORPIO:

Love Clue: Honesty is the best policy at the moment. Speak what is on your mind and in your heart. Prepare to kiss goodbye to a load of old nonsense.

Singletons Consider: Water signs Cancer and Pisces understand you and make you feel great. Libra is funny and great company. Outdoorsy pursuits boost love chance.

Charm SCORPIO: Complex Scorpio is tricky. Very obvious, but possibly quite individual, so do not wade in too quick. Scorpio likes to run the show & control the pace of things: allow this and you are sorted.

SCORPIO Turn on: Passion has to be intense, or the Scorpion will not bother. If you are half hearted, do not go near this sign, for the sting in the tail is not pretty. Take charge in the bedroom, and act out your fantasies. Anything goes here.

Erogenous Zone: THE GENITALS. Do I really have to spell this out? Fairly obvious really, but spin it out and make it last. Tease and avoid the hot spot for extra powerful lovemaking, finally.

SAGITTARIUS:

Love Clue: Do not focus too much on commitment issues. Have fun and keep your sense of humour active!

Singletons Consider: Virgo and Capricorn are sensual, earthy possibilities. Pisces is all over the place, but most appealing.

Charm a SAGITTARIAN: Find the Zodiac Archer in the great outdoors. Do not be afraid to make the first move: they like the upfront, in-your-face approach.

SAGITTARIAN Turn on: Sagittarians are adventurous and lots of fun. They like surprises, so use your imagination. Introduce a copy of the Karma Sutra and work your way through the pages over time. Prepare to be wild.

Erogenous Zone: HIPS AND THIGHS. Wrap yourself around the waist area & be generally touchy-feely below the waist.

CAPRICORN:

Love Clue: Try not to expect so much and you will get what you wanted all along. Let your loved one be themselves – you need to be more accepting. Ditch expectations.

Singletons Consider: Water signs Cancer and Scorpio get emotionally interesting: can you handle the intensity? Taurus is sensual earthy fun.

Charm CAPRICORN: Warmth and serenity win the Capricorn heart. They are cautious and can spot insincerity a mile off. So do not bother unless you mean it. Talk about your ambitions and reveal your game plan.

CAPRICORN Turn on: Build up the Capricorn's confidence. Flattery is good, but you have to mean it, or you will repel the Goat. Well-placed compliments and sophisticated romancing gets the Goat. Be stylised and a tad old fashioned for the best results.

Erogenous Zone: KNEES AND SKIN: well that covers most things. Get busy, and kiss your loved one all over. Pampering massages and lots of TLC suit sensual Capricorn. Lots of foreplay hits the spot.

AQUARIUS:

Love Clue: Trust your intuition above all else. It will guide your love style and your decisions. You can be the grand seducer/seductress. Choose wisely.

Singletons Consider: Libra is humorous and lots of fun. Virgo is earthy, sensuous and full of surprises. Sagittarius will keep you on your toes.

Charm AQUARIUS: This Air signs loves to see your independence and success. Strong opinions and the ability to keep Aquarius guessing are your weapons of massive distraction. It starts in the head, so looks are not that important.

AQUARIUS Turn on: Variety is the spice of life for this sign. Captivate the Aquarian mind and the rest will follow. Steer clear of what is predictable and boring. Equality is important, so swing it both ways for sexy times.

Erogenous Zone: ANKLES AND CIRCULATION. No this does not mean get intravenous. Use your mind with Aquarius and the rest will follow. Ankles are made to be tied up, me thinks.

PISCES:

Love Clue: Learn from past mistakes. Do not accept the blame for everything, but do be willing to forgive and forget. Move on and be happy!

Singletons Consider: Capricorn is sexy and very with it. You will enjoy the natural authority of the goat. Leo and Gemini provide lively social fun

Charm PISCES: Pictures, photographs, etchings: if you get an invite for coffee, you are in. Sensual, romantic vibes will hook the Zodiac fish. Show emotion in the eyes, for words may not be needed.

PISCES Turn on: Romance, watery backdrops, and emotional warmth seduce Pisces. Take it easy, slow, and turn it on by following your intuition. A Polaroid camera should be near-by, but look after those intimate shots.

Erogenous Zone: The FEET: Toe sucking, foot massage and nice shoes will have Pisces eating out of your hand. Play with feet under water and the bathroom becomes the main place of seduction.

♉ ♊ ♋
♌ ♍ ♎ ♏
♐ ♑ ♒ ♓

13 GASTROLOGY

Find how to seduce the different Star Signs with food in this chapter. Use this for Valentine's Day, or for any candle light meal you wish to organize. Get your juices flowing with this Astrological approach to food. Suggested menu for seducing your favorite Star Signs.

Fire Signs ~

ARIES:

Aries is not a food snob, and loves all kinds of gastronomic delights. Aries loves hot, heady flavours and is up for most things. This sign will try anything once. So you can safely follow your own preferences if they are not too sloppy, salad-y or sweet.

Aries usually loves meat and spicy foods. But do not go too mad and present something that takes the roof off your mouth. Eating is functional for the Ram and must satisfy the appetite completely. Serve up anything you need a microscope to see, and you will be calling in the Pizza boy later. Do not bother with fiddly little dishes that would not feed a mouse. Food that sits in the middle of the plate, looks pretty, but merely titillates the taste buds does not impress Aries. A mountainous dish hits the spot. You do not want to witness Aries chasing silly, sickly, slippery morsels with a fork.

The Ram is not pushed on healthy eating and likes to tackle serious food with serious portions. Besides it all gets burned off in the bedroom, or the gym, so you cannot really lose.

Starters: Chipolata Sausages, Scallions and Mash. **OR**: Garlic Bread and Beef Pate.

Main Course: Irish Stew and Dumplings. **OR**: Roast Beef and Yorkshire Pudding.

Desert: Rich Creamy Bread and Butter Pudding. **OR**: Sherry Trifle…or both!

LEO:

Leo loves food that has captured the essence of the sun. Mediterranean food, Fruit and hot dishes hit the spot for Leo. This is a decadent, extravagant sign, so you can afford to push the boat out. Serve up a dish fit for a King or Queen and you will be rewarded in kind. Rich sumptuous dishes go down a treat, but try to use dairy foods sparingly. Okay it will not hurt just once, but do not make a habit of it or your Leo will conk out or fall asleep and will not be fit for anything.

Leo requires the best of everything. So if you are not up to the challenge go to the nearest posh restaurant and let them do the foody bit. Save up your energies for later. If your cooking is not Cordon

Bleu standard, there is really no point. The Zodiac Lion has a huge appetite. So cook for a family of five, and do not expect any leftovers. Typically the Lion may have to nap before they get down to business, which gives you time for the washing up. Yep the restaurant beckons.

Starters: Caviar and Oat Cakes. **OR:** Quail's Eggs and Fresh Bread.

Main Course: Mediterranean Lamb and Spicy Vegetable Rice with Sweetened Carrot. **OR:** Prime Rump Steak with Mushroom, Pepper and Onion Sauce.

Desert: Queen of Puddings. **OR:** Red Berry Pavlova.

SAGITTARIUS:

This dynamic Fire sign loves to experiment and will not really mind what you serve up. So long as you are on the menu for afters. Anything does and you will quite literally get away with anything. Go for it and cook what you like, for the Zodiac Archer appreciates freedom of expression and imagination. Even if you fail in your attempt you will feel like a winner. Concentrate on feisty hot dishes that are a challenge to eat. The most controversial Vindaloo you can muster up is always worth a shot. This will capture the Sagittarian's attention. Though do remember that if you are planning some action for afters, you might want to take it easy on the spices.

Remember the Sagittarian has to quell the fire within and needs a drink or two, especially if you have gone mad with the chilli powder and garlic. Have plenty of larger and water on tap and expect to take your time with the ceremony of eating. It constitutes a philosophy and an art form for the hungry Sagittarius a serious business indeed.

Starters: Carrot and Coriander Soup with Selection of Crisp Breads. **OR:** Nachos and Chilli Dip.

Main Course: Pork Chops and Basmati Rice with Roast Vegetables. **OR:** Chicken, Coconut and Peach Curry with Nan Bread.
Desert: Ice Cream and Hot Chocolate Sauce with Marshmallows.
OR: Syllabub and Apricots.

Earth Signs ~

TAURUS:

Taurus loves the finer things in life. Rich, heavy, fat laden foods hit the spot. Go easy on cholesterol forming substances. But little suggestions of indulgence are fine. Remember that too much excess expands the waistline and reduces sex appeal. So don't rush through courses and stick to titbits if you are watching your figure, or someone else's.

Taurus is more prone to weight gain than most. But for special occasions a little of decadence does not hurt. Taurus loves to relax and take time over food. Background music, seductive aromas and a magnificent visual display set the scene. You may of course not get around to the food until you have reclined on the sofa or made use of the nearest bed. When you eventually start eating the following menu should do the trick. Oh, and Taurus loves to use the body as a table!!!

Starters: Marine aphrodisiacs: Scallops and Lemon, Oysters and Tabasco. **OR**: Cockles and Muscles with Tangy Red Pepper Sauce.

Main Course: Veal, Venison, rare Red Meats and choice of Game delicacies for the carnivores. **OR:** Creamy Spinach Pasta, Salad and Feta cheese.

Desert: Red Berries (Strawberries, Raspberries, Loganberries) and a Fondu of warm Belgian White and Dark Chocolate Sauce with Ice cream or Cream on the side. **OR:** Crème Brule.

Fine Red fruity wines, Cognac, Baileys Irish Coffee.

VIRGO:

This earth sign is sensible and possibly unimaginative when it comes to food. So prepare to cater for a faddy, fussy eater, who may be quite critical of what you serve up. Make things easier on yourself and ask what food they like. It would be a shame to make a great secretive effort that blows up in your face.

Virgo is appreciative of wholesome, healthy food and is very conscious of fibre intake. Copious amounts of earthy fruit and vegetables go down well. And this sign is quite likely to be vegetarian: Do find out! Carnivore Virgos is a rare breed that expects organic meat and fish straight from the local farm or nearest ocean. Try not to use foods out of the freezer, as short cut options don't cut it with this perfectionist Zodiac Sign. Keep things tidy as you work and try to have most of the washing up done before you serve up, or your Virgo will be heading for the kitchen sink rather than the bedroom.

Starters: Bean Soup (Tomato and Basil base). **OR:** Nut Loaf and Salad.

Main Course: Stir Fried Fish and Vegetables with Wild Rice. **OR**: Rainbow Trout and Root Vegetables.

Desert: Stewed Apples and Tangy Citrus Marscapone. **OR**: Frozen Fruit Yoghurt.

CAPRICORN:

The Zodiac Goat is very practical and may not be too impressed if you have blown the monthly budget on a seduction bid. Okay so Capricorn is not easily bought. But this sign is going to be suitably pleased you have made an effort. Mm, is it worth the bother? Possibly not. But if you do go for it, serve up functional food with a twist. Use your creative imagination and concoct your own dish, if you dare. But remember this Sign usually prefers recognisable food that hits the spot. Capricorn likes a healthy hearty choice and appreciates simple presentation. So you could do worse than traditional fare such as Steak, Peas, and Chips. A word of warning: The Goat has quite an appetite that is not easily satiated. Have plenty of food on standby and make sure that have energy left for the bedroom too. Do not burn the food and do not burn out making it.

Starters: Chicken Liver Pate and Bread Sticks. **OR:** Prawn Cocktail.

Main Course: Steak with Red Wine Sauce, Peas and Chunky Chips. **OR:** Salmon in Filo Pastry and Rich Cheese Sauce.

Desert: Black Forest Gateaux. **OR:** Mars Bar Cheesecake.

Air Signs ~

GEMINI:

Geminis are a bundle of nervous energy. So if you can get your partner to sit still long enough to savour a luxurious meal you are doing well. Do not expect the setting up of the menu and the planned seduction to go entirely to plan.

Gemini's are unpredictable live wires who change on a whim. It is not that your hard work will go to waste. But do not have mad expectations of how the evening should pan out. That is your quickest way to head wreck, not the fast track to a heaven sent connection. Once you have done your bit, let Gemini take over and think it was all their idea. Then you are on to a winner. Perform with the minimum fuss and you will get your just deserts. Never mind your best efforts; you can still expect Gemini to either eat rather quickly, or else pick at their food because they're talking too much. It all depends on the day that is in it. Still worth a shot though.

Starters: Crispy Avocado and Bacon Salad with Sesame Seed Rolls. **OR:** Caesar Salad with Olive and Tomato Bread.

Main Course: Chicken Satay and Boiled Wild Rice with lightly roasted Seasonal Vegetables. **OR:** Risotto and Mozzarella

Desert: Melon and Fresh Grated Ginger with cream. **OR:** Blueberry Cheesecake.

LIBRA:

Libra can be a fussy eater, but is usually grateful and interested by anything served up by you. Just do not expect Libra to eat it if it is too over the top. They might be impressed, but they will not be hungry if you pull out Gordon Ramsey's latest cookbook. So keep it simple and go for quality produce. Do not scare off cautious Libra with anything too hot and spicy, though the milder flavours of some Mexican foods go down well.

Serve up a selection of foods as Libra is picky and likes to put together their own plateful. Even the buffet bar of a kiddies tea party would do if you run out of imaginative ideas. Bring on sausages, pineapple and cheese on a stick, plus cucumber sandwiches and you are laughing. Well, perhaps not. Oh, and Librans love to drink. So if all else fails have a good variety of wines and beer on tap: who needs to eat?

Starters: Thinly chopped Carrot, Pepper, Cucumber, Celery with dips of cream cheese, garlic, Lemon and Tomato. **OR:** Melon and Parma Ham.

Main Course: Mexican Foods: Tacos, Nachos, Refried beans, Chilli, etc. **OR:** Chicken and Apricot fruit curry, with Nan bread.

Desert: Strawberries and Ice cream. **OR:** Apple and Blackberry pie.

AQUARIUS:

Aquarians love snacks of all descriptions. Yes, Aquarius is a veritable picker of foods. So use your imagination and tantalise those taste buds. This Air sign is quite lazy with food preparation and cooking. But this time you are doing the work and laying on a spread. Just do not expect to be given a hand. To be honest Aquarius is perfectly happy with anything you serve up. So if the menu is not coming together and you feel embarrassed by your efforts the nearest Pizza takeaway will do just fine.

Aquarians love all kinds of fruit and especially enjoy Mediterranean food. They are also happy with food straight out the freezer, which is good to know for those days when you cannot be bothered. Having said that, Aquarius is very appreciative of any special effort you dare to make. Food is a token of love after all. So get busy and don your favourite chef's hat and apron.

Starters: Greek Salad. **OR:** Mediterranean style Tomato and Olive bread with Gazpacho soup.

Main Course: Tapas selection: Meatballs, Roasted Peppers and Onions, Chorizo Sausage, Garlic Mushrooms, Prawns in Brine, Squid in Tomato Sauce, with fresh Bread Rolls. **OR:** Parma Ham, Pasta and Parmesan.

Desert: Fruit Salad. **OR:** Orange and Lemon Sorbets with Ginger Snaps!

Water Signs ~

CANCER:

Cancer loves home cooking. So if you can perform in the kitchen just like mammy did, you are likely to make a good impression. Comfort food is top of the list for this sign that craves homeliness and security. Make your Cancer feel loved and treasured with a mound of Mash and you will be graciously rewarded later on. Cancerians actually make brilliant chefs themselves. But you do not need to go Cordon Bleu to impress them, though it might help.

The Zodiac Crab is impressed by fancy flavourings and well-seasoned food. So consult hip cookbooks for timely tips. Also foods with high water content provide good sustenance for this sea creature. But it is perhaps best to avoid serving up fellow Crustaceans. Steer clear of obscure seafoods that might turn the stomach of your Cancer. Offend the senses of this Zodiac sign at your peril It is probably best to play safe: Back to the Bangers and Mash.

Starters: Avocado, Prawn and Mayonnaise Salad. **OR**: Salmon Mousse.

Main Course: Lemon Chicken and Potatoes with Cream and Onion Sauce. **OR**: Seafood Paella

Desert: Banana Cream. **OR**: Knickerbocker Glory.

SCORPIO:

Scorpios are intense sensual creatures whose taste buds need to be stimulated by strong flavours and bold colours. Food must have a definite and distinctive flavour to impress the Scorpion. Cold foods are pretty repellent to the bold Scorpio who likes to whet and satiate the appetite with piping hot dishes. Chances are Scorpio will either love or hate what you serve up. There are no half measures. So take intelligent risks and do your homework.

This Zodiac sign is more than up for healthy measures of garlic and ginger. Also deep, dark red dishes smack of seduction. There may be absolutely no need for desert: it's usually cold after all. But have something hot and sticky ready for later just in case. You are not likely to fail in your quest for seduction with Scorpio. For if this sign has accepted the invite you are more than half way there already. Answer the door without a stitch on and you won't even have to cook.

Starters: Hot Shellfish Platter and Salad. **OR:** Curried Chicken Soup.

Main Course: Pasta with Chorizo, Garlic and Tomato Sauce. **OR:** Thai Chicken Satay and Lemon Grass Fried Rice.

Desert: Hot Red Currant Pie and cream. **OR:** Strawberries mouth to mouth.

PISCES:

Pisces loves sea-food and will happily eat creatures of the deep, the shallows and possibly even the contents of the nearest rock pool! Anything goes, so long as it is aquatic and breathes under water. Food for this Zodiac sign must be fresh and organic. For additives and pungent tastes upset the delicate constitution of Pisces. So long as it was caught, picked or harvested yesterday Pisces will eat it! Steer clear of additives, and packaged foods if you want to seduce this Star Sign.

The Zodiac fish also loves meat, though may have made a conscious decision to become vegetarian for commendable reasons. Do check whether or not your target eats food that used to have a face before you serve up the best rump steak.

Deserts are no problem, since Pisces has the sweet tooth of a five-year-old. Anything goes, so long as it's thick, creamy and stodgy.

Starters: Squid in Tomato and Garlic Sauce. **OR:** Lobster with Lemon and Butter.

Main Course: Ham and Pineapple with Roast Potatoes and Cheesy Veg. **OR:** Swordfish in Garlic, Pepper and Cream Sauce.

Desert: Lemon Meringue Pie. **OR:** Hot Treacle Pudding.

14 GASTRO POWER FOODS

Find out here which power foods most support your good health. Have you been lacking in energy lately, or feeling under par? Then this Gastro section should help you. Use if you are nursing a loved one back to health, preparing for a pregnancy, supporting a young family, feeding the elderly. All stages and ages benefit from a Gastrological approach to food. Check out this section to find your Zodiac power foods and beneficial dietary plan. Yes, you will notice there is some overlap between the elemental categories Fire Signs in general benefit from spicy foods; so long as they are not overly fired up already! Water signs need water based foods and sea foods are great for added nutrition. Earth signs respond well to root vegetables or anything grown in the ground. Whilst Air signs may enjoy quite dry, crisp foods and the odd Aero Bar! Zodiac signs ruled or influenced by the same planet may also have some overlap. Your power foods are almost like medicine to your system; though remember to get the balance right. Rotate your foods for optimum health benefits and do not ever fixate on one particularly favourite as you are likely to be intolerant to such a food. Always follow your intuition and eat what your body requires from day to day. You need to feel cool and happy about your diet; not that it is like some form of prolonged torture of avoidance. But do be a little bit disciplined and draw the line at over indulgence.

ARIES:

Good food is vital to your life source and equilibrium. You need to keep well stoked-up to feed all that surplus energy. Eat regularly and do not scrimp on any major food group.

You require a well-balanced, full bodied diet in order to function at your best. Potent foods like meat, beans, nuts, bread and pasta serve you well. Your Arian constitution copes well with junk food; and you rarely suffer from indigestion. But that is no excuse. You are active, love to keep busy, and find it easy enough to burn off the fat.

Do not be tempted to over-tax your system though; or you will eventually succumb to middle aged spread and a beer belly. If you choose to lay-off the meat, that is fine; for your constitution also copes well with a vegetarian diet. Just remember to keep your protein intake high (beans and pulses etc). Your fiery nature adores curries, spices, Mexican dishes, and fried food. Do not overdo it though, and calm things down with plenty of cool fluids; just not too much beer!

POWER foods: Ginger, Horseradish, Red Pepper, Chillies, Leeks, Onions, Garlic, Mustard, Watercress, Paprika, Beer, Tomatoes, Juniper, Milk Thistle, Nettle, Rhubarb, Peppermint.

TAURUS:

With your tendency to plod along, you are prone to laziness and inertia. Inclined to comfort eat; you put on weight easily. Lack of exercise only makes matters worse. Be careful to avoid rich foods, particularly dairy products. If you can supplement Dairy with Soya replacements containing added calcium, your waistline will greatly benefit. Many of the world's large, big, and beautiful are Taurus: you get the picture? But the Zodiac old bull is reluctant to give up its pleasure zone and usually accepts the consequences of overeating: what are a few extra pounds amongst friends? If you do wish to lose weight a vegetarian regime suits you. Even a diet of fish and chicken with plenty of fruit and vegetables does the trick. But many Taurus bulls love their red meat, and are most unlikely to make such a sacrifice.

If you love your dairy and sweet foods, make sure that you boost good cholesterol levels with a high intake of porridge, dark chocolate, lecithin, and cranberry juice.

POWER foods: Cereals, Berries, Spices, Beans, Cloves, Mint, Gooseberries, Thyme, Rosemary, Olives, Apples, Pears, Grapes, Rhubarb, Green Beans, Cherries, Cabbage.

GEMINI:

You burn up fat much more quickly than most people, but this does not mean that you should overdo it. Your system does not tolerate overload and you should not overtax your digestion with too much heavy food. You need light, nutritious fare, little and often for optimum health. Watch out for that sweet tooth and do not indulge your penchant for sticky puddings too often. Do avoid meals and drinks with additives: you are already wired to the moon and quite hyper enough.

Eat plenty of protein, for this has a grounding effect and strengthens you. meat, nuts, fish, eggs and beans work well for you. But do be very careful with dairy products. The calorific content you can handle; it's the effect of dairy on the lungs that does you a great disservice. If you have asthma or breathing difficulties avoid dairy products like the plague. They form mucus on the lungs and compound these problems. Remember too that apple juice is very good for de-sensitizing the airways.

POWER foods: Carrots, Dill, Marjoram, Valerian, Hazelnuts, Walnuts, Oats, Fish, Liquorice, Apricots, Squash, Turmeric, Peanuts, Most Nuts and most Vegetables (except Cabbage).

CANCER:

Being Cancer, you have an extreme love of dairy laden profoundly sweet puddings. One of the Zodiac's main chocoholics, you cannot contemplate a diet that does not include your daily fix. I'm sure you already know all about it; but these foods make you highly susceptible to excess stomach acid. Keep the digestion aids handy if you are not willing to cut down on such indulgences. You will certainly know all about it if you do not limit such heavy foods. If you were born on a Full Moon, you will be even more likely to retain weight if you eat the wrong foods; so try to find out the position of The Moon at your time of birth (or perhaps you can already see the evidence around your waist!).

Ruled by The Moon and connected to the sea, you need to keep up your daily intake of water. Drink plenty, but not with your meals or you will hamper your digestion. A glass of water half an hour before a big meal will help you eat less food, if you cannot face a proper diet.

POWER foods: Cabbage, Pumpkin, Cucumber, Seaweeds, especially Kelp, Mangoes, Bananas, Mushrooms, Melon, Strawberries, Watercress, Lettuce, Melon, Mushroom, Pumpkin, Turnip.

LEO:

The king of the Zodiac beasts cannot survive on meagre rations. You are a proud, regal creature who needs the best of everything. If money were no object you would dine out every night and eat caviar for breakfast! A natural carnivore, your intake of foods is likely to be high in protein and rich in fat. You also have a hearty appetite, and tend to eat for two. Sometimes you are inclined to be lazy, and if your stomach is over laden with fodder, you're not inclined to waddle far. Exercise *has* to be a part of your regime if you want to keep your pride in-tact.

Your fine appearance is part of your appeal, after all! You put weight on easily; whilst too much fat and sugar puts your heart under strain. Drink plenty of cranberry juice and eat porridge regularly to keep good cholesterol levels high. A vegetarian diet makes you feel short-changed, and you were never any good with half measures. If you ever want to lose weight cut out the cream and high fat stodge.

POWER foods: Olives, Citrus Fruits, Almonds, Saffron, Corn-meal, Pineapple, Mangoes, Honey, Cinnamon, Bananas, Meat, and most Vegetables with high Iron content.

VIRGO:

Being Virgo, you are likely to be a fussy eater. You cannot cope with huge meals laden with intense protein. Grazing suits your sensitive digestion and intestinal system. Be careful to avoid the foods you are intolerant to; but be aware that a lot of your faddy habits are point-less. You probably are *not* allergic to everything under the sun. Being so aware of your health can have a positive or negative effect. You are disciplined about what you put into your mouth; but you also stress too much.

Worry of course, plays havoc on your ability to digest food. A diet that is high in carbohydrates suits you, though try to go for grains like spelt, rye and barley if you cannot tolerate wheat. A huge variety of fruit and vegetables keeps you sweet. But make sure you rotate your foods to guard against sensitivities that may develop if you overdo things. Let little-and-often, be your maxim, and you will not go far wrong. Just do not overload your system with toxins (additives and gluten).

POWER foods: Parsnips, Green Beans, Parsley, Carrots, Water-cress, Dill, Marjoram, Mint, Caraway Seeds, Alfalfa, Brown Rice, Po-tatoes, Roots Vegetables, Fish and most Nuts (similar to Gemini, also ruled by Mercury).

LIBRA:

Naturally enough, you thrive on good food. For the best quality pro-duce, your fruit and vegetables should be organically produced. Sim-ple recipes and styles suit your system well: anything too fussy just smacks of pretension. Not that you are adverse to posh meals. It is just that you like to know what you are eating and where it is come from. You are quite prone to weight gain if you over do the good life. Understandably you love a good quality wine with your meal; but endless candle lit dinners are bound to hit the waist-line eventually. Your strong drive to retain your good looks and gorgeous appearance usually keeps you in check. Though if you become complacent in life or in your relationships, you may become rather cuddly if not rotund. You love sweet things and you are another of the Zodiac's chocoholics. Belgian chocolates hit the spot, but also tend to produce them on your face. Lighten things up with tasty vegetarian food; you do not *really* need much meat.

POWER foods: Basil, Cinnamon, Raspberries, Blackberries, Artichokes, Sorrel, Pennyroyal, Pears, Almonds, Cashew Nuts, Dates, Fruits and Milk, Starchy foods, Sugar, (similar to Taurus, also ruled by Venus).

SCORPIO:

For optimum health you need a wide and varied diet. Like Leo, you should not restrict your protein intake. You do not particularly benefit from a vegetarian or vegan diet as you thrive on the extra oomph that meat bestows. Balance is important though and you probably *do* need to up your intake of vegetables and fruit. You tend to think you have eaten enough when you tackle a juicy prime rump steak. But you do need to eat its accompaniments too.

Make sure you have an abundant salad and at least three types of vegetables per day. If you cannot face a multitude of apples; get the smoothie habit.

Smoothies are a great way to up your fruit consumption. One for breakfast will set you up for the day. Mix Berries with bananas, orange and wheatgrass for a real kick. Stodgy cakes and breads may not be your thing, so make sure you get your carbohydrates from Rice, Oatcakes, and Porridge with Honey. Spanish Omelettes are a painless way to boost your veg. consumption.

POWER foods: Watercress, Kelp, Brown Rice, Aloe Vera, Beets, Onions, Garlic, Potatoes, Carrots, Brazil Nuts, Tomatoes, Spices especially Cayenne, Paprika, and Chilli, (similar to Aries).

SAGITTARIUS:

Boy do you love your food. General abstemiousness is *so* not you. Thankfully you expend a large amount of energy running from place to place. Your system is quite hyper and you can cope with a certain amount of overload. But quite often, you do feel off colour because of over indulgence. Do learn not to overdo the animal produce, for an excess of protein is liable to make you hot and sweaty. Indeed if you really over do things over time, you may be at risk from high blood pressure, and shortness of breath.

Do not assume you can get away with eating what you like for ever. Be sensible and disciplined with your choices, at least some of the time. You are not the most health conscious of the Zodiac signs, and tend to think you can eat whatever you feel like with no repercussions.

Curries, spicy foods and fried platters are probably your favourites; but do make sure you up your intake of fresh fruit and vegetables. Drink more Water and lay off the spirits. Balance holds the key.

POWER foods: Asparagus, Mint, Olives, Dandelion Leaves, Mulberries, Hawthorn, Rosehip, Chestnuts, Maple Syrup, Sage, Thyme, Nutmeg, Celery, Leeks, Tomatoes, Cinnamon.

CAPRICORN:

Your digestive system can be somewhat sluggish and you do not digest big heavy meals easily. Sometimes your eyes settle on something your stomach just cannot handle. You love food in theory; but must learn what suits you and what does not. As you grow older, your appetite becomes heartier; but Capricorn children can be quite a pain to cook for!

Fussy eaters all, Capricorn needs to learn the habit of grazing for optimum health. If you really cannot face big meals, acquire a taste for healthy titbits like nuts and raisins. soups, smoothies, and casseroles present food in an easily digested form. Try to steer clear of high protein dairy rich dishes that will lie on your stomach for about a week. If you can handle salads learn to create elaborate platters with fish or chicken and 101 types of lettuce. Drink plenty as you are prone to dehydration and choose foods that are light on the stomach but pack a punch on the energy system. Root vegetables and fruits ground you and fill you up.

POWER foods: Raisins, Beech Nuts, Pine Nuts, Barley, Turnips, Sloes, Tamarind, Spinach, Carrots, Beets, Malt, Meat, Starchy Foods, Rye, Onion.

AQUARIUS:

You are quite likely to get into bad habits with your eating. Once you find a meal or two you love, you are inclined to stick to it, until you realise you have eaten the same thing for about a month. You are also quite eccentric in your tastes.

A picky eater, you can be quite strict with yourself about what you should or should not eat. To give you credit, you usually go for healthy choices; but you probably do not get enough *variety* in your diet. Remember there are many different foods out there you usually do not even consider. So do not be lazy in your choices. Do supplement your food intake with a good quality multivitamin though. If you are not allowed to eat certain foods for medical reasons, you tend to become over meticulous about everything on the menu. You are inclined to get quite rundown through not eating enough. Make sure your diet packs a punch and get into foods that nourish your brain power. Introduce more fish, nuts and cod liver oil and ease off the dairy products.

POWER foods: Oily Fish, Coconut, Walnuts, Hazelnuts, Sunflower Seeds, Carrots, Liquorice, Caraway Seeds, Parsley, Wheatgerm,

Apples and Citrus Fruits, Dried Fruits and Frozen Foods (similar to Taurus)

PISCES:

Being an emotional sign, you can be quite erratic in your eating patterns. You may adore a particular food one minute and go off it suddenly, the next. You are the Zodiac fish that swims in two different directions. So your reactions and eating habits are inclined to be either one thing or the other. You alternate between two options in all things. If you are upset, you comfort eat; or else you cannot muster up an appetite at all. There is also an addictive streak to your personality which makes you inclined to fixate on certain foods. Watch that you don't overdo the sugar, coffee or fizzy drinks and steer clear of bad habits. Your sensitive system is hyper reactive and you are quite likely to have food intolerances. Strong flavours and additives do not do you any favours either. Keep your diet sensible and tuck into lots of plain and simple hearty home-cooking. Avoid pre-packaged dinners like the plague. Make sure you get a varied diet high in minerals, seafood and water content.

POWER foods: Watercress, Brown Rice, Cucumber, Dandelion, Poppy Seeds, Sesame Seeds, Oily Fish, Seaweeds, Melon, Sea Foods and high Water content Fruits and Veg. (similar to Cancer).

15 ZODIAC KIDS

Check out this section to find out what your kids or siblings are likely to be like as they grow. You may recognize yourself and your own development in some of the stages mentioned. Zodiac babies, Kids, and age elevenses to early teens are covered here.

ARIES

If you are parents to an Aries child you really have to be ready for anything. Ruled by Mars, these kids are unpredictable, and full of energy. Expect erratic behavior and all sorts of shenanigans. A healthy mischievous streak bestows this child with a wicked sense of humor too. You can expect pranks galore and endless madness to keep you busy. Life is not dull with an Aries child in the house, that is for sure.

BABY: Aries babies love stimulation, lots of activity and noise; ideal really if you have a busy family. These munchkins get bored easily, and need constant attention. Their senses must be stretched, so take note of what they are looking at, listening to and touching. Aries babies respond to different textures, mad colors and frantic music. Exhausting indeed.

You may ask; do they ever sleep? Well, of all the Zodiac babies, Aries is the most wakeful when put to bed alone. Your Aries baby ironically gets more rest when you stop creeping around. Dare to put the cot in the front room; or at least let them share with a sibling. The more wound up you get; the crankier these babies become. Do yourself a favor and do not be precious with your Aries baby; or you will be the one who suffers.

CHILD: This child is very strong willed, so prepare for much friction as you begin to lay down the ground rules. Aries kids do not respond well to discipline; but they do need to be contained somehow. Only you know what the boundaries for your child will be. But be assured they will push you to the limits as they test them out. Young Aries easily develops bad habits such as untidiness, bad manners and playing-in-the-dirt.

These kids make it their mission to see what they can get away with. So you could usefully ignore them most of the time. If they are free from harm; then remember the rest is just an excuse for boldness. Aries generally knows what is right and what is not, so you needn't worry on that score. Most of the time they are just winding you up; do not rise to the bait.

ELEVENSES: Once the temper tantrums have stopped, you can enjoy the intelligence and brightness of your young Aries. These kids need to keep physically active, and there is certainly energy to burn most of the time. But as the sensitive, creative side to Aries develops, you will notice your youngster becoming more thoughtful and reflective. (Well, on a good day anyhow).

Aries children are quite dramatic, so you can expect a fair quota of drama queen behavior, and a natural flare for performing in front of the adults. Young Arians are quick learners, so good schooling is a must. These clever kids can easily reach the top of the class with the right encouragement and a good education. But, it is the same old story, if they get bored, there will be lots of mischief to compensate.

TAURUS

Little Taurus is a real home-bird. If you are parents to a Taurus child you will never be rid of them. No, they do not remain child-like, and they do pull their weight. But Taurus is hopeless at letting go of the past. So leave their bedroom in place, even when they are long gone and married with kids of their own. Taurus is reluctant to leave home turf, and needs family to stabilize and harmonize their existence.

BABY: Baby Taurus is a demanding little creature. With a strong will and stubborn temperament, you will soon wonder where the tranquil days went. But this delightful Zodiac baby will repay you with oodles of affection and lots of tactile action. The best way you can reassure your Taurus child is with a cuddle. Remember, what you say is not half as important as what you DO with this baby. Soft, sensual tranquil environments with great smells and warm, comfortable fabrics are what this baby needs.

The mellow, peaceful and relaxed vibe of a family home speaks to the heart of little Taurus. But this baby needs to know there is love in abundance; so will test your reactions often in the bid for yet another cuddle. Irregular sleeping patterns will be taxing; so be patient; and cuddle!

CHILD: Taurus kids are adventurous and keen to understand. Their inquisitive streak kicks-in early and no secret is well enough hidden. These children have intense instincts and will just *know* what you're up to. Taurus needs to maintain the Status Quo and gets insecure when things change. But, you can expect a battle of wills once they have made up their mind about something. Be warned; they will not budge. Do not bargain with young Taurus. There really is no point. Nor should you withhold your physical touch as they find that very difficult to forgive. Do not gloss over the endless questions, or spurn Taurus child's affection. The best thing is to remain straightforward. Emotional trauma upsets them, so try not to argue in front of this kid, as they internalize an awful lot.

ELEVENSES: Taurus teens work hard when a subject grabs their interest. Their sheer tenacity and determination means that they will get the grades needed to pursue the career that makes sense. Despite their home-loving ways; Taurus is an independent creature who needs to roam free. You will find Taurus individuality develops quickly from the age of six. This Sun Sign often struggles with mathematics and physical education; but is meticulous, so grasps details and stores a lot of info in that expansive brain. Music elevates the Taurus soul, and it is a good idea to pay for your child's music lessons as soon as they express an interest. Taurus teen is a sensuous being who is likely to have a string of admirers. But there is a heartless streak too; if they are not interested – that is it.

GEMINI

Little Geminis are exhausting company; but they are entertaining and intelligent too. You will certainly benefit from a sense of humor, for Gemini provides many a belly laugh. If you are a parent to a young Gemini it is important that you really *listen* to that endless chatter. Huge offense will be taken if you switch off. So try to appreciate their earnestness, even when you're knackered!

BABY: Gemini babies are lively souls who will communicate in whatever way they can. You can expect to have quite a dynamic, expressive baby on your hands. Somehow Gemini manages to connect in profound, surprising ways, well before the first words. Gemini baby also has a wicked sense of humor and quite a chuckle which will delight you in its heartiness. There is a knowing contained in this young soul and a willingness to muck-in and see what happens. You do not really need a rigid routine with Gemini babies, for they are flexible and willing to go with the flow. In fact it is better not to impose a strict regime on this child. Gemini is an endless source of entertainment and destined to bring you many laughs and plenty to think about. Enjoy experimenting; it is an adventure.

CHILD: Gemini youngsters love to shred things, so you would be well advised to leave precious items out-of-reach. If you want to keep your toddler quiet, a pile of old magazines and newspapers in the corner should do the trick. Hours of fun.

Gemini kids have a special way of communicating and often words are not necessary. One look from those expressive eyes will let you know what is going on. Learn the language of those eyes and you will not go far wrong. Gemini loves to day dream and you will often catch your youngster looking out the window, gazing ethereally into space. Gemini is not always that grounded, so learn when to step in before your child floats off entirely. The Gemini youngster has many real friends and a myriad of imaginary ones too. Cute!

ELEVENSES: Gemini kids question everything. They have intelligent, enquiring minds that want to fully grasp what is going on. These children are creative, with a love of the arts. So, paint-box, crayons and paper will keep them happy; well, for about five minutes anyway. Gemini is enthusiastic and loves to day dream. But this child's imagination is so profound that fantasies are become just as vivid as reality once they get a grip. These kiddies are nifty little liars when they want to be too. It is not usually done out of badness. But the blurring of what *actually* happened is easy enough when the truth hurts. Little Gemini's are independent souls who absorb information like a sponge. Let them wander as they will as their energy levels allow them to cope with just about everything.

CANCER

Parents of little Cancers are blessed with caring, considerate children. Ruled by The Moon, these lunar creatures are sensitive, psychic beings with a protective emotional shell. Do not let this child down; you will never be allowed to forget it. These kids have a strong sense of loyalty. But, they are great at emotional blackmail too. Their techniques wear you down and inevitably they get their way.

BABY: Cancer babies are invariably gorgeous, cuddly creatures. With the typical button-features of a perfect child, these little cutiepies are guaranteed to melt your heart.

Cancer kids generally sleep well; except on a Full Moon when they are likely to be exceptionally energized. Also, Cancer babies are easily amused. You do not really need to splash out on pricey toys. Besides, these babies are usually so fixated on mammy they won't be distracted by fancy goods. The cute-but-clingy phase lasts until the etheric cords linking mother and child begin to loosen-up (age three). Then the cheeky stuff begins to kick-in; but if you thought cutting the umbilical cord was easy. It is a good idea to breast-feed your Cancer baby for as long as possible to boost optimum health.

CHILD: The monsters come out to play in the Cancer psyche when school and outside commitments require stretches apart from mammy. It is important to be disciplined with your child and explain things gently. Chances are your little cuddle-bunny will need a lot of reassurance as the big wide world beckons. If these adjustments take place smoothly, you may then experience the opposite problem. Walkabout syndrome is probably *not* a big rebellion. But, the new-found freedom of your increasingly independent child leads to interesting developments. Keep a beady-eye on your child during this phase. Explorative Cancers are expert at slipping through any precaution you care to put in place. They are skilled at outwitting you, for their psychic sense detects how to slip through the net!

ELEVENSES: You will have noticed from a young age that your Cancerian has a knowing-air. Despite Mammy-fixation, these little lovelies are very in-tune and able to discern what is what in all sorts of obscure situations. Do not think you can hide things from your child. They will invariably sniff out your worst secrets, so the straightforward approach is the best one. Let your child come up with the complexities. There will certainly be enough going-down to keep you busy (and worried) for quite some time. "Why" is Cancer's favorite word; so prepare intelligent answers to your child's annoyingly perceptive questions. Your child is innately wise, so you can expect to raise a little oracle. Your lunar-child is an old Soul who needs to be nurtured and trusted.

LEO

If you are parents to little Leo, you have your work cut-out. Leo's are shameless attention-seekers with a heart of gold. This kid performs for effect and needs a constant, patient audience. You do not overlook Leo unless you want endless flak. For sanity's sake, keep Leo at the hub of family activity. Ruled by the Sun these kids are colorful with a sunny disposition and great sense of humor.

BABY: Baby Leo needs lots of hugs, reassurance and attention. These are cute babies with a wicked chuckle and mischievous glint in the eye; which I defy you to resist. Little Leo is very interested in what is going on, and responds well to stimulation, so long as the environment is not too hectic and noisy. Little Leo is a baby to be proud of. Gorgeous, with a lovely disposition, these bundles of joy keep themselves entertained for hours. If they are aware of you in the background watching, they will feign disinterest and perform to impress. Do not forget to heap praise upon them later, as this will ensure at least some gaps of peace and quiet. Leo is quick witted and intelligent. But when the chat starts, you will be on the receiving end of endless ideas, reports and jokes. Hours of fun.

CHILD: Leo kids are natural leaders and you will find them running rings around you from a very early age. You can expect to be shown the way by your little Leo, and more often than not, they are right with their hunches and intuitions. Full of heart and courage, these kids have natural strength and a love of life. Do not be afraid of spoiling them; you will not be able to resist lavishing lots of attention and gifts upon them anyhow. It is their birthright to land on their feet with lots of sensual trappings in the future, so they might as well get used to it from an early age. You will not affect them adversely by providing them with what they require. Denial is not really the best way to discipline these kids. Besides, too much discipline just makes them feel unloved, uncomfortable and miserable.

ELEVENSES: Nurture your Leo kid. They are open-hearted and full of unusual, creative ideas. Natural leaders and performers, quite possibly fame awaits them down-the-road. Leo does have a lazy streak though, so getting them to contribute to household chores is likely to be a chore in itself. Your kid is bound to be demanding of your time, money and attention. But the up-side is that you will be rewarded in bountiful ways in years to come.

Little Leo does reach a stage of self-containment and independence soon enough. Leo expends high amounts of energy putting their all into things. So you will notice quiet times of reflection and introspection during the teen years. This is nothing to worry about; it is just Leo recharging the batteries for the next attempt at gaining recognition.

VIRGO

Being parents to a Virgo child is a fairly joyful experience, though you may sometimes wonder if you have spawned an old head on young shoulders; well, what is new? You *have*. You really do not need to nag or criticize your Virgo child. These kids are very self-aware, introspective and self-critical. You do not need to enforce rules to keep them on track, and you may in fact find they are better behaved than you are.

BABY: Your Virgo baby is bound to be beautiful with gorgeous rounded features and a knowing look in the eye. These children are usually Old Souls incarnated to make the world a better place. Very evolved, and easy to look after, your baby responds well to routine and a cool, tranquil environment. You can expect your baby to beat all records and probably develop a step-ahead of its peers. But, Virgo babies can be little control freaks, and you will notice that they do not like their routine to be upset. They are flexible enough if you need to travel, or if there is a change of plan. But do try to stick to regular hours, feeds and sleeps, wherever you may be. Virgo baby has delicate digestion, so will not thank you for missing a feed, or heating up the milk to the wrong temperature.

CHILD: You can expect your Virgo child to run a tight ship! Yes, at times it will feel like this kid is running the family home. But, the beauty of it is; you will find that your child is right most of the time. You would be well-advised to swallow your pride and hang on their every word. You might as well accept that you have produced a little oracle and get on with it. Test it out, and see what goes wrong when you ignore your little Virgo's hunches. These kids are wise souls sent to help you and make your life easier; you might as well get used to it.

Virgos are practical, earthy old souls with a matter-of-fact approach to life. But they do need lots of reassurance and TLC. It is lonely for them sometimes with so-called friends who get jealous of their talents, knowing-ways and good looks.

ELEVENSES: It is a myth that Virgo is prim and proper. These kids are actually earthy, sensuous beings with a great connection to Mother Earth. If you have any doubt how to bring out the best in your teen Virgo, encourage their innate link with nature. Virgo kids are perfectionist and thorough in their work, play and relationships. But they are quite serious-minded, so could use some cajoling sometimes to spark up their sense of fun.

Ruled by Mercury, these kids are very intelligent and seem to carry the whole weight of the world on their shoulders. It is as if they already understand what they are being taught at school. Little Virgo really has heard it all before. Like a sponge, this child responds well to new ideas, so you more than likely have a Grade A student on your hands.

LIBRA

Libran kids are obtuse, so you can expect lots of contrary behavior and bizarre disagreements from your little angel. Yes, the Libran child invariably looks gorgeous; like butter-would-not-melt. But as all parents know, appearances can be deceiving. Libran kids will argue the point ad infinitum; so you really have to make sure that no means "no." Stick to the boundaries that feel right, and do not budge an inch.

BABY: Baby Librans are witty and amusing with a real feel for music. Indeed it is music that will calm their souls before sleep; so before you try any of the usual tricks give your child a blast of Beethoven. It will work quicker than all the soothers in Mother Care! Libran babies are shy little things and may need their confidence boosted as they start to emerge into the big wide world. A squeeze of the hand at well-chosen moments should do the trick. But be warned, Libran kids are very good at playing off both ends against the middle. They will approach the favored parent with a request, and invariably win them over with general cuteness. Previous denials and resistance from "Bad-Cop" parent will then have no impact. Do guard against being out-maneuvered by your nifty child.

CHILD: Little Librans are creative and intelligent beings possessing profound imaginations. Here is another child of the Zodiac likely to have a plethora of imaginary friends. Do not discourage the make-believe aspect of your child's psyche; for it is the dreams and visions of this kid that make life bearable. Play-time boosts your child's confidence and allows them to assert control on their environment. The imagination is literally a haven from adverse pressures, people and experiences. But, Librans become increasingly self-willed and stubborn as their equilibrium stabilizes. You can expect a few screaming matches and temper tantrums as moodiness kicks-in. Librans get seduced by the latest craze or gadget; so expect to be worn-down until you relent. Just say yes!

ELEVENSES: Your Libran child is clever, but tends to excel at one or two subjects rather than across the board. There may be some angst and loss of confidence on account of subjects that do not gel with the Libran mind (usually math and science). But gentle coaching can get your kid over most of the hurdles. Arts, media and music suit Libra well indeed. You can expect your child to shine in one area, which will set them up for a successful career. Your little Libran is bound to have a wicked sense of humor and gets easily distracted by the opposite sex. Anyone who takes their fancy gets put on a pedestal which can lead to scanty school reports and dodgy grades. Eventually of course, reality dawns and your B student will be able to concentrate once again, and get a few A's.

SCORPIO

Being parent to a Scorpio is an uncomfortable privilege! This child is a cute little thing, who can read your mind and anticipate your next move. Once they get the measure of you; you can expect your buttons to be merrily pushed until you relent to that impressive will. There is a bewitching quality to this kid, which serves them well. You needn't have too many fears on account of little Scorpio.

BABY: Your baby Scorpio is an alluring, charming creature, who will captivate you with just one look. You will notice a knowing glint in your child's eye and realize you have spawned a mind-reader; or perhaps a mind-bender! Do not be daunted, but do be careful. This youngster does not understand the meaning of the word "no." The sooner you lay down ground rules and impose a routine, the better. Scorpio loves to control things and loves a bit of drama too, so you can expect many a temper tantrum in the supermarket if you try to avoid the latest fad.

Scorpio child is destined to play a dominant role in family life, and you will find that older siblings are quite charmed by the new arrival. This viper-in the-nest is a bossy little thing, who will stir things up big time. Brace yourself.

CHILD: Watch out for your child's tendency to exaggerate. This bundle of brooding mischief loves gossip and drama, so it is important to check the facts before you run to other parents or teachers complaining about injustice in the play-ground. Your child loves to wind up unsavory characters and is likely to get into a scrape or two. But Scorpio kids with their innate psychic ability are street wise and canny. It is advisable to stay in their good books, for the infamous sting-in-the-tail is no myth. Your little Scorpio is excellent at pushing buttons and sensing weak spots; and their behavior can be unpredictable as well as mysterious. Scorpio has their own reason for doing things and those well-honed instincts will get them out of all sorts of trouble, even as they land their mates right in it.

ELEVENSES: Your Scorpio child is well able to cast a spell or two. Their stories and shenanigans are captivating. They are likely to be surrounded by all sorts of mates in awe of their charisma. Do not be surprised if your kid is a ring-leader for many a rebellious uprising, as they are particularly good at making teacher's lives a misery. Of course their political awareness is not that well developed yet. But just wait until they hit student age.

Young Scorpio will ignore what makes them feel uncomfortable and responds only to what is understood. The opposite sex gets torture not romance at this stage; for Scorpio is not adverse to a bit of intimidation. Life with this child is certainly weird and wonderful; and you can expect to be kept on your toes. Scorpio makes the rules up; get used to it.

SAGITTARIUS

Young Sagittarians are lively and fun. If you are parents to a little Sagittarian, you are in for lots of laughs. But will need boundless energy to keep up with the mad shenanigans. These kids have a well-developed sense of adventure; so you *will* need to keep an eye on them. They are likely to wander. It is a good idea to encourage your child to sublimate all that excess energy with lots of physical activity.

BABY: Needless to say, it is quite tricky to get this baby to unwind enough to sleep. Innately restless, this is the baby you will have to push around the block, hoping the land-of-nod will descend a.s.a.p. But, the extra exercise and fresh air is just what you both need, so get into it. You really have no choice. You will have to come up with endless ideas to keep your child amused. This baby needs attention, stimulation and constant activity. At a later stage, you may be relieved to notice a lazy streak develop. But really, for your child's benefit it is better to encourage positive activity. If you notice lethargy kicking-in, it is usually a sign of listlessness and despondency, so do be hands-on when it happens. Go to a film, go for a drive, have a giggle, or go kick a ball, together!

CHILD: This kid is a bundle of vibrant energy, destined to run rings around you for many hours of the day, and many years to come. You will get respite, but only once your little dynamo has collapsed into a heap of exhaustion in the corner. This physical sign scoots around like a mad thing until the batteries run low; which they do at a moment's notice. It is a good idea to learn the art of cat-napping if you have a young Sagittarian on your hands. Grab your moment. You are also likely to have wakeful nights once that overactive imagination starts on the night-time terrors. The best way to calm the mind of this frantic creature is with a lilac-colored bedroom and a charming nightlight of the moon. Learn to pace your child if you have a tight schedule; a workable routine is crucial.

ELEVENSES: Your child is a natural sporting champ, which is a great use of all that surplus energy. Intelligent, with a lively mind, young Sag is also good at studies. But, the opposite sex is likely to be a distraction from an early age. Thankfully, the school work does not suffer too much. These kids really do have energy for everything. Your child's insatiable curiosity gives them a hunger for travel and adventure.

Sagittarius has a love of life and embraces it in all its glory. Your kid is not likely to get into serious trouble. But there will inevitably be the odd scrape. Your child's humor is their saving grace, so do encourage it at every given opportunity. At least your Sagittarian is great at looking on the bright side, and more often than not they are the tonic you need at the end of a weary day.

CAPRICORN

Little Capricorns love their home life. If you are parents to young Capricorn, you are lucky to have a youngster who will really treasure family life. Indeed, this Earth Sign finds it difficult to detach from its roots. So when the time comes to flee the nest, your son or daughter will certainly need a gentle nudge. If you do not manage this, chances are they would still have their own room upstairs, aged 42.

BABY: Baby Capricorns are as good as gold. They respond well to a practical routine and adore home life. These babies sense what is best for the family, and are great at settling down for the night, unless they are unwell. In fact if you have a cranky Capricorn baby on your hands, chances are they need to be checked over by your doctor. In the fullness of health these babies sleep so well, you are likely to get a full night's sleep right from the off. Indeed, you may well have to *wake* them up in the mornings; they really do love their comfortable nest.

If you are planning a baby, you could do worse than aiming for a mini-Capricorn. The only potential problem is the inevitable teething saga. Your baby Capricorn is bound to get frustrated that sleep is no longer straightforward.

CHILD: This child hates to be unsettled and needs the grounding of home life to function effectively in the adult world. The formative years set Capricorn up for life and they are eternally grateful for a set-tled, comfortable home-life. Depending on the Zodiac Signs of the family, your little one may sometimes get over-shadowed. Make an effort to include them if this happens a lot. But generally these kids are happy watching and observing from the side-lines. It is the way they learn what is acceptable and what is not.

Capricorn kids are quite placid; but the good news is they are obe-dient and love to do as they are told. You are lucky indeed to have such an obliging child. The only frustration or concern may be their lack of independence and slightly serious-minded nature. Aim to lighten them up a little.

ELEVENSES: Young Capricorns are studious and hardworking. They are never rebellious for the sake of it, except perhaps when they have been hurt. But these placid, docile kids are not a complete pushover, and they sometimes do something controversial to make a point. Take note when this happens, as they are more than likely upset and need a good old-heart-to-heart. As young teens, Capricorns begin to show more oomph, creativity and develop a taste for life. Their years watching and observing begin to pay off and their confidence increases. It is difficult to fault the performance of this Grade A student. But there may be clashes with the most authoritative parent as the need to assert independence kicks-in. This may be a shock after the many docile years; but it passes.

AQUARIUS

The young Aquarian has an opinion on everything. If you are a parent to this intelligent Air Sign, you certainly have an intelligent child on your hands. Indeed the incessant chat is likely to drive you bananas after a while. But be mindful that it is very important to nurture this trait in your little Aquarian. In time to come, when they have talked their way into a lucrative career, you will be glad you did!

BABY: This little dote is a gorgeous baby who thrives on attention and interesting company. Mature and independent from a young age, this child still hates to be left alone. Aquarius babies need company for speedy development and enjoyable vibes. This little one would happily sleep through a party in the corner, rather than pine upstairs knowing there is fun going on down below. Of course this does not mean you can never go out. But do make efforts to keep your child up-to-speed with your plans. Your Aquarian baby is really an old soul in a little body, so you must not ignore or overlook them. Besides, the joyful disposition of your wee dote will keep you amused and repay you handsomely. Do not bother with fancy toys; that old cuddly bear or comfort blanket is what matters.

CHILD: Your Aquarian kid is a born entrepreneur, and stands to make a mint. Encourage this child's lively mind and wicked sense of humor. If you tolerate all the chat and do not say 'hush' the whole time; you will really help set your baby up for life. Patience and a listening ear really is the best gift you could possibly give. These old souls are generous and spirited too; so you can only benefit in the long run if you support them beyond the call of duty now. Your little

Aquarian has an experimental, quirky nature and needs a certain amount of privacy. If there are many siblings to contend with, your little one will love the company. But also need quality time and special gestures of affection. Apart from that they are independent, resourceful, and good at staging their own entertainment.

ELEVENSES: Your Aquarian child has strong instincts and is able to sense what to do next without any prompting from you. Don't be tempted to interfere; you won't be thanked. Little Aquarians are popular and well-loved; and your child will want to join in with all sorts of activities. Aquarius is a team player who loves to be included. But, there is still occasional need to withdraw. The quiet moments are the prime time to subtly check that all is well.

Aquarians like to follow their intuition and do not respond well to routine. They perform well with the subjects they like; but will not be pushed along with those they do not. Your child is a gadget whiz and is likely to spend hours on the computer. Do not expect them to be tidy while they are absorbed; the chores can wait.

PISCES

You have your hands full if you are parent to the Zodiac Fish. Your little Piscean is highly psychic and you will not get away with anything. This little one can read your mind and will often tell you what you have just done, or who you have just talked to. These kids come alive at night, so you can expect fitful nights with your baby and endless nights lying awake waiting for your teenager to show face.

BABY: This baby is a gorgeous, sensitive creature. But, you will have your work cut-out adjusting to their sleeping pattern. Pisces comes alive at night and the Moon does strange things to this baby's delicate system. There is something very special about your other-worldly baby. You will soon appreciate this when their extra-sensory perception starts to develop. These kids have a natural zest for life. But you will also notice a tricky duality in their behavior. On the one hand you have a cute, obliging little child; and on the other, the monster who just won't settle comes out to play. Pisces has a golden, endearing nature one minute and a petulant, impatient nature the next. Pisces babies are exhausting, but entertaining. They are mystical, magical babies who are also very human.

CHILD: Your Zodiac Fish is very cute, and loveable. But you can expect a battle of wills if you impose unreasonable boundaries. Pisces needs *some* structure; but generally, these kids do not respond well to discipline. They simply need to know where they stand. You may sometimes notice a selfish streak when it comes to sharing thoughts, possessions and affections. Pisces child will not be forced to do go against their natural inclinations. You can be assured there is a reason for this; but it is no excuse for bad behavior. Never forget that your little fish is very susceptible to energies, so may take an unexpected dislike to certain people. Pay attention to this and don't assume that they are just being rude. Pisces has plenty of imaginary friends and does not need weird human ones.

ELEVENSES: Your Pisces child is likely to be an avid reader, so do line up an interesting array of books to keep them busy. These intelligent kids respond well to the arts. But Pisces learns at a measured pace, and may find it tricky to retain facts and figures. Exam time can be stressful and coursework seems to suit the Piscean psyche rather better. Your child will likely have quite far-fetched dreams. But these are treasured and fiercely guarded; so do not try to steer them away from their chosen career. This would only make them more desperate and determined to prove you wrong. When this Zodiac Sign sets its heart on a course of action, nothing will deter or discourage their resolve. There is a touch of genius about your Pisces and wicked instincts too. Wait and see.

16 ZODIAC KIDS HOLIDAYS

Check out this section to find out what your best options for the holidays are. KIDS RULE OKAY! Where to go and what to do? Are you planning to take the kids away with you or to swan off into the sunset together (having called in the grandparents)? Of course you are probably going to brave it. The holidays are about the kids and these are valuable times for bonding and oodles of family fun

ARIES

If you are parents to an Aries child you really have to be ready for anything, especially on holiday. Ruled by Mars, these kids are live wires; unpredictable and full of energy. Expect erratic behavior and all sorts of shenanigans. A healthy mischievous streak bestows this child with a wicked sense of humor, so you can expect pranks galore and endless madness to keep you all entertained. Even Aries babies love stimulation, lots of activity and noise; ideal if you already have a busy family.

As I am sure you are aware, your Aries child is very strong willed. This stubborn streak will come to the fore on holidays, so you will have to get the balance right between indulging their whims and keeping some boundaries of discipline in place. On holidays especially, these kids will make it their mission to see what they can get away with.

Think action packed holidays, full of fun and adventure. If you want to quiet them down a bit take them away to hot, hot beaches. Just make sure to avoid the severe sunstroke temper tantrums.

TAURUS

You will have to try to find some kind of home from home for the holidays. Taurus does not like to roam too far afield, unless there is a sense of taking "home" along with you. If you do not have much of a budget for travel, these kids could quite happily stay local. They can always catch up with friends or generally hide away causing mischief upstairs. The bedroom is an important haven of security for a Taurus child, so make sure that when away they are happy with their corner of the room, villa or apartment. They will need a place to retreat for quiet times, deep thinking and of course sulking.

A young Taurus is a demanding little creature, with a strong will and stubborn temperament. Be careful not to spoil them on holidays though for the sake of a quiet life. Taurus kids are creatures of habit; so even really nice changes if too overwhelming can unsettle them.

The mellow, peaceful and relaxed vibe of a family home speaks to the heart of little Taurus, so a cute holiday cottage in the midst of lots of greenery works wonders. Guard against boredom though. Taurus kids are adventurous; keen to explore and understand new environments.

In moments of indiscipline, you can expect a strong clash of wills. Do not be tempted to bribe or tempt these kids. It will be cast up for ever if you forget or change the plan. Do not bargain with Taurus; manipulations are bound to back fire.

Despite their home-loving ways; Taurus is an independent creature who intermittently needs to roam free. Relax about them scrambling off across the moors or up the hills if they are in safe enough company. Letting them off the leash satisfies their sense of adventure and gives you room to breathe as well.

GEMINI

As if you had not realized already, Geminis are exhausting company. They love to travel though and will be up for any adventure you care to expose them too. In a way these kids are easiest to please, and you could nearly please them is by pleasing yourself. I suspect their tolerance would stop short at a trip to Vegas though.

Geminis are entertaining and intelligent too. At whatever age they are lots of fun to take on holiday. You will certainly benefit from their mad maverick nature. Just a word of warning though, you will get tired and so will they. So remember to listen to that endless chat and respond with a nod and a wink, even on that endless motorway drive.

If you are short on holiday ideas see what your Gemini child has to say. They probably will have decided on several suitable destinations already. (At least they pay attention in geography).

You do not really need a rigid routine with Gemini kids. You can easily travel to the far corners of the earth without them getting overly fractious or freaked out. These kids are self-contained little units, who will not be too clingy if you need to call in the baby minder so you can go out for a romantic dinner. It is potentially a win: win situation.

CANCER

Cancer is emotional, and they make for considerate, sweet kids, for the most part. Very sensitive, they will pick up on your need to be alone and will be very considerate about your holiday plans. Generally as long as it is somewhere by the sea, they will be happy. You can choose between the northern coast of Scotland, Montana, or the Costa Del Sol, your child will be equally content.

Remember though these kids need to be studied. Overly hectic environments will not be suitable for too long and they may not really like the idea of Disneyland Florida on an overly hot summer's day. Those huge queues would kill all their fun and yours. Fainting fits and temper tantrums are a likely consequence. Not fun for anyone; right?

Cancer kids are great manipulators and are particularly good at emotional blackmail. If they have a particular notion on holiday, chances are they will get their own way. You might as well make it easy on yourself, even if you do not quite agree on the timing of their idea. Just say yes.

LEO

These kids are the Zodiacs shameless attention seekers with a heart of gold. They perform for effect and need a constant, patient audience, even on holiday. Sibling rivalries are likely to be interesting if you have a Leo kid. They are likely to be fractious and extra demanding if they feel their siblings are getting more breaks.

These kids cope well enough in the sun, but they do need a measure of activity too, so get the balance right. Do not overlook your Leo unless you want endless flak. For sanity's sake, keep Leo at the hub of family activity on holiday. They are likely to lead a rebellion in the ranks if they do not get some in-put as to what happens from day to day. Do not spoil them; but do listen to them

They love holidays which involve animals. Go on Safari if the budget stretches that far; but if not, the Lions of Longleat in the West Country would go down well. Alternatively, visit the local zoo or Sea World, or an aquarium, if you are abroad.

Remember Leo kids are natural leaders, so adventure holidays with the school are always a good idea. Think of this during term time and you might have more bargaining power over the destination of your choice come the summer.

Your Leo kid will have extravagant taste and could well be a drain on your resources if you let them. Be careful not to spoil little Leo, but they will require a certain level of treatment. Think Macey's, rather than Target.

VIRGO

Taking a Virgo child on holiday is a fairly joyful experience, though you may sometimes wonder if you have spawned an old soul. These kids are not boring; but they can be quiet and reflective on holidays. They love to merge with the landscape in remote places and can be quite dreamy when left to their own devices. They will not take up much of your time or money. These kids are independent and self-sufficient. You are more likely to have great chats and sort the world out on holiday with your Virgo. Not a bad option really.

You should find that these kids do not need too much discipline. They find their own way within reasonable boundaries In fact if you have a group of kids heading off somewhere on their own with a Virgo in the company, they pretty much have a parent with them anyway. You can leave a Virgo and siblings alone and not worry too much. These kids are very self-aware and you do not need to enforce rules to keep them on track. You may in fact find they are better behaved than you are.

Camping is a great holiday if you have a Virgo or two in the mix. They are not too precious bout their surroundings; but love to be linked to nature and places of historical interest. Any quaint or magical place will fire their imagination. Places like New England or Sedona, or Devon and Cornwall would go down a treat.

LIBRA

Little Librans can be fractious company on holiday. These kids are obtuse and difficult to please if they are out of sorts. You can expect lots of contrary behavior and bizarre disagreements from your little angel if they end up in a place they do not like. I would suggest pooling family ideas before you head off if you have a strong Libran contingent at home.

Remember Librans love music, so you might get the holiday you all really want if you use a bargaining tool or two before you go away, such as family trips to the odd musical or concert. If they are old enough, the summer music festivals with Dad might give mum a good enough excuse to get some "away time," with the girls.

If you are away with a Libran Baby, make sure you have a ready music supply to lull the kids to sleep if you are in a strange place or a strange land. It works every time.

Remember that Libran kids are very good at playing off both ends against the middle. They will approach an amenable parent with a special request and invariably win them over with general cuteness. Previous denials and resistance will then have no impact. Do guard against being out-maneuvered by your nifty child. Agree a strategy in advance.

These kids can cause merry havoc and entertaining though it may be in retrospect, you do actually want to have a relaxing time. It will pay to let them have their way, within reason.

SCORPIO

Of course you will be well aware that there is a bewitching quality to this kid, which serves them well. They like to be in control and need to feel secure. Their input on the family holiday destination is quite important. There is no point in going where they do not want to go. Remember you have spawned a mind reader, so there is no pulling the wool over this little one's eyes.

On holiday, the sooner you lay down ground rules and impose a routine, the better. Scorpio loves to control things and loves a bit of drama too, so you can expect many a temper tantrum if things are too out of the ordinary. Watch for the discontent of the Scorpio's siblings, for if there is an on-going issue, this viper-in the-nest will stir things up. Watch out for your child's tendency to exaggerate and create a drama. Scorpio is excellent at pushing buttons and sensing weak spots.

These kids need a holiday that will captivate their imagination. Explore old ruins, dungeons and prisons if you can find them. History and old haunted houses inspire them, as do sophisticated mind games and treasure trails. You will have to dig deep to entertain Scorpio on holiday. Do not let them get bored, with temperamental siblings. That is a recipe for disaster.

These guys love to taunt and tease, so long journeys by trains, planes and automobiles could be fractious. They really need a good thriller or mystery to read.

SAGITTARIUS

Young Sagittarians are lively, fun and love to travel. Like little Geminis these Zodiac kids are the easiest to entertain on holiday. If your family contains a little Sagittarian, you are in for lots of laughs. But you will need boundless energy to keep up with the mad shenanigans. These kids have a well-developed sense of adventure; so you *will* need to keep an eye on them. They are likely to wander.

On holiday, it is a good idea to encourage your child to sublimate all that excess energy with lots of physical activity. Treks, water sports and rock climbing et al can all at various points be thrown into the mix. Exercise and fresh air galore is necessary to tire them out and keep them entertained. Activity holidays hit the spot, for languishing on a beach is not really the Sagittarian style, except for an hour or two.

You will have to come up with endless ideas to keep your Sagittarian kid amused. If you notice lethargy kicking-in, it is usually a sign of listlessness and despondency, so do watch for signs of depression. Go to a film, go for a drive, have a giggle, or go kick a ball.

You will get respite, but only once your little dynamo has collapsed into a heap of exhaustion in the corner. This physical sign scoots around like a mad thing until the batteries run low; which they do at a moment's notice. It is a good idea to learn the art of cat-napping if you have a young Sagittarian on your hands. Grab your moment.

You could always pack your Sagittarian kid off to a sporting summer activity or training school. This really is the best idea all around, for these kids do not inevitably want to be hanging from the apron strings for the bulk of the holidays.

CAPRICORN

Little Capricorns love their home life, so may weirdly be reluctant to go on holiday unless it is to a home from home destination. Trips involving the extended family are good, especially if Gran and Grand Pa live in the countryside. This youngster really treasures family life and group activity. This kid hates to be unsettled and needs the grounding of home life to function effectively. Travel to places of cultural interest when they are old enough works. But generally these kids are happy watching and observing from the side-lines.

Of course they will tag along on a family holiday; but do not be surprised if they are a little bit quiet. They will enjoy the getting home as much as the holiday itself. Indeed for them it might be the best part of going away.

These kids are not particularly independent, so may need your company whatever you are doing. They will not get in your way in fact they are pretty good at fading in to the background. You could probably take them along to a seminar and they will not be fazed.

As young teens, Capricorns begin to show more oomph. Their creativity kicks in and they develop a taste for life. Their years watching and observing begin to pay off and their confidence increases. On holiday they will take more interest. But they are good enough company at any age. Just see if you can get them to have some *fun!*

AQUARIUS

The young Aquarian has an opinion on everything, and will most certainly want to have a say in where you all go on holiday. If you are a parent to this intelligent Air Sign, the incessant chat is likely to drive you bananas from time to time. If you are in a place of interest, there will be endless questions; but that is much better than the shut-down which occurs when this child is bored. Do not even go there.

Mature and independent from a young age, this child still hates to be left alone. Aquarius kids need company to spark their imagination. You can take this kid anywhere. They would happily sleep through a party in the corner, rather than pine upstairs on their lone-some.

Your Aquarian baby is really an old soul in a little body, so you must not ignore their spiritual side. Take in the local churches, cathedrals and ancient monuments. If there is a local crystal shop or slate mine, go and have a look. Aquarius possesses curiosity for all sorts of places and even apparently boring museums or exhibitions will captivate even a young child.

Your little Aquarian has an experimental, quirky nature and needs a certain amount of privacy. But if there are many siblings to contend with, they will love the company. Just do not ignore them.

PISCES

Like all water signs the Pisces kid loves the water in all its guises. Waterfalls, rivers, lakes, and the sea are fundamental to Pisces enjoyment of life, never mind just on holiday. Fishing trips and boat rides hit the spot. Seeing others have fun also brings the Pisces joy, so these kids are team players on a family holiday. They will be polite and helpful, so long as they do get their own way in some part.

Remember that your little Piscean is highly psychic. They absorb their environment like a sponge, so it is advisable to keep things varied and not incessantly hectic. They may go a bit introspective in airports and other busy places; but their own shades and smart phone will give them a world of their own to get lost in whilst travelling.

Be aware that Pisces may actually need these props to be comfortable, so do not get too cross at what is apparent anti-social behavior. It really is not; it is the Pisces survival mechanism. Look after them in this respect and they will be all yours again once you land.

Pisces has a golden, endearing nature one minute and a petulant, impatient nature the next. Do not give this changeability too much thought, it is par for the course and will only drain your energy as a parent if you fret about it. Do not sweat the small stuff.

17 LOCATION, LOCATION

Zodiac Cities and Countries. Use this information to identify a suitable holiday resort. You should find that the energy of these places particularly suits your Zodiac sign. Where to go…what to do…so many places, such little time!

ARIES:

Countries: Denmark. France. Germany. Poland. Syria. Japan. England. Palestine.

Cities: Brunswick. Birmingham (UK). Naples. Marseilles. Krakow. Verona. Utrecht. Florence. Capua.

TAURUS:

Countries: Cyprus. Ireland. Switzerland. Egypt. Iran. Iraq (perhaps not!) Capri. Greek Islands.

Cities: Dublin. Bologna. Mantua. Hastings (UK). Eastbourne (UK). Palermo. Lucerne. Leipzig. St. Louis.

GEMINI:

Countries: Belgium. Corsica. Egypt. Wales. Sardinia. Armenia. United States of America.

Cities: Cardiff. Bruges. Plymouth. London. San Francisco. Versailles. Nuremberg. Cordoba. Melbourne. New York.

CANCER:

Countries: Holland. Mauritius. New Zealand. Northern and Western Africa. Scotland. Paraguay. Algeria.

Cities: Amsterdam. Berne. New York. Manchester. Milan. Genoa. Venice. Tunis. Stockholm. Mahebourg. Cadiz. Algiers. Istanbul. New York.

LEO:

Countries: Italy. France. Southern Iraq. Sicily. Czechoslovakia. The Alps. Romania. The Lebanon.

Cities: New York. Blackpool. Oxford. Bristol. Portsmouth. Chicago. Philadelphia. Damascus. Madrid. Los Angeles. Bombay. Bath. Rome. Syracuse. Prague.

VIRGO:

Countries: Brazil. Crete. Turkey. Switzerland. Virgin islands. Yugoslavia. Mesopotamia. Greece. Iraq.

Cities: Venice. Boston. Corinth. Heidelberg. Athens. Boston. Jerusalem. Paris. Lyons. Reading. Health Resorts - wherever you care to mention.

LIBRA:

Countries: Canada. Austria. Burma. Tibet. China. Indo-China. South Pacific Islands. Northern Egypt. Japan.

Cities: Egypt. Frankfurt. Vienna. Freiburg. Leeds. Nottingham. Lisbon. Antwerp. Copenhagen.

SCORPIO:

Countries: Algeria. Morocco. Norway. Uruguay. Transvaal. Syria. Korea. Bavaria.

Cities: Dover. Fez. Halifax. New Orleans. Washington DC. Newcastle (UK). Liverpool. Hull. Cincinnati. Baltimore. Valencia. Stockport. Milwaukee.

SAGITTARIUS:

Countries: Australia. Hungary. Yugoslavia. Arabia. Spain.

Cities: Bradford. Oregon. Cologne. Toledo(Spain and USA). Sheffield. Nottingham. Naples. Toronto. Stuttgart.

CAPRICORN:

Countries: India. Afghanistan (perhaps not!). Shetlands. Orkneys. Albania. Bulgaria. Mexico. Macedonia. Lithuania.

Cities: Delhi. Oxford. Mexico City. Brussels. Ghent. Port Said. Administrative centers of major cities.

AQUARIUS:

Countries: Ethiopia. Lithuania. Iran. Israel. Sweden. Russia. Poland.

Cities: Brighton. Moscow. Salzburg. St. Petersburg. Hamburg. Bremen.

PISCES:

Countries: Portugal. Philippines. Greek islands. Scandinavia. Mediterranean. Sahara.

Cities: Venice. Alexandria. Seville. Santiago.

18 HOLIDAY HEAVEN

Look here for the types of holidays that best suit the different Zodiac Signs.

ARIES: Action packed holidays jam-packed with interest suit Aries. This restless spirit needs entertainment and is not likely to be happy sitting on a cruise ship, .or at the top of a mountain; unless of course they climbed there by rope across a precipice. Aries likes to live life to the full and close to the edge. This sign needs adequate stimulation, even when chilling out! Relaxation does not really come into the frame: Okay slight exaggeration. But do not expect to get away with sitting on a beach for days on end if accompanied on holiday by an Arian.

TAURUS: Earthy, sensual connections hit the spot for Taurus. Mediterranean countries with fine culture, scenery and beautiful local talent, are what Taurus requires for a good time. They also love to holiday *en famille* and need to see that everyone is catered for before they can even think about relaxing. Taurus loves to unwind and luxuriate in sumptuous surroundings. Good food is of the utmost importance and if the holiday is self-catering or the fayre is low standard, the Zodiac Bull will be very difficult to please. Taurus is liable to put on weight whilst having fun. So needs to be careful if the object of the trip is to attract the opposite sex.

GEMINI: Variety is the spice of life for Gemini, who is always inclined to believe the grass is greener. Of course singletons are set up for endless fun in places like Ibiza. Since Gemini remains a child at heart, whatever the age, the scope for holiday enjoyment remains broad and exciting. Take your pick. Mad exotic locations suit Gemini with oodles of love and fun thrown in for good measure. This sign is highly susceptible (I do not think vulnerable is the word.) to the holiday romance. Care should be taken of course if said Gemini is already spoken for. But apart from that there is a free license to go (responsibly) mad.

CANCER: Seaside resorts or any place with sufficient supplies of Aqua suit Cancer. Of course the salty variety best suits this Zodiac crustacean. The Caribbean is ideal territory with wonderful food and plenty of options for scuttling around. Lay on island hopping, along with water sports galore and exciting evening events and you have a happy holiday crab on your hands. Sun, sea and sex are what Cancer expects during holiday season. Indeed whatever terrain they find themselves in, it has to be home from home, with all the extras thrown in. The grumpy crab is not a pretty sight. So if you have one in your party, make sure there is plenty of choice from day to day; plus the facility to beat a hasty retreat for private moments from time to time.

LEO: Designer togs and five star hotels do it for Leo every time. Warm, sunny climes are the order of the day; not many Leo's head for Lapland (unless there are 24 hour Jacuzzis on tap!) The Zodiac Lion loves to splash out, splurge, and generally indulge every whim whilst on holiday; and woe betide any killjoy who stands in the way. Leo heaven requires luxuriant surroundings, soft bathrobes and a butler on constant standby with Champagne and strawberries. Relaxation is the order of the day. For the Lion in chill out mode becomes positively lazy. Action packed ideas and package holidays fall short of this sign's ostentatious pretensions. Though occasionally Leo ventures out on the prowl: On the pull, if not on Safari.

VIRGO: Virgo should head for the nearest health farm as an emergency measure. For by the time this sign agrees to a holiday, it is two months too late. Holidays are a stressful idea for this practical earth sign. Workaholic tendencies incline the Zodiac Virgin towards business rather than pleasure. Whilst everyone else is off having fun, Virgo will be exercising a different indulgence: This is not martyrdom, but some bizarre preference, which Virgo would do well to modify. Virgo must be disciplined about relaxation and learn when to head for the hills. Earthy connections recharge Virgo batteries. So walking holidays suit the Zodiac Virgin down to the ground. This sign loves to pamper Mind, Body and Spirit. So anything that expands the aura, if not the wallet is worth Virgo's time and energy.

LIBRA: Hang gliding, Balloon Riding; or any bizarre recreational activity that gets this sign air born is to be welcomed. Libra loves to holiday *en famille* or in a group of bosom buddies. The sign of balance needs convivial company and fun times in order to recharge. Social events of all kinds hit the spot, so long as there is plenty of alcohol on tap and high jinx for entertainment. To have a laugh is the aim of the Libran holiday. This sign does not really need peace and quiet. Indeed too much time alone can drive the Libran nuts. Holiday romance becomes the quest of the season. Along with anything unforeseen that makes the spirit fly. Libran holidays do not have to be planned; spontaneity and a go-with-the-flow groove turn this sign on. Libra is ready for anything or anyone when the sun goes to the head. Be careful out there.

SCORPIO: Deep-Sea diving in the Caribbean does it for Scorpio. But so does the hectic pace of any metropolitan city. Variety, places of interest and unusual activities are needed along with ample opportunity to unwind. Links to water along the way are fundamental or this water sign's batteries will not recharge. Intrigue, mystery and sexy encounters are crucial to satiate the Scorpion appetite. So whatever your relationship status, make an effort to spark up the unexpected on holiday. This sign needs a honeymoon every year: use your imagination. In a way location is not madly important to Scorpio. So long as there is a sense of adventure thrown in, whether it be between the sheets or not, all will be well. Haunted houses, eerie hangouts, and dark nightclubs all appeal to the subterranean depths of Scorpio; especially in restless mode.

SAGITTARIUS: So long as the Zodiac Archer's appetite for adventure is satisfied, this fire sign is a happy holiday bunny. This restless spirit is easy to please, so long as an element of surprise is maintained throughout the season. Not too much to ask for really. Yes, in fact the friendly Sagittarian is not the most relaxing company if you want to unwind! Leave this one to their own devices and they will hit on what is required: usually it lies over the next hill where the grass is greener. Hot spots do it for Sagittarius, who needs to be stimulated at every turn. Whether it be the sweltering heat, the white-knuckle ride, or beneath the sheets, this sign wants to live life close to the edge, and would feel short changed on a reflective retreat with the grand-parents.

CAPRICORN: Posh hotels in beautiful surroundings suit the earthy Capricorn with the Midas touch. Vegas and the Casino world is an acquired taste that may appeal to male Capricorn's in theory. Certainly demonstrations of wealth, fine food and extravagant romantic gesture all happen on the ideal Capricorn holiday. But even those not yet in their material prime enjoy the pretense of being so. This sign attracts financial issues. So in some shape or form holiday enjoyment succeeds or not because of the filthy lucre. Watch out for arguments and stress re money: do not let the same old problems spoil the fun. Holidays are about switching off, indulging a bit and perhaps letting rip with the odd fantasy or two. Go on live dangerously.

AQUARIUS: Long-haul flights to interesting exotic places please Aquarius. But too much hectic, frantic activity is not up this Air sign's street. Remote hot sticky environments suit, so long as the humidity is not too desperate. Aquarius needs variety and stimulation; but only when the privacy groove has been satiated. Holidays have to be on their terms. Part of this prerequisite is that everyone else is happy too...so there should not be too much grumbling in the camp. Family holidays are very important in secret, special places if at all possible. Aquarius can be a bit of a holiday snob and hates to feel part of the rabble. Holiday packages and tours are not ideal for this sign that hates to be dictated to. Aquarians are not boring holiday chums. Their general kookiness and sense of humor provides hours of endless fun. But where there is discord, they will suit themselves.

PISCES: Pisces likes all sorts of nonsense on holiday, so long as there's water involved. Swimming with dolphins, water sports and fishing all suit Pisces. For water signs need to connect with their element to get the best benefits of a proper rest. After dark the Piscean likes to socialize and to connect with the local flora and fauna. Going out and about to see what's on offer appeals to Pisces curiosity. An element of go with the flow is important and Pisces does not like regimented regimes. Boot camp is definitely not an option. Unusual or spiritual places provide the necessary nosiness fix. Pisces likes to experience what it would be like to live elsewhere. So tends to fully absorb the holiday environs, whatever they may be. Psychic sensitivity means that Pisces should be discerning and careful with holiday choices.

19 CAR SIGNS

If you are bit fed up of approaching the cute chick or hunky lad at the bar and asking them their star sign in an attempt to get familiar? Well then, try this! "Hey babe what's your Car Sign?" A prominent company did some recent research, asking over a hundred thousand of their motor insurance customers to assess their driving style. Based on their date of birth. Penalty points were subjected to the rigors of an astrological analysis and it was found that Scorpios make the worst drivers. If offenses on the road are an indication of driving style, Scorpios, with their passionate urge to be in control and obsessive need to have the upper hand, got the top spot. No surprise there then. The survey was only a bit of fun. There was not a hugely diverse range between the main offenders. But Aquarians landed somewhere in the middle, along with Capricorn, and Virgo who apparently drive like grannies. While Taurus was to be found at the bottom of the ranks, making them apparently the best, most careful drivers on the roads. Surprisingly Aries, with their natural spontaneity and risk taking inclinations were the next best behaved at the bottom of the list. This can only mean one thing, because to be honest Aries is probably the astrological sign most inclined to break the law on the roads. Where Sagittarius, second from top, clearly gets caught for speeding; the quick reactions of Aries, get them out of trouble in the nick of time. Their natural understanding of mechanics and how the car works also helps.

The car we choose is a form of self-expression and how we drive it reveals ALOT about our approach to life. Find your Car Sign here below and see if it matches up to your driving style. Watch out for your drive safely clue too!

ARIES: You are impulsive and prone to risks which makes you
vibrant behind the wheel. You love to pull off a stunt and know how to make the car you drive work with you. You are the type who shows what a car can do. You understand the workings of the vehicle you lovingly choose and you know how to get the best out of it. Probably you break the law on occasion but clearly you do not get caught thanks to your ability to move quickly out of situations that compromise you! Your quick reactions are key. As in life, so behind the wheel.

KEY SAFE DRIVING HINT ~ Pay attention and heed others.

TAURUS: Although you are the best behaved of the zodiac
signs when it comes to penalty points, you are in fact a mass of contradictions behind the wheel. One thing is for sure you are methodical and safe. Even when you speed you pride yourself on your safety and you know what you are doing behind the wheel. Top Gear's James May is a Taurus and got the tag of "captain slow" because of the way he dithers on the road. However he was clearly capable of high speeds and was not the one of the team who has had near fatal accidents.

KEY SAFE DRIVING HINT ~ Harmony behind the wheel: at one with your vehicle

GEMINI: One Gemini confessed to me to be alternately speedy and granny behind the wheel. On any given day you can be erratic and changeable as you drive from A to B. If you are in a bad mood it would translate into your driving choices and responses. A grumpy Gemini will cut someone up and leave them by the way side. When you are on a mission to get somewhere, nothing will stop you. But on a sunny day you can be lackadaisical, playful if not a little bit stupid and childish.

KEY SAFE DRIVING HINT ~ Do not get distracted from the task in hand.

CANCER: Cancer on a bad day can be grumpy, temperamental and highly strung. Not exactly safe traits to bring out onto the open road. Watch out for that indecisiveness when driving. Road safety requires focus and definite reactions, especially in dangerous fast moving situations. As in life, so on the highway you can get thrown off track by other's actions. So watch that reactive streak and pay attention to your own way of being. Third from the top in the survey, clearly you need to avoid drink driving also.

KEY SAFE DRIVING HINT ~ Do not drink and drive #nobrainer.

LEO: Leo love the finer things in life, and this applies to their car and king of the road style when behind the wheel. Leo loves to be seen and will make a big noise when not respected. Fellow drivers need to let you do your thing and all will be well. You deserve regal attention and everyone must defer to you and let you take the lead. It is not your style to give way nor to bow out of the race. You are fiery, dynamic and bring a lot of energy to the table. All great qualities for road trips and long distance travel.

KEY SAFE DRIVING HINT ~ Avoid getting annoyed #patience.

VIRGO: It has been said you drive like a granny. But at least this would make you meticulous and careful if not a little nervous on the roads. Develop more self-confidence and settle into your place on the road. You have as much right to be there as anyone. so do not play the meek humble Virgo as this can actually be dangerous when behind the wheel. Translate this into a metaphor for life and you have a pretty good instruction on how to better yourself. Your perfectionist streak is desirable, but that over caution can be a nuisance.

KEY SAFE DRIVING HINT ~ Move over granny!

LIBRA: It is no surprise that you are one of the safer zodiac signs behind the wheel. Ever the strategist, you usually have a game plan of getting safely from A to B in record time. You are balanced and fair and your slightly manipulative streak translates well behind the wheel. Your positive energy gives you the run of the road and traffic parts ways for you as if instinctually. Not much gets in the way of a Libran driver. You do not suffer fools and you get your way. Fair cop.

KEY SAFE DRIVING HINT ~ Focus on your game plan.

SCORPIO: Well the passionate scorpion came of worst in the survey. But it is not all bad. Your need for controlling outcomes and impatience when you do not get your way may be something to do with it. But on a good day, your passion will take you places. You are competitive and determined so of course, you are not inclined to give way to people that should not really be behind the wheel in the first place. Best to recognise that it takes all sorts and then life can run more smoothly, on and off the road.

KEY SAFE DRIVING HINT ~ Modify that unyielding temperament.

SAGITTARIUS: You did not do so well in the survey, and came off next to Scorpio at the top of the table. Why would this be? Well possibly something to do with your spirit of adventure and spontaneity and somewhat loose reactions and behaviour. The rules of the road need to be strictly adhered to for optimum safety. You are someone who marches to your own drum, therefore following rules does not come easy. Hence your penalty points.

KEY SAFE DRIVING HINT ~ Follow the rules as best you can.

CAPRICORN: You came off pretty well in the survey and Capricorns along with Virgos tend to be the granny drivers of the zodiac. You are controlled and purposeful and cautious. This could make you annoying to others who need to see definite moves and decisions. You seem to be always hiding your next move, which also does not make you an easy driver to observe or contend with. Try to be a bit more transparent both on and off the road and you will get better responses from people. Have confidence in you and what you know and this will make you a better more dynamic driver. The go slow is not always safe in life.

KEY SAFE DRIVING HINT ~ Step on the gas a little more.

AQUARIUS: You were pretty much centre stage in the survey which makes some kind of sense of your altruistic tendencies. Your individualistic streak however comes to the fore and no one can see you for dust. You can be a bit touch and go on the roads therefore. Sometimes safe and sometimes a bit spacey and erratic. But always performing on your own terms and in your own style. You are perfectionist and often have OCD type tendencies. So this makes you meticulous on the roads but always on your own terms.

KEY SAFE DRIVING HINT ~ The highway or the by-way?

PISCES: You are the dreamy one in life and behind the wheel, which is okay as you seem to function well enough in your own little world. You would be flexible and give way to other drivers most of the time. But boundaries are always an issue for you. So if pushed for time, you are quite likely to push your luck and your fellow drivers. You would be sometimes obliging, and other times ill-tempered and impatient. Generally you adapt to the conditions of the road and you are safe enough. Just take your time with things.

KEY SAFE DRIVING HINT ~ There is no rush?

20 FEMALE ZODIAC FANCIES

Want to know the best way to treat your mother, wife, or girlfriend on a special day? Follow the guidelines here for assured success with flowers, perfume and other magical tokens. It is important to know how to treat the most important women in your life. So chose with care and give it a lot of thought. Presents from the heart always hit home and your lady friend or relative will be so delighted to be appreciated on any given day.

Fire Signs ~

ARIES: Aries favors anything fast, hot and furious, so red flaming colored clothing always goes down a treat. If you really want to impress an Aries female, a diamond choker or ring does the trick. Alternatively, anything that honors her unique Arian nature shows you care. Aries females have very definite ideas about what they want. The Buzz word for Aries is "I am," so Aries likes to make a statement. Go for materials and clothing in red or gold and remember blue is a color which attracts professional opportunities for Aries.

Always look for sophisticated classic styles. Choose strong definite classy smells if you are buying perfume. It really is best to find out her favorite rather than be too adventurous.

Perfume ~ Chanel no 5 or Tweed is a safe bet.
Flowers ~ Honeysuckle

LEO: It is easy to shop for your Leo female friend if you have ready cash. She loves expensive things and anything that smacks of opulence, luxury or grandeur will hit the spot. If you can afford gold jewelry or ornaments all the better. Classy or monogrammed items work well. So Macey's or Tiffany's vouchers will work if you really cannot decide what to buy. Regal items and rich colors work in head-scarfs, accessories and costume items. The kind hearted queenly lion will appreciate your efforts and anything which suggests luxury will hit the spot. Leo is all heart too, so any outfit that speaks volumes and taps into a quality emotion will win her over. Garments suggestive of sunny climes work well. Motifs and colors containing lion or sun imagery are appropriate. Clothing does not have to be subtle but it does have to be tasteful.

Perfume ~ Decadent perfumes like Opium titillate the taste buds
Flowers ~ Sunflower

SAGITTARIUS: Open-minded Sagittarius loves the whole buzz and adventure of fashion, shopping and unwrapping. so really you will not go too far wrong if you choose something unusual and unexpected for your woman.. She will love any surprise you spring on her and she will simply appreciate the thought you put into it and the gesture. Anything jazzy or slightly mad and off the wall is good. Costume jewelry or clothing that captures the imagination and has a story behind it will suit very well. Ethnic items from foreign shores linking to diverse cultures allow Sagittarius to carry off unusual ideas and looks. Materials and clothing in oranges and peach. Vibrant colors

and exotic fabrics work well. Also any item that reflects Sagittarian spontaneity and sense of humor hits the spot.

Perfume ~ Clarins Eau Dynamisante is fresh and spirited without being too heady.
Flowers ~ Dandelion

Earth Signs ~

TAURUS: Your Taurus woman loves earthy looks and materials, but really any quality item hits the spot. Ruled by Venus, being well turned out is a treasured priority for the sign that requires the best of everything. Rich sumptuous fabrics and deeply regal or earthy colors are favorites. Anything that smacks of luxury is sure to please her. She can be quite conservative with her tastes, so nothing too mad. She loves to feel cossetted and comfortable, so even slippers if all else fails will work! Practical Taurus will not suffer discomfort in order to look good, so be practical in your choices. Clothing in tans, beige, camel, earthy colors, rose and some greens give a splash of color. Remember when choosing gifts that Taurus responds to anything 'Touchy Feely'.

Perfume ~ J' Adore by Christian Dior
Flowers ~ Lily of the Valley

VIRGO: Think Earth mother or nature goddess for your Virgo lady, and you will not go far wrong. Modest gifts and styles that are not too flash or embarrassing will go down well. So do be practical and you really do not have to spend too much to show your appreciation to this zodiac goddess Any style or gift that honors their powerful, but discreet identity will be well received. Virgo go for under stated glamour which gets people talking, but which preserves mystery and privacy. Clothing and jewelry in moss, terracotta, bronze, plus mulberry or berry colors suit Virgo.

Perfume ~ Paris by Yves Saint Laurent is romantic and distinctive.
Flowers ~ Crocus

CAPRICORN: Clothes and gifts that smack of opulence and status will hit the spot for your lady friend. Look for classic labels and subtle lines. Anything of lasting value will be appreciated. Understated classy items that spell class and wealth suit Capricorn down to the ground. If you can even find a well-chosen antique this will be impressive. Remember Capricorn rules the skin, so soft fabrics that skim the skin, or skin treatments and special creams will be much appreciated. Candles, materials and clothing in warm autumnal tones or rich colors like purple and deep blue work well.

Perfume ~ Miracle by Lancome means business
Flowers ~ Carnation

Air Signs ~

GEMINI: Gemini woman needs to receive something curious and interesting. She likes to be kept interested with books, videos, tickets and anything linked to travel. If buying clothes go for cute, busy airy fabrics and styles. You Gemini female loves a talking point, so use your imagination with pressies for her. Any item that makes an impression whereby she can express her personality works well. Clothes which restrict movement are not a good idea. Ditch the corsets and stick to floaty chiffon. Airy, spacious clothes cut imaginatively suit Gemini. Candles, materials and clothing in Quartz Green, Silver, Pale Yellow, Florals, Prints & Stripes.

Perfume ~ Angel by Thierry Mugler
Flowers ~ Lavender

LIBRA: Your Libra female appreciates elegance. New clothes and gifts are appreciated, especially anything with a top-notch designer label. So try to avoid as new and second hand items. Libra has a great sense of humor, so will enjoy quirky, fun gifts. Clothes in unusual colors and light fabrics sit right. Tea dress materials and pastel shades look lovely in the summer. Go for items in pale mauve, lilacs, pastels and all shades of pink. Treat your lady friend to a gift token for a massage and a spa day. Libra loves to receive anything which enhances their beauty.

Perfume ~Arden Beauty will restore Libran balance.
Flowers ~ Foxglove

AQUARIUS: Your Aquarius female possesses a unique personal and sometimes eccentric style. As with everything, she will call the shots and makes a statement without much effort. You need to find things to match her personality and you will know her taste by now. She is very fixed in her ways and not much will change that. So check out her perfume, makeup and cosmetic creams and simply boost her supplies. Your Aquarius lady appreciates comfortable clothing really from any time or era, but it has to be clean. Retrograde styles suit her, and the Bohemian groove works well. Clothing does not have to be modern, so long as Aquarius likes it, it looks good. Go for items in powder blue, aquamarine, cornflower, sky blue, lilac and violet.

Perfume~ DKNY. Any scent that stands out and gets her noticed.
Flowers ~ Orchid

Water Signs ~

CANCER: Your Cancer woman enjoys antiques and anything of historical interest, so styles and gifts that are modern with a hint of times gone by are just perfect. Cancer does not like old moldy items worn years ago, so second hand goods are out unless they are very well preserved. This sign loves anything romantic, floaty and steeped in antiquity. She does not like anything too formal. Look for a tasteful piece of jewelry or an unusual signature scarf. She will not like anything too common or what everyone else is receiving, so do make a real effort. Your Cancer lady is a one-off, and has to be appreciated as unique. Go for the colors of the sea, purples, lilacs and 40 shades of green. Pearls and silver make an impression, and delicate jewelry will buy you many favors. Avoid gold.

Perfume ~ Givenchy's Very Irresistible is romantic, sensual
Flowers ~ Lilies

SCORPIO: Your Scorpio female is easy to please as long as you make a significant effort to save and put her before all others on this fine day. Only slightly kidding here! Anything sensual and expensive will impress. It does not have to be too pricey, so long as it is quite sexy it will work. Anything you buy should be designed to make her feel like a million dollars. Of course if it is from you, that is half the battle won. The obvious choice is lingerie or under wear, so team up with Dad for a sumptuous gift box. Anything smart works and a nice pair of ear rings will hit the spot. Colors to go for are pinks, purples, indigos and black.

Perfume ~ Samsara or Poison are exotic and very Scorpio
Flowers ~ Chrysanthemum

PISCES: Seeing as Pisces rules the feet, shoes are of the utmost importance to your Pisces lady. See what you can find out there for her, but keep the receipt as she is quite picky when it comes to her foot ware. Quite plain clothing works for your Pisces woman, so you could even get a crisp white shirt or some other classic item. It is worth clubbing together with siblings to get something really nice for her. Bright colors and risky styles in shoes and costume jewelry suit your lady, and she expresses herself with the little items and trinkets that make her feel special. More of the same gratefully received. Clothes or items that have a fairy or angelic quality suit your magical Pisces female very well

Perfume ~ Elizabeth Arden Beauty, Eau de Parfum: it is floral, light & refreshing.
Flowers ~ Lotus Blossom

21 HEAVEN SCENTS

Just as each astrology sign has recognisable personality traits, so each is prone to specific physical strengths and weaknesses. The ancient physician Hippocrates recommended compatible herbs and plants for the treatment of the typical zodiac complaints he identified. Medical Astrology now is a respected and reputable practise which yields incredible results. Aromatherapy is a powerful way of capturing the healing essences of flowers and herbs in oily suspension. These oils can be used to anoint candles, burned in diffusers, or added to a steaming bath. Learn how to work with the oils which support your personality and physical ailments. Your zodiac sign has a specific connection to certain oils, aromas and plants. This is a complex healing system, but the basics are applicable to all of us in some shape or form.

Here below I have outlined the signature oils for each zodiac sign. This is the oil which will lend you the most support in your daily life. But remember your natal chart is sophisticated. So if for example you are having a tough time emotionally, find out your MOON sign in the earlier chapter, and use the oil which specifically resonates with that Zodiac Sign. If you are trying to attract love into your life and you know the Zodiac Sign of the person you find compelling, use the oil which best resonates with their energy. Want to boost your luck at a particular time of year? Then use your own oils in combination with the oils which resonate to the specific month involved. There are many applications for using these magical oils. So get creative and use your imagination.

ARIES: Signature Oil ~ Rosemary

Rosemary is warming and no nonsense. It supports Aries energy when extra power and commitment is needed. It hits the spot and directly mirrors the impact an in-your-face Aries often makes. Rosemary is great for headaches. A few drops in some boiling water makes a great inhalant in a bowl with a towel over the head. Aries is high energy and always on the go. Rosemary has a soothing affect and stills the mind.

Companion Oils ~ Lavender & Bergamot

Lavender calms the mind and soothes the soul, and it is highly protective also. A few drops on the pillow at night with sort out the most stubborn case of insomnia. This oil is very supportive of mad frantic Aries, who sometimes finds it difficult to unwind. Bergamot calms the temper, and works well for the hot headed Aries who has sometimes has trouble controlling their anger and off the wall reactions.

TAURUS: Signature Oil ~ Rose

Rose links to the planet of love Venus which of course is the ruler of Taurus. This scent is beautiful, sumptuous and highly erotic. It suits the Taurus earthy groove, and is both intoxicating and alluring. Taurus loves luxury and needs to feel appreciated and expensive. Rose oil plays to this drive and supports Taurus with all their emotional and physical needs. Rose oil is pricey, but Taurus does not mind spending on the best, as long as it serves them well.

Companion Oils ~Sandalwood & Frankincense

Taurus needs to feel safe and secure and reassured. Sandalwood and Frankincense banish insecurity. These scents and oils inspire self-confidence and a sense of innate well-being. Both are luxurious and perform with depth and sincerity, which totally suits Taurus sensibilities. Highly sensual, these products offer a hint of decadence also.

GEMINI: Signature Oil ~ Basil

Gemini is a highly focused sign, prone to being obsessive re ideas, goals and inclinations. Basil has a great "chill pill" effect on this highly strung zodiac sign. Gemini cannot put something down once it is begun and will work mad hours until a task complete. Basil offers a sense of perspective, and encourages the recognition that tomorrow is another day. Basil revives a flagging bran also where there is a deadline to complete. It works towards the best outcome for the user. It has a variable application which is perfect for the versatile and multi-tasking sign Gemini.

Companion Oils ~ Clary Sage & Rose

Gemini is prone to over thinking and worry too much. Clary Sage is great at dispelling angst and anxiety. Rose is a good balancing oil for the Gemini twins. The conflicting voices vying for predominance do not get a word in edgeways and calm descends. The dual nature of Gemini responds particularly well to Rose which primes the heart for decisive action.

CANCER: Signature Oil ~ Blue Camomile

Family is fundamentally important to Cancer. The need to love and be loved is the *raison d'etre* of this nurturing sign. Blue Camomile is highly relaxing and sensual. It suits this water sign's need to unwind and de-stress. This mothering oil is supportive and comforting. It is calming, soothing and a great oil for use on children. Cancers often have upset stomachs caused by worry and stress. This oil relieves stomach cramps, and brings a warming effect to the solar plexus when rubbed directly into the skin.

Companion Oils ~ Sandalwood & Cinnamon

Cancer is known for their moodiness and they can become easily annoyed by the slightest irritant. Sandalwood is a great leveller and excellent at diffusing a bad mood. Cancer is also highly sentimental and they find it difficult let go of anyone or anything at all. Cinnamon evokes the memories and encourages a healthy perspective. Very evocative of Christmas, Cancer finds the scent heart- warming and supportive emotionally.

LEO: Signature Oil ~ Jasmine

Leo is of royal lineage and only the best will do. This zodiac regal creature loves luxury and does not scrimp on extravagant gestures. Jasmine oil is the best of the best, aptly called the king of oils. Jasmine resonates with the sun and is highly compatible with Leo who needs to feel special. Leos are born at the height of summer, and they need the warmth and nurturing of this exotic oil. Bergamot inspires self-confidence and self-love, which may or may not be a good thing.

Companion Oils ~ Bergamot & Ylang-ylang

Leo loves to be adored, and when the zodiac lion goes unappreciated, the consequences are not pretty. Bergamot is a great aroma for lifting the senses and the spirits. Directly associated with the Sun, Bergamot inspires a sunny disposition and brings a heart-warming glow to the user. Ylang-ylang is supportive of the throat centre, very important for the lion who needs to be self-expressive and above all *heard.*

VIRGO: Signature Oil ~ Lavender

Virgo is always the first person to offer support and a helping hand to those in need. Virgo links to the summer harvesting, abundance and horn of plenty. Not so much the zodiac virgin, as the prolific and productive nature goddess. Virgo is closely associated with inner healing and vibrant health. Lavender oil is a great for destressing, and is highly protective. Virgo can be over fixated on their own health and can become quite neurotic. Lavender has a powerful calming effect which stills the mind and supports deep sleep.

Companion Oils ~ Peppermint & Cedarwood

Peppermint stimulates the Virgo creative drive, making this hard working sign, productive and unstoppable. Virgo is often over worked and overloaded with responsibility. So Peppermint instils natural balance, and the impulse to ease off the gas a little. This scent encourages Virgo to be less compulsive and more selective. Cedarwood is balancing and calming, so also very helpful to a stressed anxious Virgo.

LIBRA: Signature Oil ~ Geranium

Libra requires inner equilibrium, fairness and justice to dominate their world. For peace of mind and tranquil resolution, Geranium is a great balancer. Venus bestows a love of fine things, appreciation of beauty and the determination to keep things in harmony. An off balance Libran is not a pretty sight. Geranium in perfume or aromatic products gives Libra a great boost and ensures inner serenity. This scent suits Librans refined sensibilities, and enhances their expression of beauty and honesty.

Companion Oils ~ Rose & Marjoram

Rose is a scent and oil directly linked to the planet Venus which rules Libra. Geranium is an acquired taste, so its replacement with delicious, comforting Rose, works well. Librans often suffer from back pain, so Marjoram is a great one for the medicine cabinet when mixed with a carrier massage oil.

SCORPIO: Signature Oil ~ Patchouli

Patchouli is dusky, distinctive and sensual. A great match for seductive Scorpio, this scent and oil gets powerful results. This energy works deeply and is transformative at a profound level. It is therefore perfect for the phoenix-rising-from-the-ashes phenomenon that is Scorpio. Scorpio is a private zodiac sign that finds it difficult to trust. Patchouli encourages the expression of real emotion and has great healing potential for a shut-down control freak. Patchouli is also a great aphrodisiac, greatly compatible with erotic, intense Scorpio. Use this oil in the bath for the best results.

Companion Oils ~ Ginger & Lemon

Ginger has an unmistakable and lively tang. Associated with the planet Mars it does not mess about and it urges a result and quickly. Ginger is intensely energizing and a great aphrodisiac also. Lemon oil supports the heart which is good for opening up energies which maybe a little closed down. For overly secretive and self-protective Scorpio, this is significant.

SAGITTARIUS: Signature Oil ~Black Pepper

Black Pepper is a great vibrational match for the determined Sagittarian, who is set in their ways and fixed on their direction. Black Pepper does not mess about with the senses. It is in your face, and makes a direct hit. It is a great tonic for tired muscles and an over fatigued mind. Like the Archer's Cupids bow, it shoots the target head on. Sagittarians are physical, active and up-for-it personalities. They have a quick flowing energy and although they seem to have great reserves, all of a sudden they crash and burn. Black Pepper is great for massage in combination with other oils, soothing intense aches and pains with ease. It is a great pick me up for those who suffer from jetlag also.

Companion Oils ~ Rosewood

Sagittarius has a lot of surplus enthusiastic energy which can make this fire sign somewhat hyper at all the wrong moments. Rosewood oil calms the jitters and is calming. Also associated with Jupiter the ruling planet of Sagittarius, Rosewood is a good luck booster and general tonic.

CAPRICORN: Signature Oil ~ Vetiver

Vetiver is an oil which directly supports the earthy nature of Capricorn. In the far east Vetiver is known as the oil of tranquillity. This mellow grounded and relaxing aroma supports the ever busy Capricorn, who always has some place to be. Capricorn often gets overloaded with stress and an exaggerated sense of obligation. Vetiver disperses the angst and corrects that inner tension. Capricorns often suffer joint problems and structural skeletal issues. Vetiver is a great anti-inflammatory which can be directly rubbed into painful areas.

Companion Oils ~ Amyris & Lemon

Capricorn is always striving and busy. Life is one endless responsibility involving achievements and tasks. Amyris oil aids relaxation and peace of mind which is invaluable for Capricorn. Lemon helps keep an already busy bran alert and on point. A great anti fatigue oil, Lemon supports Capricorn with a heavy work load.

AQUARIUS: Signature Oil ~ Neroli

Aquarians can appear to be quite detached, cool and aloof. This is a very independent sign, which prides itself on its self-sufficiency. The Aquarian is quite happy to keep his or her own company. Neroli has an aromatic and meditative energy which appeals to the Aquarian's soul. Also an aphrodisiac, this scent supports the sex life, and gives a warm tingling feeling all over. Aquarius needs to remember the importance of acknowledging personal needs. Relationships tend to be more social for the Aquarian. Neroli brings another more interesting suggestion into the mix.

Companion Oils ~ Marjoram & Cinnamon

Aquarians can be prone to nervous disorders, so a soothing mellow oil like Marjoram is just perfect. This oil helps to disperse stress and has a calming influence. Cinnamon supports the great cerebral brain activity of the Aquarian who lives largely in their head. This oil boosts focus and concentration and is great where there is a deadline to deliver.

PISCES: Signature Oil ~ Melissa

Pisces is the water sign of the fish, and Melissa the most watery of oils is a great support for the two fish that swim in different directions. The Lemon balm plant which yields the fragrance has a high water content, so it takes a lot of compression to create just a small amount of this precious oil. Pisces is typically a compassionate sign, often sacrificing much personal energy for the sake of others. Melissa is an oil that encourages the nurturer to look after themselves a little more. It is a soothing comforting way to destress. Pisceans can also be prone to depression and Melissa is uplifting and is said to disperse dark thoughts and intense oppressive moods.

Companion Oils ~ Cinnamon & Fennel
Cinnamon will enhance the natural and latent psychic tendencies of Pisces, while Fennel is useful to ease addictive tendencies, giving inner strength when tempted to overindulge.

22 ZODIAC TRAITS

Want to understand the main traits of your Zodiac Sign, and those of your loved ones? Here below is a comprehensive list.

ARIES: Assertive, Urgent, Spontaneous, Energetic, Forthright, Enthusiastic, Decisive, Quick Witted, Confident, Active, Restless, Vibrant, Instinctive, Rash, Physical, Impetuous, Irresistible, Impulsive, Mind Blowing, Dynamic, Street Wise, Impressive, Gorgeous, Selfish, Pioneering, Bold, Courageous, Resourceful, Aggressive, Survivor, Impatient, Egocentric, Emotional, Out-spoken, Hot Tempered, Extroverted, Excitable, Domineering, Thoughtless, Strong Minded.

TAURUS: Stoic, Reliable, Stubborn, Determined, Loyal, Sensual, Cautious, Methodical, Practical, Possessive, Self-indulgent, Warm, Tactile, Commonsensical, Fixed, Materialistic, Astute, Patient, Systematic, Compelling, Persuasive, Focused, Willful, Persistent, Judgmental, Faithful, Permanent, Dedicated, Enduring, Inert, Immoveable, Ingrained, Predictable, Trustworthy, Passive, Steady, Tenacious, Introverted, Domesticated, Sturdy, Lazy.

GEMINI: Flexible, Versatile, Multi-Talented, Multi-Tasking, Curious, Mutable, Mercurial, Intelligent, Easily Bored, Stimulating, Cerebral, Funny, Interested, Interesting, Mischievous, Inquisitive, Fun, Charming, Beguiling, Skillful, Communicative, Canny, Witty, Sharp, Restless, Adaptable, Changeable, Enigmatic, Quick, Attentive, Impatient, Flirtatious, Flighty, Lively, Highly Strung, Independent, Mentally Active, Unemotional, Cool, Highly Expressive, Adaptable.

CANCER: Sensitive, Emotional, Affectionate, Caring, Protective, Moody, Loving, Nurturing, Maternal, Comforting, Changeable, Grumpy, Manipulative, Controlling, Imaginative, Compassionate, Psychic, Deep, Nostalgic, Possessive, Spiritual, Vindictive, Sharp, Kind, Demanding, Empathetic, Melancholic, Forgiving, Quiet, Sullen, Sentimental, Taciturn, Lunar, In-Tune, Security Conscious, Self-Interested, Black and White, Attentive

LEO: Generous, Expansive, Bossy, Impressive, Self-Assured, Emphatic, Full of Heart, Leader, Kind, Loyal, Creative, Colorful, Friendly, Dictatorial, Performing, Impressive, Powerful, Regal, Dignified, Self-Centered, Dramatic, Catty, Proud, Compassionate, Abundant, Energetic, Fearless, Committed, Firm, Flamboyant, Theatrical, Humorous, Fierce, Authoritative, Persuasive, Bright, Lazy, Sumptuous, Scrumptious, Luxurious, Magnificent, Bitchy.

VIRGO: Analytical, Critical, Modest, Intelligent, Discerning, Clever, Smart, Efficient, Eloquent, Articulate, No-Nonsense, Reasonable, Wry, Witty, Charming, Captivating, Facilitating, Passionate, Earthy, Motivated, Diligent, Effective, Talented, Oracular, Always Right, Infuriating, Meticulous, Grafter, Conscientious, Fastidious, Mentally Agile, Vibrant, Unique, Compelling, Evolved, Worrying, Restless, Anxious, Intuitive, Straight-forward.

LIBRA: Refined, Elegant, Gracious, Balanced, Sociable, Lively, Fair, Just, Charming, Easy Going, Diplomatic, Gullible, Resentful, Sympathetic, Strategist, Seductive, Romantic, Flirtatious, Courteous, Suggestive, Team Player, Discrete, Democratic, Non-Confrontational, Distinctive, Polite, Impractical, Cool, Low key, Quietly Confident, Self-seeking, Refined, Indecisive, Uneasy, Harmonious, Musical, Loving, All-Embracing, Cute.

SCORPIO: Passionate, Intense, Intuitive, Magnetic, Profound, Compulsive, Secretive, Insightful, Psychologist, Super Savvy, Canny, Obsessive, Charismatic, Hypnotic, Confident, Mysterious, Jealous, Controlling, Powerful, Charmed, Magical, Kinky, Sarcastic, Fearless, Enduring, Willful, Imposing, Cruel, Sadistic, Transformative, Suspicious, Curious, Private, Deep, Determined, Resilient, Loyal, Shrewd, Irresistible, Spell Bound.

SAGITTARIUS: Free thinking, Philosophical, Adventurous, Up-for-it, Optimistic, Intellectual, Explorative, Tactless, Indiscrete, Casual, Searching, Inquisitive, Truthful, Logical, Humorous, Flirtatious, Witty, Charming, Grandiose, Vivacious, Outspoken, Independent, Fun Loving, Chatty, Lively, Changeable, Affectionate, Extrovert, Naïve, Child-Like, Hilarious, Sociable, Non-Judgmental, Accepting, Obliging, Sweet, Inoffensive.

CAPRICORN: Serious Minded, Authoritative, Earthy, Softly Sexy, Matter-of-Fact, Conventional, Conservative, Prudent, Calculating, Practical, Disciplined, Ambitious, Querulous, Dignified, Discrete, Cautious, Successful, Businesslike, Commonsensical, Masterful, Shy, Restrictive, Controlling, Staid, Classy, Sensible, Dutiful, Earthy, Reliable, Cold, Insecure, Measured, Mighty, Astute, Articulate, Smart, Winner, Systematic, Unhurried.

AQUARIUS: Independent, Honest, Original, Inventive, Distant, Unconventional, Quirky, Eccentric, Detached, Objective, Humane, Distant, Knowledgeable, Private, Discrete, Clever, Sharp, All-Seeing, All-Knowing, Visionary, Wise, Genius, Paradoxical, Stubborn, Generous, Compassionate, Intellectual, Inscrutable, Revolutionary, Friendly, Humane, Unemotional, Gifted, Aloof, Cool, Uncanny, Maneuvering, In-Control, Timeless, Old Soul, Self Sufficient.

PISCES: Dreamy, Imaginative, Vague, Kind, Soft, Intuitive, Psychic Sponge, Easily-Led, Duplicitous, Esoteric, Spiritual, Impressionable, Ambiguous, Emotional, Complex, Ambivalent, Indecisive, Companionable, Mystical, Channel, Dual Natured, Self-Sacrificing, Escapist, Confused, Artistic, Introverted, Potentially Deluded, Ungrounded, Floaty, Ethereal, Other-Worldly, Space-Cadet, Too Nice, Obliging, Deceptive, Aware, Higher Consciousness.

23 ZODIAC IDENTIFIERS & TIPS

Want to understand the main markers and identifiers of your Zodiac Sign, and those of your loved ones? Here below is a comprehensive list. Find your Zodiac day of the week, your Zodiac Guardian Angel, and the main features of your Star Sign.

ARIES

Ruling Planet: Mars
Gender/Duality: Masculine - Positive
Element/Triplicity: Fire - Inspirational Level
Quality/Quadruplicity: Cardinal – Enterprise, Ambition
Primal Desire/Planetary Principle: Leadership/Action
Day of the Week: Sunday
Zodiac Angel: MACHIDIEL – Self-esteem, Assertiveness, Individuality

Life Tip: You are a born survivor and have the energy to achieve great things. Always busy, you can appear to be quite self-absorbed. However when you fall in love (or lust you are quick to pounce. Be careful that this passionate drive within you does not land you in trouble.

Aries can burn out quick, which is fine if you want to love them and leave them. In the long run though you should think of your reputation and go for someone who can handle your sense of mischief and fun. Try to develop your tolerance levels. You do hate people to disagree with you, and are well able to find ways to convince them to change their minds. Watch out for this tendency to manipulate just because you want your own way. Learn to live and let live.

Your mantra is very much "I am" and that is that. This is admirable, as we have to take it or leave it where you are concerned. But do not be in such a rush, or you stand to miss out on many of life's experiences. Do not be afraid to take action with someone you are unsure about and see where you get to with each other. The partner who looks uneasy is just overwhelmed by you, not repulsed. If your love has problems or a broken heart give them a chance as they are worth the effort. You will be duly rewarded.

TAURUS

Ruling Planet: Venus
Gender/Duality: Feminine - Negative
Element/Triplicity: Earth - Practical Level
Quality/Quadruplicity: Fixed – Strength, Willpower
Primal Desire/Planetary Principle: Stability/Production
Day of the Week: Friday
Zodiac Angel: TUAL – Patience, Stability, Security

Life Tip: Taurus is a charming, and sensual being, who loves to feel secure and in control. If you are Taurus, you will have to watch that possessive streak with partners, and lose the tendency to assume ownership of your conquests. With your tender touch it is unlikely that lovers will complain too much. A surprising aspect of your nature is your shyness when it comes to making connections sexually.

You are quite passive and need the opposition to take the initiative-well, you prefer it.

Taurus does not like to put itself on the line for love. If you are not a sure thing- forget it, Taurus will not even come close Your good looks and natural charm open many doors. But be careful not to accumulate a string of flirtations that come to nothing.

Keep your options many and varied, but remember to decide eventually. If you have a partner take a breather now and again. Make sure they do not cramp your style. Do not allow jealousy to mess up important relationships. You are caring, considerate and love sex. What more could a lover wish for? If you do not treat your partner as a possession there is every chance you will keep them for an eternity.

GEMINI

Ruling Planet: Mercury
Gender/Duality: Masculine - Positive
Element/Triplicity: Air - Mental Level
Quality/Quadruplicity: Mutable – Flexibility, Versatility
Primal Desire/Planetary Principle: Communication/Versatility
Day of the Week: Wednesday
Zodiac Angel: AMBRIEL – Adaptability, Communication, Relationships

Life Tip: Gemini can do and think several things at once- always useful! You have boundless nervous energy and need variety and stimulation to keep you sparkling. Your nature is naturally flirtatious and lively which puts you streets ahead when it comes to scoring with the opposite sex. Watch out for superficiality and try not to flit around quite so much.

Commitment is an alien concept for Gemini and future lovers and friends will have your dual personality to contend with. An outlet is needed for that logical positive mind and its accompanying nervous tension. Deception and fraud are a highly likely if you do not nip questionable behaviour in the bud.

CANCER

Ruling Planet: The Moon
Gender/Duality: Feminine - Negative
Element/Triplicity: Water – Emotional Level
Quality/Quadruplicity: Cardinal – Enterprise, Ambition
Primal Desire/Planetary Principle: Security/Love
Day of the Week: Monday
Zodiac Angel: MURIEL – Reticence, Self-reliance, Contentment

Life Tip: Cancer can be like the changeable sea – calm and tranquil one minute, brooding and threatening the next. "Crabbie" is an apt nickname for you when you hide under that shell silent and scowling. But to those you love, you are kind, receptive, caring and protective.

Your imagination is second to none. Just be careful it does not invent worries and dilemmas that do not exist. Use it positively and your natural psychic ability will blossom and never let you down. You are a true romantic and lovers are in for a treat when you get going. But love needs to be equal and returned or things will get ugly. Do not waste your time on losers Claustrophobia in relationships is not good. You do not want to chase people away with too much love and kindness.

Your big heart gets over enthusiastic at times so watch that tendency to smother. Those Crab pincers can puncture holes in things if you hold on too tight. Give people room to breathe and all the love in the world is yours to play with.

LEO

Ruling Planet: The Sun
Gender/Duality: Masculine - Positive
Element/Triplicity: Fire – Inspirational Level
Quality/Quadruplicity: Fixed – Strength, Willpower
Primal Desire/Planetary Principle: Power/Creativity
Day of the Week: Saturday

Zodiac Angel: VERCHIEL – Courage, Leadership, Loyalty

Life Tip: Leo expects lots of attention and loves being centre stage. You are generous hearted and a great friend. Be careful you do not choose mates and lovers who always agree with you. Variety is the spice of life. Leos are the performers of the universe - a little proud and arrogant perhaps, but charming and full of life at the same time. You need people around you who can match your enthusiasm and exuberance. If the love you give is not returned you get deeply wounded, so choose wisely. For lesser mortals (other zodiac signs) your passion for life can be overwhelming. Go for the person who gives you the eye, then follows it through with definite action. The 'wishy-washy' approach will not do it for you. So if he/she does not match you 100% back off – only real men/women need apply.

VIRGO

Ruling Planet: Mercury
Gender/Duality: Feminine - Negative
Element/Triplicity: Earth – Practical Level
Quality/Quadruplicity: Mutable – Flexibility, Versatility
Primal Desire/Planetary Principle: Crystallisation/Purity
Day of the Week: Wednesday
Zodiac Angel: HAMALIEL – Physical Health, Social and Administrative Skills

Life Tip: Strangers would call you aloof and cool, but those who know you will vouch for your warm loving nature. You are practical and intelligent and very little escapes your attention. Try not to be so self-critical. Develop your self-confidence, as this will serve you well in years to come. You are much better looking than you appreciate. Believe the compliments and then you will not waste time doubting or undermining yourself. Modesty is attractive but not when it gets in the way of love action! You are faithful and kind. Any person lucky enough to bed you will surely wed you. Virgos are fussy in love so if there is a lack of available talent, hang in there. Do not be tempted by the serial seducer! In matters of the heart intensity is your middle name. If you are in love remember it is cool to be cool - let your man/woman do the running.

LIBRA

Ruling Planet: Venus
Gender/Duality: Masculine - Positive
Element/Triplicity: Air – Mental Level
Quality/Quadruplicity: Cardinal – Enterprise, Ambition
Primal Desire/Planetary Principle: Union/Balance
Day of the Week: Friday
Zodiac Angel: ZURIEL – Straightforwardness, Balance, Conformity

Life Tip: Librans love company and your gregarious nature thrives on social activity. Do not be afraid to be lonely as you never will be, but do learn to be alone and content in your own space. Be careful to make gestures of love and friendship from the heart without expecting a return. Love is freely given and it will find you if you give up the frantic search. You fall in love easily so do not mistake flirtation for a declaration of devotion. Romance is heaven sent for Librans and you give everything when you love someone. Be prepared for surprises in love and do not believe all the cliches - it could be Mr-nice-guy who strings you along and forgets your birthday, whilst Jack-the-lad turns up on the doorstep with bouquet and sheepish grin! Alternatively the flirtatious lady could turn out to be just right for you, while the shy girl is tedium personified! Reserve judgement and follow your gut instinct in matters of the heart. Let the hormones do the talking for once. And ignore that endless chatter in your head.

SCORPIO:

Ruling Planet: Pluto/Mars
Gender/Duality: Feminine - Negative
Element/Triplicity: Water – Emotional Level

Quality/Quadruplicity: Fixed – Strength, Willpower
Primal Desire/Planetary Principle: Control/Power
Day of the Week: Tuesday
Zodiac Angel: BARAKIEL – Risk taking, Opportunity and Self-development.

Life Tip: You have a reputation as a sexy creature. But you can be a bit impatient and intense. So do ease up on the control and security issues.

Do not shoot yourself in the foot and miss romantic opportunities: you can be too cautious at times. Be careful not to avoid someone because of shyness. Although it shows you are seriously interested, it might also send them running. You are meant to be the demon love god/goddess remember?

Watch out for jealousy and trust your partner a little bit more. A fresh start is always a good idea for you, so do not be afraid to wipe the slate clean and begin again. Lose your nervousness if you want to attract that person – a sense of humour and a nice smile should do the trick. Fix them with those eyes of yours and hypnotise to full effect.

Mystery is fine and attractive: intense negative behaviour is not. Expect stormy times and make the most of passion. Scorpio must ride a roller coaster of emotion, but it can be fun.

SAGITTARIUS

Ruling Planet: Jupiter
Gender/Duality: Masculine - Positive
Element/Triplicity: Fire – Inspirational Level
Quality/Quadruplicity: Mutable – Flexibility, Versatility
Primal Desire/Planetary Principle: Liberty/Expansion
Day of the Week: Thursday
Zodiac Angel: ADNACHIEL – Optimism, Power of Vision, Expansion

Life Tip: Freedom is so important to Sagittarius that any form of confinement can drive you quite nuts. You need to feel there are endless options and possibilities open to you. Make sure you do not break too many hearts in your quest for greener pastures. You can be quite difficult to pin down, so someone to keep you on your toes is the best option for long term happiness. If you can find the partner you cannot quite understand all the better. Your exuberant sexiness will win many admirers so enjoy the ride as you have the pick of the field.

Keep your options open and Jupiter your ruler will guide you in the right direction. Others might be watching you hoping that you trip up. Not a chance. Plan your strategy and the game set and match is all yours. Guard against boredom, as this is the one thing that can undo all your good intentions. Endless stimulation is a pressing need for Sagittarius, so if you have found what you are looking for do not blow it. Single Sagittarians should go with the flow and trust the universe to deliver.

CAPRICORN

Ruling Planet: Saturn
Gender/Duality: Feminine - Negative
Element/Triplicity: Earth – Practical Level
Quality/Quadruplicity: Cardinal – Enterprise, Ambition
Primal Desire/Planetary Principle: Attainment/Crystallisation
Day of the Week: Wednesday
Zodiac Angel: NADIEL – Confidence, Thoroughness, Determination

Life Tip: Self-confidence is your birth right but this can be daunting for those with insecurities or silly agendas. Use your humour to win others over, if you can be bothered. Slow to fall in love, you savour the flowering of your emotions. There is plenty of fun to be had when you relax, but you need to know where you are headed first. Chill out a bit, or your ambitious, controlling streak may be your romantic downfall. Sometimes you can be too proud for your own good. Be prepared to admit mistakes and move on.

Remember that with enough determination you can conquer any mountain you wish to climb. Focus gets you absolutely everywhere.

Dare to be brave and wear your heart on your sleeve - the rewards will be huge. When you fall in love it is usually for keeps. A sure thing is what you both offer and expect. Fair enough! Just make sure that you do not miss out on all the fun.

AQUARIUS

Ruling Planet: Uranus
Gender/Duality: Masculine - Positive
Element/Triplicity: Air – Mental Level
Quality/Quadruplicity: Fixed – Strength, Willpower
Primal Desire/Planetary Principle: To Know and Understand/Truth
Day of the Week: Saturday
Zodiac Angel: CAMBIEL – Ambition, Principles, Ideals

Life Tip: Aquarians love to live life on their own terms and guard their privacy fiercely. Because of this you can be difficult to get up close and personal to, never mind dangerous with. Be careful of sending mixed signals to the opposite sex. You do not want Mr or Miss Right to pass you by! Be aware that like a magnet you can repel and attract in equal measure. So smile extra sweetly and spell out your interest to a loved one. Playing hard to get may help you win the heart of Mr or Miss Popular. But do not shoot yourself in the foot and miss out completely! Be aware that you will always need a certain amount of freedom. So stay away from partners, friends and careers that cramp your style.

Guard against a tendency to come across as obnoxious. You often are right, but others will not thank you if you live as if you are always so. You mean well and have a loving, compassionate heart. But feel as if you can always sort things out when push comes to shove. This personal confidence is sometimes overbearing, so learn when to keep silence.

PISCES

Ruling Planet: Neptune
Gender/Duality: Feminine - Negative
Element/Triplicity: Water – Emotional Level
Quality/Quadruplicity: Mutable – Flexibility, Versatility
Primal Desire/Planetary Principle: Unification/Sacrifice
Day of the Week: Thursday
Zodiac Angel: BARAKIEL – Sensitivity, Imagination, Thoughtfulness

Life Tip: Pisceans are the dreamers of the Zodiac. You are clever, visionary and creative and tend to put the needs of others before your own. This will make you a loving parent and provider. Be careful not to tax your mind with needless worry as you have the tendency to conjure up many scenarios with that vivid imagination. Certainly avoid sending the opposite sex running for the hills with unfounded accusations. Try to relax.

You are sensual and loving, but put the brakes on if you sense that your partner is getting claustrophobic. Give someone a chance and allow a relationship to take off. Attract lovers who let you act out your fantasies, who respond to your warm attentions. Do not beat yourself up over your inherent indecisiveness. It is part of your Piscean legacy and you will need to go-with-the-flow of your changing emotions. Make the most of your creativity, cleverness and poetic vision. But try to stay awake and keep your feet on the ground; if you can find them!

24 ZODIAC GUARDIAN ANGELS

You may or may not be aware that each Zodiac sign has its own special Guardian Angel. But of course we also have our own Guardian Angels who assist us with our particular wants and needs. As you open up and get to know your Angels, why not start with your Zodiac Guardian? Find more information on your Zodiac Angel and be open to how they can help and guide you.

Can Angelic Light help you to connect with your Soul Mate? Help you track down the ideal career? Or even help you find those keys? Do not be surprised to hear that the answer is a big resounding "yes!"

Our Angels are ever ready to work with us and assist us with our concerns. But we do have to ask. As well as connecting with us through prayer and religious ceremonies, they also want to become involved in our daily lives. Angels respect our free will and do not make themselves known to us unless we *actively* honor their presence. However, if we are in a life threatening situation, and it is not yet our time to shake off this mortal coil, they *will* intervene to uphold God's will. Aside from their role of protection, Angels are God's messengers and they are able to help us in so many different ways. As long as our requests are within the remit of the heavenly order, we really should not be afraid to ask.

No, Angels are *not* a substitute for belief and faith in God, or our own particular religious inclinations. But they are available to us to work with, to guide us, and to open up our hearts and minds; if only we dare risk it. Never mind the skeptics in our midst, working with supernatural guidance is in fact a completely *normal* phenomenon; more normal perhaps than trundling through life blindly without any heavenly assistance at all. Now who in all honesty really wants to do that?

Get to know your Angels by listening to the promptings of your heart. You may at first dismiss the impressions you get as mere imagination or fantasy. But learn to trust what is happening and you will open up to a world of wonderment and magic. No, it is not some kind of madness; though you do have to learn to test the guidance you receive to make sure it is legitimate, and from the light side. The Bible urges us to "test the spirits," and if we are working closely with our Guides and Angels, this is *very* important indeed.

Angels communicate with us through our dreams, through daily signs and wonders, and through our intuition. Learn to trust the whisperings of your intuition and the link with your Angels will continue to grow and develop. It is important to ask for *protection* and *grounding* when you are working with your Angels. This is where the prayer bit comes in. Simply ask to be guided as you go about your day, and do not be afraid to trust the heavenly hosts with your big issues and problems either. Miracles do happen. You will find that the more you belief and trust, the more you will be assisted and guided in amazingly natural ways. It really is worth taking that leap of faith. What do you have to lose?

ARIES

Zodiac Angel: MACHIDIEL
Self-esteem, Assertiveness, Individuality

With Machidel by your side, be vigilant and do not run headlong into situations that you have not thought through properly. You are daring, brave and dynamic, but need to be more circumspect. Allow Machidel to guide you forward. Ask to be shown when a leap of faith will pay off. Equally be open to the guidance that your latest mad idea may not actually be a good one. Do not be too proud to listen to your guidance. Machidel may indeed save you from embarrassment time and time again. So look before you leap and ask to be shown when a risk would backfire spectacularly.

Remember, your Guides will not let you go too far wrong; unless of course there is a valuable lesson to be learned. One thing is for sure; with Machidel as your Angel you will be picked up, brushed down and sent back out into the fray fairly lively.

Use your confidence to great effect and do not be afraid to make brave decisions. Just be careful not to get too bogged down in material concerns at the expense of your spirituality. Machidel is on hand to remind you of your higher purpose and of the great things you can achieve, if only you would trust a little bit more.

TAURUS

Zodiac Angel: TUAL
Patience, Stability, Security

Tual is an Angel who supports your systematic, measured nature. This Angel connects with those who plod through life. People who have a strong Taurus element to their Natal Chart are tenacious and determined, but tend to get blocked when they start to panic. An off balance Taurus can be possessive and obsessive, holding on emotionally in fear of change. Taurus needs to maintain the Status Quo, and can get very stuck when resistant to matters out-with personal control. For this reason Taurus is a past master at burying his/her head in the sand.

For passive Taurus, Tual's stabilizing influence is indeed a God send. Call on Tual for help, particularly when you feel wobbled by a person, situation, or big adjustment. Tual assists your inner security and self-reliance; stabilizing you whenever you feel shaken. But to reap the full benefits of this Angel's guidance, you must learn to surrender control re material worries and concerns. Trust Tual to demonstrate that you will always be looked after and provided for by the heavens above. Tual will also assist any Taurus going through traumatic adjustment or profound change. Allow Tual to open your heart and mind, enabling you to embrace life in all its glory.

GEMINI

Zodiac Angel: AMBRIEL
Adaptability, Communication, Relationships

Ambriel is an Angelic messenger who assists our flexibility within relationships as well as our ability to communicate. This Angel has a wicked sense of humor and loves to help you analyze situations as well as elevate your consciousness. Ambriel loves to get caught up in mind games; so you can expect this Angel to run merry rings around you. This may not sound like much fun. But Ambriel will help you to lighten up and not take things quite so seriously. Your link with Ambriel warns you to avoid taking on too much. Be careful not to absorb the negative energy of those who seek out your terrific wit, intelligence, and mind power.

Guard against burn out and trust that Ambriel will prompt you when you are taking on too much, or being too nice. One of your lessons for this life is to learn when to say 'no'. You cannot be all things to all people, though there is no doubt you will have fun trying! With Ambriel's help, you must be ever mindful of how grounded you are. One thing is for sure, you love to put your ideas across. Ambriel will help you discern when to speak and when to remain quiet.

You will not go far off track with this loving, but mischievous Angel at your side.

CANCER

Zodiac Angel: MURIEL
Reticence, Self-reliance, Contentment

Muriel encourages you not to sit on your feelings, ideas and intuitions. You must learn to trust your gut reaction, for it represents Muriel's guidance in your life. The more you tune in and listen to what you know to be correct; the more your inner-tuition, or inner teacher will guide you. For all those with a strong Cancer element to their Natal Chart; family, hearth and home are very important. Muriel helps you to appreciate your loved ones and connect with them whole heartedly. Watch for those moments when you are too self-sufficient and self-contained. Of course these are admirable qualities. But sometimes you need to steer clear of "cutting off your nose to spite your face." Try not to be too fixed in your outlook and trust that Muriel will teach you greater flexibility and forgiveness.

Your biggest challenge is the restlessness or grumpiness that hits you every so often. When this happens, ask Muriel to guide you quickly to its cause (for the sake of everyone who lives or works with you). With patience, you will learn to see a pattern and will be so much of a victim to moodiness you do not even understand. Muriel will help you develop your self-awareness and psychic abilities if you choose. Trust the process.

LEO

Zodiac Angel: VERCHIEL
Courage, Leadership, Loyalty

Verchiel is a messenger of God who supports courage, leadership and loyalty. With the guidance of this Angel you are likely to be all heart, generally up-for-it and very creative. You have an inspirational spirit which attracts others. When in balance you are filled with compassion and love for your fellow man. But on the down side are inclined to be too readily available. In your anxiety to please and make heartfelt connections, you sometimes strive too hard and consequently waste a lot of energy.

Work with Verchiel to find a workable equilibrium; then discern who is worthy of your time, and who is not. You have a particular frequency that leads you into challenges requiring sound judgement and vision. Despite your upbeat and strident nature, you possess inner insecurities that occasionally force you to test people's loyalty. But you are able to rise above life's trials and will always use the full force of your imagination to extricate yourself from situations that are not working.

Learn to take more time with Verchiel's help. If you learn patience and think things through, you will not get into half the scraps that you do! Your strong emotions and open heart are a God send. Use them to full effect, and embrace the good stuff.

VIRGO

Zodiac Angel: HAMALIEL
Physical Health, Social, Administrative Skills

Hamaliel encourages you to be very health conscious and aware of your physical reality. It is no accident that off balance Virgo can be something of a hypochondriac. But at least your interest in all things healthful puts you on the right track for a long life. You are a stickler for detail and very hands on with the practical stuff. Ever the diplomat, you have great skills of empathy and are able to appreciate all sides of an argument.

Hamaliel assists you in juggling your commitments and enables you to keep all your balls in the air. You are easy to get on with and very flexible; just watch that you do not become too soft though. A pushover does not demand much respect after all. Attend to your needs and give yourself equal priority to everyone else. Access a bit of oomph and do not feel so obliged to help. If you open up to Angelic guidance, Hamaliel will help you find the way forward in even the most contentious situations. Choose your moment and you will easily make the right links.

With all your issues, actively ask for this Angel's guidance and stop that tendency to overanalyze things. Hamaliel will steer you to the quickest most effective solution at breakneck speed. Stop ruminating and trust life's intrinsic simplicity.

LIBRA

Zodiac Angel: ZURIEL
Straightforwardness, Balance, Conformity

Your inner balance is so important to you, that you sometimes miss out in a bid to maintain your equilibrium. Your tendency to prevaricate means that life can sometimes pass you by. With Zuriel's help, learn to pin point what is worth going for, and what you should avoid. Until you learn to trust Angelic Guidance, you are likely to come unstuck time and time again.

When you dither in your pursuit of beauty and harmony, you often miss out. Life's rough edges have a certain charm after all; so perhaps learn to redefine your definition of beauty, and foster your sense of humor. Your skills of judgement and ability to conform are without question. But loosen up a little with Zuriel's help and you will gain a whole lot. Find the still small voice within and learn to identify the moment when it is safe to act. Once you have that intuition or prompting, you must not waiver.

When you are out-of-sync, you are inclined to continually weigh up the positive and negative aspects of your options. This may sound like a good ability to have, but after a certain point, it really gets you nowhere. Access the love factor and give fear short shrift. You do not always have to act within the expected boundaries of what's acceptable.

SCORPIO

Zodiac Angel: BARAKIEL
Risk taking, Opportunity and Self-development

Barakeil assists Scorpio with astute decisions and personal development. If you are Scorpio, you naturally have impressive psychic and spiritual savvy, which can be developed to quite formidable levels if you choose.

Barakeil provides you with Angelic guidance and inspiration, nudging you forward and encouraging you to take risks. This Angel helps you materially with business ventures and practical decisions. But also steers you towards enlightenment and renewed consciousness. Barakeil helps you to wake up to the truth on many levels. So prepare to open up to Barakeil's prompting and be surprised at what you can achieve and where you can get to. Tap into your intuition and use your great focus to make dreams and visions a reality. You will begin to appreciate the formidable personal power that you possess. Just be careful not to fall into the temptations of manipulation and control.

The down side of being Scorpio is the likelihood that life will deal you a blow now and again. Scorpio is inclined to get flattened every so often to learn the lessons of trust and inner strength. Fear not though! Like the phoenix rising from the ashes Scorpio is a master of regeneration and survival.

SAGITTARIUS

Zodiac Angel: ADNACHIEL
Optimism, Power of Vision, Expansion

Adnachiel supports your eternal optimism and sense of adventure. Life is never dull in the arms of this Angel's loving care. Ruled by Jupiter, you have determination, vision and are intrinsically lucky. But with Adnachiel's help, you can achieve even greater things and be a brilliant inspiration to others. This Angelic guidance will bring you boundless opportunities in the form of travel, relationships and mad ideas. You are a fun filled character, with a wicked sense of humour and nose for mischief! On the down side though, you can be quite pushy and domineering. Your stubborn streak is legendary, and you will not take "no" for an answer. When you feel restless, bored, or out-of-sorts, ask for Adnacheil's assistance. Then sit back and await inspiration, for your next big idea is bound to be divinely inspired.

Try to soften your approach within relationships and don't tease loved ones so mercilessly. From time to time your blunt, outspoken nature is likely to get you into trouble. But you are a great communicator; at least others know where they stand! Allow Adnachiel to refine your energies and your inner and outer life experience. This will take you on a fulfilling spiritual adventure and lighten you up.

CAPRICORN

Zodiac Angel: NADIEL
Confidence, Thoroughness, Determination

Being Capricorn you have a tough, focused exterior. Your air of natural confidence makes you very determined and focused as you go about your business. Generally, you know what you want and how to go about getting it. As you project good stuff into the ether, you are clever at concealing any anxiety and insecurity lurking beneath the surface.

Nadiel, your Zodiac Angel is there for you to help you heal from the inside out. Under this Angel's guidance you are encouraged to soften up a bit, and not to be so hard on yourself. Let go of past trauma and disappointment. There is no need to remain bogged down by what went on in times gone by. Lighten your load and cast your burdens onto your Angelic assistant.

Trust Nadiel to guide you on the right track and learn to heed your hunches when it comes to big decisions. You may feel the logical route usually makes sense. But as you get to know your Angel better, you will discover that heaven has a completely different agenda that works wonderfully well; bringing you even more than you ever thought possible. You are an independent, thoughtful soul, who could benefit from giving something a little bit different a fighting chance. Allow Nadiel to guide you.

AQUARIUS

Zodiac Angel: CAMBIEL
Ambition, Principles, Ideals

Being looked after by Cambiel you are a great visionary, who can see the ins-and-outs of all situations, people and possibilities. Your skills of objectivity and detachment are enviable. But you also possess great sensitivity, which makes you vulnerable to hurt from time to time. Cambiel, your Angelic assistant inspires you to be compassionate and principled.

Your innate altruism is supported by your heavenly guides, and you are destined to do great work for all humanity if you choose to befriend your best self. Cambriel helps you to connect more closely with your Divine purpose. But this does not have to be a grand or daunting prospect. Keep your feet on the ground, and you can be of practical help too. As your intuition develops, your spiritual antennae may also become more sophisticated. Just do not get lost in out-of-this-world notions.

Appreciate the little things in life and allow the heavenly hosts to guide you. Trust Cambiel's ability to help you balance commonsense with lofty insights. Then you really can have the best of both worlds! Your best achievements occur when you ditch the emotional issues that block your progress. Prepare to receive Cambiel's healing and so embrace a great future.

PISCES

Zodiac Angel: BARAKIEL
Sensitivity, Imagination, Thoughtfulness

You share your Zodiac Angel with Scorpio; but Barakiel brings you different life experiences and lessons to your fellow water sign. Being Pisces, you possess great sensitivity and imagination. But you do struggle with the duality of your nature. The fish that swim in two directions, symbolize your place in the heavens. This makes life tricky when you are off balance. You can be changeable, deceptive and unfocused on a bad day. But on a good day, your mutability, thoughtfulness and gentle nature put the rest of us to shame.

Call on Barakiel to help you balance your sometimes contradictory nature. This Angel is on hand to inspire you creatively, psychically and spiritually. You possess great natural gifts that can be developed for the good of all. And of all the Zodiac signs, you are the most awake spiritually. You incarnate with an innate understanding of what makes the universe tick. Barakiel your Angelic assistant will help you to access your best self and inspire you to make the best choices.

Barakiel will also help you overcome your phobia of commitment and your tendency to get caught up in inappropriate notions. Try not to drift aimlessly through life. Learn to trust Barakiel to define the best way forward.

25 ASTRO HEAVENLY HELPERS

What Spiritual Guidance and Messages do your Celestial Guides have? No task is too major for the heavenly hosts, so why not surrender your problems and issues to the powers that be and allow the angels to work miracles in your life. Can the Heavens above help you to be recession proof? Yes I am pretty sure they can. Remember, God and his winged messengers are bigger than the recession and every other hardship that we may be experiencing. Relax a bit and give the heavens a chance to intervene. Step back and see what happens. Here are some more heavenly helpers your Zodiac Sign can call on, as you feel the need.

ARIES

Angel Oriel looks after your destiny and guides you fully. Do listen to your intuition about what to do and when as you assess your life game plan. Trust that still small voice within as your intuition has the answers. Angel Tabris honors your free will and asks you to think things through. You can be proactive with your own destiny. God will give you the answers you need, but you must keep a look out for the messages which occur along the way. Those synchronicity moments are clues about what your priorities should be. You must think on your feet.

Angel Zeruch supports you physically bringing you extra strength. Call on Zeruch for extra help as you go about your business. Angel Zeruch helps you to meet challenges head on and brings you divine inspiration for the road ahead. Hang in there in situations which test your patience and be assured. You will get great results. Prepare to be very pleased, very soon.

Zuphlas is the Angel of nature, who links especially to trees. When you feel things are too hectic get out and about in a wooded area to shift your angst and stress. Be assured that any negativity around you will shift very quickly if you get out into nature as soon as possible. Feel your problems melt away.

TAURUS

A new level of heavenly support is coming at you, as long as you are ready to receive it. Can you handle it? Embrace what is on offer and be delighted at how things work out. You will triumph. Ask Angels of abundance to help you release fears re not having enough money or resources. Trust that you will be provided for in perfect ways. Understand that on a deep level God provides for you however fraught you feel your circumstances to be.

Allow the Angels to work their magic in your life, and be thrilled at the answers you get. Watch and listen out for clues as you what you should do. Do not doubt what you know to be true. The skeptics of the world would have us believe there are no such things as Angels. Prepare to see them wonderfully disproved, and keep your faith in the magic of life. Ask the Angels of abundance to support you. It is faith in God's provision that ensures a steady supply of what you need. Do not wobble; be grateful. Do not hold onto fear.

You are looked after in all areas of life. The Angels see your concerns. Remember you have to ask for their help to receive. They will not interfere with your free will. All of your prayers will be answered in one way or another, so do not feel ignored by the Heaven's above.

GEMINI

You will attract every good thing if you simply trust your Angels and God to guide you. Say yes to what the Universe requires of you at the moment. Archangel Chamuel will help you fall in love with life all over again. If you have been down hearted do not despair. You are very much loved by the Heavens Above.

Archangel Raphael is on hand to help you breathe away old trauma and the out worn patterns of behavior that hold you back. Prepare to be revitalized by Heavenly help and breathe on your problems and issues. If you need guidance, your Angels speak through hunches, ideas, intuitions and dreams. If you are in any doubt, stay still and be silent. You will then receive impressions re what to do next.

Archangel Uriel will support you and confirms that your best idea on a matter of importance was your most recent. Go full steam ahead and follow your hunches. You will not make a mistake. Go for it. Archangel Chamuel will support you with an immanent career change. Embrace new opportunities whole heartedly. These will link you up with the right people and places. Chamuel sees situations clearly. If you ask this Angel for clarity, you will be shown what to do and when to do it.

CANCER

The Angels are not limited by time or space. They will be there for you; but you do have to ask. What do you need help with? No doubt it will be very evident. Ask for the help you need. Balance schedules and let the Angels help you find the right balance. Give equal weight to love, work, family and friends. Most importantly give equal weight to you. If you feel overwhelmed by current responsibilities, ask the Angels to help you find the space for productive time-out. Trust that you will be shown the way forward; you will be. If life is off balance you will understandably feel tired and drained.

Remember there is enough time for everything. Ask for an Angelic time warp to give you a breather and lighten up your way. It works. Accept that there is Heavenly Help for what troubles you. There will be a natural solution soon. Archangel Michael is a warrior Angel who is God's heavenly bouncer. He will protect and look after you if you call on him. Stay true to yourself as you encounter your current life challenges. Do not allow bullies or subversive people to get the upper hand. Stay light and bright; you will conquer all.

LEO

Do not be too proud to ask and listen to guidance. Machidel will save you from embarrassment, so look before you leap and ask to be shown when a risk would backfire. Machidel will pick you up, brush you down and send you back out into the fray fairly lively. Be confident and do not be afraid to make brave decisions. Ambriel loves to get caught up in mind games. This Angel will run merry rings around you. Ambriel will help you lighten up and not take things quite so seriously. Your link with Ambriel warns you to avoid taking on too much. Do not absorb the negative energy of those who seek to drain you.

Angel Hamaliel encourages you to be health conscious and aware of your physical reality. Do not become a hypochondriac; but do take an interest in all things healthful. Hamaliel assists you in juggling your commitments and enables you to keep all your balls in the air. Be easy to get on with and flexible; but not too soft though. Angel Adnachiel supports eternal optimism and a sense of adventure. Life is never dull in the arms of this Angel's loving care. Be determined, have vision and access you innate lick factor. With Adnachiel's help, you can achieve great things and be a brilliant inspiration to others.

VIRGO

Barakiel will help you overcome a phobia of commitment and a tendency to get caught up in inappropriate notions. Try not to drift aimlessly. Embrace the best way forward. Our Angels are ever ready to work with us and assist us. But we do have to ask. They want to become involved in our daily lives. Until you learn to trust Angelic Guidance, you are likely to come unstuck. Loosen up with Zuriel's help. Find the still small voice within and learn when to act. Once you have that intuition you must not waiver. Do not bother to weigh up the positive and negative aspects incessantly. Access the love factor and give fear short shrift. You do not always have to act within the expected boundaries of what is acceptable. Angels do not; why should you?

Barakeil provides you with Angelic inspiration, nudging you forward, encouraging you to take risks. This Angel helps with business ventures and practical decisions. Barakeil helps you to wake up to the truth on many levels. Prepare to open up to Barakeil's prompting. Be surprised at what you can achieve and where you can get to.

Tap into intuition and focus to make your dreams and visions a reality. Appreciate your personal power; but be careful not to be too controlling. You cannot be all things to all people, though there is no doubt you will have fun trying. With Ambriel's help stay grounded. Learn to chill out a little bit more. Stress bites. Ambriel will help you discern when to speak and when to stay quiet. You will not go far off track with this loving, mischievous Angel at your side.

LIBRA

If you are an independent, thoughtful soul, who could benefit from giving something a little bit different half a chance. Allow Nadiel to guide you wisely. Ask the Angels to enhance your vision so that you can see the ins and outs of all situations, people and possibilities. Cambriel sparks up sensitivity and guides you in wonderful ways. Appreciate the little things in life and allow the heavenly hosts to guide you. Trust Cambiel's ability to help you balance commonsense with lofty insights. You can have the best of both worlds if you ditch the emotional issues that block your progress. If you are an independent, thoughtful soul, who could benefit from giving something a little bit different half a chance, allow Nadiel to guide you wisely.

Ask the Angels to enhance your vision so that you can see the ins and outs of all situations, people and possibilities. Jeremiel helps you to review life. If you need a new game plan for life. Call on this Angel for insights you had not yet thought of. Jeremiel is expert at prompting memories and insights. Those with selective memory syndrome will be quite surprised at the revelations Jeremiel brings up. There is no hiding from the truth with Jeremiel on side.

Jophiel can help you with creativity. Call when you need novel ideas and a heavenly muse. Jophiel is expert at lifting negativity and restores peace amidst chaos. Call on Jophiel when things appear to be beyond repair, when you are weighed down and burdened. This Angel will shift what is holding you back..

SCORPIO

Cut ties with those who drain your energy with Archangel Michael's help. When you feel tired for no reason, the chances are someone is tapping into your energy field negatively. It is probably unconscious, but do call on Michael to sort it. No one will come to any harm and you will feel a whole lot better.

Jeremiel heals emotions and gently stirs up suppressed issues so that they can be finally forgotten. Jeremiel assists development of clairvoyant ability and vision too Call on this Angel when you need a dose of inspiration to get you past creative blocks. Things will move along and come unstuck.

Call on Angel Jophiel if you feel in need of a make-over. Jophiel appreciates beauty and will guide you to the right colours and styles for YOU. A divine input in your choices could make all the difference to your confidence. Also, when your thought processes are confused call upon Jophiel to restore inner-peace.

Raziel helps with spiritual understanding. He guards God's secrets and can assist you with complex questions. If you are feeling blocked ask Raziel for clarity now. Equally if you wish to develop your gifts ask Raziel to lead you to the people who will assist you. Archangel Jophiel assists you as your dreams become realized. You really can make a great impact in life and must persist to make things happen. Have you been exploring material routes to happiness? Let the Angels guide you onto a more fulfilling path for life, which will bring you everything you wish for.

SAGITTARIUS

Feel the passion of what is going on your life and embrace love completely. Breathe out negativity and be inspired with all the opportunities coming your way. Azrael will enable you to find empathy for difficult people. Archangel Ariel will help give you the courage of your convictions. Hold fast to what you know. The right understandings and circumstances will arise to assist you.

Archangel Michael will help you manifest your heart's desire. He will protect you as you find the best way forward. Focus and be clear about what you want to happen. Archangel Sandalphon urges you to find peace within. Just switch into the Angelic Zone and all will be well. Be still within and remain confident that things will pan out wonderfully well. There are no mistakes only lessons that will stand you in good stead. Transform those problems NOW. Do not engage in conflict or needless niggles.

Angel Sandalphon will guide your decision-making process. There is really no rush, so take your time with your next moves. Listen to gentle music to soothe your mind and soul. Sandalphon speaks to you through music so take note of lyrics when you turn the radio on. Love will find a way and you will get the answers you are looking for. Remain open hearted and open minded as you prepare to receive this month's gifts from God. Remember, you deserve to receive. Raphael urges you to assess your lifestyle, diet and exercise regime. Are you doing all you can?

CAPRICORN

Still your soul and await developments. Archangel Jeremiel confirms you have done a Trojan job overcoming setbacks and difficulties thus far. The worst is now behind you. You have doubtless learned a lot and will be now able to help others and yourself more. Use empathy and understanding this summer. To attract new and loving situations into your life, stay positive. Jeremiel will help you find solutions to tricky problems. You will triumph quite spectacularly.

Archangel Haniel renews your passion and zest for life. Claim a fresh start and attract new people, places and circumstances. When you are stuck in the midst of a tricky problem, the answers may elude you. Ask your Angels to light the way forward. You might as well hand it all over to heaven for the time ahead. You may need a break from pressing routines. Ask your Angels to create a gap that makes sense.

Archangel Jophiel reassures you that your dreams are coming true. Be patient as the seeds you have planted ripen and do not panic that it is all going to fall apart at the last minute. Archangel Ariel confirms that the time is ripe. You are ready to spread your wings and fly. Change is daunting at the best of times. Be assured that with the help of your Guardian Angel, you will be able to fully embrace new opportunities.

Archangel Haniel supports you as your sensitive nature develops. Protect yourself as the insights and intuitions flow. Archangel Michael will look out for you. All you have to do is ask. There will soon be cause for celebration, so stand firm with what you know to be right. Your intuitions will be validated and the Angels will bestow many blessings upon you. Accept the clean slate on offer. Every day is a new day.

AQUARIUS

Angels will light your way forward. Tread brightly into the future and trust what is happening. It is bound to be good, so let things pan out and let the Angelic realm look after the details. You just need to be receptive to guidance and be willing to follow through with the next appropriate action. Ask the Angels for a clear sign if you are supposed to make definite moves at this time. There is no rush; but you do not want to miss out on something important, right? Be comforted that your Angels surround and protect you at all times. Nothing much can go wrong really; you must worry less. Believe in yourself and know that the Angels are on hand to help you. Stay grounded and remain as humble as possible; though I am sure you will soon have reason to feel very smug indeed. Pay special attention to your dreams.

Your Angels will be relaying important messages to you at night. Be mindful of your waking emotions. This will give you a clear clue as to how you really feel. You are being helped by the heavens, even if it does not always feel like it. Trust that what you are experiencing is in your best interests. See what you can retrieve from it a situation. Your prayers for special love will be answered and a Soul Mate is on the way, if not already with you. Angel Love supports you and will turn things around in good ways. Stay positive.

Let go of anger and any simmering resentment you are holding onto. It is not doing you any good. Archangel Michael protects you from lower energies; you are safe. You do not need to fret about the unseen and things beyond your control. Your guidance now is to concentrate on what you can influence. You know what to do.

PISCES

Test the waters with a new idea and ask for Angelic guidance to confirm whether or not it is the right way forward. It is Okay to experiment and assess how you feel as you go. If you need to consult a professional, legal, medical or financial, ask Angels to lead you to the right person. Magical energy surrounds you now. Make a wish and trust for its outcome. Focus on what you want to happen and listen to your heart.

Your ability to manifest is potent. Let go of limitation and see yourself succeeding; your Angels will guide your way forward. You will soon have an amazing offer. It is okay to be powerful as long as you are powerful with a good hear.

Develop your personal power with the Angels help and nurture your talents. Be careful whom you trust. Archangel Michael will protect you. Do not be victimized or bullied for a moment longer. Let go of all self-blame going back into the deep distant past. Ditch resentment; there really is no point holding onto hurt. Let all that residue emotional pain go. It may well be time to consider your options as you assess the possibility of a new direction.

Gabriel will help you ask the right people the right questions. Do not be shy; follow through. You may need healing re father or authority issues if you feel confined or compressed in your circumstances. Ask your Angels to heal any outstanding problems or issues between you. Difficult karma can be sorted at any point if you show willing. Let your Angels lighten your load. Chamuel brings you peace and comfort. Be assured and take stock.

26 CELTIC ASTROLOGY

CELTIC Astrology. I'm a Tree! What tree are you? Our ancient ancestors on this fair emerald isle resonated strongly with the trees around them. Every month was assigned a tree rather than an astrological sign. Find yours here below.

BIRCH
24th December – 20th January

You are trustworthy and courageous. It takes lot to bring you down as you are innately optimistic and quietly confident. You cope with the rough stuff quite effectively, remaining efficient amidst life's trials and tribulations. You are a born survivor who knows how to melt into the background when required. Your wicked sense of humor inspires many people. Even though you are a traditionalist at heart, you are not boring.

Life Stuff: Life is designed to strengthen you and test your mettle, so as a Birch you are likely to have had severe tests in family situations. You understand feelings of isolation and loneliness, but once you have weathered life's trials not much then gets you down. Your wit and fun side enrich your days and you are able to put things behind you quickly.

Love Stuff: Love, romance and passion come and go for you. And even within your most established relationships there is likely to be an ebb and flow. Do not stress about the apparent changeability of your love life. Simply adjust to each phase and stay as relaxed as possible.

ROWAN
21st January – 17th February

You are a unique individual with a great sense of humor. Difficult to read, you keep the rest of the world guessing. Your maverick nature stretches what is possible and on the back of not much at all, you get results. You hate authority and make the rules up as you go along. But you are a compassionate soul, who will step in to help whenever possible. Even though you have a calm exterior, you feel things deeply and hide intense passions.

Life Stuff: You are a live wire, with an experimental nature. Your creativity and imagination stand out, and your talents will inevitably take you far. A bohemian soul, you are off beat and quirky. But you have the qualities of a natural leader. Others rely on your composure and integrity, and you are great in a crisis. Laziness *really* annoys you.

Love Stuff: A free spirit, you do not commit easily. Old fashioned romance and tradition are not your style. But for the lucky partner who captivates your heart, you are a great catch. Unconventional love moves make you unpredictable in the sack, and you are never boring.

ASH
18th February – 17th March

You are a funny mixture. Highly intuitive and sensitive, you also tell it like it is. Though not exactly a push over, you are quite easily swayed. Like the Ash, you bend in the wind; but you do not break easily. People are attracted to your empathetic nature, and natural charm. But you see the light and dark within personalities, remaining non-judgmental and compassionate. Wise, spiritual and discerning, you are not in the least bit dismissive.

Life Stuff: You are artsy, but not pretentious. Despite your great creativity, you are surprisingly conventional and unpretentious. Structure is important to you as you feel vulnerable when things are out-of-sync. Channel your energies effectively, and you stand to make oodles of cash. You have the Midas touch, but must guard against being hurt.

Love Stuff: You do not play by the rules in your love life. The dual aspects of your nature often conflict and you do not settle easily. In fact you can be quite fickle and changeable until you decide what it is you want. Intense and romantic, you are just not very reliable.

ALDER
18th March – 14th April

You are a dynamic, competitive character who hates to take "no" for an answer. With terrific courage and panache you are destined to achieve great things. You take the initiative in life and your faith is reflected back to you in spectacular ways. Sometimes impatience gets the better of you, and others may find you arrogant. But you are loyal, effective, and good to have on side. Just do not let that stubborn ego block your progress.

Life Stuff: Your entrepreneurial skills will take you far. You thrive on intelligent risks, and are a great instigator of projects. Be careful that you do not get seduced by flattery though. You are a sucker for adoration, and tend to play it cool so people fawn around you. But you are magnetic and make a formidable opponent. There are no flies on you.

Love Stuff: You are independent, thrilling and *love* sex. You may marry on a whim, even though co-dependent relationships do not really grab you. Commitment does not give you a buzz, but your sexiness makes up for it. You are a spectacular lover; but as for spouse?

WILLOW
15th April – 12th May

You are extremely loyal and will defend those you love to the hilt. Although you like well-defined boundaries and value the Status Quo, you adjust to swift change when you have to. Your keen intuition advises you what to do and you instinctively know when to act. Although you love the safety and comfort of what is familiar, you also know when to walk away. Psychic and mysterious, you live on your wits and keep us all guessing.

Life Stuff: You are generally healthy and stoic. But for your sanity's sake, learn to forgive and forget. Worry and stress may accumulate if you do not learn to let go of old emotional trauma. Undo the knots of a power struggle; then life will improve hugely. A restless spirit, you are destined for great success *only* when you have found your niche.

Love Stuff: You are intense and passionate, and it is difficult to fathom your complexity. If you marry young and get stuck, your children become a lifeline. You are likely to experience attraction to someone *much* older or younger. The *right* person brings balance.

HAWTHORN
13th May – 9th June

You are a spontaneous spirit, but you also know how to come up with a strategy. Clever at spotting people's weaknesses and strengths; you make a supportive sympathetic friend, or a manipulative, exploitative opponent. Inspirational with a great sense of humor, others seek out your company. Your charisma and charm bring many blessings. But when you feel threatened it is a different story. Do not rise to the bait; tap into positive creativity.

Life Stuff: Your mind power and willingness to experiment are your great gifts. You are destined to remain mentally agile well into old age. Always trust your hunches and act on impulse when it feels right. This is your lucky charm for this life, giving you the edge in competitive situations. You love to perform and have a well-developed altruistic streak.

Love Stuff: Your great bond with your lovers is your ability to be a great friend first and foremost. You need variety and can be quite restless, so you are only likely to settle for good when you connect with your true soul mate. You are destined to have fun searching.

OAK
10th June – 7th July

Your generosity of spirit is legendary, and you have a wicked sense of humor that puts a light spin on even the heaviest situation. Your charm takes you places, and when you *focus* you can bring about spectacular events. You are honest and possess unique integrity. But when hard-done-by or off balance, you can be quite egocentric, attention-seeking, and inclined to gossip. Trust in your optimistic streak and you will win out.

Life Stuff: Because you value the truth, you can be naïve and say too much in contentious situations. You do put yourself through it, shouldering more blame than perhaps you have to. Not very street wise, you are willing to play the martyr on a matter of principle. With your big dreams and cunning plans, things can go either way, but you inevitably hold-fast

Love Stuff: Your high standards make you picky in your love life and vulnerable to heartache. You set yourself up time and time again, by expecting too much from people. Try to understand that human failure and betrayal are part of life's rich tapestry, and chill.

HOLLY
8th July – 4th August

You are a strong, resilient character who is loyal and reliable. But sometimes you put conditions on your time and energy. You have an iron will and can be *very* bloody-minded. When off-balance, you are quite needy and overly sensitive. Tap into your hidden strength and develop a perverse sense of humor; that should help. Keep your heart and mind open, for you are an affectionate and trustworthy soul. Why change that?

Life Stuff: You possess a meticulous, careful streak. Very with-it financially, you have an eye for an investment. But you steer clear of mad ideas that have no substance. Privacy and time alone are important, since your problem solving abilities mean that people often pull at you for answers. You are generous and funny, but you *do* know when to step back.

Love Stuff: Commitment is crucial to your equilibrium. You are quite religious and certainly you are the marrying kind! For better and for worse, you see things through. But you are not in the least bit boring. Caring and kind; what more could a lover wish for?

HAZEL
5th August – 1st September

You are too nice for your own good. The problems you face often derive from people who are not as straightforward as you. Usually, kind and considerate, when off balance, you can be nervous and a little paranoid. But you are highly sensitive and extremely intuitive. For this reason your relationships get complex, as you see through even the most subtle lie. However, you are diplomatic, genuine, and usually suffer in silence.

Life Stuff: You are organized and clever, with a great eye for detail. You honor your commitments and maintain a high standard. But you sometimes inspire jealousy and sabotage from those less capable; which hurts. Private moments keep you sane, though you do love to travel. Recoup your energies frequently, and protect yourself at all times.

Love Stuff: A genuine soul, you care deeply for loved ones. Under that cool exterior, you are earthy and sensual. Others often misread you, assuming you are aloof and unapproachable. Actually you are loyal, warm and highly affectionate once you get going.

VINE
2nd September – 29th September

You have an individual style and unique way of doing things. But you are changeable and your moods are a wonder to behold. More than a bit clingy when off balance, you have been known to have the odd temper tantrum. On a good day, you are kind and caring; on a bad day, you have tunnel vision and cannot see past your own agenda. Even though your emotions keep you on the edge, you are good company and your laughter is infectious.

Life Stuff: You need variety and there is always lots going on around you. Of course, life throws challenges at you, but you are a born survivor. When you commit to something, do see it through. For when you find the right career, you are destined to be successful if you persist. Mix and match clothing and hobbies, but be consistent with the work stuff.

Love Stuff: You are a passionate, feisty being, full of fire and energy. You do not often experience burnout when you are up-for-it. But when you do lose interest, or get diverted, you are off fairly lively. Lovers find it difficult to keep up with your earthy sensuality.

IVY
30th September – 27th October

Sometimes you stand out from the crowd; other times you pale into the background. It all depends what mood you are in. In general, you are stoic, consistent and low key. But you have your mad moments, and you do not miss a trick. Your quick wit weeds out anyone fake or phony and you are likely to be quite psychic. On occasion you attract dubious company and weird experiences. But you move on quickly and it takes a lot to defeat you

Life Stuff: Light, airy places, people and experiences help you balance your tendency to attract the dark stuff. You are compelling, fascinating and reel in a wide variety of friends and options without even trying. Sometimes you're rolling in cash, other times you have not a bean. But you are essentially magical and lucky, so expect good things.

Love Stuff: You are romantic dreamer, who can be quite ruthless when the loving is done. Love grabs you quickly and things get intense super-fast. But on waking up the next morning, you may wonder what all the fuss was. Only kidding, but you catch my drift.

REED
28th October – 24th November

You are overwhelming, dominant and forceful; a powerhouse indeed! With great energy and inspirational ideas, you are destined to multiply your resources and talents, way beyond the scope of your original expectations. Your imagination and flare annoys certain people. But you know how to be subtle and seduce those who resent your brilliance. Charisma, charm and your ability to squash nonsense, win you a great many friends. And once you set your heart on something; it is yours within minutes.

Life Stuff: Hardy and resourceful, life throws a lot at you. But you are courageous, fearless and not much fazes you. You like to be kept on your toes, because inner confidence assures you, it will work out just fine. Adjustments come easy to you, and until you land in a scenario that fulfills your (fairly normal) expectations, you keep busy.

Love Stuff: You are an intense bundle of passions! Persistent and tenacious, you will not let go until you have landed your prize. Learn to back off though, or your suspicious nature and possessive streak may cause problems. Pace yourself: Can you keep it up?

ELDER
25th November – 22nd December

You are patient, and possess oodles of discipline, which is great for your focus. Generally you achieve impressive results, and fulfill your ambitious nature. But you can be quite autocratic and difficult to persuade. You are the one who runs the show. If things are going your way, you keep people on side with your wicked sense of humor. But if there is a rebellion in the ranks you will manipulate and scheme to retrieve the situation.

Life Stuff: You love people and accumulate a wide range of friendships throughout life. Fame and fortune attract you, but you must not be seduced by it. You can go far if you do your thing. People respect you, but do not take their support for granted. Watch that extravagant streak. You do not need to buy favors or give into desperation. Trust life and relax.

Love Stuff: You have it made. Relationships do not faze you. You can enjoy them on your own terms and do not take things too seriously. Your light approach protects you and you do not get involved to the point of no return. Marriage is cool, but you will always travel.

THE NAMELESS DAY
23rd December

Sorry nothing much to say here. You are an enigma and a mystery and undoubtedly special. Enjoy your unique path and make your impression on life creatively. You do not do things by the book, so don't even try to conform. You decide what is going to work, and follow it through with inimitable style and panache. When you fall in love it is for keeps and whoever grabs you is lucky indeed! That is all you need to know.

27 WALK LIKE AN EGYPTIAN

EGYPTIAN DEITY alternative astrological guidance. Search below for the wisdom and guidance of your Egyptian Birth date. Find the Guide animal linked to your month of birth and see what this creature has to say about your love life.

SPHINX
27 December - 25 January

Your artistic temperament and diverse talents ensure that you do not miss a trick. A photographic style memory serves you well. But, watch you do not lose perspective. Even Super humans need to keep a grip on reality. You make a reliable and committed partner, but only when you have reached a respectable position. You are highly motivated and disciplined. Nothing blocks your route to the top of the tree. And you possess a ruthless streak that comes into play if someone attempts to sabotage or undo your good work- understandable. A true perfectionist, you have a brilliant mind. There is indeed a touch of genius when you are in full flow. An exceptionally creative and powerful personality, you cast a spell. When you want to impress, you surely will.

Guide Animal: Lion

You love to rumble in the jungle at every given opportunity, and hate to be confined and constricted. Tedium does not float your boat. In the right relationship you look after your brood and can be very nurturing and protective of your loved ones. Keep balance and watch out for power struggles. Do not let the mind games go too far, even though they do turn you on.

SHU
26 January - 24 February

Lively and quick-witted, your mental agility is impressive. Liable to be academic and highly intelligent, you happily grapple with most topics. With great eloquence, you are rarely lost for words. You hate to admit mistakes so will store up excuses just in case. But that perfectionist streak makes you your own worst critic. A true Renaissance man or woman, you need a lot of stimulation or boredom sets in. Very sociable but intensely private, you are complex. Adaptable and willing to work in unusual conditions and in unusual ways, you will try anything once. Flexibility is your middle name whilst you amuse and amaze. You respect life, humanity and see the best in everyone, without being wet.

Guide Animal: The Ostrich - You get bored easily and
need variety in your love life. Lovers have an obligation to keep you interested. They must have stamina and oodles of oomph in the sack. Needless to say, you do not commit readily, though you are the type to hook up and fly to Vegas on a whim. Your relationships get in-

tense quickly, and you are hot-to-trot. Beauty and good looks in a mate are crucial.

ISIS
25 February - 26 March

You are a gentle, nurturing soul. Above all you are caring, sharing and kind. A beautiful person indeed, the finer feelings of love, romance and perception encapsulate your *raison d'etre* There is no active deception or nastiness hidden away. Okay, so everyone has a shadow side. But it is difficult to find it in your case. With a talented and unusual disposition, you possess a refined, artistic nature. You are a creative and poetic personality, skilled enough to make a fortune by not doing very much at all. Being very psychic and intuitive, it is impossible to lie to you. And with your great intensity and heightened sensitivity you are exceptionally powerful. Not much stand in your way, once you are committed to a plan of action. Your great intelligence identifies you.

Guide Animal: The Goose - You thrive on intense and meaningful connections. Not afraid to commit, you are a trustworthy, loving partner. But in long term links, lovemaking can become routine. Make a concerted effort to avoid the sofa and slippers syndrome. Never give up on intensity in the bedroom. Keep developing and experimenting. Sex is not a household chore, so continue to express your inner naughtiness.

OSIRIS
27 March - 25 April

You are a natural leader who can be forceful and convincing. Others find you annoying but inspiring. So curb that determination to get your own way. You have boundless energy and get things done. But there is no need to be too pushy when you want victory. Simply stating your case in no uncertain terms should do it. With focus, you can achieve great things. For you are destined to win or else go down fighting. Watch that tendency to be overly stubborn though. Feisty as you are, a mellow demeanour will usually be more potent and effective than a confrontational one. You are a crusader: a pioneer. With a head full of ideas, you are ever ready to spring into action.

Guide Animal: The Bull

You have an eccentric, unpredictable approach, which makes you experimental and exciting in the bedroom. Your libido is huge, a veritable powerhouse of sexual oomph in fact. Try to calm down a bit, and spin-out your love making skills. Do not play away from home (too often), and watch that tendency to mix business and pleasure. Learn to sublimate some of that sexual energy.

AMUN
26 April - 25 May

Highly creative, you possess a rare artistic sensibility. Your intuition is sensitised which ensures that you do not miss a trick. With refined taste and high expectations, you can be unexpectedly shy. Even though you are easily wounded, you have an unbending, unswerving Will that triumphs at every turn. As a born survivor, you feel things deeply but can move on when required. Your complex character is both earthy and perfectionist. But you are inclined to bury your head in the sand rather than deal with something tricky. Stay real and monitor unrealistic expectations. Your high ideals and sense of purpose guarantee that you will find what you are looking for – eventually.

Guide Animal: The Ram - Your mystery and allure keep your mates entranced. They may intend to just test the water, but in fact lovers become hooked very quickly. Once they have slept with you, you run the show. But until then, rely on your charisma and charm to captivate your prey. Scenarios of capture and struggle appeal to your psych; and you love to be overwhelmed, so long as you adore the person doing the deed.

HATHOR
26 May - 24 June

You are quite "out there" and always on the look-out for new experiences. For you, reality is one big joy ride that occasionally becomes the ghost train. As an eternal optimist, you have visions and dream dreams, each one more magnificent than the last. Your natural intensity means that you experience life by the minute. You are a law unto yourself in true maverick style. Your upbeat groove does not have to indicate immaturity. But there is a part of you that will never grow up. Uncompromising as ever, you will stick your neck out, rather than damage your personal integrity. You are a powerful figure with the Midas touch, who can quite literally run the show without being there.

Guide Animal: The Cow - Stability and reliable relationships are crucial to your equilibrium. You do not loosen up easily with potential partners, and you need to know you are onto a sure thing before you get deeply involved. Committed love obviously suits you and you get off on lavishing oodles of care and attention on your mate. Just be careful what you expect in return and watch out for the green-eyed monster.

PHOENIX
25 June - 24 July

You are a mysterious and enigmatic personality: a passionate and deep individual who feels everything on an intense level. Life is exhausting but exhilarating for those connected to you. Certainly, there is never a dull moment. At times you feel like an alien in a strange land. You are highly psychic with many overwhelming perceptions and intuitions. For sanity's sake, find an outlet so that your incredible imagination can express itself. You are liable to implode and beat yourself up when things go wrong. But to an extent you thrive on hardship and respond well to a challenge. Resilient and defiant, you are fiercely independent and treasure your privacy.

Guide Animal: The Heron - In love you need an understanding, beguiling mate. One who will allow you to remain independent and care free, yet who provides the nurturing, supportive environment you crave. You need commitment, as well as an intense connection. Needless to say, if you find such mate express your gratitude as much as possible. Sex is a psychic, spiritual thing for you; you are positively Tantric.

ANUBIS
25 July - 28 August

You are a powerful compelling character, possessing great charisma and appeal. With incredible magnetism, you know how to command attention, and you are skilled at getting your own way. You are never likely to be ignored, even when incognito.

Ego is an issue. But you automatically instil respect in both loved ones and opponents. Using humour and witty rhetoric you manoeuvre situations to maximum effect. Loyalty, generosity, and restraint make you a regal creature that never stints on affection and support. Your warmth of character and skills of performance attract the limelight. Express yourself on the stage of life; and expect the spotlight to shine upon you.

Guide Animal: The Jackal - You love to mate. Sex is important to your equilibrium and emotional fulfilment. You make your most intimate links physically and have terrific stamina.

Flirting and seducing come naturally to you. But you are slow to trust when it comes to intimate connections. Others have to win your heart, and you must see their love in action before you launch into a full commitment.

THOTH
29 August - 27 September

You are a veritable force to be reckoned with. There is no point trying to pull the wool over your eyes; you can see around corners. With your exacting standards and strong ambition, you are inclined to take life quite seriously. As well as being determined and focused, your organisational skills are second to none. It is virtually impossible to fault you. You are a master of discernment, with an innate understanding of human nature. And since you never take 'no' for an answer, your success is guaranteed. You are reliable, honest, and not in the least bit ruthless. There is an on-going sense that anything can happen in your life, and probably will. You carry infinite possibilities within.

Guide Animal: The Ibis - You attract many different lovers; whether or not you follow through is your choice. But people are drawn to your sexual prowess, chemistry and self-assured nature. You inspire deep feelings and possess intense sexual energy. But you hate to feel obligated or responsible for someone else's happiness. Clingy types, need not apply. You can take it or leave it; and this may be bewildering to those who love you.

HORUS
28 September - 27 October

As a cool customer, you are willing to calculate your moves. You are nobody's fool. Independent and candid, you are not afraid to tackle things head-on. Not much is beyond you. You keep a cool head in a crisis, and know when to act for maximum impact. Logically minded, you are not liable to get carried away. You are free spirited. But, you do not compromise readily. Things have to be on your terms, or they tend not to happen. Outgoing, popular and approachable, you never want for company. And your in-built protection is that inherent likeability. Your originality holds the key to wealth and riches. Whilst honed instincts will propel you to the level of success you choose.

Guide Animal: The Hawk - You do not settle for second best in relationships, and your high standards are difficult to fulfil. Concentrate more on your independence and self-sufficiency and you will not feel so let down when others get distracted. You are upfront and readily able to communicate your deepest feelings. But others find you too easy and available.

Try to be more mysterious and hold something back. Long term links suit you best. You need to know your efforts are going to be rewarded. There is no point if there is no guaranteed return. Keep the faith.

WADJET
28 October - 26 November

Your dynamo personality is captivating and compelling. And your powers of persuasion are irresistible. Not one to give up easily. Nothing will defeat you, whilst your heart is open and compassionate. You bring warmth, discipline and passion to your relationships. Whilst your magnetic charisma means there is no need for words – one look from those soulful eyes does the trick. Insightful, but non-judgemental, you get straight to the point. And are great to have around in a crisis. Your level head and sensible demeanour sorts things out. And you are able to wriggle out of compromising situations in a most charming way. Complex, but utterly adorable, nothing escapes your eagle eye.

Guide Animal: The Snake - A natural, sensual extrovert, love making comes easy to you. Not threatening at all, you are eager to experiment and do not have a problem demonstrating your preferences. You love to have a bit of a giggle which is great for flirty connections. Then when things get intense, you rise to the occasion with style and panache. Not afraid to take the lead, you do not dominate, but you do conquer. You know how to build something durable and strong in subtle ways.

SEKHMET
27 November - 26 December

Determination will see you through – But life is hard work. So expect character-forming challenges to occur regularly. A true survivor, your achievements are precious indeed. Stoic qualities serve you well. And much effort goes into the attainment of your dreams. With grounded equilibrium, you are a formidable force when focused. Your tenacity and discipline win every time. When up against it, keep your head down. Expect to reach the dizzy heights of success. But first prove your durability. Fame awaits you if you are patient and do not give up. You are sensual and practical: a skilful, considerate friend and lover. Appreciate the view along the way, and learn to value the little things in life.

Guide Animal: The Lioness - Your self-effacing attitude extends to the bedroom, which means that your partner has lots of fun. But do you? Certainly you are one of life's givers; but you will gain even more if you dare to verbalize your own desires. Make an effort to tap into your own needs for greater all-round fulfilment. You are easy going and relaxed in love; but politeness does not really have a place once you engage sexually.

28 AZTEC ASTRO PROFILES

AZTEC ASTROLOGY. AZTEC LOVE STYLE ORACLE

Could Ancient America hold the clue to your destiny? The Aztec Zodiac is based on an ancient astrological system which uses 13 day cycles to yield 20 signs. The Aztec symbols are Crocodile, Wind, House, Lizard, Serpent, Owl, Deer, Rabbit, Water, Flower, Monkey, Grass, Reed, Ocelot, Eagle, Vulture, Earthquake, Flint, Rain, and Dog. Find out which symbol will reveal your Aztec personality and Soul Mate by following the five simple steps in the appendices at the back of the book. Using the simple counting system, follow the instructions, calculate your Totem Animal, and then read your Aztec Profile here below. You can also check your compatibility with loved ones using the same system.

CROCODILE

Aztec You: You are a natural leader, who is inclined to be a bit snappy. Dynamic, passionate and full on, you fear rejection and hate to have your good intentions trampled upon. Tap into your positive spirit and use your creativity to full effect. Do not worry so much about what others think and you will naturally shine bright. Your focus will take you places. You have a fearless nature and will tackle most things head on. Just watch that your pushy, stroppy ways don't get you into trouble. Trust your instincts and do not be afraid to show your true feelings. Life will reward your bravery.

Relationships: You love to rumble in the jungle at every given opportunity, and hate to be confined and constricted. Tedium doesn't float your boat! In the right relationship you look after your brood and can be very nurturing and protective of your loved ones. Keep balance and watch out for power struggles. Do not let the mind games go too far, even though they do turn you on.

Compatibility: MONKEY'S creativity and mischief is very attractive to you. But you need to feel secure, whereas MONKEY is inclined to love all and sundry. DOG provides loyalty, companionship and commitment.

WIND

Aztec You: You are changeable like the wind and your variable moods keep the world guessing. When you are angry you blow the competition away. When calm and settled; you are soothing beguiling company. Witty and open, people love your company when you are on form. You can get your head around most subjects and it takes a lot to faze you. Creative, free and easy, you have a vivid imagination, which is great for your professional life. Flexible and amenable, you fit in well. But you can also be flippant, superficial and flighty, which doesn't always bode well for the love stuff.

Relationships: You get bored easily and need variety in your love life. Lovers have an obligation to keep you interested. They must have stamina and oodles of oomph in the sack. Needless to say, you do not commit readily, though you are the type to hook up and fly to Vegas on a whim. Your relationships get intense quickly, and you are open and well connected. Beauty and good looks in a mate are crucial.

Compatibility: GRASS is your opposite sign, so you can expect mad shenanigans with those who blow in the wind. But you are likely to get into a power struggle with GRASS. MONKEY is lots of fun and it works over time.

HOUSE

Aztec You: Your home environment is crucial to your equilibrium. You need firm foundations, stability, and security in your life's circumstances. So you build things up over time, and get very rattled when your dreams and schemes do not work out. Your personal presence is powerful, sometimes over-bearing, and others may find you imposing and intimidating. But you command respect and at least you are not the kind of person who gets overlooked. Privacy is important to you, and you often need time alone to recoup your energies. Warm and caring too, you are loyal and comforting.

Relationships: You thrive on intense and meaningful connections. Not afraid to commit, you are a trustworthy, loving partner. But in long term links, lovemaking can become routine. Make a concerted effort to avoid the sofa and slippers syndrome. Never give up on intensity in the bedroom. Keep developing and experimenting. Sex is not a household chore, so continue to express your inner naughtiness.

Compatibility: REED, your opposite sign suits you down to the ground. You provide each other with a stable environment, enabling you both to flourish. You make more sense together than apart. GRASS suits too, but is more staid and traditional.

LIZARD

Aztec You: You are great at getting things started with your big ideas and tenacious approach to life. Indeed, you are a live wire of vibrant energy, who can seduce and beguile just about anyone! Ambitious and impatient, you must learn to calm down and finish what you've started. Otherwise, you are likely to leave a trail of unfinished business behind you. Learn patience and put your perfectionist streak to good use, remaining focused until the job is done. Your mind power is formidable, and you attract people with your unusual perspectives and outlook.

Relationships: You have an eccentric, unpredictable approach, which makes you experimental and exciting in the bedroom. Your libido is huge, a veritable powerhouse of sexual oomph in fact. Try to calm down a bit, and spin-out your love making skills. Do not play away from home, and watch that tendency to mix business and pleasure. Learn to sublimate some of that sexual energy.

Compatibility: You make a hot, potent mix with your opposite sign OCELOT. But you are likely to burn out quickly and get on each other's nerves when the daily grind kicks in. REED brings serenity and calm, which compliments your frantic nature.

SERPENT

Aztec You: You are powerful with a magnetic personality that keeps people transfixed once they fall under your spell. Stoic and intense, your skills of survival and strength are enviable. Life may test you repeatedly. But you are destined to shine and develop in spectacular ways as you come through a trial of fire. Deeply passionate and intense, you possess a compelling and hypnotic presence. Likely to be psychic and deeply spiritual, you understand life and willingly use your profound insights to help others. Guard against too much stress and worry and you will never get rattled beyond your remit.

Relationships: Your mystery and allure keep your mates entranced. They may intend to just test the water, but in fact lovers become hooked very quickly. Once they have slept with you, you run the show. But until then, rely on your charisma and charm to captivate your prey. Scenarios of capture and struggle float your boat (within reason). And you love to be overwhelmed, so long as you adore the person doing the deed

Compatibility: EAGLE, you opposite sign is a powerful sign that attracts your profound, intense nature. But you are likely to conflict and disagree about everything outside of the bedroom. OCELOT brings privacy and peace of mind, plus good loving.

OWL

Aztec You: You are a conscientious character, who is inclined to put social concerns and obligations before selfish desires. Very admirable! But do remember that life is to be enjoyed. You do not want a host of simmering resentments deriving from self-denial to haunt you; right? Your political inclinations mean that you're likely to be active in community settings. Getting involved in public issues inspires you, and you do like to complain to the powers that be on behalf of everyone. You are a stickler for routine and your commonsense is commendable. Just do not become too boring.

Relationships: Stability and reliable relationships are crucial to your equilibrium. You don't loosen up easily with potential partners, and you need to know you're onto a sure thing before you get deeply involved. Committed love obviously suits you and you get off on lavishing oodles of care and attention on your mate. Just be careful what you expect in return and watch out for the green-eyed monster.

Compatibility: VULTURE your opposite sign shares your community concerns and together you can build a life of good deeds and worthy service. Save some time for each other though. EAGLE is more liberating, less dominant, and offers a lighter touch.

DEER

Aztec You: You are a generous hearted creature, who has a lot of love to give. You nurture and cherish loved ones; supporting to the max all those you are close to. But you are a paradox. There are many people, you cannot be bothered with, and you are very selective with your affections. This may sound discerning, but to those who are excluded from your world, you come across as cool and aloof. You are a free spirit who needs a safety net. Willing to experiment, you wander aimlessly, but only if there is a secure base to return to. Your intuition guides you through life's trials. Never ignore it

Relationships: In love you need an understanding, beguiling mate. One who will allow you to remain independent and care free, yet who provides the nurturing, supportive environment you crave. You need commitment, as well as an intense connection. Needless to say, if you find such mate express your gratitude as much as possible. Sex is a psychic, spiritual thing for you.

Compatibility: EARTHQUAKE, your opposite sign offers an earth-shattering, intense connection. Find common-ground, with your Soul Mate and you will go far. VULTURE shares interests and provides a safe, respectful environment.

RABBIT

Aztec You: You are a bundle of energy; restless, hyper active, and always on the move. Your lively, captivating character keeps people buoyant and in good humor. You are agile in mind and body, with lots of bright and unusual ideas. But you can be perverse. You love to mix it up with controversial gossip or insights. Plus you do have a self- destructive tendency, and can be a little paranoid at times. Rest assured you do not have to fret; people generally love you. Just hold back with the unpopular points of view and you will not alienate those who are important. Your outspoken nature is a mixed blessing.

Relationships: You are a RABBIT, so you love to mate! Sex is important to your equilibrium and emotional fulfillment. You make your most intimate links physically and have terrific stamina. Flirting and seducing come naturally to you. But you are slow to trust when it comes to committed connections. Others have to win your heart and you must see their love in action before you go the whole hog.

Compatibility: FLINT, your opposite sign attracts you. But over time, there may be a clash of wills and differences of opinion. You like a bit of antagonism; but fighting all the time? No thanks. EARTHQUAKE supports your changeable nature.

WATER

Aztec You: You have a great sense of humor, off beat imagination, and enviable talents. Your extreme sensitivity makes you highly intuitive, a little bit psychic and very emotional. Also you have an artistic streak and a hint of genius if only you would choose to develop it. Trust me; your ability to express yourself creatively is in there somewhere. You are a powerful character, whose charismatic presence permeates the room. Once you gain control of your strong emotions, you possess formidable focus and determination. But until then, you're not the most responsible, reliable character.

Relationships: You attract many different lovers; whether or not you follow through is your choice. But people are drawn to your sexual prowess, chemistry and self-assured nature. You inspire deep feelings and possess intense sexual energy. But you hate to feel obligated or responsible for someone else's happiness. Clingy types, need not apply. You can take it or leave it; and this may be bewildering to those who love you.

Compatibility: RAIN can handle your strong, intense emotions. Your mutual watery energies forge a life-long bond, which is difficult to severe. FLINT provides great companionship, and a listening ear. But is not so much on your wave length.

FLOWER

Aztec You: You are a stubborn soul with high expectations. But you are not demanding; just rather gauche and socially awkward. You get hurt easily by tactlessness and inconsiderate behavior drives you nuts. You hate to be over-looked, but you do not pass judgement. You simply simmer, storing up the misdemeanors in your memory bank. You are devoted, faithful, loyal and true, and would like to think that others are the same. Welcome to the real world! Lighten up and do not take umbrage so easily. Remember, you are intrinsically lucky, but just need to be a tad more realistic.

Relationships: You do not settle for second best in relationships, and your high standards are difficult to fulfill. Concentrate more on your independence and self-sufficiency and you will not feel so let down when others get distracted. You are upfront and readily able to communicate your deepest feelings. But others find you too easy and available. Try to be more mysterious and hold something back. Long term links suit you best.

Compatibility: DOG is your attractive opposite sign. You make a loyal, devoted, reliable mix. But where is the oomph? MONKEY introduces more mischief and humor. This sign provides fun, laughter and an element of surprise. Can you handle it?

MONKEY

Aztec You: A natural performer, you have a wicked sense of humor and well developed mischievous streak. You love to be at the center of things, and with your skills of communication and great talent, you often are. Loud and proud, you dominate whatever room you find yourself in. But you can be quite reserved one-to-one. Is your public face all bravado, or is there some substance beneath it? You are not inclined towards introspection, but deep thought would not go amiss from time to time. You are highly intelligent and not in the least bit superficial; just easily distracted.

Relationships: A natural, sensual extrovert, love making comes easy to you. Not threatening at all, you are eager to experiment and don't have a problem demonstrating your preferences. You love to have a bit of a giggle which is great for flirty connections. Then when things get intense, you rise to the occasion with style and panache. Not afraid to take the lead, you don't dominate, but you do conquer!

Compatibility: CROCODILE is your opposite sign and the old CROC can exert a strong influence over you. You may not like to be dictated to; in which case choose FLOWER who understands your changeable, apparently fickle nature rather better.

GRASS

Aztec You: You are a sociable, considerate soul with tons of friends and many interests. Quietly ambitious, you can achieve great things with concentration and focus. Hang in there with treasured dreams, and never take "no" for an answer. You are sensitive and thoughtful to everyone; but must also learn to give yourself equal time and attention. Sometimes you get over involved in other's problems and don't leave yourself enough time for reflection. Preserve your boundaries better and guard your heart a little more. You will then thrive and be far more effective with the stuff that really matters.

Relationships: Your self-effacing attitude extends to the bedroom, which means that your partner has lots of fun. But do you? Certainly you are one of life's givers; but you will gain even more if you dare to verbalize your own desires. Make an effort to tap into your own needs for greater all-round fulfillment. You are easy going and relaxed in love; but politeness doesn't really have a place once you engage sexually.

Compatibility: WIND, your opposite sign is a compelling connection. But this frenetic energy is likely to wear you out. Your serious mind responds well to CROCODILE who is supportive and open hearted. CROCODILE's solidity makes you feel safe.

REED

Aztec You: You are a full-on character, who loves to pioneer a just cause. Your great integrity and balance means that you get results where no one else can. The champion of hopeless cases, you always have a bee your bonnet about something. Of course you annoy certain people who can't be bothered with anything but themselves. Just make sure that you're not compensating for emptiness deep inside. Sometimes your frantic nature may distract you from suppressed issues you need to acknowledge. Be honest with you as well as everyone else; then get set to conquer the world. You are totally unique.

Relationships: You love a challenge, so when you have your eye on someone exciting, you do not give up on a connection that is right for you. Persistence is absolutely key. You are not afraid to follow through a powerful connection, and you do not get hurt that easily. In love you win out, and you make a formidable opponent. When you are engaged in the full force of your powerful emotions, you let it rip. If you're treated right; everyone's a winner.

Compatibility: HOUSE your opposite sign, offers strength and security. So long as you agree to disagree, you will get on like a house on fire! WIND allows you to feel more in control and you can run things on your own terms. Is that a good thing?

OCELOT

Aztec You: Your presence is comforting and your voice soothing. Your aura radiates a warm glow and no none feels left out when you're around. You have a sharp mind and spot-on intuition; so not much gets past you. But you must get your facts right before speak up. You love intrigue, gossip and secrets, so long as they do not harm anyone. Do be careful with all that, and do not assume you know what is what. When you want to make something happen, you can be extraordinarily pushy. This takes people by surprise and you are often successful by default. Shock tactics work every time.

Relationships: You are very tuned in and able to sense who is interested and who is not. Open and in touch with your emotions, you do not have a problem being chased, or doing the chasing. Either is just fine with you, so long as you land your prize at the end of it. You do not let pride get in the way of a good time, and you easily make intense, meaningful connections. You captivate and seduce with subtle, gentle moves.

Compatibility: LIZARD your opposite sign is a challenge, but very attractive to boot! You love compelling connections, so look for the most intense, sexy signs if you're on the hunt. HOUSE provides stability and a safe environment when you are knackered.

EAGLE

Aztec You: A unique, independent spirit, you find it difficult to see someone else's point of view. Sometimes you baulk under a challenge and head for the hills. But you are quietly ambitious and get things done. Guard against rigidity and learn to bend a little or you may alienate useful contacts. You need to play a nifty game to get workable results in the real world. Yes, you are full of fancy ideas. But if you stay grounded and remain as focused as possible, things will actually happen. Your free and easy nature attracts like-minded souls. Mysterious, spiritual and shamanic experiences link you to the other side.

Relationships: You love to surrender to the moment. When you feel comfortable, you are not in the least bit shy. Relationships are a voyage of discovery for you, and you relish all kinds of connection. Just be careful of projection though. You are quite prone to fantasy and obsessive dreaming, and tend to put potential lovers on a pedestal, which may mess up your chances in the real world. Keep it real and enjoy the thrills on offer.

Compatibility: SERPENT your opposite is fiery and dynamic, just the way you like it. But you need to spread your wings and fly free, so SERPENT may feel restrictive after a while. LIZARD lets you be and will not threaten you or cramp your style.

VULTURE

Aztec You: You have a formidable intelligence and rapier wit. Your strong powers of judgement serve you well, and nothing escapes your notice. Others seek out your spectacular insights. But your innate power and commanding persona, makes you inclined to clash with authority. Be careful in your professional life, and learn to be more flexible. You like to do things in your own way, but must try to adapt just a little, or you could alienate important people. You are brutally honest and not afraid to tell it like it is. But do work on your sensitivity if you don't want to scare off gentle souls.

Relationships: Your privacy and personal freedom are important. It's not that you get up to all sorts, but prospective mates need to understand your lonesome nature. Within a secure, committed relationship, you love to roam far and wide. You need the best of both worlds. But you are loyal and not afraid of linking forever with the right person. Bossy too, you manage to have a laugh once your perverse sense of humor is engaged.

Compatibility: OWL your opposite is traditional and stable; a good match. OWL helps you take on life and fulfill your potential, but does not invade your space or privacy. SERPENT is compelling, and dynamic, keeping you entertained and satiated.

EARTHQUAKE

Aztec You: You are always two steps ahead of the competition. Your mind power is immense and your wit is razor sharp. But your skills of empathy could be better developed. You sometimes get stuck on a one-way-track, and miss out on worthwhile connections. Being stubborn and resolute, you are not great at compromise. But at least people know where they stand. Always trust your judgement even when it comes to big risks. You have brilliant instincts and "lucky" is your middle name, so what can go wrong? Develop your emotional responses and do not always rely on logic to solve problems.

Relationships: You can be quite self-centered, so you do not want a demanding long term mate who takes the attention off you! No, you are not selfish, but you are very aware of your needs, wants, and desires from minute to minute. And it would take someone quite formidable to displace your priorities; that is for sure. Your Soul Mate reads you well and is no doubt very different indeed. It is the mind power factor that does it for you.

Compatibility: DEER is your opposite and this gentle soul is highly suitable. Able to fade into the background and be independent, you are well matched in intellect and inclination. OWL also makes the link, being socially with it and very cool.

FLINT

Aztec You: You can be hard work to relate to, but you have great energy and your heart is in the right place. You tend to question things too readily and are not always very relaxing company. As you go about your business, you are practical and meticulous. But flexible, you are not. When things do not go as planned, it throws you off big time. And you can be quite desperate and domineering when you're trying to maneuver things. Take a chill pill and be less dependent on outcomes. Channel your focus and intensity into work stuff and foster your free spirit for play time.

Relationships: You are in love with love and when relaxed, you make a great lover. You are good in the bedroom, and there are never likely to be complaints in the bedroom department. Allow your free and easy manner to translate into your daily life, and you'll be onto a winner. But do keep your wants and needs in focus, and don't let your lover take over completely; as if! Get the balance right, and use your charms to full effect.

Compatibility: It is an extreme case of love or hate with your opposite sign RABBIT. Give things a chance, because it will likely be very intense and passionate. But if the fighting does not calm down, move on. DEER is less frantic, mellow company. You respond more evenly to a gentle soul.

RAIN

Aztec You: Your mind is a veritable machine. In other words, you rarely allow yourself the luxury or head space of not thinking. Great at making other people's ideas happen, you are a popular character. Few problems and challenges defeat you, and you really are a gift in a crisis. Do try to still your mind and see what happens from time to time. Who knows, you may get even better insights. A warm, nurturing soul, you love to love and it means the world to you to see your loved ones happy and sorted. Sometimes though, you may interfere and help too much. Learn to leave well enough alone when you have to.

Relationships: You are a lucky soul, young at heart and probably great looking too. You age slowly and will always maintain your optimistic spirit. Just watch that tendency to interfere, and don't spoil your connections with too much input. Love-making is very important to you, and you perform to the maximum in a committed relationship. Boring you are not, and you will always attract lots of attention.

Compatibility: WATER your opposite sign is a great match. But the moodiness and intense emotions you both experience will keep you on your toes. RABBIT is exciting, sensual and never boring. Either way, you will have lots of fun.

DOG

Aztec You: You love to be caught up in the social whirl, so loved ones who demand your intense attention get short shrift. Loyal and patient as you are, you like to keep life, light and bright. Intense issues and ridiculous rows are not your cup of tea. You rightly do not have much time for those who do not know how to enjoy themselves. Peace and harmony are important to you, and you are great at diffusing tricky situations with your humor and charm. Definitely a team player, you also know how to fulfill your own needs. But in reality you do not need too much privacy or introspection. Variety keeps you buoyant.

Relationships: You are great in a committed relationship, so long as you feel valued. If you get short changed, you move on, and may even put it about a bit until you are sure. Watch out for your suspicious streak, in the early days of a connection. It would be a shame to sabotage a good thing. Give love a chance, and relax as things heat up. Do not let fear get a foot hold. Be mature and circumspect, then love will grow.

Compatibility: FLOWER your opposite sign shares your love of all things cultural, and you will have endless chats designed to stimulate the intellect. Remember to give the love stuff a good portion of your time. RAIN is also up for travel, adventure and exploration.

29 VEDIC INDIAN ASTRO PROFILES

Discover your Indian Love sign and rev up your love life with ancient insights from Asia. No, the symbols and esoteric tools of another culture do not invalidate our own Western Astrology. But these different insights from the Indian Tradition reflect the diversity of our universe as well as an esoteric truth. Vedic Astrology serves up food for thought and an unusual way of looking at life, love and what makes us tick.

Vedic Astrology provides a psychic map enabling the seeker to gain deeper understanding of personality, relationships and the love stuff too. This system uses 27 Moon Signs, unlike our western Astrology, which of course uses 12 Sun Signs. The 27 Moon signs, called NAKSHRATRAS, are symbolized by different animals, which may be male or female. This approach offers a useful tool to help us discern who we are well matched with, and who we should perhaps give a wide berth to.

If you are born on the cusp of a Moon Cycle read both creatures either side of your date and see which you feel rings most true for you. You may indeed have elements of both power animals in your persona. So, calculate your date and month of birth in the simple tables at the back of the book to find your Vedic power animal. Then proceed to calculate your options Vedic Style.

ASHWINI + The Male Horse
13th April – 27th April

Vedic You: You are always up-for-it and need your adventurous, independent spirit permanently stimulated. Yes, you can be quite exhausting! But you're never dull. Sometimes you come unstuck in the pursuit of perfection. Though, generally your intuitions are spot-on. It's when your heart is fully engaged and distracted that you do not always make the best judgement-calls. Always on the look-out for the next thrill, you move through people, circumstances and options quickly. But you are not afraid to commit when it makes sense. Just watch out for that grass is greener syndrome when the terrain gets tough. You do not want to baulk at the first fence now do you?

Love Style: You are a passionate thoroughbred that will not be tamed; not inside, nor outside the bedroom. Lovers have to run to keep up with you, and you are always several leaps ahead of the pack. Normal you are not. You are curious and experimental. But somewhat idealistic about the love stuff, so you understandably get very hurt when someone disappoints you. Watch those expectations though, and try to cool the emotional responses once in a while.

Best Match: Bharani's sensuous style gets a grip of you in no time at all. Bharani and Ashwini are also highly compatible over time. There is no fear of commitment as the natural ease between you disperses potential jitters. Bharani can deal with Ashwini's fear of rejection and occasional insecurities.

Steer Clear: Hastas are over bearing and horribly practical. Ashwini feels stifled and there is a potential battle over keeping the

347

sex life scintillating. Ashwini needs adventure and excitement. Hasta is not that bothered.

BHARANI + The Male Elephant
27th April – 11th May

Vedic You: You are a well-balanced creature. In touch with your feminine side, you are nurturing and kind. But you are also strong and resilient when up against it. Your independent streak is phenomenal, and you can even be a tad pushy or aggressive when you are focusing on a result. Your self-sufficiency makes you very competitive professionally, and you have great levels of stamina. You are certainly not one to crumple when the going gets tough. Thankfully your softer side redeems you time and time again. You are not unavailable emotionally; nor are you stilted in your responses. Open, and empathetic to others; you are also quite happy in your own company.

Love Style: You are a skilled lover who is charming and attractive. Well-able to turn it on at the drop of a hat, you like the thrill of chasing after your prey. The love stuff absorbs you fully and you are relentless until you land the object of your desire. Very like the Western Taurus Bull, you respond to a sensuous atmosphere, good food and fine wine. Sex is important to you, but you do not forget that romance must come first. A full-on loaded situation turns you on; once committed though you are inclined to be lazy.

Best Match: Ashwini returns the favor offering you excitement and stimulation. Life is never dull. You can expect to be treasured, nurtured and protected; though this must be an equal bond for the best level of fulfillment to be achieved. Revati matches you in the bedroom and lights the eternal flame.

Steer Clear: Chitra brings out the worst in you. You are likely to get mighty wound up in the company of Chitra. Jealousy, obsessiveness and possessiveness all come out to play. Best stay away.

KRITTIKA + The Female Sheep
11th May – 25th May

Vedic You: Warm, witty and responsive, you are well-able to be all things to all people. Within a family context, you are loyal, supportive and loving. Your friends get the full treatment and you never forget birthdays or what is meant to happen next. Yes, you can be quite organized on everyone else's behalf; just do not neglect your own wants and needs. You love without expectation, so your time, money and energy is freely given; one big reason why you are so loved! When you first meet new faces your timid side comes to the fore. But you can be quite fiery and dynamic when your mind gets going on a topic. Matter-of-fact and undemanding, you are not generally the jealous type.

Love Style: Your sexual responses are intense, though you are not often the one to make the first move. Highly sexed as you are, you do not generally instigate the deed. Passive and mellow in your approach, there is not a hint of desperation about you. This sparks up your mystery and allure, and you rarely have to do much more than smile to attract the right kind of lover. Your great belief in Destiny reassures you through the lean patches and you are always assured of action at the perfect time. Once committed; you are sorted.

Best Match: Jyeshtas is inspirational and brings out your best qualities. Kind, fun and nurturing of your heart and soul; here you will find true understanding. You will both fulfill each other's wishes and desires; why look elsewhere? But, Pushya is also great for sexual shenanigans and longevity.

Steer Clear: Shravana and Purva Ashadha leave you mighty confused. The mischief of this type unsettles you and would be no peace of mind in such a union. Uttara Ashadha is as bossy as you are, so there would be an ongoing battle of wills; do not bother.

ROHINI + The Male Serpent
25th May – 8th June

Vedic You: You are a romantic spirit; quite Byronic and ethereal actually. Often troubled by intense torment, your chaotic emotions and ruminations leave you in a spin. Not the most decisive creature on the planet, you deal with tricky situations by becoming detached and distant. Frequently to be found in a public place with a huddle of people hanging on your every word, you are charismatic, enigmatic and popular. But, you are a changeable character, and there is no knowing what mood might descend within a minute. You are a compelling challenge indeed for those who find you attractive; and you are loving and romantic when you warm up.

Love Style: Getting close to you can be heavy-weather. I'm sure you have driven many unrequited passions nuts in your time. You actually have very high standards when it comes to love and you do not mess around with your heart. Material well-being is important to your laissez-faire; so a mate with refined sensibilities and preferably lots of money suits well. When you have spotted your ideal lover, you won't relent until you have wooed them heart and soul. Watch jealousies though; do not blow it.

Best Match: Anuradha is your ideal lover, though you may never set foot out of the bedroom once you get started. You are mutually besotted and bring out the best in each other. Do work sensibly to get past the first row though. It could be devastating. But pass this test and you're together forever. Anuradha is a successful genius; good choice

Steer Clear: Magha and Mula are insensitive and do not appreciate your refined sensibilities. When you are not treasured, you get insecure. Plus, you find it impossible to forgive gross negligence and selfishness; oops!

MRIGASIRA + The Female Serpent
8th June – 21st June

Vedic You: You are a restless, refined spirit with spiritual awareness and an artistic temperament. Charismatic, witty and entertaining too, you are never short of an audience. In fact, you have quite an army of fans who respect you to the max. You are also very good at manipulating others for your own ends. But it is always done with the utmost cool and no one's complaining. Your high intelligence means that you get bored easily, and you are always looking for the next pet project or soul to way-lay. You are inclined to question your circumstances too much. Do try to calm down and enjoy your surroundings a bit more; instead of always wondering what to buy or decorate next.

Love Style: You tend to be quite analytical with your love style, so you need a mate who can tolerate your endless ramblings. Intelligent as you are, your love life often gets the third degree. It does not mean you're not having fun, but perhaps it does mean you could be having more (of everything.). Try not to criticize your lover or yourself too much. Unwind and enjoy sensual moments and don't bother with so much speculation; well not in the bedroom anyhow. Read each other War and Peace in the Living Room instead.

Best Match: Ardra excites you and hits the spot on every level. This is a fulfilling union to match the best of them. Between you, you sort the world out. Ardra is an equal in body, mind, and spirit. You talk for hours and share the same sense of humor. Hasta opens up to you. But you may get a little bit bored in the long run.

Steer Clear: Dhanishta is not on your wave length. You do not feel understood or heard and this is a completely frustrating mismatch in the long term. The fights could even get out of hand, so do not get waylaid if you can help it by Dhanishta.

ARDRA + The Female Dog
21ˢᵗ June – 5ᵗʰ July

Vedic You: You are very good at spotting the people who will be helpful to you. Understandably you foster friendships which will take you places. This is your great strength; but sometimes your main weakness too. Your desire to get ahead makes you of course very ambitious. But problems arise when you think too much about the next phase when you should instead be concentrating on a finer feeling. Do not overlook your emotional and sexual needs at the expense of status. It is not worth it. Your inner-self and inner-child need nurturing. Is it time to concentrate on some good clean fun? Do not sacrifice the real you. The impact you make in the big wide world is only part of the story

Love Style: You have a great need of appreciation, and often lap up the attention of many lovers before you meet your match. If you're lucky enough to have found your Soul Mate early on; you will have found someone who reaches you deep inside; who recognizes when you are vulnerable and who understands your hidden emotions. You do tend to suppress a great deal. But your true love will lure you out to play and you are bound to feel well-loved and comfortable in their company. Wait for the right one.

Best Match: Mrigasira is good news for you. This is a mutually exclusive and fulfilling union. You keep Mrigasira amused with your wit and intelligence; and they return the favor by teaching you how to open up to love and life. You balance-out each other's weak spots and develop each other's good points.

Steer Clear: Jyeshta is dominant and will run rings around you. Can you handle it? It is okay if you are in lazy groove. But it is not a marvelous idea in the long run. Ashlesha is an ego on the loose when you're around and way too selfish for you.

PUNARVASU + The Female Cat
5th July – 19th July

Vedic You: You are a sensitive, nurturing creature, who gives a lot of love to life's waifs and strays. Always ready with sound advice and endless cups of tea, you are a great friend indeed. You are likely to be the office shoulder-to-cry-on too. Your strong instincts give you the edge, and your intuition is formidable. It is a rare day when you are wrong about something; it just does not happen. But in the midst of this great strength lurks your Achilles Heel. Do be careful of burn-out and don't allow people to pull at you in an abusive or disadvantageous way. It is okay to save up favors, and you're never short of company. But, you do need more privacy and better ways to preserve your energies.

Love Style: You are inclined to feel lonely in a crowd. You spend so much time tending to everyone else that they often assume you're completely resilient and overlook your needs. Your Soul Mate knows different. Only your true love sees your vulnerable, needy side. Lucky them! Independent and self-sufficient as you are; you do not like to be restricted or possessed. Mates have to understand you attract a lot of interest, so must not feel threatened by stiff competition. You're quite a flirt; but you do remain faithful when spoken for.

Best Match: Ashlesha is a sexual dynamo who compliments you well. But there may be a quick burnout with this union if you cannot keep up with Ashlesha's demands. Bharani is a great teacher; mature, sensual, committed and loving. But not in the least bit dull. Also Pushya is supportive and loyal, providing great stability and surety.

Steer Clear: Jyeshta is compelling and charismatic. But will drive you to distraction and wind you up with game playing and general unavailability. Great if you like the emotional roller coaster. Not great for a peaceful life though.

PUSHYA + The Ram
19th July – 2nd August

Vedic You: You are a walking dictionary with very high standards. Responsible and caring, you do not like to see your loved ones go without. Often times you will overlook your own needs to make sure others are comfortable. Even from a young age, you are a natural parent waiting to happen. Likely to have had a correct, proper up-bringing, you have a well-developed sense of right and wrong. Your home environment primed you for life in many good ways. But, sometimes you find it difficult to find the humor in life. It is a serious business as far as you're concerned. Though you would perhaps benefit from a smidge more levity; for the sake of self-preservation, if nothing else.

Love Style: Interestingly sex is your saving grace. You are light-hearted, playful and adventurous in your established relationship. But, even though you enjoy frivolous encounters, you will not do much about it if it's not right. You tend to save your best self for your Soul Mate only. You are perfectionist when looking for love, so you may get hurt along the way, when others do not return your enthusiasm. Hold back a bit when making the first tentative moves; then swing into action when you know what is what.

Best Match: Ahswini is your ideal love. But this may be a tale of unrequited love if you're not careful. It can really work if you stay cool and let things unfold slowly. You are likely to put Ashwini on a pedestal; which is okay as Ashwini loves to be adored. Ashlesha stirs your soul deeply. This is a sensual, lasting bond.

Steer Clear: Dhanishta is a dominant creature and you react badly, even violently when you're dictated to. This will not work unless you can understand Dhanishta's need for freedom and somewhat hypocritical nature.

ASHLESHA + The Male Cat
2nd August – 16th August

Vedic You: You are a dominant, proud creature, who loves an audience. Like the Western Zodiac pussycat Leo, you respond well to life in the spotlight. Fiercely independent, you do not like your style to be cramped personally or professionally. You are strong, clever and competitive, but you also have a restless streak and hate to be dictated to. Not great at taking orders, your restlessness often gets the better of you. In relationships, you baulk if things get heavy. Anything for an easy life. You do have a lazy streak, and like to keep things as straightforward as possible. Simplicity really appeals to you, though you love luxurious surroundings and sumptuous food. Fair enough.

Love Style: Your analytical mind makes you indecisive and that restless streak does not always help either. You find it difficult to make lasting connections and can get quite jaded and cynical about love. But your heart is strong and you are always up for a fresh attempt. Modify your expectations and try not to be so demanding of your lover. Then happiness is but a breath away, and probably much closer than you think. Love does not equal imprisonment, so give it half a chance by relaxing into the connections you make.

Best Match: Pushya is up-for-it, sexy and alluring. This intense creature pushes all the right buttons and leaves you panting for more. Pushya is warm, witty and lots of fun. There is never a dull moment. Ashlesha creates a deep bond with you, once you get past the initial game playing. It is a lasting union.

Steer Clear: Magha stirs your hormones intensely, yet is too aloof in other ways. Insecurities re) how much you are needed will haunt this union. Mostly you just feel rejected and out-in-the-cold. What's the point?

MAGHA + The Male Rat
16ᵗʰ August – 30ᵗʰ August

Vedic You: You are a powerhouse of energy and knowledge. A born leader, everyone loves you. For you retain natural humility and genuine spirit in all situations. Fair and kind, no one gets overlooked when you are around. You are compelling, interesting and it is hard to match your intelligence. Life is for living as far as you are concerned; and you certainly live it to the maximum. Because you make such a great effort with everything you attempt, you get very frustrated when your labors of love go unnoticed. It is not that you do things for a return. But you do need to be affirmed and appreciated, even as you conquer the world. Your talents are diverse and you can turn your hand to most things.

Love Style: Your deep-seated urge is to make that special connection with your Soul Mate. Only the best will do. No, you're not overly perfectionist, but you do need to find the magical ingredients of high-octane chemistry matched with a commitment that will run and run; or else you feel short changed. Not too much to ask for! You enjoy sex and passionate links stir your heart and soul into action in all areas of life. Your burning desire is to feel special, nurtured and desired. Good luck; it's out there somewhere.

Best Match: Jyeshta makes you feel whole and completely fulfilled. There are no questions asked. This union is a prime example of unconditional love. Jyesthta knows how to charm you into submission, and leave you hungry for more. Sexually and emotionally this match hits the spot.

Steer Clear: Shravanas are complex creatures and love doesn't come easy between the two of you. Shravanas take a while to warm up and are perhaps too introverted for your tastes. Go right ahead if you like a challenge.

PURVA PHALGUNI + The Female Rat
30th August – 13th September

Vedic You: You are a gracious, grounded creature; vivacious and fun to be around. Family and friends are of supreme importance and you generally bend over backwards to please them. But you do have a cut-off point, which is invariably brutal. Your boundaries are well in place, so if the support, camaraderie and love are not equally returned, you can be quite the drama queen. Creative and lively, you get hurt when those you love do not match your enthusiasm, and you Do hate to be neglected or overlooked. Although you are not an insecure character, you really cannot be bothered with too much time on your own. You are comfortable with you; but life is too short for too much alone-ness.

Love Style: The family unit is a crucial cornerstone for you. Although you love sex, you find fulfillment within the confines of family life. Commitment is not an eternal imprisonment as far as you're concerned. You are mature enough to express your needs within a life-long partnership. But you do make sure that there is lots of action and fun between the sheets. Lucky in love as you are, you always hit the jack pot in your relationships. You are great at keeping things light, bright and well-on-track.

Best Match: Magha is passionate and powerful. More than enough to turn you on when required. You love the intensity and natural authority of Magha. They can order you about and you won't even notice (too much). Magha offers emotional security and comfort as well as a happy family life.

Steer Clear: Dhanishta is hard work. This heavy, loaded creature will put you through the emotional ringer if you allow. It is not easy to share Dhanishta with others. So, this can be a potentially destructive union. Steer clear or learn to back-off.

UTTARA PHALGUNI + The Bull
13th September – 26th September

Vedic You: You are a solid, warm, responsive creature. Always on the go, you have oodles of energy and mountains of stamina. Sometimes though, you get over-preoccupied by what is going to happen tomorrow. This invariably detracts from what you should really be dealing with. Try not to get so distracted and focus more on the present. You are grounded enough, and it is probably a reflection of your busy ways that you need to think ahead so much. But you do often feel restricted by circumstances and hate to be in situations you cannot control. Unplanned events unsettle you; you need to know what's coming next. Routine is crucial to your equilibrium as is excitement on your own terms.

Love Style: Like the proverbial old Bull, you are a bit full of it! You have a powerful sex drive along with a predictable tendency to think the grass is greener. You desperately need the security of a relationship. But you do get lazy with your responses when settled. You definitely do not lose interest; but you do become a bit difficult to reach and can't always be bothered to get busy. The thrill of the chase excites you though, and you like to reel in prospective conquests even if you're spoken for. You will not do anything about it though.

Best Match: Purva Phalguni is a Soul Mate. This creature touches you as no other can and reaches every fiber of your being. Practically it all makes sense too. You make a good team from day to day. Anuradha will bend over backwards to please you. But perhaps this is a tad unequal. Love is reliable and consistent though.

Steer Clear: Shatabhishak is a defensive creature who is difficult to relate to. The barriers come up very quickly. It is as if, they do not want to be known at all. If you are determined, you may penetrate their heart; eventually.

HASTA + The Female Buffalo
26th September – 10th October

Vedic You: When everything is running smoothly, you are charming, generous and nicely confident. You have many friends and people generally respond well to you. But, you can be quite unapproachable and preoccupied when things aren't going your way. Fair enough! But you should find that distracting yourself by considering how others need your help works much better than a whole load of unnecessary angst. Clever as you are, your Achilles heel is this occasional introspection and vulnerability. You do become quite out-of-sorts and unsettled when things are challenging. More faith and trust in the support of unseen forces would serve you well indeed. You're great at self-promotion.

Love Style: Powerful and earthy, your sex drive is dependent on how appreciated you feel. You are reticent and shy until you know you're onto a winner. But, underneath that homely exterior is a rampant creature desperate to get-it-on. Relationships make you uneasy. Your fear is that love won't be reciprocated. You monitor your lover's responses for quite a time before you feel settled enough to let rip. More faith in you would really help your sex life. You have a lot to offer; there is no need to watch things so closely.

Best Match: Mrigasira is a vibrant creature who nurtures you and teaches so much about unconditional love and self-acceptance. This is an equal match, and your self-esteem is never better than when you are in Mrigasira's company. Mrigasira acts like a charm on your life, bringing abundance and luck

Steer Clear: Ashwini is a nitpicker when you are in the room. The incessant fault-finding is sure to wear a bit thin. If you want to make a go of it, you will have to learn decorum and detachment. Even so, it is a sweat and hardly worth it!

CHITRA + The Female Tiger
10ᵗʰ October – 23ʳᵈ October

Vedic You: You are a hectic, intense creature, always on the look-out for a party. Your life is full of mad, frantic activity and you have many interesting contacts stored on your phone or computer. You get bored quickly and need to be constantly stimulated; spare a thought for those who need to breathe-easy now and again. You are exhausting company and difficult to keep up with. Easily distracted, commitment is not your favorite word. You take a long time to settle down and prospective partners have to honor your independent spirit, or things will not last long. Your intuition is jumping and your creativity is your best friend. You rarely spend time on something that is not highly beneficial to you.

Love Style: It is a rare creature who can pin you down long-term. Your Soul Mate has to be formidable indeed to grab and keep your interest. You are not intrinsically afraid of commitment; it is just that it takes you quite a time to meet your match. In theory you are faithful and true. But the reality is in the wrong relationship, you are easily distracted. More often than not, you hook up with fellow free spirits, who are just as restless as you are. It does not make for peaceful Holy Matrimony; but the excitement quotient is high.

Best Match: Hastas is inspirational, cultured and refined. This is a classy, spirited creature who will keep you on your toes for as long as you like. Hastas is warm, earthy and generous. You will want for nothing. Hastas is attentive, creative, and more often than not loaded. Where can you go wrong?

Steer Clear: Uttara Bhadra is not the most spontaneous creature in your company. You certainly rub each other up the wrong way. But, you can improve things by not retaliating to their incessant teasing and bullying. Why bother?

SWATI + The Male Buffalo
23rd October – 6th November

Vedic You: You are an inspirational character, who thrives on knowing everybody's business. A natural politician, you are diplomatic and kind. Your concern for the greater good always wins-out as you have a way with words and leadership qualities that work in most situations. Your positive outlook inspires people, for you are a comforting presence with natural charisma and a soothing, earthy quality. Quite happy to step back, you have in-built humility and do not need to take the credit for your efforts. Your altruistic sensibilities are well-developed and you are a wonderful family member. Are you human? Fair play; but do not always gloss over your needs for the sake of others; right?

Love Style: You have the love style of a hunter and pursue your love interests relentlessly. Often your sex life gets put on hold, as you always have a lot to be getting on with. Once you get the chance though, you're up there with the best of them. Sensual and earthy; you are a great lover. There are no complaints or mumbles from the bedroom in your house. When on the prowl, you are dynamic, even aggressive. Plus, you are inclined to be possessive, needing the assurance of your lover's fidelity incessantly at the start.

Best Match: Bharani has a hypnotic effect on you. Passionate and intense, there is no room for boredom. This is a great sexual match with lots of experimentation to keep it interesting. Your earthiness compliments Bharani's general gumption, and zest for life. An empowering inspired union.

Steer Clear: Revati puts you on a pedestal which brings out the worst in you. Not normally bullish or abusive, you don't like anything too easy, so you rebel. This just does not work very well. You do not live up to their expectations.

VISHAKHA + The Male Tiger
6th November – 19th November

Vedic You: You are an intense over-bearing character who makes heavy-weather of most things. It is okay though, you get away with it, for you are usually likeable and productive. Constantly busy though, even your relationships have to run-to-schedule. This is where you should perhaps lighten up, as people often do get oppressed by you over-time. The upside is that you offer a stable and reliable presence. You are not particularly demanding, as you do not dictate to others. But you do set yourself high standards, and those who do not like it, can go elsewhere as far as you are concerned. You are dogmatic and you take things a little bit too seriously. Slow down and do not criticize.

Love Style: You are an arduous love challenge who sees a relationship through to the bitter end. You just do not know when to let go. Identify when something's not working and move on. There are no mistakes. Your Soul Mate is a tolerant being, with a broad grin and wicked sense of humor. They need both qualities; the one to melt your heart and the other to drag you out of the doldrums. Change unsettles you, which is why you hang on. But, your desire for fulfillment is strong and your sex drive is a slow burner.

Best Match: Chitra is a sexy creature who will keep that wily smile fixed firmly upon your face. Passionate and exciting too, there is a soothing quality about Chitra which suits you down to the ground. Chitra calms your soul and revs up the hormones; a potent mixture which paves the way for lasting love.

Steer Clear: Revati is a critical creature, and the two of you in combination invariably rip each other to shreds. You may try to compensate and end up not being yourself at all. There really is no point if it is such an effort.

ANDURADHA + The Female Deer
19th November – 2nd December

Vedic You: You are a bundle of laughs; probably because you are a bundle of contradictions. Your complex character certainly keeps us all amused. On the one hand, you plan things meticulously; whilst on the other, you are magically spontaneous and lots of fun to be with. It all depends on your waking mood, what kind of day it is going to be. Sometimes you are a fearful, over emotional creature, afraid to bare your soul lest it get in the way of a productive day's work. You tend to distract yourself with endless projects when you are going through a rough patch. Spiritual and kind as you are, life is not always easy, and you have jaded cynical responses which surface from time to time.

Love Style: You are a true romantic with a real love of refined gestures and sumptuous settings. In love with love, you fall quickly in love and get bitterly disappointed when things go wrong. Likely to be a bit transparent with your emotions, you are not much of a challenge. You get downtrodden when neglected, and too often your emotions are unrequited when you attract the wrong type of lover. All is well when you hook up with your Soul Mate, for they share your aesthetic sense and love to love as much as you do.

Best Match: Jyeshta is everything you could wish for. A passionate, sexy, and sensual package, you really would be daft to look elsewhere. Jyeshta is tailor made for commitment, and does not mind your changeable, sometimes flighty nature. This creature sees you and likes everything about you.

Steer Clear: Chitra is a stickler for detail and likely to be very nit-picky in your company. You really will not have a moment's peace. This creature is not very good at flying high, and your spirit gets crushed fairly quickly by Chitra.

JYESHTA + The Male Deer
2nd December – 15th December

Vedic You: You are a formidable creature. Charismatic and spiritual, you love to be challenged and enjoy living life to the full. Spiritually well-developed and mature, you have an innate understanding of the way things should be. Talented and creative, you invariably demonstrate true genius in whatever you attempt. You do not need to be competitive; things come naturally to you. Others find you daunting and those who are less than secure often get jealous of what you are able to do, without even having to think. What riles such people is that you don't even notice how clever and effortless you are. You have everything deep-within and therefore need nothing; an enviable life indeed.

Love Style: Your high intelligence means you can be very cool in the love stakes. Just as well you have integrity. Your brilliant mind has oodles of allure and compassion, so those who do not find you threatening find you very attractive indeed. You do not have to do much to seduce your lover. Your sex life is potent and passionate. Indeed, you won't make love unless it is going to take you to that other place. Your spirit has to fly, or else you will not bother. Passion and soul connections go hand in hand for you. Very Tantric!

Best Match: Magha is warm and loving; a gentle soul who will nourish your often battered spirit. Magha provides security and support. You really will want for nothing as your every need will be tended to. Even your extreme sensitivity is nurtured and valued. Magha calms you down and spurs you on.

Steer Clear: This is a combustible union. Ardra is difficult to trust and has a completely different take on what is acceptable. You are likely to react by being dominant and aggressive. Then Ardra retaliates and its general mayhem.

MULA + The Male Dog
15th December – 28th December

Vedic You: You are a productive, intelligent, hard-working character. But you do have a self-destructive tendency, which manifests as grumpiness or petulance in your closest relationships. Even though you are intrinsically loyal, you cannot bear to be wrong, and you do sometimes border on paranoia. Because of your well-honed instincts, you rarely miss a trick. But be assured, it is pretty messy when you do. Your cleverness is your saving grace, and you have good staying power as well as discipline. When your interest is engaged, you make a great and reliable employee. But when you are listless or restless, you can become snappy, aggressive and untamed. You bite!

Love Style: Your dangerous, snappy side makes you uneasy re sexual experimentation. Part of you is worried about taking things too far too soon. Do not panic even as you make your suggestions. It is okay to test the water; no one can reprimand you for that. But, you do indeed have some interesting fantasies. You need an understanding, up-for-it partner who supports your wicked ways and allows you to reach your fullest potential in-the-sack. Loving stability brings out the worst in you, and I mean that in a positive way.

Best Match: Purva Ashadha provides a tranquil environment and calms you down. You do not feel quite so wound up and angry about everything. This is an unconventional union. As a couple, you do what you want; when you want. Other Mulas understand you. But it is a bit dull in the long-run; you're too similar.

Steer Clear: Punarvasu winds you up to the point of no return. They then become demanding, possessive and hypocritical. Punarvasu will not commit in a hurry. But will expect you to behave. Arguments are memorable and entertaining.

PURVA ASHADHA + The Male Monkey
28th December – 11th January

Vedic You: You are a talented, creative creature with oodles of nervous energy. Your natural flare and panache ensure you top the class effortlessly. Those who do not know or trust you, frequently get jealous; stirred by your self-assurance and ease of expression. Thankfully, you do not really notice. Courageous as you are, you are also quite changeable. Flexible and well able to move on quickly if required; you are also pretty nifty at shifting the goal posts to suit yourself. This is confusing for your conventional, staid friends and loved ones, who find it difficult to keep up with your latest whim. But you are usually validated by your choices which inevitably lead to great success.

Love Style: You love mind games and mental connections. If someone doesn't grab you intellectually as well as physically, there is unlikely to be much action in the bedroom. You need to be stimulated from the head down; and a wicked sense of humor works every time. Exclusively cerebral relationships you find stifling and restrictive. You need fun and laughter with plenty of high jinx to keep you coming back for more. Sexual union is a way to express your-self heart and soul; so it has to makes sense on all levels.

Best Match: Revati compliments you well, and can read your mind brilliantly. You can be serious-minded one minute, wickedly mischievous the next. Revati is sensitive to your needs, loves sex. But can be pushy at clever moments. Revati allows you to be; is not in the least bit clingy and loves you up in the right way.

Steer Clear: Your union with Dhanishta has a quick burn-out factor. Things get intense quickly. But the rot sets in when commitment issues surface. Dhanishta can be thoughtful and caring, so try to enjoy the positive bits.

UTTARA ASHADHA + The Mongoose
11th January – 24th January

Vedic You: You have an arid, dry humor, so you are not the best flirt in the world. Your natural intelligence makes you over-analytical. But you love a good argument, so long as it is civilized. You find it very difficult to cope with aggression one-on-one, and avoid confrontation at all costs. But, you are direct; up-front and straightforward. What you see is what you get. You have a way of getting to the heart of a problem. Your advice is always relevant, so loved ones frequently turn to you for support. But, because you are so sorted, others assume you do not need the same reassurance and security as they do. Not in the least bit insecure, you often get overlooked. Tell them you need cuddles too.

Love Style: You are complex creature when it comes to love-stuff. You have many needs and a spiritual connection is just as important to you as a sexual one. Quick to make your move when you fancy someone; in your established relationships, you can be quite passive. You generally prefer a lover to make the running. But, when you are on the prowl it is all systems go. Day-to-day concerns are a turn off for you, and you really can't be bothered with mundane nonsense. Love has to make your spirit fly; or you are off into the middle-distance very quickly.

Best Match: Uttara Bhadra loves you deeply, so don't doubt their sincerity. Their calm, even temperament wins you over slowly but surely. This creature understands your vulnerable side, and is patient and kind too. You can work through all life's challenges confidently with Uttara Bhadra at your side.

Steer Clear: Magha is so different from you, that this normally reasonable creature gets right under your skin; and not in a good way. Vicious anger and irrational aggression flare up when the negative influences kick-in.

SHRAVANA + The Female Monkey
24th January – 6th February

Vedic You: You are a complex creature with a strong maternal instinct and developed feminine side. Although you are very loving, others find it difficult to keep up with you. Changeable and unpredictable; when the fancy takes you, you are off. Thankfully, your concern for loved ones means that you stop short of disaster. But it is an important part of your psyche to pursue your fantasies and daydreams. Despite your inclinations, you know when to back-off, and you are not overtly prone to obsessive behavior. People do not always understand you; you do not explain yourself very well. But you are an old softie as well as sentimental through and through. Only mind-readers need apply.

Love Style: You are a jumpy, edgy lover who finds it difficult to settle. Relationships may come and go, but you still hold the ideal of a blissful family life close to your heart. Are you are looking too hard for perfection? Why not relax and run with what you have got? Love has more chance if you deal with what is what. Do not leap too far ahead and spoil it all before it even gets off-the-ground. Your playful streak is lots of fun. But generally, your light-side comes out for an airing only when you're sorted.

Best Match: Purva Ashadha is in tune with your body, mind, and spirit. This is an intense sexual union, which can develop on all levels given enough time and patience. Try to get past the physical aspect and see what else is there. Uttara Bhadra makes a great life-partner. Love grows and matures over time.

Steer Clear: Magha is not tolerant of your wants and needs. Magha has an agenda. Not many manage to pin down or fluster this flighty spirit. Your own emotions may get overlooked and this relationship makes you wobble.

DHANISHTA + The Lioness
6th February – 19th February

Vedic You: You are an idealistic spirit who is very good at fighting everyone else's battles. A Trojan, stoic character, you are great at shaking off the doldrums and coming up with a game-plan for tackling the latest dilemmas. Your largesse and grand persona hates to be restricted, so you get stressed out by unnecessary nonsense and agendas. You often wonder why the whole world is not as straightforward and kind hearted as you. But you are no push over and you do see things for what they are; as well as what you want them to be. Your childlike hope and excitement often surfaces and takes over. But it is this wonderful quality that redeems you and everyone else you meet, time and time again.

Love Style: You are a passionate but cuddly creature; a great mixture that brings you a whole lot of loving. Your sex drive is strong and you are ardent in the expression of love. While someone is loyal to you; you are loyal to them. But if you get double-crossed, you come up with a revenge plan, which usually involves a long wait so you can serve the dish cold. You love the thrill of the chase and when single you see a good bit of action whilst you make your mind up who is right for the long-haul. A lucky love star indeed.

Best Match: Shatabhishak is compelling, mystical and mysterious. This creature will keep you fascinated for hours on end. You're both independent, and neither of you has a problem with the other doing what they will. This is a balanced, mature union. Committed yet not stifling; perfect bliss in fact.

Steer Clear: Uttara Bhadra is a stubborn, tricky customer who brings out the worst in you. The thick skin of the Elephant is oblivious to your refinement and sophistication. Do you like being unappreciated? Hardly!

SHATABHISHAK + The Female Horse
19th February – 4th March

Vedic You: You are a mysterious, ethereal creature who loves to fathom the depths of life itself. As well as being many layered and complex yourself, you love to understand what makes others tick. Your life's mission is to glean as much knowledge as possible, and you delight in the quest of wisdom. Oftentimes your spiritual nature distracts you from more earthly pursuits; like a sex life. Developing your persona and furthering those aspirations is your main aim. But of course, you need love and affection just like anyone else. Quite perfectionist, you have high expectations of yourself and others. The sickening thing is; you always pass life's trials and tribulations with flying colors.

Love Style: You are fussy when it comes to your love life. But you are no prude. It is just you prefer to hold back until you are absolutely sure of someone. You come across as quite traditional and subdued. The truth is there are hidden depths to you that come out to play once you get into gear. You are up for excitement and stimulation within your relationships, despite all appearances. But, your expectations let you down. Love would come easier, if you would only chill. No one is perfect, so work with what's real.

Best Match: Rohini is a true romantic who restores your faith in love. Like soothing balm for the troubled soul, Rohini nurtures you. You feel affirmed and appreciated. Prepare for a sexy rollercoaster ride with Dhanishta. Your feet will not touch the ground, and your heart welcomes this love match with ease.

Steer Clear: Punarvasu is a complicated, slippery creature. Difficult to understand Punarvasu blows hot and cold. One minute you feel smothered; the next neglected. Your own inconsistency does not help; a definite miss-match.

PURVA BHADRA + The Lion
4th March – 17th March

Vedic You: Relationships are your be all and end all. If you are not experiencing quality connections, you feel shortchanged. Ambitions, material goods and status are all very well; but what really floats your boat is great company. Passionate exchanges are more important than major success or lots of dosh. Of course you would like all of the above; but you are genuinely not too bothered. You can take or leave the good times, so long as you have deep, lasting love links. The inbuilt irony is that you often receive everything you think you don't need, anyhow. Life is good to you. You are lucky, self-contained and well-blessed. In return you support and sustain those you love; no questions asked.

Love Style: You give your all to relationships, especially passionate ones. Your sex drive is strong and you have stamina left to burn. Your ideal partner has their work cut out to keep up. But you are tender, loving and kind, so there are never too many complaints. Love rarely gives you much cause for concern. Your luck is such that the pain of unrequited love usually eludes you. It is thankfully not a huge part of life's game plan. Even when relationships get stressful, you always have a tactic ready to improve things.

Best Match: Uttara Bhadra balances your refined, majestic, untamed nature. Practical and eminently sensible, Uttara Bhadra brings out the best in you. Together, you can have it all. This is a lucky, abundant union full of promise and goodness. Stop hankering after what will never be and enjoy what is.

Steer Clear: Jyeshta stirs you up profoundly, but in quite disturbing ways. Do not go near this creature if you want a quiet life. Passionate at first, Jyeshta keeps you guessing; but ends up pushing all the wrong buttons. Pure torture, really.

UTTARA BHADRA + The Cow
17th March – 31st March

Vedic You: You are a sensuous, soulful creature with hidden depths. Others tend to underestimate you, as you are much more complex than you first appear. You love your home comforts and feel under-par in sparse surroundings. Control and having things "just so" is important to you. You do not want to come across as too demanding, so you pride yourself on keeping your desires under wraps. Spirituality is important to you, and you are prepared to make certain sacrifices in life to preserve your integrity. Do remember that it's okay to loosen up and have fun. You are a mature character, but there is nothing to lose if you enjoy the medicine of a good laugh now and again. No one is watching.

Love Style: Love and sex go hand in hand as far as you're concerned. You do not get one without the other; well, one shouldn't be happening without the other. To find lasting happiness is your game plan, and if you do not find love, you are self-contained enough for it not to matter too much. Whilst single, you are not adverse to a touch of experimentation. You are not totally devoid of fun and adventure; not by any means. But the ultimate prize is the conglomeration of love, commitment, and loyalty.

Best Match: Revati makes a great match; together you can conquer the world. You are both willing to put the work in and your natures fit snuggly. This union is special and sacred. You include and help many along the way; your relationship is all-embracing. Pettiness and silliness don't get a look-in.

Steer Clear: Bharani finds you a bit off-balance. You are inclined to give more than you gain in this union. In your company, Bharani becomes one of life's takers. They are compelling and sensual, but not compatible.

REVATI + The Female Elephant
31st March – 12th April

Vedic You: You are a creature of huge integrity and high standards. Those who know you are lucky indeed, for you find the best in everyone. You are inspirational and kind with a delicate sensibility and soft heart. Your spirituality is well-developed and you have a sophisticated code of conduct by which you live; which is not in the least bit contrived. Your heart and soul are genuine; one could not ask for a better companion. Often though, you get disappointed by others and by life itself. You are not oblivious to the trials and tribulations of our existence. But you do have an amazing resilience and optimism that sees you through most things. Your stubborn streak is your saving grace!

Love Style: The union of sex, romance and love is very important to you. You will not usually have sex for the sake of it. But you do relish the activity when in a meaningful relationship. You are a perfectionist and very intense, so early on in love, you can be a tad overbearing. Sometimes you over analyze new links. Just be careful not to miss out on true love. When love is fully reciprocated, you sense how to balance things much better. It is the knowledge that you are truly loved that enables you to give selflessly.

Best Match: Uttara Bhadra is a special, comforting companion. Together, you create a lasting, union that touches many. Peaceful and happy, Uttara Bhadra keeps you serene and smiling all your days. There is barely a cross word between you. But it's not in the least bit boring.

Steer Clear: Vishakta is very full-on sexually, and you respond better to more subtle moves. Vishakta is also not big on commitment, so if you're getting it together steer well clear of ultimatums.

30 CHINESE ZODIAC LOVE STYLE

According to legend the origins of Chinese astrology evolved from Buddah himself. Apparently only twelve animals turned up in response to Buddah's invitation for the naming of animals. Hence the twelve Zodiac signs have a different complexion in the Far East. The correct order of attendance was the RAT, the OX, the TIGER, the RABBIT, the DRAGON, the SNAKE, the HORSE, the GOAT, the MONKEY, the ROOSTER, the DOG and finally the PIG. Consequently Buddah decided to name various years after the animals that bothered to show up. The idea being that people born in any given year would inherit many of the characteristics of the relevant animal.

As with all esoteric tools, Chinese Astrology offers another fascinating system based upon the laws of synchronicity and Universal law. Expect to see significant traits reflected in your relevant sign, but be aware that there are also five different categories of each animal to consider. It gets more complicated, but bear with me. Each of these sacred creatures has a connection to either METAL, WATER, WOOD, FIRE, or EARTH. These elements are prominent in the art of Feng Shui..

There is not the scope in this chapter to go into much detail about the specific differences between the Water Rabbit and the Wooden one. But use your powers of inference, and be aware that the Water Rabbit would be a fluid and emotional animal; while the Metal Rabbit would be tougher and more steely! It is of course more intricate than this, but use your imagination, and it will give you the right idea. Keep in mind the quality of the element that describes your power animal and work around it accordingly.

NB. Please note that some books refer to the OX as the BULL or BUFFALO, the RABBIT as the CAT or HARE, and the GOAT sometimes passes as the SHEEP. The Chinese New Year always begins at some point between the end of January and mid- February, depending on the year in question.

Years re Chinese Horoscopes

TIGER = 1938 (Earth), 1950 (Metal), 1962 (Water), 1974 (Wood), 1986 (Fire), 1998 (Earth), 2010 (Metal)

RABBIT = 1939 (Earth), 1951 (Metal), 1963 (Water), 1975 (Wood), 1987 (Fire), 1999 (Earth), 2011 (Metal)

DRAGON = 1940 (Metal), 1952 (Water), 1964 (Wood), 1976 (Fire), 1988 (Earth), 2000 (Metal), 2012 (Water)

SNAKE = 1941 (Metal), 1953 (Water), 1965 (Wood), 1977 (Fire), 1989 (Earth), 2001 (Metal). 2013 (Water)

HORSE = 1942 (Water), 1954 (Wood), 1966 (Fire), 1978 (Earth), 1990 (Metal), 2002 (Water), 2014 (Wood)

GOAT= 1943 (Water), 1955 (Wood), 1967 (Fire), 1979 (Earth), 1991 (Metal), 2003 (Water), 2015 (Wood)

MONKEY= 1944 (Wood), 1956 (Fire), 1968 (Earth), 1980 (Metal), 1992 (Water), 2004 (Wood), 2016 (Fire)

ROOSTER= 1945 (Wood), 1957 (Fire), 1969 (Earth), 1981 (Metal), 1993 (Water), 2005 (Wood), 2017 (Fire)

DOG= 1946 (Fire), 1958 (Earth), 1970 (Metal), 1982 (Water), 1994 (Wood), 2006 (Fire), 2018 (Earth)

PIG= 1947 (Fire), 1959 (Earth), 1971 (Metal), 1983 (Water), 1995 (Wood), 2007 (Fire), 2019 (Earth)

RAT= 1948 (Earth), 1960 (Metal), 1972 (Water), 1984 (Wood), 1996 (Fire), 2008 (Wood), 2020 (Fire)

OX= 1949 (Earth), 1961 (Metal), 1973 (Water), 1985 (Wood), 1997 (Fire), 2009 (Wood), 2021 (Fire)

LIFE HINTS

TIGER

Tigers can expect steady and respectable progress, along their life path. There is no point in getting ahead of things if you are a Tiger. Remain measured, magnanimous and modest. The proceedings may be initially drab and colourless which will frustrate the colourful Tiger.

Action and dynamic events are stimulating for this magnificent creature. But the tendency towards low-key events will give the Tiger time to consolidate recent gains. The chance to reflect and build on past success should be gratefully received. Make progress slowly but surely. The extension of your network of contacts will ensure a stable and profitable future. Tigers should feel free to take the initiative. But must remain sensitive to the delicate infra structure of their private life.

Expect interesting challenges and possible developments. Tigers should show commitment to a specific plan of action. Make intelligent decisions and do not waiver once under way. Consistency is everything. Socially, life can be a mellow but rewarding time for Tigers. Take the opportunities that arise organically and make the most of apparently unexciting invitations.

Singletons can expect a rewarding early start to new relationships. But they must not rush things along. Accept people at face value or not at all. Tigers will need to be adaptable, patient and tolerant. Ingratiate yourself with good behaviour and there will be benefits from the most uninspiring scenarios. Avoid judging the book by its cover. Be open to events however banal. Pleasantries will be tedious but serve you well.

There may be a tangible flow of creative energy courtesy of your own self. Simply access it for great results. Be brave enough to forward your inspirational ideas and have the courage of your convictions. Confidence in your abilities will serve you well at this time.

Pay attention to a fitness regime. The Tiger is prone to feeling intermittently sluggish and lethargic. Exercise will keep energies topped-up. Overall, enjoy life with a laid back approach. A mellow attitude will benefit the outcome of potentially difficult scenarios. Occasional breaks from routine will help Tigers prepare for life's challenges. Invest in the future and prepare to yield an abundant harvest; eventually.

Compatibility: TIGERS are well suited in personal relationships with the HORSE, the DOG, and the PIG. In Business and work situations the HORSE is good to have around. Be cautious of the SNAKE, MONKEY and OX in love relationships. Of course it does not mean "do not go there." Forewarned is forearmed: conflict is likely. In competitive situations avoid fellow TIGERS, The SNAKE, The ROOSTER, and the OX.

RABBIT

The Rabbit is all set for an enjoyable pleasant lifetime courtesy of their own initiative. Rabbits have a certain amount of control and can dictate the way things roll. They have the luxury of being able to keep some semblance of order. After changeable volatile times, the Rabbit is always able to make a concerted effort to find stability. Rabbits will always be able to relax and thrive. A renewed ease to the Rabbit demeanour is always fortuitous. Simply by letting things go and letting things be, the Rabbit falls on its furry feet.

The Rabbit should ignore knocks and disappointments, and not give them too much energy. Set-backs will organically adjust and right themselves. Rabbit talents will always be stretched, and opportunities to flourish will present themselves. Prospects for the Rabbit are good. But as a Rabbit you will need to find your direction, and make pertinent, sensible decisions.

Rabbits must not be afraid to take the initiative in work situations. The good stuff will not fall out of the sky. But do not appear to be too eager to push for self- advancement. Finding fine balance is the key to success. If you are a Rabbit make the most of established contacts. Use in-house people who value your judgement to promote your cause. Genuine opportunities will arise if you are keen and enterprising. Eliminate feelings of frustration and failure- these hold you back, and hamper your progress.

Rabbits must allow their creativity freedom of expression. If the Rabbit is willing to develop and use its intuition, not much will stand in the way of success. Hobbies may unexpectedly turn into lucrative work pursuits if Rabbits take a risk or two. Pertinent action will be rewarded. Finances need care and Rabbits should be sensible as per! Allowances should be made for unexpected expenses linked to travel and accommodation.

Financial folly is never advisable, though Rabbits have an innate survival system, and they are intrinsically lucky. However the Rabbit must remain cautious and circumspect when it comes to money. Do put a stop to lavish or unnecessary expenditure. But sniff out openings and do not miss out on genuine opportunities.

Compatibility: RABBITS are well matched personally to the GOAT, the DOG, Fellow RABBITS, and the Snake. They should stay well away from the ROOSTER in relationships, and the HORSE, ROOSTER and MONKEY in business. Good business links for the RABBIT are with the GOAT and PIG.

DRAGON

Dragons can expect a pleasant enough life-time, depending on how they play it. Dragons would always be well-advised to be flexible in the midst of changing circumstances. They should learn to adjust and adapt as and when things arise. Attitude is critical to the level of success Dragons may reach. Significant events will have an important knock-on effect. What the Dragon accepts, lets-go of, or develops will as always need careful consideration. Personal and professional issues must be thought through properly. Action taken in the right spirit will bring inspirational results. But reckless or impatient choices will only make matters worse.

Dragons should embrace opportunities for further training. New skills will always serve the Dragon well. Lessons learned are destiny moments that will radically shape the Dragon's future. Dragons would do well to broaden their horizons. New roles, requests and opportunities are worth following through to the hilt. Originality of thought will be well rewarded; and the Dragon should use its vivid imagination in controversial situations. Finances must be dealt with for order to descend. A savings plan or further investment would not go amiss for Dragons. Vigilance in practical matters is advisable.

Balance in a Dragon's life is crucial. The temptation to focus fully on work will lead to accusations if loved ones are neglected. Enjoyable social activities are worthwhile, and any chance of a break should be accepted. Dragons must not become too engrossed in their work at the expense of personal relationships. All diversions should be gratefully received for entertainment's sake.

Romance is ever possible for singletons, and new connections will progress quickly for Dragons. Be open to love, and do not be alarmed at the speed of some of the developments. Expect romance, work and head wreck; possibly in that order. Start as you mean to go on. Find personal balance and do not waste your time heading down glamorous blind alleys. Discrimination will serve the Dragon well. So use wisdom, patience and intuition for the best results.

Compatibility: DRAGONS are well suited to the RAT, the SNAKE, and the MONKEY. They should avoid the DOG in both business and personal relationships. DRAGONS also work well with the RAT, the SNAKE and the MONKEY.

SNAKE

Snakes will do well to be reasonable, dedicated and disciplined. The Snake should stick to what is familiar and comfortable. Risks are inadvisable, as a rule-of-thumb. There will be plenty of scope for social and romantic enjoyment, for Snakes attract this kind of attention. But be selective with encounters of the close kind. Opportunities will be many and varied on the social scene. But there will often be traps, agendas and competition to deal with. Use that wily Snake like discretion, and slither away when the going gets rough.

Snakes can make great progress with their individual thinking. Opportunities to expand personal skills, and training should always be welcomed. If you are a Snake, keep your eyes peeled for opportune moments. Snakes would do well to pay attention and make judgements only when the evidence presents itself. Premature or hasty decisions will back fire. So stay alert all you Snakes!

Your best chances are rooted in what you already know. Beware of fanciful notions or dreams and visions that threaten to cloud your perception. Give yourself regular reality checks as time progresses. Mixing business and pleasure is oddly well advised, as partnerships can cope with many layers of expression. Timely information will surface from the most unlikely sources. Always be responsive and ready.

Your Snake like charm and intelligence will take you far. But do not be tempted to resort to manipulation or devious behaviour. All links with creativity, the arts or design will be lucky for Snakes. If you are a Snake take the advice of a professional if you find yourself legally or financially strapped. Snakes should be vigilant and sensible in money matters. Snakes should exercise financial caution and wise investment is advisable if possible.

Snakes are intrinsically lucky and can expect good return from time and money well spent. New friends and acquaintance will enliven your time, as always. Creative ideas will come thick and fast, if you open your mind and allow things to flow.

On a personal level the Snake will always face challenges. Contentment will derive from family ties. But expectations will have to be fulfilled to keep loved ones sweet. Commitments must be met, or the Snake could run into trouble.

Snakes must avoid retreat when the going gets rough; and be ready to compromise for the sake of harmony and peace. Settling down and consolidating past progress is eternally advisable. Snakes are typically cautious regarding personal commitments. But good energy will inspire Snakes to trust, relax and try a little bit more. Intimate environments will become a breeding ground for self-expression. Look out for that glint in reptilian eyes as you go about your business.

Compatibility: SNAKES are well suited to the ROOSTER, the DRAGON, and the OX re personal connections. They should avoid the TIGER, the PIG, and fellow SNAKES. SNAKES work well with the ROOSTER and the DRAGON.

HORSE

Horses can expect to be singled out for recognition during their colourful lives. Focus is always important for the Horse. So decisions need to be made about general direction. If Horses are willing to follow guidance and do what is asked, they stand to reach a spectacular level of achievement.

Other Zodiac signs are well disposed towards the Horse. So this equine creature should make the most of the good vibrations. Horses should not be afraid to express themselves or their talents at any time the urge takes them. They must concentrate on what comes naturally rather than force issues.

Irrational risk taking will not pay off for the Horse. Horses must not follow through on a whim and a prayer. But a meticulous and careful approach will yield positive results. The Horse must decide what it wants and pursue it relentlessly through to the end. Finances need due care and attention. Location is an issue that will have to be addressed.

Control and focus are the keys to success for the Horse. But they should remain flexible and allow for swift and sudden change. Material matters will be challenging but interesting. Avoid panic if you are a horse. A bolt from the blue may send you into a spin. But breathe deeply and calm down quick. Home improvements or a move will be worth the effort. Rewards from time and money invested at this point will bring enjoyment for many years to come.

Domestically life will be fulfilling but changeable for Horses. There will always be unusual opportunities to socialise. So accept all invites with enthusiasm.

Single Horses can look forward to interesting connections and several new relationships will manifest at unexpected moments. It is constructive for the Horse to always embrace the unusual or the challenging. As a variety of experiences will maintain interest. Make the most of talents, imagination and creativity. The rewards will be, well, rewarding.

Compatibility: HORSES relate well to the DOG, the TIGER, and fellow HORSES. They should steer clear of the RAT, the MONKEY, and the RABBIT. In business the HORSE connects well with the TIGER, the DOG and the ROOSTER. But should distrust the RAT, the OX, and the RABBIT.

GOAT

Every year is a great year for the Goat. But organisation is needed in order to take advantage of the opportunities therein. All levels and aspects of Goat life are permanently well favoured. But Goats should concentrate on where they are headed; and good progress can be made despite recent disappointments. Goats should develop their ideas, as their unique perception will be well received.

Goats are the masters of their destiny, and should realise the power that lies within. The energy invested in worthwhile projects will be highly advantageous. Deep thinking and intelligent decisions are advisable. Goats must not be tempted to drift on or waste precious moments. They should follow through hunches and intuitions. If you were born in Goat time, you would do well to assess what is truly for you.

Financially Goats must not act on impulse or behave recklessly. Be selective re what seduces the purse strings. The development of a current hobby, or interest always has the potential to bring equilibrium and balance to the Goat. Goats can expect times of personal fulfilment and happiness. But they will need sensitivity in dealings with temperamental loved ones. The foibles and eccentricities of others will be challenging.

The key factors that guarantee a bumper stretch of success for the Goat are action and initiative. Brave moves will bring recognition. But reckless impulsiveness should be avoided. The balance is fine, and you must spot your moment. Random acts are not the best route to enlightenment. However, intelligent risk taking will always be very profitable.

Compatibility: GOATS are well suited to RABBITS, fellow GOATS, and PIGS. They should avoid ROOSTERS, DOGS, RATS, and the OX in personal relationships. In Business GOATS connect well with RABBITS and fellow GOATS.

MONKEY

The Monkey must watch its wicked sense of mischief. Over eagerness or indiscriminate rampant enthusiasm could get the better of this tricky creature. Monkeys beware! As long as the Monkey keeps a rein on its more adventurous tendencies all will be well.

If you are a Monkey do not over reach or over extend yourself. Acrobatic as you are, you would not want to swing too high and miss your footing now, would you? Monkeys should build on current foundations and elevate their present position slowly but surely.

Monkeys must give all opportunities their best shot though. There is always a measure of unpredictability, if you are a Monkey-condition normal.

Keep your eyes peeled for unsolicited information, which is always! Never trust your luck to the point of folly. But do be aware that progress may happen upon you, so a little opportunism is absolutely fine.

Monkeys should build on links with what they already know and love. Logical developments will guarantee success in any case, never mind the spooky stuff. Things will happen and advancement in the Monkey universe is assured.

Monkeys can benefit themselves by referring to past achievements to sell a point. Do not be afraid to sing your own praises as a Monkey, but not too eloquently. Shine out just enough to get attention. But do not repel others with egocentricity. Guard against lavish spending and unnecessary extravagance. Be sensible about what you can achieve. Travel is always advised, and well-starred for the Monkey; so perhaps budget for trips as an on-going discipline. The Monkey's need to wander will have to be satiated somehow, but keep it clean.

Relationships are delicate for the Monkey. Monkeys will have to guard against selfish behaviour; and they must consider the desires, wants and needs of loved ones, or things could get messy. Efforts will be rewarded in a domestic situation. But neglect may sadly strain important relationships. Forewarned is forearmed. Monkeys can expect a full and active social diary. Balance is the key to keeping things sweet.

New relationships are always on the horizon, as the Monkey circle extends itself. Scandal, gossip, surprises, and interesting scenarios inspire endless chatter. Allow new links the space and time to develop. Rushing in too quickly will not serve the Monkey well at any time. But discipline will definitely enhance the Monkey's luck. There are always a myriad of directions life could take. Sometimes, Monkey should just decide on a course of action, and be disciplined enough to see it through.

Compatibility: MONKEYS do well in love with RATS, DRAGONS, and fellow MONKEYS. They should avoid the TIGER and the ROOSTER in love connections. In business MONKEYS connect well with the RABBIT, the SNAKE, and the ROOSTER. They should avoid doing business with DRAGONS and RATS.

ROOSTER

Roosters can look forward to a prosperous lifetime. It takes a while for the momentum of change to kick in. But Roosters can expect positive motion; steering them ever onwards and upwards.

If you are a Rooster build on all positive experiences, think clearly and take up all invites. Precious opportunities lurk in unexpected corners for Roosters. Take definite action to address outstanding problems, and nip any hassle in-the-bud. Do not allow negativity to fester, as this will undermine progress. Make the moves and the rest will follow. Pay extra attention to the moods and wishes of loved ones; and generally stay ahead of the game.

The Rooster can expect many make-or-break opportunities. So guard against laziness that could easily scupper your position. Never allow the rut of complacency a look-in. Roosters should make strides by being as charming as possible. Be open as a Rooster and hold on-to a modicum of humility, or you may alienate people. Pride comes before a fall, remember?

Unexpected interest in your talents and image will leave you feeling like the cat that got the cream. Roosters only stand to remain in a rut if they choose to do so. There is so much potential for the Rooster that it would be a sin to miss out. Do not be afraid to follow through hunches. Use your intuition and you will be the victor in complex situations.

Roosters must not let the past hold them back. Remain open to progress and take your chances. Watch energy levels and sleep when tired. Eat properly and take sufficient exercise. The scales will directly reflect your state of mind. So keep yourself in peak condition.

Personal relationships will benefit from a conducive and comfortable domestic environment. Create harmony in your living space and so create good vibes with loved ones. Home improvements will bring the Rooster great contentment and a sense of fulfilment. The Rooster must watch the hectic schedule however. As priorities will be challenged at various points. The Rooster would do well to learn more flexibility. Rigid and fixed attitudes will create difficulties and prevent the importance of a compromise.

The Rooster must be eternally ready for anything. Activity social, romantic and professional will keep Roosters very busy indeed. Anything that enriches life and broadens the Rooster's experience should be fully embraced.

Compatibility: ROOSTERS do very well in relationship with SNAKES, the OX, the DRAGON, and the HORSE. They should take it easy with the RABBIT, the RAT, and fellow ROOSTERS. In business, ROOSTERS connect well with the OX and the SNAKE. But not with other ROOSTERS.

DOG

The Dog must always guard its interests carefully. More haste, less speed is the maxim that comes to mind. Dogs should put effort into whatever makes sense re their specific needs, wants and requirements.

If you are a Dog let things unfold in their own time. But do concentrate on what you really want. The right things will take root, but only if you focus and visualise the desired outcome. Dogs are well advised to consolidate their position. But adding to their current field of experience will also bring rewards.

Major advancement will not happen overnight, except in very unusual circumstances. Dogs would do well to check out the problem areas and stumbling blocks along the way. A bit of lateral thought will help the Dog unravel complex situations.

New training is always a great idea for Dogs, if the timing makes sense. Learning new things should always be a major priority, never mind the supposed barriers of age, finance, or culture. The Dog should expand its horizons and keep the grey matter stimulated.

Teamwork is potentially rewarding for Dogs. Calling-in the support of family and friends will help the Dog through the challenges that arise. Dogs must watch that they do not speak out of turn. They surely value their independence. As always, the Dog needs support and companionship to give life extra oomph and enrichment.

Dogs must find solutions to the sometimes unfair demands on their time, energy, and emotions. They should guard against others taking advantage of their amenable nature. The Dog will always be noted for its persistence, dedication and tenacity.

Dogs need courage and they will find it worthwhile to circumnavigate unnecessary pressure. Transform current lessons to serve you well in the years to come. Dogs should watch, listen and learn with genuine enthusiasm. The Dog life-time is all set to be rewarding, if not a little bitter-sweet. When the going gets tough. Woof!

Compatibility: DOGS make great romantic connections with the TIGER, The HORSE, and the PIG. In business they work well with TIGERS and HORSES. DOGS should avoid connections with DRAGONS, or at least be well guarded around this fiery opposition.

PIG

Pigs can expect a golden lifetime. Domestically there is always the need to reorganise, prioritise and generally get moving. Pigs must delegate between loved ones and friends, and not be afraid to call in favours. Pigs must not even attempt to shoulder all the burdens. The various degrees of responsibility are negotiable.

If you are a Pig, be open to discussion, and stay upbeat when the challenges arise. The Pig's social life will be rewarding. But balance is needed- there is work to be done.. Pigs must be willing to bury the hatchet regarding past hurts and disappointments. Make emotional detachment and personal development a priority if you are a Pig. All will be well if you take things honestly, sweetly and from the heart at all times.

Pigs should take advantage of offers arising in the work place. There will be opportunities to progress, but they will be subtle and apparently indiscernible.

Pigs should learn to spot their moment and make nifty moves at the appropriate time. Finances look blessed so long as the Pig remains cautious and sensible. Money will flow in and out of accounts like water. It is always timely for Pigs to develop their investments and savings plan.

Pigs can always find ways to improve their luck and expand their resources. Creative initiative will get the Pig everywhere, always. Life will bring many blessings along with challenges that will stimulate personal growth. So snort around and be as prolific as possible.

Compatibility: PIGS are well suited to the DOG, the TIGER, the RABBIT, and the DRAGON. They should be very wary of the SNAKE. In business and work situations PIGS like the GOAT, fellow PIGS, and the RABBIT.

RAT

Rats can always get things started, if they so decide. Much drive and creative energy will give rise to good opportunities. Rats should learn from experience and integrate past failures and disappointments. The future looks inspiring, so long as the Rat can leave mistakes firmly behind.

A new and positive approach will often inspire the Rat. Determination can be renewed, but it will take a deliberate decision, and a change of outlook to bring about fundamental changes. Rats can make great strides, but it takes a massive personal effort to manifest the magic. Acting on impulse can also bring its own reward. Rats have the power and commitment to turn their lives around at any time they decide. They must be simply prepared to take responsibility for initiative, and their enterprises will be duly rewarded. Things will not fall into the Rat's lap. But personal commitment and endeavour will guarantee results.

Rats must find the time to relax amidst frenetic activity. Schedules will become hectic, so the unwind in the eye of the storm, will be fundamentally important.

The Rat's personal life will get controversial at points. But it is always exciting and decisions must be made. Rats should not run and hide, but face things head on. Their responsibility must be honoured, but it is important to give "number 12more attention.

The Rat can achieve great things using wit and charm. Rats have impressive qualities and can influence the toughest opposition. So if you are a Rat take your chances. Reel in whatever, or whoever you want- you may regret any further delay.

Rats must always take the opportunity to move away from personal grief, sadness, or difficulty. If this is achieved when the need arises, not much will shake the Rat.

Compatibility: RATS are well suited to Fellow RATS, The OX, the DRAGON, and the MONKEY. They should avoid the HORSE in business and relationships, or at least be careful!. In business the RAT works well with the OX and the DRAGON.

OX

Life can be a mixed experience for the Ox. This endurable beast can expect recognition if not notoriety over time. The strong Ox spirit is worthy of success; and the Ox will survive the twists and turns of fate- guaranteed. The Ox would be well advised not to panic amidst the radical change.

If you are an Ox adopt a wait-and-see attitude rather than get overly stressed by "if only". Assess all your options when the ride gets bumpy. You have more imagination than you appreciate. So use the full range of resources at your disposal and play your wild card.

In-house contacts will benefit the Ox career path for the duration. Call in favours. New challenges should always be welcomed and major adjustments will be worthwhile. The Ox may well find itself up against stiff competition. But persistence will pay off, and sheer hard work will manifest the desired results. Guard against becoming demoralised. There is no need! Simply maintain your position rather than slip back through resentment, anger or frustration.

Renewed focus will benefit the Ox handsomely in the long-term. Whilst relationships will bring diversion and light relief. Home life and domestic bliss are re-balancing factors. But some discipline and organisation may be needed.

The Ox will have to call in favours or rely on team effort at times. Although the Ox is not one for sharing its burden, there will be noticeable rewards deriving from inter-dependency. The Ox will certainly make bigger strides as part of a unit for a change.

The private life of the Ox will flourish in the most unexpected circumstances. New contacts will bring forward thrills, excitement and stimulation, so be selective. The Ox often has the luxury of some quite enviable choices in life. Make the most of these! Regrets are futile, so be imaginative with your options. And Adventurous...

Compatibility: The OX mixes well with the SNAKE, the ROOSTER, and the RABBIT. The OX should avoid the TIGER in personal relationships; and the TIGER, the HORSE and the GOAT in business connections. The OX works well with the ROOSTER and the SNAKE.

The Elements:

EARTH

Earth contains us. It is the nurturing environment in which we grow, develop, and hopefully flourish. Earth interacts with the other elements Wood, Fire, Metal and Water in many and varied ways. Earth represents fairness and equality in positive mode. But negatively tends to smother or gets overly stressed before the main event.

Earth types are loyal, reliable and will support you come what may. Earth takes its time and will not be rushed. These grounded personalities are persistent and determined. They will not give up and methodically move forwards until they attain their goal. The enduring qualities of Earth mean that generally you know where you are with this element. But there is the potential for the rare earthquake in areas of seismic stress. Inner strength marks this element in the positive. But Earth types are prone to finding fault and nit-picking within arguments. Many hairs tend to be split by this slightly obsessive energy. On the plus side you will not find more patient, tolerant and loyal people born with the blessing of Earth.

WOOD

Wood symbolises **Spring**, and the sprouting of roots and shoots. New life links with this energy. In fact any new or on-going growth be it animal, vegetable or mineral has a close connection with Wood.

Yin Wood is supple, pliable, and flexible, whereas Yang Wood is rigid, sturdy, and often ancient! Wood can of course be used to stoke a life-giving fire, or it may be used to spear the enemy in battle. Wood has endless possibilities, and may be used for good or bad according to inclination. It is versatile, expansive and nurturing.

Wood personalities are co-operative and think of the community first and foremost. They consider other people equal to themselves, and always, make attempts to be all-inclusive. Plenty of ideas fly around, for Wood is both creative and constructive. Wood knows how to win people over to their way of seeing things, which is usually practical and full of common sense. Wood characters are also visionary. They visualise possibilities. But would be slow to commit themselves, for fear of alienating endless possibilities. Here we find the artists and writers of the Zodiac. Wood ensures a personality that takes the rough with the smooth, and embarks on tasks with positive energy.

Enthusiasm is a given quality of Wood. But negatively, Wood can get impatient or overly tired when energy if expended. Wood tends to lose patience quickly, so may leave a trail of unfinished work in its wake. A bit of application along with the inherent enthusiasm would give Wood types the edge.

FIRE

Fire of course brings light, warmth and feelings of security. The link to the **Summer** season connects Fire to the life-force of The Sun. Happiness and joyous times are represented by Fire energy. However, Fire also explodes, destroys and causes devastation when it is not contained. There is an inherent danger when you mess with Fire. Positively Fire brings fairness, dynamic approach and integrity. Conversely, this molten lather manifests in aggression, war and conflict.

Fire personalities are the leaders of the Chinese Zodiac. They are always active and rarely run out of energy. Unless of course they overdo it, and burn themselves out. These characters know no boundaries and often lead themselves and others into hot water. Fire dislikes rules, regulations and any kind of confinement. You can expect challenges events and times when you mix with Fire. This energy lives in the moment and pays no heed to the future. The time is now.

Fire, therefore does not plan ahead, nor is it very clever at anticipating events. A law unto itself, Fire will rampage through the neighbourhood if you do not keep it in its rightful place. In the positive Fire signs are humorous and passionate. But give them free reign, and they can be impatient, demanding and exploitative.

METAL

Metal connects us to **Autumn** and brings the energy of strength and steely resolve. Metal is strong but compliant when the engineering is skilful. This is a molten material that can be moulded into many shapes, forms and structures beautiful or useful. Metal represents solidity and has the ability to hold and contain the other elements. It is also a conductor, so has the inherent capacity to protect or destroy depending on where you are standing! Positively Metal enhances communication. It brings justice, force and is an energy that is not to be messed with. Metal is full of inspiring ideas and has the capacity to attain lofty heights. In its negative aspect Metal can bring destruction, sadness and danger. It has the potential to be quite beautiful. But can also manifest as a lethal weapon that will run you through if you are not careful!

Metal personalities are very matter-of-fact and strong in their resolve. This elemental type gets things done. There is an in-built desire to be the best and to achieve ambitions come what may. Metal inspires the dogmatic approach to life, so arguments with this element should be averted if possible. There is a tendency for metal to have quite an inflexible attitude when up against it. This element is single minded. Organisational skills are good and Metal is very self-sufficient, content to function in its own sphere of influence. Not much will budge the Metal mind when it is set on a particular course of action.

Metal has an inherent self-belief, so does not take kindly to personal challenges or someone questioning their judgement. Perhaps surprisingly, Metal does respond well to change and weathers well. Metal types are serious minded and do not accept help lightly. They are strong, determined and intuitive in the positive. But in the negative can be lacking in sense of humour and tend to take themselves a little too seriously. Metal elements should also watch for dips into melancholy. But this is a formidable steely personality type that measures up in most respects when balanced.

WATER

Water relates to **Winter** and the element of water in whatever form, be it drops of rain or the ocean deep. Water is artistic, beautiful and serene. It is all encompassing and reaches everything in some shape or form. There would be no on-going life without Water: it is one of the main elements we need to survive. In the positive, Water nurtures, embraces and understands. But it also has the capacity to overwhelm, drown and swamp when there is no escape.

Water consequently can wear you down and be quite exhausting in the wrong environment. Water holds our emotions and on a deep, buried level it connects us to the unconscious and our buried secrets. It may therefore contain and understand our hidden fears, possibly heightening stress and nervousness. Water has the ability to see a little more than it should, so other elements find it disarming, incapacitating and not a little threatening at times.

Water people are great communicators. They know how to win people over and get their own way. Watery powers of persuasion are second to none. Water is perceptive, intuitive and highly sensitive. This element is likely to have innate psychic ability, and would be able to read your mind given half the chance. Call on Water types to negotiate a deal, for they can have people eating out of the palm of their hand in a short space of time. Water types are flexible, adaptable and great company too. Water is able to see the bigger picture, as well as able to penetrate to the heart of a problem very quickly.

Water is holistic and covers everything; no stone is left unturned when Water is in the environment. Positively, Water people are artistic, sociable and empathetic. They are great people to confide in. When off balance however, Water can be invasive, intrusive and a little bit too much. The sensitivity of Water can at times backfire, for this personality is prone to reading too much into situations that are inherently straightforward.

31 CHINESE ZODIAC TRAITS

The Chinese Zodiac Animals have different elements associated with them. Explore further in this chapter, the traits and features that make up your loved one's personalities, Chinese style.

General Profiles of The Animals

The TIGER
Associated Element: Wood

Tigers are independent and powerful. They have a rebellious and unconventional streak that makes them a bit of a handful. Tigers love acting on impulse and they are a dynamic, fun loving sign. Never distrust a Tiger, unless you want to cause offence. Tigers are genuine, affectionate and sincere. Passion runs close to the surface when a Tiger is around; so do not wind them up unless you want to be pounced upon. These creatures are passionate, stealthy and graceful. So needless to say, they make wonderful lovers. Watch out for dramatic displays of emotion and the slight loss of control in hairy moments. But Tigers are usually composed and make great leaders. It is important to monitor personal direction as a Tiger, and to guard against becoming embroiled in petty distractions.

Tigers have warmth of heart. They are generous creatures with a lot to give. Just watch those claws do not kill you with kindness.

Tigers are strong willed and determined. They love a challenge and are possessed of incredible energy and stamina. Be careful as a Tiger not to be too hasty with risky situations. Although you are not afraid to take a chance, you need to assess carefully when risks are justifiable, and when they are just plain crazy.

Restlessness is a scourge Tigers have to adapt to. Sometimes they move on too quickly if something is developing too slowly for their impetuous nature. Some patience would not go amiss. And do not be too proud as you are a creature who will often need to call in favours. Tigers are meant to connect with their fellows and experience the interchanges of love, loyalty and affection; whenever possible.

The RABBIT
Associated Element: Wood

The Rabbit is a very lucky sign. You will find as a Rabbit that things often come good for you at the last minute. You will notice a recurring pattern throughout your life. Just when things look like they are going belly up, expect a miracle; it will surely manifest. Think of the times when everything looked like it was falling down around you. Is there not always some kind of incredible break through?

Rabbits symbolize grace and beauty. Their nature is charming and refined, without being prudish. Rabbits are polite and know the value of mutual respect and good manners. Do not expect the Rabbit to be a pushover however. Their strength of character and will power, are legendary. Take one on at your peril. Rabbits are very smart and sophisticated, and have a way of making you look bad without even trying; but only if you cross them first.

The Rabbit is very shrewd and knows how to get its way. Their charm is very seductive, and they are liable to nibble their way through the toughest opposition. Rabbits love peace and harmony; and will wander off very quickly at the first sign of conflict. They prefer to negotiate; because they know they can win through with their magic talk and wily wiles.

Rabbits possess a calm, unflappable exterior, that is often mistaken for aloof snobbery. Think again! Rabbits are actually very kind and considerate. They are simply cautious about whom they connect with and do not suffer fools gladly. Anyone who knows and loves the Rabbit will vouch for their charming, inquisitive, and special nature. The twitching nose gives them a special propensity for magic!

Rabbits dislike change, and can feel unsettled when their security is threatened. Bolder behavior would not go amiss at times. For unscrupulous people are apt to take advantage of this sweet nature. Rabbits are agreeable beyond the call of duty. But just remember, once they clock what is happening, it will become apparent they should never have been underestimated. A Rabbit would be well advised to develop a thicker skin. This would prevent the odd skinning and serve them well. The less time spent in the soup/stew/casserole the better.

The DRAGON
Associated Element: Earth

Dragons are very magnanimous and proud. They have plenty of energy at their disposal. Dragons are financially generous and love to spend money. Assertiveness and self-confidence are great Dragon qualities. Watch out for an overtly selfish streak though. At times the Dragon gets carried away and will champion the cause of fire creatures with too much enthusiasm. Sometimes excitement can get a grip of the Dragon. Watch out for pushiness at the wrong times, when the determination to, "make things happen" gets the better of you.

Dragons can be fussy and too snobby with certain expectations. Things have to be just right, or the Dragon will have something to say about it. If conditions are not perfect for the anticipated scenario, the Dragon will feel uncomfortable and will baulk. Avoid an argument with this one. Dragons are dogmatic and will not be told. They make good leaders and are mature in their outlook on life. If you have an old head on young shoulders, the chances are you have inherited some Dragon energy from somewhere. Dragons are fearless and not afraid to take on formidable responsibilities. They can be a little forthright with the wind in their sails. But they are not easily defeated, so make great friends and partners.

Dragons can be a bit indiscreet, so do not confide in a hurry, unless you have worked out exactly whom you are dealing with. Having said that Dragons are not afraid to tell it like it is. They are brutally honest and will not hold back when making a point. Expect to be hurt by a Dragon and if you cannot handle the truth stay well away. What you see is what you get with this fiery creature.

Dragons should definitely develop their skills of tact and diplomacy. Curbing the urge to splurge, and overspend, would also be lessons well learned.

Your lively independent manner means that as a Dragon you are well liked. But do guard against overly impulsive behavior. Use your many talents wisely and you are destined for major success. Dragons are unusual and powerful creatures, not easily defeated and great to have on side.

The SNAKE
Associated Element: Fire

The Snakes are the hedonists of the animal kingdom. They love to slink around hissing when it pleases them and of course love to indulge in a great variety of temptations. The Snake knows how to enjoy life on its own terms. But snakes are also highly intelligent and intuitive. Nothing passes the attention of this mind-bending mind reader. Try to deceive one at your own expense. *That* kind of selective behaviour is the preserve of Snakes alone. Never return the favour, it can be fatal; certainly a big mistake!

Snakes of course only trust their own judgment. They are invaluable friends as they are rarely wrong about human nature, and know how to work the system. Snakes choose their words carefully and rarely speak, unless it serves their interests.

Sometimes disarmingly quiet, the Snake watches, observes, and notes the behaviour playing out in its field of vision. Very economical with its energy, the Snake only moves tactically, and does not miss an opportunity to further its interests. Having said that this is not a selfish creature. But the Snake *is* self-serving if that does not sound too much like a contradiction.

The Snake persona is charming, beguiling and enigmatic. There is also elegance in movement. This creature knows how to glide to perfection, so can certainly make quite an entrance.

Snakes tend to see the drama in life, and have a head for gossip and scandal. They can get things out of proportion, and often read too much significance into harmless events. When a Snake is off-balance, possessiveness, and tenacity kick in quite unattractively. Never cross one of these creatures. Snakes know how to milk a revenge scenario to perfection. If you cannot handle the intensity of the Snake, you would be advised to keep a healthy distance, and approach only when you know it is not hungry!

The HORSE
Associated Element: Fire

The Horse is a happy, content and intelligent creature. Those born in a horse year are usually popular, bright and well able to pace life sensibly. However, the Horse has an impulsive and tempestuous streak that craves adventure. Occasional grazing may suddenly turn into a bolt across the field, for no apparent reason.

The Horse has a quirky sense of humor, and is open to a wide variety of experiences. This elegant creature has a wicked idea of what constitutes fun, and has an inherent capacity to shock in quite unexpected ways. Eloquence is a key word in the Horse world. The Horse knows how to convey a point or two, and adopts an unusual angle when making a convincing case. The Horse can certainly call the kettle black, and argue a point until the cows come home.

In matters of the heart, the Horse is not fussy, so much as discreet and choosy. A great variety of mates may catch the Stud's attention, but once settled the Horse is loyal, unto the moment therein! This animal is a creature of habit, except when that urge for a wild spin kicks in. Not possessive, mistrustful or jealous, the Horse will live and let live. It is accepting of others and will not be overly demanding when in a relationship. The Horse has high standards for its own behavior, but will not expect very much from others.

One point that will rile the Horse is not getting its own way. Clearly this animal's agreeable nature ensures this kind of conflict rarely happens. But you can expect scenes of irritability if you go back on an agreement you made with a Horse friend or lover. The Horse is not a drama queen, but short shrift is what you will get if you are unreliable. I guess loyalty towards such a magnificent companion is not much to ask for.

Apart from the occasional flare of temper, the Horse is desirable. If you are a Horse avoid alienating loved ones with undignified moody displays. Make the most of your many talents, and build towards a successful future. You have a great temperament that will contribute to a rewarding and fulfilling future. Just keep those four trotters on the ground and do not rush too far ahead of yourself. A full-paced gallop will certainly cover a lot of ground. But you will be finished at the end of it. The playing field might just peter-out. Put the brakes on, and work methodically towards the achievement of your goals.

The GOAT
Associated Element: Earth

The Goat is an honest and reliable animal. Sincerity is this creature's middle name. But you may not believe it, as the Goat can come across as quite smug. A misunderstood Goat is introspective and apparently unapproachable; a veritable Billy Goat Gruff! But get past what you think to be the case, and you will find a charming and refined sensual creature.

The Goat can appear to be pessimistic and aloof. However, underneath the thick coarse skin is a romantic soul, quite ready and willing for intimacy. The Goat is surprisingly tolerant and able to forgive with ease. This typifies a generous and open heart. The Goat gives this personal leeway, not as an excuse for his own bad behavior. But out of a genuine unconditional way of being. Baa aaaah!

Goat's hate strict schedules, and do not perform well under pressure. They are discipline in their own way, but would not respond well to a dictatorial regime. Goats hate to be put under pressure, and will run and hide if they are obliged to perform. They love domesticity, and a sense of security in their own home.

The Goat makes bonds for life, and it would be very rare for the Goat to be mistreated or abused. Perhaps that aloof exterior serves a purpose after all! This creature attracts only those it can work with and connect to. There is no nonsense, and no funny business with the Goat. This creature shapes its own destiny. Anything can happen!

Be careful if you are a Goat to build on the positive vibes in your life. Say "no" to negative thinking, and embrace the future fearlessly with good faith. Disappointment is a rare occurrence. But if you do get a knock along the way, learn from it, pick up and start over. You have the power to turn things around Do so!

Watch out for your tendency to be a little haphazard in your approach to life. Find some discipline but always function on your own terms, in personal and business relationships. Show your true feelings to enliven your connections; and give your best for a great reward on all levels.

The MONKEY
Associated Element: Metal

The Monkey is of course warm, spontaneous and funny. An infectious sense of humour will have this animal laughing even in the midst of adversity. The Monkey loves life, and this creature is very energising company. The Monkey is not one of life's vampires who would leave you drained and crawling out the door. Quite the opposite: If you are down? Find a Monkey to cheer you up.

The Monkey is elegant and stylish and has great taste. This animal is not mercenary or materialistic, but loves comfortable and tasteful surroundings. Show me a Monkey who is not stylish and well turned out!

The Monkey has a sharp and intelligent mind and an irascible wit. Do not take on this animal with a competitive banter, or repartee, as you may well lose face.

The Monkey is a great improviser and can talk its way out of most compromising situations. This animal is not actively deceitful, but the Monkey does know the fast track away from trouble. A street-wise little fluff-ball you might say.

The Monkey is inventive and gymnastics of all kinds come naturally to this animal. A great mover in more ways than one is the monkey. This animal is a master of lateral and illogical thinking. Present a riddle or puzzle to the Monkey, and it will be sorted very unconventionally, but brilliantly nonetheless. The Monkey is able for complex scenarios and situations that would normally defeat the best of us. Indeed this Chinese animal thrives on the unexpected. And comes into full power and self-expression when up against it. Look to this creature for a solution.

The Monkey learns quickly and absorbs information like a sponge. As a Monkey you will be a success at whatever you turn you hand to. What a luxury of choice you have at your finger-tips. Nothing eludes you.; and you can do great things if you concentrate your boundless energy in one direction. Some hope there? Ah go on then; just do it all!

Watch out for that arrogant streak. Sometimes your competence gets a bit much for us lesser mortals. Do have mercy. We will catch up eventually. Do not be too crafty or nifty in your bid to succeed. You do not want to get caught now, do you? Having said, that even if you were found in a "red-handed" situation, you would have a plausible get-out clause.

Do *try* to concentrate on one thing at a time. You are a great social animal, and are destined to be well loved experiencing a lifetime of mischief and laughter.

The ROOSTER
Associated Element: Metal

The Rooster is a neat and precise creature, who likes to peck around making sure things are' just perfect. Needless to say this power animal is proud and colourful. The appearance of things is important to the Rooster. If something does not measure up to expectations, this creature will feel short-changed and most annoyed.

The Rooster is very organised and tidy. Perhaps unrealistically it expects those who inhabit the same air space to be equally responsible. The Rooster has a great eye for detail and will not miss the intricacies of an argument. This animal will not easily forget a wrong and is quite self-critical as well as fussy with loved ones. The Rooster has no time for impatience, and yet is one of the most impatient creatures in the universe.

Powers of observation are truly a blessing from heaven for the Rooster. This gives them the edge in career situations that involve playing ball and pleasing the powers that be. Roosters are hard workers and are very meticulous and patient within a working environment. Their steely determination to succeed will inevitably reap a reward in the long term. But not necessarily as quickly as this one would like.

The Rooster is blessed with an innate capacity to get out of trouble and difficult situations. Resourceful and intelligent, it will seem as if the Rooster was absent, even whilst mingling in the thick of it. A master stroke indeed. With patient application the Rooster is able to arrive on its own terms. This takes determination and tenacity. But believe me the ambitions will inevitably be fulfilled as long as there is no wavering. (There will not be!)

Watch out for a certain prudish element in your relationships. You're not exactly one for getting down and dirty! Your refined nature takes offence at such suggestions. Do not let this emotional prickly streak tamper with good connections. Rise to the occasion in every sense and make a link. Not everyone is as polite as you granted. But you do not want to be stuck in a liaison of interminable boredom and tedium. Do you? Keep your options open, and become aware of the many types of emotional expression. Be unafraid.

Be careful also that your pedantry does not make life overly tense. Accept that others have a different way of being and go get you some. Take good advice about decisions that make you uneasy. When you are in a tight spot your thinking tend to become a little fussy. So do not be too proud when you need a guiding hand. You are a brilliant planner. But watch out for the expectation that your wishes be followed to the letter. It is not going to happen, especially not within a group situation. Make allowances for the inadequate performance of other power animals. They have a different set of circumstances to contend with. Your outgoing personality and inevitable success will make life very rewarding. There are plenty of good friends who worship the ground you walk on. So what can go wrong?

The DOG
Associated Element: Wood

Dogs are sincere and intelligent animals. They are as loyal as they come, and there is a strong unconditional element to the love they express. Dogs are sticklers for justice, and will champion a worthy cause to the hilt. They play by the rules, and you will not find a dog looking for loopholes. Having said that Dogs do have a certain independence. They are not boring despite their conventional streak. You can count on a Dog. They are extremely reliable and their word is their bond. A Dog will die before it lets you down. A slight exaggeration perhaps, but you get the picture.

Dogs are diplomatic, but will never gloss over the truth. They are not afraid to speak their mind on controversial and complex subjects. A lie tripping from the Dog's mouth would be a rare occurrence indeed. Tact, along with the fearless defence of what is right, are trademark Doggy traits. Dogs are able to objectify most situations and always listen to problems with interest and respect. They are great confidants when you feel like the whole world is against you. Dogs preserve secrets and can be trusted to keep silent, even with the juiciest gossip. So if you want the Chinese whisper effect, do not make a Dog part of the chain. It will stop with them. Woof!

When Dogs get annoyed or lose their temper they are quick to make amends. They are so obliging, they even have a habit of taking on other people's mistakes as if they were their own. If you hurt a Dog, it will wonder whether it hurt you first. There will be great demonstrations of affection, and huge remorse until you have kissed and made up. Dogs will forgive and forget very quickly once the problem has been sorted. You will never find a Dog bearing a grudge. Once a solution is found, there is the end of it. It will be as if it never happened. Dogs have a tendency to be a bit pessimistic. They wear a slightly sulky look at times. But they are the world's realists, so the serious face is often justified.

Dogs are not superficial or flippant, and out of respect they do take life seriously. If you are Dog try to be a little more light hearted. We do not expect you to carry the burdens of all. Though we are certainly grateful for your friendship when we need a listening ear, oodles of affection, and great company. Watch out for a tendency to be stubborn over particular issues that bother you. Be careful not to be too bloody-minded. You cannot win them all.

Guard against anxiety and a propensity to think quite negatively at times. You have an admirable character, so observe and be proud of your personality. A healthy self-esteem would not go amiss. Be accepting of who you are, and realise that enjoyment of life is equally important as the attempt to sort everything out.

The PIG
Associated Element: Water

Pigs are open, sincere and strong creatures who shuffle around achieving great things, almost without being noticed. Pigs will avoid a fight at all costs and prefer to keep a low profile in controversial situations. They will walk away from hassle, as they wound easily and don not need that kind of grief. Pigs are very adaptable and know how to blend in to the background. They are not shy, but they are clever. A Pig could be a leader within a group situation without anyone being particularly aware of the fact.

Pigs are not good at any kind of confrontation. They do not respond well to the pressure to sort out a problem, whether it be emotional, financial or romantic. Pigs hope for the best and expect things to sort themselves out. More often than not their *laissez faire* attitude works. But Pigs scream and holler when pursued with a view to slaughter!

Pigs have a tendency to store up resentment, and will not forget a wrong doing in a hurry. They are prone to simmering resentment which can be quite soul destroying and destructive. So do guard against this if you are a Pig, as you are only hurting yourself. Objectify and forgive, for your own sake.

Pigs are loyal and make wonderful companions. They love socialising and meeting people. A great variety of connections keep them interested. They need the stimulation of harmless fun and gossip. Indeed Pigs give fun and frolics so much importance, that they are in danger of frittering away opportunities for serious progress. Pigs need to watch their priorities and find balance in their lives. They are capable of good work. They just do not particularly want to do it. If you are a Pig, so do be aware of your responsibilities, and remember to fulfil your obligations. At least sometimes.

Pigs hate to disappoint people and sometimes promise too much before failing to deliver. Keep track of your commitments and try to avoid letting others down. Actions speak louder than words so watch that the neglect of duty does not alienate you from loved ones. Pigs need to watch out that their charming naivety does not trip them up. They can be a little too child-like and trusting at times. Pigs do learn quickly from their mistakes however. So the same *faux pas* will never happen twice; there just might be another one to take its place.

Pigs should monitor self-indulgence and extravagance. Pigs are pleasure seekers, and will be the life and soul of social events if they feel comfortable. Pigs have great integrity and mean well. But they need to be careful not to promise the world when they can only deliver gestures of intent. The destiny of the Pig is to be loved and respected by many. You are lucky as a Pig, for you will be forgiven most of your misdemeanours- there is something irresistible about you!

The RAT
Associated Element: Water

The Rat is a charmer that knows how to get its way using the nicest possible techniques- well usually. Do not forget this rodent can chew its way through the most impervious materials and possesses the means' to invade your most unsuspecting, intimate places. It does not pay to be complacent about the Rat. This is a persistent and tenacious creature. The Rat is a master and there is no stopping this animal when it wants to get under your skin, and make an impression.

The Rat is a hard worker, and is not afraid of the graft needed to guarantee impressive results. This creature is sincere and direct to the point of brutality if necessary. The Rat is an all or nothing type of being. If you do not float this animal's boat, forget it. The Rat is not a time waster, and hates any kind of slack behaviour in its associates. Financially, the Rat is a genius and certainly possesses the Midas touch. The Rat knows what to do and when to do it. This power animal is an expert at discerning the right time to make a Splash. The Rat can expect maximum impact in its chosen field.

The Rat is also very intelligent and likes the stimulation of good social company. But the Rat also needs down-time, and enjoys its own thoughts and privacy at pertinent moments. Rats are very generous to their nearest and dearest. This animal is slow to trust and will be very wary until it is comfortable in your company. Because the Rat is often misunderstood, it has learned to be slightly shifty and slippery in personal dealings.

The Rat is difficult to pin down amidst uncertainty. Usually it is better to leave the Rat alone and not ask for favours. But surprising displays of generosity will inevitably occur, just when you have given up! Needless to say the Rat likes to operate in its own way, and is quick to drop people who don't fit in with the game plan. Loved ones are safe as houses however. The Rat is loyal in defending its own, and will destroy anyone who threatens the status quo.

Rats are great party animals and enjoy throwing very lavish occasions to verify their social status. They take care of friends and families without question. But be careful you do not assume a connection with this quite private creature. Wait to be chosen, or forget it.

Rats are sentimental and may feel things on a deep emotional level. They have fine sensibilities and are usually culturally aware or politically minded. Engage the Rat in conversation and you will not budge for many hours.

If you are a Rat do not fret unnecessarily about security and the safety of loved ones. Sometimes you over burden yourself with stress, so confide in good friends when the going gets tough. Be aware though that certain associates have their own agenda, and may not have your best interests at heart. A rude awakening may sometimes demoralize you. But never lose faith. The Rat is a born survivor that can process the dark and difficult side of life very effectively. Rats inspire respect from most people. Ignore those who find you too intense or self-obsessed. They do not see *you*.

Rats when they are committed, will not let go, even in the midst of defeat. They will never walk away from a commitment, however rough the road gets. Rats would therefore benefit in recognizing the time to let go. A lot of stress and aggravation is eliminated, if as a Rat, you can discern what is going on at a deeper level.

Channel your energies wisely. Or you may find that at times you work against yourself unwittingly. Monitor self-defeating tendencies, and use your irresistible charm to get you everywhere.

The OX
Associated Element: Earth

The Ox is not afraid to work very hard to achieve its birth-right of prosperity. This power animal is systematic, disciplined and leaves no stone unturned. The Ox is patient and trustworthy and makes a great friend and reliable companion. This creature hates ostentation, and obscene displays of decadence or wealth. The Ox has refined taste but likes to live a simple life with minimal fuss and clutter. Very little will shake the constitution of the Ox, and very little will throw this creature off track.

The Ox is slow and steady and gets long-term results. He prepares for meticulously for the inevitable harvest further down the road. The self-confidence of the Ox is second to none. The Ox possesses oodles of charisma and doesn't even need to speak to make an impact. The sheer presence of the Ox ensures all eyes look in its direction.

A magnificent animal, the Ox commands respect and admiration, but never insists on it. This creature is a reluctant star in his own sphere of operation. But the Ox is also prone to naïve displays of bad judgement. Emotionally the Ox can get deeply bruised by bad treatment. This creature is all heart, and is prone to be too open in relationships. The Ox needs to guard its privacy a little more, and not be quite so giving when the return is not mutual.

The Ox respects tradition and does everything to the best of its ability. This animal is not afraid to take on major tasks, and will always perform well amidst difficulty.

If you are an Ox, be careful that this tendency to say "yes" to everything, does not leave you with too much of a burden to shoulder. Even the Ox can only bear so much weight. Admittedly you can carry more than your fair share of heavy-duty demands. But keep the balance right. Make sure that your nature is not abused. Opportunists may come and go, but your durability is worth more than this kind of abuse. Do everything to the best of your ability as always. But expect an equal return from others. You give others great respect, and must expect the same honour for work well done.

As an Ox you bring great stability and security to your relationships. You are a brilliant provider, and attend unquestioningly to the needs of loved ones. Try to be a bit more open to the ebb and flow, of life's circumstances. The Ox hates the shift and change of the tides of life; and needs the reassurance that all is well.

Watch out that you do not stress yourself with unnecessary panic, and be wary of the negative self-fulfilling prophecy. Try to be more verbally expressive to loved ones. They all know that your loyalty is guaranteed, but would appreciate greater displays of affection from time to time. Be careful not to become too preoccupied with your ambitions, and so neglect your personal responsibilities. Always stand up for what you believe in. Never waiver once you have decided on a course of action. Your sheer determination will guarantee you a result.

鼠　牛　虎　兔
RAT　OX　TIGER　RABBIT

龍　蛇　馬　羊
DRAGON　SNAKE　HORSE　GOAT

猴　雞　狗　豬
MONKEY　ROOSTER　DOG　PIG

Celebrity Chinese Zodiac

Famous TIGERS: Victoria Beckham, Phil Collins, Jon Bon Jovi, Neil Morrissey, Alanis Morissette, Terry Wogan, Robbie Williams, Tom Cruise, Cheryl Crow.

Famous RABBITS: David Beckham, Drew Barrymore, Nicolas Cage, Emma Bunton, Bertie Ahern, Roger Moore, Angelina Jolie, Fatboy Slim, Kate Winslet, Sting, Tiger Woods, Enrique Inglesias, Neil Jordan, Whitney Houston, J.R.R Tolkein.

Famous DRAGONS: Jeffrey Archer, Maeve Binchy, Roald Dahl, Tom Jones, Ringo Starr, Dave Stewart, Elle MacPherson, David Hasslehoff, Kirk Douglas, Clive Anderson, Alicia Silverstone, Sigmund Freud, Courtney Cox.

Famous SNAKES: Liz Hurley, Bob Dylan, Tony Blair, Pierce Brosnan, Kim Basinger, Bjork, Ruby Wax, Shania Twain, Courtney Love, Sir Alex Ferguson, Brad Pitt.

Famous HORSES: Rowan Atkinson, Rolf Harris, Lou Reed, Mike Tyson, Will Young, John Travolta, Annie Lennox, Bob Geldof, Chris Evans, Clint Eastwood, James Cameron, Cherie Blair, Billy Connolly, Helena Bonham Carter.

Famous GOATS: Julia Roberts, Cilla Black, Angus Daeyton, Billy Idol, Jerry Springer, Keith Richards, Bruce Willis, Michael Palin, Mel Gibson, Julio Inglesias, Robert De Niro, Sinead O'Conner, Whoopi Goldberg, Noel Gallagher.

Famous MONKEYS: Christina Aguilera, Jennifer Aniston, Gillian Anderson, Michael Douglas, Rod Stewart, Daina Ross, Lisa Marie Presley, Celine Dion, David Copperfield, Roger Daltrey, Tom Hanks, Bob Marley, Kylie Minogue, Jerry Hall.

Famous ROOSTERS: Michelle Pfeffer, Dawn French, Yoko Ono, Steve Martin, Britney Spears, Paul Merton, Byran Ferry, Catherine Zeta Jones, Joan Rivers, Daniel Day Lewis, Michael Caine.

Famous DOGS: Bill Clinton, Chris Tarrant, Holly Hunter, Michael Jackson, Brigette Bardot, Cher, Naomi Campbell, Kate Bush, Jennifer Lopez, Madonna, Elvis Presley, Barry Gibb, Claudia Schiffer, Sylvester Stallone, Sharon Stone, Prince William.

Famous PIGS: Byran Adams, Iggy Pop, Meat Loaf, The Dalai Lama, Luciano Pavarotti, Ewan McGregor, Steven Speilberg, David Letterman, Kevin Kline, Carl Gustav Jung, Billy Crystal, Hillary Rodham Clinton, Woody Allen.

Famous RATS: George Bush, Bono, Ben Affleck, Buddy Holly, William Shakespeare, Geri Halliwell, Chris de Burgh, Hugh Grant, Gareth Gates, Cameron Diaz, Liam Gallagher, Shirley Bassey, Gary Lineker.

Famous OXES: Antony Hopkins, Diana, Princess of Wales, George Clooney, Saddam Hussein, Billy Joel, Kate Moss, Meg Ryan, B. B. King, Billy Ocean, Sigourney Weaver, Meryl Streep, Adolf Hitler, Walt Disney.

TABLES AND APPENDIXES

1) TABLES FOR MERCURY RISING P. 67

Find Your Mercury Sign here below. It could be the same as your Sun Sign, but equally may not be. The tables below indicate when Mercury switched signs in your year of birth. Find your year of birth below, then look up the date before your birthday and note the Mercury Zodiac Sign. There may be more than one date under each sign because of the Mercury Retrograde phases (when Mercury retreats backwards for three weeks at a time three or four times a year).

1945

14th January	Capricorn
5th February	Aquarius
23rd February	Pisces
11th April	Aries
17th May	Taurus
4th June	Gemini
18th June	Cancer
3rd July/17th August	Leo
26th July/10th September	Virgo
27th September	Libra
15th October	Scorpio
4th November	Sagittarius

1946

10th January	Capricorn
29th January	Aquarius
15th February/2nd April	Pisces
4th April/17th April	Aries
12th May	Taurus
27th May	Gemini
10th June	Cancer
28th June	Leo
4th September	Virgo
19th September	Libra

8th October/21st November	Scorpio
30th October/ 12th December	Sagittarius

1947

3rd January/27th December	Capricorn
22nd January	Aquarius
8th February	Pisces
16th April	Aries
4th May	Taurus
18th May	Gemini
2nd June	Cancer
11th August	Leo
27th August	Virgo
12th August	Libra
2nd October	Scorpio
7th December	Sagittarius

1948

1st January/19th December	Capricorn
14th January/21st February	Aquarius
2nd February/18th March	Pisces
9th April	Aries
25th April	Taurus
9th May/29th June	Gemini
28th May/12th July	Cancer
2nd August	Leo
17th August	Virgo
4th September/18th October	Libra
27th September/10th November	Scorpio
29th November	Sagittarius

1949

1st January/11th December	Capricorn
6th January	Aquarius
14th March	Pisces
2nd April	Aries
17th April	Taurus
2nd May	Gemini
10th July	Cancer
25th July	Leo

9th August	Virgo
29th August	Libra
4th November	Scorpio
22nd November	Sagittarius

1950

16th January/5th December	Capricorn
1st January/15th February	Aquarius
8th March	Pisces
25th March	Aries
8th May	Taurus
15th June	Gemini
2nd July	Cancer
17th July	Leo
2nd August	Virgo
28th August/10th October	Libra
11th September/27th October	Scorpio
15th November	Sagittarius

1951

1st January/2nd December	Capricorn
10th January	Aquarius
1st March	Pisces
16th April/2nd May	Aries
2nd April/15th May	Taurus
9th June	Gemini
24th June	Cancer
8th July	Leo
28th July	Virgo
3rd August	Libra
20th October	Scorpio
8th November	Sagittarius

1952

12th January	Capricorn
2nd February	Aquarius
21st February	Pisces
8th March	Aries
15th May	Taurus
31st May	Gemini

14th June	Cancer
30th July	Leo
7th August	Virgo
24th September	Libra
11th November	Scorpio
1st December/1st January	Sagittarius

1953

7th January/31st December	Capricorn
26th January	Aquarius
12th February/16th March	Pisces
2nd March/18th April	Aries
8th May	Taurus
23rd May	Gemini
6th June /29th July	Cancer
27th June/12th August	Leo
31st August	Virgo
16th September	Libra
5th October/7th November	Scorpio
1st November/10th December	Sagittarius

1954

1st January/23rd December	Capricorn
18th January	Aquarius
5th February	Pisces
13th April	Aries
30th April	Taurus
15th May	Gemini
31st May	Cancer
8th August	Leo
23rd August	Virgo
8th September/5th November	Libra
29th September/12th November	Scorpio
4th December	Sagittarius

1955

1st January	Capricorn
10th January	Aquarius
17th March	Pisces
6th April	Aries

22nd April	Taurus
7th May	Gemini
13th July	Cancer
30th July	Leo
14th August	Virgo
1st September	Libra
8th November	Scorpio
27th November	Sagittarius

1956

1st January/2nd February/8th December	Capricorn
4th January/15th February	Aquarius
11th March	Pisces
28th March	Aries
12th April	Taurus
29th April	Gemini
6th July	Cancer
21st July	Leo
5th August/29th September	Virgo
26th August/10th October	Libra
31st October	Scorpio
18th November	Sagittarius

1957

1st January/2nd December	Capricorn
12th February	Aquarius
4th March	Pisces
20th March	Aries
4th April	Taurus
12th June	Gemini
28th June	Cancer
12th July	Leo
30th July	Virgo
6th October	Libra
23rd October	Scorpio
11th November/28th December	Sagittarius

1958

14th January	Capricorn
6th February	Aquarius

24th March	Pisces
12th March/10th April	Aries
2nd April/17th May	Taurus
5th June	Gemini
20th June	Cancer
4th July/23rd August	Leo
26th July	Virgo
28th September	Libra
16th October	Scorpio
1st January/5th March	Sagittarius

1959

10th January	Capricorn
30th January	Aquarius
17th February	Pisces
5th March	Aries
12th May	Taurus
28th May	Gemini
11th June	Cancer
28th June	Leo
5th September	Virgo
20th October	Libra
9th October/25th November	Scorpio
1st January/31st October/13th December	Sagittarius

1960

4th January/27th December	Capricorn
23rd January	Aquarius
9th February	Pisces
16th April	Aries
4th May	Taurus
19th May	Gemini
2nd June/6th July	Cancer
1st July/10th August	Leo
27th August	Virgo
12th September	Libra
1st October	Scorpio
1st January/7th December	Sagittarius

1961

1st January/20th December	Capricorn
14th January/21st February	Aquarius
1st February/18th March	Pisces
10th April	Aries
26th April	Taurus
10th May	Gemini
28th May	Cancer
4th August	Leo
18th August	Virgo
4th September/22nd October	Libra
27th September/10th November	Scorpio
30th November	Sagittarius

1962

1st January/12th December	Capricorn
7th January	Aquarius
15th March	Pisces
3rd April	Aries
18th April	Taurus
3rd May	Gemini
11th July	Cancer
26th July	Leo
10th August	Virgo
29th August	Libra
5th November	Scorpio
23rd November	Sagittarius

1963

1st /20th January/6th December	Capricorn
2nd January/15th February	Aquarius
9th March	Pisces
26th March	Aries
9th April/10th May	Taurus
3rd May	Gemini
4th July	Cancer
18th July	Leo
3rd August/16th September	Virgo
26th August/10th October	Libra
28th October	Scorpio

16th November	Sagittarius

1964

1st January/30th November	Capricorn
10th February	Aquarius
29th February	Pisces
16th March	Aries
2nd April	Taurus
9th June	Gemini
24th June	Cancer
9th July	Leo
27th July	Virgo
3rd October	Libra
20th October	Scorpio
8th November/16th December	Sagittarius

1965

13th January	Capricorn
3rd February	Aquarius
21st February	Pisces
9th March	Aries
15th May	Taurus
2nd June	Gemini
16th June	Cancer
1st July/1st August	Leo
31st July/8th September	Virgo
25th September	Libra
12th October	Scorpio
1st January/2nd November	Sagittarius

1966

7th January	Capricorn
27th January	Aquarius
13th February/22nd March	Pisces
3rd March/17th April	Aries
9th May	Taurus
24th May	Gemini
7th June	Cancer
26th June	Leo
1st September	Virgo

17th September	Libra
5th October/13th November	Scorpio
1st January/30th October/11th December	Sagittarius

1967

1st /24th December	Capricorn
19th January	Aquarius
6th February	Pisces
14th April	Aries
1st May	Taurus
16th May	Gemini
31st May	Cancer
8th August	Leo
24th August	Virgo
9th September	Libra
30th September	Scorpio
5th December	Sagittarius

1968

1st January/16th December	Capricorn
12th January/11th February	Aquarius
1st February/17th March	Pisces
7th April	Aries
22nd April	Taurus
6th May/13th June	Gemini
29th May	Cancer
13th July	Leo
15th August	Virgo
1st September/7th October	Libra
28th September/8th November	Scorpio
27th November	Sagittarius

1969

1st January/9th December	Capricorn
4th January	Aquarius
12th March	Pisces
30th March	Aries
14th April	Taurus
30th April	Gemini
8th July	Cancer

22nd July	Leo
7th August/7th October	Virgo
27th August/9th October	Libra
1st November	Scorpio
20th November	Sagittarius

1970

1stJanuary/3rd December	Capricorn
4th January	Aquarius
5th March	Pisces
22nd March	Aries
6th April	Taurus
13th June	Gemini
30th June	Cancer
14th July	Leo
31st July	Virgo
7th October	Libra
25th October	Scorpio
13th November	Sagittarius

1971

1st January/14th January	Capricorn
7th February	Aquarius
26th February	Pisces
14th March/18th April	Aries
1st April/17th May	Taurus
7th June	Gemini
21st June	Cancer
6th July/ 29th August	Leo
26th July/11th September	Virgo
30th September	Libra
17th October	Scorpio
2nd January/6th November	Sagittarius

1972

11th January	Capricorn
31st January	Aquarius
18th February	Pisces
5th March	Aries
12th May	Taurus

29th May	Gemini
12th June	Cancer
28th June	Leo
5th September	Virgo
21st September	Libra
9th October/29th November	Scorpio
1st January/30th October/12th December	Sagittarius

1973

4th /28th December	Capricorn
23rd January	Aquarius
9th February	Pisces
16th April	Aries
6th May	Taurus
20th May	Gemini
4th June	Cancer
27th June	Leo
28th August	Virgo
13th September	Libra
2nd October	Scorpio
1st January/8th December	Sagittarius

1974

1st January/21st December	Capricorn
16th January/2nd March	Aquarius
2nd February/17th March	Pisces
11th April	Aries
28th April	Taurus
12th May	Gemini
29th May	Cancer
5th August	Leo
20th August	Virgo
6th September/26th October	Libra
11th November	Scorpio
2nd December	Sagittarius

1975

1st January/14th December	Capricorn
8th January	Aquarius
16th March	Pisces

4th April	Aries
19th April	Taurus
4th May	Gemini
12th July	Cancer
28th July	Leo
12th August	Virgo
30th August	Libra
6th November	Scorpio
25th November	Sagittarius

1976

1stDecember/25th January	Capricorn
2nd January/15th February	Aquarius
9th March	Pisces
26th March	Aries
10th April/19th May	Taurus
29th April/13th June	Gemini
4th July	Cancer
18th July	Leo
3rd August/21st September	Virgo
25th August/10th October	Libra
29th October	Scorpio
16th November	Sagittarius

1977

1st January/1st December	Capricorn
10th February	Aquarius
2nd March	Pisces
18th March	Aries
3rd April	Taurus
10th June	Gemini
26th June	Cancer
10th July	Leo
28th July	Virgo
4th October	Libra
21st October	Scorpio
9th November/21st December	Sagittarius

1978

13th January	Capricorn
4th February	Aquarius
22nd February	Pisces
10th March	Aries
16th May	Taurus
3rd June	Gemini
17th June	Cancer
2nd July/13th August	Leo
27th July/9th September	Virgo
26th September	Libra
14th October	Scorpio
1st January/ 3rd November	Sagittarius

1979

8th January	Capricorn
28th January	Aquarius
14th February/28th March	Pisces
3rd March/17th April	Aries
10th May	Taurus
26th May	Gemini
9th June	Cancer
27th June	Leo
2nd September	Virgo
18th September	Libra
7th October/18th November	Scorpio
30th October/12th December	Sagittarius

1980

2nd January/25th December	Capricorn
21st January	Aquarius
7th February	Pisces
14th April	Aries
2nd May	Taurus
16th May	Gemini
31st May	Cancer
9th August	Leo
24th August	Virgo
10th September	Libra
30th September	Scorpio

1st January/5th December   Sagittarius

1981

1st January/17th December	Capricorn
12th January/16th February	Aquarius
31st January	Pisces
8th April	Aries
24th April	Taurus
8th May/22nd June	Gemini
28th May/12th July	Cancer
1st August	Leo
16th August	Virgo
2nd September/14th October	Libra
27th September/9th November	Scorpio
28th November	Sagittarius

1982

1st January/17th December	Capricorn
12th January/16th February	Aquarius
31st January	Pisces
8th April	Aries
24th April	Taurus
8th May/22nd June	Gemini
28th May/12th July	Cancer
1st August	Leo
16th August	Virgo
2nd September/14th October	Libra
27th September/9th November	Scorpio
28th November	Sagittarius

1983

12th January/4th December	Capricorn
1st January/14th February	Aquarius
7th March	Pisces
23rd March	Aries
7th April	Taurus
14th June	Gemini
1st July	Cancer
15th July	Leo
1st August/6th September	Virgo

29th August/8th October	Libra
26th October	Scorpio
14th November	Sagittarius

1984

1st January/1st December	Capricorn
9th February	Aquarius
27th February	Pisces
14th March/25th April	Aries
31st March/15th May	Taurus
7th June	Gemini
22nd June	Cancer
6th July	Leo
26th July	Virgo
30th September	Libra
18th October	Scorpio
6th November/7th December	Sagittarius

1985

11th January	Capricorn
1st February	Aquarius
18th February	Pisces
7th March	Aries
14th May	Taurus
30th May	Gemini
13th June	Cancer
29th June	Leo
6th September	Virgo
22nd September	Libra
10th October/4th December	Scorpio
1st January/12th December	Sagittarius

1986

6th January	Capricorn
25th January	Aquarius
11th February/12th March	Pisces
3rd March/17th April	Aries
7th May	Taurus
22nd May	Gemini
6th June/24th July	Cancer

26th June/12th August	Leo
30th August	Virgo
15th September	Libra
4th October	Scorpio
1st January/10th December	Sagittarius

1987

1st January/23rd December	Capricorn
17th January/12th March	Aquarius
4th February/14th March	Pisces
12th April	Aries
20th May	Taurus
14th May	Gemini
30th June	Cancer
7th August	Leo
22nd August	Virgo
7th September/1st November	Libra
29th September/12th November	Scorpio
3rd December	Sagittarius

1988

1st January/14th December	Capricorn
10th January	Aquarius
16th March	Pisces
5th April	Aries
20th May	Taurus
5th May	Gemini
12th June	Cancer
29th July	Leo
13th August	Virgo
31st August	Libra
7th November	Scorpio
25th November	Sagittarius

1989

1st January/30th January/7th December	Capricorn
3rd January/15th February	Aquarius
11th March	Pisces
28th March	Aries
12th April/20th May	Taurus

12th June	Gemini
6th July	Cancer
20th July	Leo
5th August	Virgo
26th August/11th October	Libra
27th September/30th October	Scorpio
18th November	Sagittarius

1990

1st January/2nd December	Capricorn
12th February	Aquarius
4th March	Pisces
20th March	Aries
4th May	Taurus
12th June	Gemini
28th June	Cancer
12th July	Leo
29th July	Virgo
6th October	Libra
23rd October	Scorpio
11th November/26th December	Sagittarius

1991

14th January	Capricorn
6th February	Aquarius
24th February	Pisces
12th March	Aries
17th May	Taurus
5th June	Gemini
19th June	Cancer
4th July/20th August	Leo
26th July/11th September	Virgo
28th September	Libra
15th October	Scorpio
1st January/4th December	Sagittarius

1992

10th January	Capricorn
30th January	Aquarius
16th February/4th April	Pisces

4th March/15th April	Aries
11th May	Taurus
27th May	Gemini
10th June	Cancer
27th June	Leo
3rd September	Virgo
19th September	Libra
7th October/22nd November	Scorpio
1st January/12th December	Sagittarius

1993

3rd January/26th December	Capricorn
21st January	Aquarius
8th February	Pisces
16th April	Aries
4th May	Taurus
18th May	Gemini
2nd June	Cancer
10th August	Leo
26th August	Virgo
11th September	Libra
1st October	Scorpio
1st January/7th December	Sagittarius

1994

1st January/19th December	Capricorn
14th January/22nd February	Aquarius
1st February/18th March	Pisces
10th April	Aries
26th May	Taurus
10th May/2nd July	Gemini
29th May/11th July	Cancer
3rd August	Leo
18th August	Virgo
4th September/20th October	Libra
27th September/10th October	Scorpio
20th November	Sagittarius

1995

1st January/12th December	Capricorn
7th January	Aquarius
12th February	Pisces
2nd April	Aries
17th May	Taurus
3rd May	Gemini
11th July	Cancer
26th July	Leo
10th August	Virgo
29th September	Libra
4th November	Scorpio
23rd November	Sagittarius

SOME MORE PRECISE MERCURY DATA EST TIME ZONE USED.

Dec 11, 1995   9:57 PM   Mercury enters Capricorn

Jan 1, 1996   1:06 PM   Mercury enters Aquarius

Jan 17, 1996   4:37 AM   Mercury Rx enters Capricorn

Feb 14, 1996   9:44 PM   Mercury enters Aquarius

Mar 7, 1996   6:53 AM   Mercury enters Pisces

Mar 24, 1996   3:03 AM   Mercury enters Aries

Apr 7, 1996   11:16 PM   Mercury enters Taurus Jun 13, 1996

5:45 PM   Mercury enters Gemini

Jul 2, 1996   3:37 AM   Mercury enters Cancer

Jul 16, 1996   5:56 AM   Mercury enters Leo

Aug 1, 1996   12:17 PM   Mercury enters Virgo

Aug 26, 1996   1:17 AM   Mercury enters Libra

Sep 12, 1996   5:32 AM   Mercury Rx enters Virgo

Oct 8, 1996   11:13 PM   Mercury enters Libra

Oct 26, 1996   9:01 PM   Mercury enters Scorpio

Nov 14, 1996   11:36 AM   Mercury enters Sagittarius Dec 4, 1996

8:48 AM   Mercury enters Capricorn

Feb 9, 1997   12:53 AM   Mercury enters Aquarius

Feb 27, 1997   10:54 PM   Mercury enters Pisces

Mar 15, 1997   11:13 PM   Mercury enters Aries

Apr 1, 1997   8:45 AM   Mercury enters Taurus

May 4, 1997   9:48 PM   Mercury Rx enters Aries May 12, 1997

6:25 AM   Mercury enters Taurus

Jun 8, 1997   7:25 PM   Mercury enters Gemini

Jun 23, 1997   4:41 PM   Mercury enters Cancer

Jul 8, 1997   1:28 AM   Mercury enters Leo

Jul 26, 1997   8:42 PM   Mercury enters Virgo

Oct 2, 1997   1:38 AM   Mercury enters Libra

Oct 19, 1997   8:08 AM   Mercury enters Scorpio

Nov 7, 1997   12:42 PM   Mercury enters Sagittarius Nov 30, 1997

2:11 PM   Mercury enters Capricorn

Dec 13, 1997   1:06 PM   Mercury Rx enters Sagittarius

Jan 12, 1998   11:20 AM   Mercury enters Capricorn

Feb 2, 1998   10:15 AM   Mercury enters Aquarius

Feb 20, 1998   5:22 AM   Mercury enters Pisces

Mar 8, 1998   3:28 AM   Mercury enters Aries

May 14, 1998   10:10 PM   Mercury enters Taurus Jun 1, 1998

4:07 AM   Mercury enters Gemini

Jun 15, 1998   1:33 AM   Mercury enters Cancer

Jun 30, 1998   7:52 PM   Mercury enters Leo

Sep 7, 1998   9:58 PM   Mercury enters Virgo

Sep 24, 1998   6:13 AM   Mercury enters Libra

Oct 11, 1998   10:44 PM   Mercury enters Scorpio

Nov 1, 1998   11:02 AM   Mercury enters Sagittarius Jan 6, 1999

   9:04 PM   Mercury enters Capricorn

Jan 26, 1999   4:32 AM   Mercury enters Aquarius

Feb 12, 1999   10:28 AM   Mercury enters Pisces

Mar 2, 1999   5:50 PM   Mercury enters Aries

Mar 18, 1999   4:23 AM   Mercury Rx enters Pisces

Apr 17, 1999   6:09 PM   Mercury enters Aries May 8, 1999

5:22 PM   Mercury enters Taurus

May 23, 1999   5:22 PM   Mercury enters Gemini

Jun 6, 1999   8:18 PM   Mercury enters Cancer

Jun 26, 1999   11:39 AM   Mercury enters Leo

Jul 31, 1999   2:44 PM   Mercury Rx enters Cancer

Aug 11, 1999   12:25 AM   Mercury enters Leo

Aug 31, 1999   11:15 AM   Mercury enters Virgo

Sep 16, 1999   8:53 AM   Mercury enters Libra

Oct 5, 1999   1:12 AM   Mercury enters Scorpio

Oct 30, 1999   4:08 PM   Mercury enters Sagittarius

Nov 9, 1999   3:13 PM   Mercury Rx enters Scorpio Dec 10,

1999   9:09 PM   Mercury enters Sagittarius

Dec 31, 1999   1:48 AM   Mercury enters Capricorn

Jan 18, 2000   5:20 PM   Mercury enters Aquarius

Feb 5, 2000   3:09 AM   Mercury enters Pisces

Apr 12, 2000   8:17 PM   Mercury enters Aries Apr 29, 2000

11:53 PM   Mercury enters Taurus

May 14, 2000	3:10 AM	Mercury enters Gemini
May 30, 2000	12:27 AM	Mercury enters Cancer
Aug 7, 2000	1:42 AM	Mercury enters Leo
Aug 22, 2000	6:11 AM	Mercury enters Virgo
Sep 7, 2000	6:22 PM	Mercury enters Libra
Sep 28, 2000	9:28 AM	Mercury enters Scorpio
Nov 7, 2000	2:28 AM	Mercury Rx enters Libra Nov 8, 2000
4:42 PM		Mercury enters Scorpio
Dec 3, 2000	3:26 PM	Mercury enters Sagittarius
Dec 22, 2000	9:03 PM	Mercury enters Capricorn
Jan 10, 2001	8:26 AM	Mercury enters Aquarius
Feb 1, 2001	2:13 AM	Mercury enters Pisces
Feb 6, 2001	2:57 PM	Mercury Rx enters Aquarius
Mar 17, 2001	1:05 AM	Mercury enters Pisces
Apr 6, 2001	3:14 AM	Mercury enters Aries Apr 21, 2001
4:08 PM		Mercury enters Taurus
May 6, 2001	12:53 AM	Mercury enters Gemini
Jul 12, 2001	6:47 PM	Mercury enters Cancer
Jul 30, 2001	6:18 AM	Mercury enters Leo
Aug 14, 2001	1:04 AM	Mercury enters Virgo
Aug 31, 2001	8:37 PM	Mercury enters Libra
Nov 7, 2001	2:53 PM	Mercury enters Scorpio Nov 26, 2001
1:23 PM		Mercury enters Sagittarius
Dec 15, 2001	2:55 PM	Mercury enters Capricorn
Jan 3, 2002	4:38 PM	Mercury enters Aquarius
Feb 3, 2002	11:18 PM	Mercury Rx enters Capricorn

Feb 13, 2002   12:20 PM   Mercury enters Aquarius

Mar 11, 2002   6:34 PM   Mercury enters Pisces

Mar 29, 2002   9:44 AM   Mercury enters Aries

Apr 13, 2002   6:10 AM   Mercury enters Taurus Apr 30, 2002

3:15 AM   Mercury enters Gemini

Jul 7, 2002   6:35 AM   Mercury enters Cancer

Jul 21, 2002   6:41 PM   Mercury enters Leo

Aug 6, 2002   5:51 AM   Mercury enters Virgo

Aug 26, 2002   5:10 PM   Mercury enters Libra

Oct 2, 2002   5:26 AM   Mercury Rx enters Virgo

Oct 11, 2002   1:56 AM   Mercury enters Libra

Oct 31, 2002   5:43 PM   Mercury enters Scorpio Nov 19, 2002

6:29 AM   Mercury enters Sagittarius

Dec 8, 2002   3:21 PM   Mercury enters Capricorn

Feb 12, 2003   8:00 PM   Mercury enters Aquarius

Mar 4, 2003   9:04 PM   Mercury enters Pisces

Mar 21, 2003   7:16 AM   Mercury enters Aries

Apr 5, 2003   9:37 AM   Mercury enters Taurus

Jun 12, 2003   9:34 PM   Mercury enters Gemini Jun 29, 2003

6:17 AM   Mercury enters Cancer

Jul 13, 2003   8:10 AM   Mercury enters Leo

Jul 30, 2003   10:05 AM   Mercury enters Virgo

Oct 6, 2003   9:28 PM   Mercury enters Libra

Oct 24, 2003   7:20 AM   Mercury enters Scorpio

Nov 12, 2003   2:19 AM   Mercury enters Sagittarius Dec 2, 2003

4:34 PM   Mercury enters Capricorn

Dec 30, 2003   2:52 PM   Mercury Rx enters Sagittarius

Jan 14, 2004   6:02 AM   Mercury enters Aquarius

Feb 25, 2004   7:58 AM   Mercury enters Pisces

Mar 12, 2004   4:44 AM   Mercury enters Aries

Mar 31, 2004   9:27 PM   Mercury enters Taurus

Apr 12, 2004   9:23 PM   Mercury Rx enters Aries May 16, 2004

2:54 AM   Mercury enters Taurus

Jun 5, 2004   8:47 AM   Mercury enters Gemini

Jun 19, 2004   3:49 PM   Mercury enters Cancer

Jul 4, 2004   10:52 AM   Mercury enters Leo

Jul 25, 2004   9:58 AM   Mercury enters Virgo

Aug 24, 2004   9:33 PM   Mercury Rx enters Leo

Sep 10, 2004   3:38 AM   Mercury enters Virgo

Sep 28, 2004   10:13 AM   Mercury enters Libra

Oct 15, 2004   6:57 PM   Mercury enters Scorpio

Nov 4, 2004   9:40 AM   Mercury enters Sagittarius Jan 9, 2005

11:09 PM   Mercury enters Capricorn

Jan 30, 2005   12:37 AM   Mercury enters Aquarius

Feb 16, 2005   12:46 PM   Mercury enters Pisces

Mar 4, 2005   8:34 PM   Mercury enters Aries

May 12, 2005   5:14 AM   Mercury enters Taurus May 28, 2005

6:44 AM   Mercury enters Gemini

Jun 11, 2005   3:03 AM   Mercury enters Cancer

Jun 28, 2005   12:01 AM   Mercury enters Leo

Sep 4, 2005   1:52 PM   Mercury enters Virgo

Sep 20, 2005   12:40 PM   Mercury enters Libra

Oct 8, 2005   1:15 PM   Mercury enters Scorpio

Oct 30, 2005   4:02 AM   Mercury enters Sagittarius Nov 26, 2005

6:53 AM   Mercury Rx enters Scorpio

Dec 12, 2005   4:19 PM   Mercury enters Sagittarius

Jan 3, 2006   4:26 PM   Mercury enters Capricorn

Jan 22, 2006   3:41 PM   Mercury enters Aquarius

Feb 8, 2006   8:22 PM   Mercury enters Pisces

Apr 16, 2006   8:20 AM   Mercury enters Aries May 5, 2006   4:28

AM   Mercury enters Taurus

May 19, 2006   4:52 PM   Mercury enters Gemini

Jun 3, 2006   7:21 AM   Mercury enters Cancer

Jun 28, 2006   3:57 PM   Mercury enters Leo

Jul 10, 2006   4:18 PM   Mercury Rx enters Cancer

Aug 11, 2006   12:09 AM   Mercury enters Leo

Aug 27, 2006   3:31 PM   Mercury enters Virgo

Sep 12, 2006   5:08 PM   Mercury enters Libra

Oct 2, 2006   12:38 AM   Mercury enters Scorpio

Dec 8, 2006   12:52 AM   Mercury enters Sagittarius Dec 27, 2006

3:55 PM   Mercury enters Capricorn

Jan 15, 2007   4:25 AM   Mercury enters Aquarius

Feb 2, 2007   4:20 AM   Mercury enters Pisces

Feb 26, 2007   10:00 PM   Mercury Rx enters Aquarius

Mar 18, 2007   5:35 AM   Mercury enters Pisces Apr 10, 2007

7:07 PM   Mercury enters Aries

Apr 27, 2007   3:16 AM   Mercury enters Taurus

May 11, 2007	5:17 AM	Mercury enters Gemini
May 28, 2007	8:56 PM	Mercury enters Cancer
Aug 4, 2007	1:15 PM	Mercury enters Leo
Aug 19, 2007	9:01 AM	Mercury enters Virgo
Sep 5, 2007	8:02 AM	Mercury enters Libra
Sep 27, 2007	1:18 PM	Mercury enters Scorpio
Oct 23, 2007	11:36 PM	Mercury Rx enters Libra
Nov 11, 2007	3:41 AM	Mercury enters Scorpio Dec 1, 2007

7:21 AM   Mercury enters Sagittarius

Dec 20, 2007	9:43 AM	Mercury enters Capricorn
Jan 7, 2008	11:46 PM	Mercury enters Aquarius
Mar 14, 2008	6:46 PM	Mercury enters Pisces Apr 2, 2008

1:45 PM   Mercury enters Aries

Apr 17, 2008	5:07 PM	Mercury enters Taurus
May 2, 2008	4:00 PM	Mercury enters Gemini
Jul 10, 2008	4:17 PM	Mercury enters Cancer
Jul 26, 2008	7:48 AM	Mercury enters Leo
Aug 10, 2008	6:51 AM	Mercury enters Virgo
Aug 28, 2008	10:50 PM	Mercury enters Libra
Nov 4, 2008	11:00 AM	Mercury enters Scorpio Nov 23, 2008

2:09 AM   Mercury enters Sagittarius

Dec 12, 2008	5:13 AM	Mercury enters Capricorn
Jan 1, 2009	4:51 AM	Mercury enters Aquarius
Jan 21, 2009	12:36 AM	Mercury Rx enters Capricorn
Feb 14, 2009	10:39 AM	Mercury enters Aquarius

Mar 8, 2009   2:56 PM   Mercury enters Pisces Mar 25, 2009

3:55 PM   Mercury enters Aries

Apr 9, 2009   10:21 AM   Mercury enters Taurus

Apr 30, 2009   6:29 PM   Mercury enters Gemini

May 13, 2009   7:53 PM   Mercury Rx enters Taurus

Jun 13, 2009   10:47 PM   Mercury enters Gemini

Jul 3, 2009   3:20 PM   Mercury enters Cancer

Jul 17, 2009   7:08 PM   Mercury enters Leo

Aug 2, 2009   7:07 PM   Mercury enters Virgo

Aug 25, 2009   4:18 PM   Mercury enters Libra

Sep 17, 2009   11:26 PM   Mercury Rx enters Virgo

Oct 9, 2009   11:46 PM   Mercury enters Libra

Oct 28, 2009   6:09 AM   Mercury enters Scorpio

Nov 15, 2009   7:28 PM   Mercury enters Sagittarius Dec 5, 2009

12:24 PM   Mercury enters Capricorn

Feb 10, 2010   4:06 AM   Mercury enters Aquarius

Mar 1, 2010   8:28 AM   Mercury enters Pisces

Mar 17, 2010   12:12 PM   Mercury enters Aries Apr 2, 2010

9:06 AM   Mercury enters Taurus

Jun 10, 2010   1:41 AM   Mercury enters Gemini

Jun 25, 2010   6:32 AM   Mercury enters Cancer

Jul 9, 2010   12:29 PM   Mercury enters Leo

Jul 27, 2010   5:43 PM   Mercury enters Virgo

Oct 3, 2010   11:04 AM   Mercury enters Libra

Oct 20, 2010   5:19 PM   Mercury enters Scorpio

Nov 8, 2010   6:43 PM   Mercury enters Sagittarius Nov 30, 2010

7:10 PM   Mercury enters Capricorn

Dec 18, 2010   9:53 AM   Mercury Rx enters Sagittarius

Jan 13, 2011   6:25 AM   Mercury enters Capricorn

Feb 3, 2011   5:19 PM   Mercury enters Aquarius

Feb 21, 2011   3:53 PM   Mercury enters Pisces

Mar 9, 2011   12:47 PM   Mercury enters Aries

May 15, 2011   7:18 PM   Mercury enters Taurus Jun 2, 2011

4:02 PM   Mercury enters Gemini

Jun 16, 2011   3:09 PM   Mercury enters Cancer

Jul 2, 2011   1:38 AM   Mercury enters Leo

Jul 28, 2011   1:59 PM   Mercury enters Virgo

Aug 8, 2011   5:46 AM   Mercury Rx enters Leo

Sep 9, 2011   1:58 AM   Mercury enters Virgo

Sep 25, 2011   5:09 PM   Mercury enters Libra

Oct 13, 2011   6:52 AM   Mercury enters Scorpio

Nov 2, 2011   12:54 PM   Mercury enters Sagittarius

Jan 8, 2012   1:34 AM   Mercury enters Capricorn Jan 27, 2012

1:12 PM   Mercury enters Aquarius

Feb 13, 2012   8:38 PM   Mercury enters Pisces

Mar 2, 2012   6:41 AM   Mercury enters Aries

Mar 23, 2012   9:22 AM   Mercury Rx enters Pisces Apr 16, 2012

6:42 PM   Mercury enters Aries

May 9, 2012   1:14 AM   Mercury enters Taurus

May 24, 2012   7:12 AM   Mercury enters Gemini

Jun 7, 2012   7:16 AM   Mercury enters Cancer

Jun 25, 2012   10:24 PM   Mercury enters Leo

Aug 31, 2012   10:32 PM   Mercury enters Virgo

Sep 16, 2012   7:22 PM   Mercury enters Libra

Oct 5, 2012   6:35 AM   Mercury enters Scorpio

Oct 29, 2012   2:18 AM   Mercury enters Sagittarius

Nov 14, 2012   2:42 AM   Mercury Rx enters Scorpio Dec 10, 2012

8:40 PM   Mercury enters Sagittarius

Dec 31, 2012   9:03 AM   Mercury enters Capricorn

Jan 19, 2013   2:25 AM   Mercury enters Aquarius

Feb 5, 2013   9:55 AM   Mercury enters Pisces

Apr 13, 2013   10:37 PM   Mercury enters Aries May 1, 2013

11:37 AM   Mercury enters Taurus

May 15, 2013   4:41 PM   Mercury enters Gemini

May 31, 2013   3:07 AM   Mercury enters Cancer

Aug 8, 2013   8:13 AM   Mercury enters Leo

Aug 23, 2013   6:36 PM   Mercury enters Virgo

Sep 9, 2013   3:07 AM   Mercury enters Libra

Sep 29, 2013   7:38 AM   Mercury enters Scorpio

Dec 4, 2013   9:42 PM   Mercury enters Sagittarius Dec 24, 2013

5:12 AM   Mercury enters Capricorn

Jan 11, 2014   4:35 PM   Mercury enters Aquarius

Jan 31, 2014   9:29 AM   Mercury enters Pisces

Feb 12, 2014   10:30 PM   Mercury Rx enters Aquarius

Mar 17, 2014   6:24 PM   Mercury enters Pisces Apr 7, 2014

11:35 AM   Mercury enters Aries

Apr 23, 2014   5:16 AM   Mercury enters Taurus

May 7, 2014   10:57 AM   Mercury enters Gemini

May 29, 2014   5:12 AM   Mercury enters Cancer

Jun 17, 2014   6:04 AM   Mercury Rx enters Gemini

Jul 13, 2014   12:45 AM   Mercury enters Cancer

Jul 31, 2014   6:46 PM   Mercury enters Leo

Aug 15, 2014   12:44 PM   Mercury enters Virgo

Sep 2, 2014   1:38 AM   Mercury enters Libra

Sep 27, 2014   6:39 PM   Mercury enters Scorpio

Oct 10, 2014   1:27 PM   Mercury Rx enters Libra

Nov 8, 2014   6:09 PM   Mercury enters Scorpio Nov 27, 2014

9:26 PM   Mercury enters Sagittarius

Dec 16, 2014   10:53 PM   Mercury enters Capricorn

Jan 4, 2015   8:08 PM   Mercury enters Aquarius

Mar 12, 2015   11:52 PM   Mercury enters Pisces Mar 30, 2015

9:44 PM   Mercury enters Aries

Apr 14, 2015   6:51 PM   Mercury enters Taurus

Apr 30, 2015   10:00 PM   Mercury enters Gemini

Jul 8, 2015   2:52 PM   Mercury enters Cancer

Jul 23, 2015   8:14 AM   Mercury enters Leo

Aug 7, 2015   3:15 PM   Mercury enters Virgo

Aug 27, 2015   11:44 AM   Mercury enters Libra

Nov 2, 2015   2:06 AM   Mercury enters Scorpio Nov 20, 2015

2:43 PM   Mercury enters Sagittarius

Dec 9, 2015   9:34 PM   Mercury enters Capricorn

Jan 1, 2016   9:20 PM   Mercury enters Aquarius

Jan 8, 2016   2:36 PM   Mercury Rx enters Capricorn

Feb 13, 2016   5:43 PM   Mercury enters Aquarius

Mar 5, 2016   5:23 AM   Mercury enters Pisces

Mar 21, 2016   8:19 PM   Mercury enters Aries Apr 5, 2016   7:09
PM   Mercury enters Taurus

Jun 12, 2016   7:22 PM   Mercury enters Gemini

Jun 29, 2016   7:24 PM   Mercury enters Cancer

Jul 13, 2016   8:47 PM   Mercury enters Leo

Jul 30, 2016   2:18 PM   Mercury enters Virgo

Oct 7, 2016   3:55 AM   Mercury enters Libra

Oct 24, 2016   4:46 PM   Mercury enters Scorpio

Nov 12, 2016   9:39 AM   Mercury enters Sagittarius Dec 2, 2016
4:18 PM   Mercury enters Capricorn

Jan 4, 2017   9:17 AM   Mercury Rx enters Sagittarius

Jan 12, 2017   9:03 AM   Mercury enters Capricorn

Feb 7, 2017   4:35 AM   Mercury enters Aquarius

Feb 25, 2017   6:07 PM   Mercury enters Pisces

Mar 13, 2017   5:07 PM   Mercury enters Aries Mar 31, 2017
1:30 PM   Mercury enters Taurus

Apr 20, 2017   1:37 PM   Mercury Rx enters Aries

May 16, 2017   12:07 AM   Mercury enters Taurus

Jun 6, 2017   6:15 PM   Mercury enters Gemini

Jun 21, 2017   5:57 AM   Mercury enters Cancer

Jul 5, 2017   8:20 PM   Mercury enters Leo

Jul 25, 2017   7:41 PM   Mercury enters Virgo

Aug 31, 2017   11:28 AM   Mercury Rx enters Leo

Sep 9, 2017   10:52 PM   Mercury enters Virgo

Sep 29, 2017   8:42 PM   Mercury enters Libra

Oct 17, 2017   3:58 AM   Mercury enters Scorpio

Nov 5, 2017   2:19 PM   Mercury enters Sagittarius Jan 11, 2018

12:09 AM   Mercury enters Capricorn

Jan 31, 2018   8:39 AM   Mercury enters Aquarius

Feb 17, 2018   11:28 PM   Mercury enters Pisces

Mar 6, 2018   2:34 AM   Mercury enters Aries

May 13, 2018   8:40 AM   Mercury enters Taurus May 29, 2018

7:49 PM   Mercury enters Gemini

Jun 12, 2018   3:59 PM   Mercury enters Cancer

Jun 29, 2018   1:16 AM   Mercury enters Leo

Sep 5, 2018   10:39 PM   Mercury enters Virgo

Sep 21, 2018   11:39 PM   Mercury enters Libra

Oct 9, 2018   8:40 PM   Mercury enters Scorpio

Oct 31, 2018   12:38 AM   Mercury enters Sagittarius

Dec 1, 2018   6:12 AM   Mercury Rx enters Scorpio Dec 12, 2018

6:43 PM   Mercury enters Sagittarius

Jan 4, 2019   10:40 PM   Mercury enters Capricorn

Jan 24, 2019   12:49 AM   Mercury enters Aquarius

Feb 10, 2019   5:50 AM   Mercury enters Pisces

Apr 17, 2019   2:00 AM   Mercury enters Aries May 6, 2019   2:25

PM   Mercury enters Taurus

May 21, 2019   6:52 AM   Mercury enters Gemini

Jun 4, 2019   4:04 PM   Mercury enters Cancer

Jun 26, 2019   8:19 PM   Mercury enters Leo

Jul 19, 2019   3:06 AM   Mercury Rx enters Cancer

Aug 11, 2019   3:45 PM   Mercury enters Leo

Aug 29, 2019   3:48 AM   Mercury enters Virgo

Sep 14, 2019   3:14 AM   Mercury enters Libra

Oct 3, 2019   4:14 AM   Mercury enters Scorpio

Dec 9, 2019   4:41 AM   Mercury enters Sagittarius Dec 28, 2019

11:55 PM   Mercury enters Capricorn

2) TABLES FOR MOON SIGNS P. 86

Now find your MOON SIGN

STAGE 1

MOON NUMBERS for the 12 Zodiac Signs

FIRST find your Moon Number by finding the month and day of your birth in charts below. The charts have been simplified to reveal your Moon number next to your day of birth.

JANUARY

Day of Birth	Moon Number
1, 2	1
3, 4	2
5, 6	3
7, 8	4
9, 10	5
11, 12	6
13, 14	7
15, 16, 17	8
18, 19	9
20, 21	10
22, 23, 24	11
25, 26	12
27, 28, 29	1
30, 31	2

FEBRUARY

Day of Birth	Moon Number
1, 2	3
3, 4	4
5, 6	5
7, 8	6
9, 10, 11	7
12, 13	8
14, 15	9
16, 17, 18	10
19, 20	11
21, 22, 23	12

24, 25	1
26, 27, 28	2
29	3

MARCH

Day of Birth	Moon Number
1, 2	3
3, 4	4
5, 6	5
7, 8	6
9, 10,	7
11, 12	8
13, 14	9
15, 16, 17	10
18, 19	11
20, 21, 22	12
23, 24, 25	1
26, 27	2
28, 29	3
30, 31	4

APRIL

Day of Birth	Moon Number
1, 2	5
3, 4	6
5, 6	7
7, 8	8
9, 10, 11	9
12, 13	10
14, 15, 16	11
17, 18,	12
19, 20, 21	1
22, 23	2
24, 25,	3
26, 27, 28	4
29, 30	5

MAY

Day of Birth	Moon Number
1, 2	6
3, 4	7
5, 6	8
7, 8	9

9, 10	10
11, 12, 13	11
14, 15, 16	12
17, 18	1
19, 20	2
21, 22, 23	3
24, 25,	4
26, 27	5
28, 29	6
30, 31	7

JUNE

Day of Birth	Moon Number
1, 2	8
3, 4	9
5, 6, 7	10
8, 9	11
10, 11, 12	12
13, 14	1
15, 16, 17	2
18, 19	3
20, 21	4
22, 23	5
24, 25	6
26, 27	7
28, 29, 30	8

JULY

Day of Birth	Moon Number
1, 2	9
3, 4	10
5, 6, 7	11
8, 9	12
10, 11, 12	1
13, 14	2
15, 16	3
17, 18,	4
19, 20	5
21, 22, 23	6
24, 25,	7
26, 27	8
28, 29	9
30, 31	10

AUGUST

Day of Birth	Moon Number
1	10
2, 3	11
4, 5, 6	12
7, 8	1
9, 10	2
11, 12, 13	3
14, 15	4
16, 17,	5
18, 19	6
20, 21	7
22, 23,	8
24, 25	9
26, 27, 28	10
29, 30	11
31	12

SEPTEMBER

Day of Birth	Moon Number
1, 2	12
3, 4	1
5, 6	2
7, 8	3
10, 11	4
12, 13	5
14, 15	6
16, 17	7
18, 19	8
20, 21, 22	9
23, 24	10
25, 26, 27	11
28, 29	12
30	1

OCTOBER

Day of Birth	Moon Number
1, 2	1
3, 4	2
5, 6	3
7, 8, 9	4
10, 11	5
12, 13	6

14, 15	7
16, 17	8
18, 19	9
20, 21	10
22, 23, 24	11
25, 26	12
27, 28, 29	1
30, 31	2

NOVEMBER

Day of Birth	Moon Number
1, 2, 3	3
4, 5	4
6, 7	5
8, 9	6
10, 11	7
12, 13	8
14, 15	9
16, 17, 18	10
19, 20	11
21, 22, 23	12
24, 25	1
26, 27, 28	2
29, 30	3

DECEMBER

Day of Birth	Moon Number
1, 2	4
3, 4	5
5, 6	6
7, 8, 9	7
10, 11	8
12, 13	9
14, 15	10
16, 17	11
18, 19, 20	12
21, 22	1
23, 24, 25	2
26, 27	3
28, 29	4
30, 31	*5*

STAGE TWO

Now find your MOON SIGN

Find your Year of Birth in the right hand column. Then trace your finger back to the correct Moon Number column. The abbreviated Star Sign you find reveals where your Moon was in the heavens at the time of your birth. (Your Moon Sign may be the same as your Sun Sign, but equally, it may not.)

Abbreviations

Ari = Aries, Tau = Taurus, Gem = Gemini, Can = Cancer, Leo = Leo, Vir = Virgo, Lib = Libra, Sco = Scorpio, Sag = Sagittarius, Cap = Capricorn, Aqu = Aquarius, Pis = Pisces

MOON NUMBER

1	2	3	4	5	6	7	8	9	10	11	12	Year of Birth
Cap	Aqu	Pis	Ari	Tau	Gem	Can	Leo	Vir	Lib	Sco	Sag	1919 1938 1957 1976 1995
Tau	Gem	Can	Leo	Vir	Lib	Sco	Sag	Cap	Aqu	Pis	Ari	1920 1939 1958 1977 1996
Lib	Sco	Sag	Cap	Aqu	Pis	Ari	Tau	Gem	Can	Leo	Vir	1921 1940 1959 1978 1997
Aqu	Pis	Ari	Tau	Gem	Can	Leo	Vir	Lib	Sco	Sag	Cap	1922 1941 1960 1979 1998
Gem	Can	Leo	Vir	Lib	Sco	Sag	Cap	Aqu	Pis	Ari	Tau	1923 1942 1961 1980 1999
Sco	Sag	Cap	Aqu	Pis	Ari	Tau	Gem	Can	Leo	Vir	Lib	1924 1943 1962 1981 2000
Pis	Ari	Tau	Gem	Can	Leo	Vir	Lib	Sco	Sag	Cap	Aqu	1925 1944 1963 1982 2001
Leo	Vir	Lib	Sco	Sag	Cap	Aqu	Pis	Ari	Tau	Gem	Can	1926 1945 1964 1983 2002
Sag	Cap	Aqu	Pis	Ari	Tau	Gem	Can	Leo	Vir	Lib	Sco	1927 1946 1965 1984 2003
Ari	Tau	Gem	Can	Leo	Vir	Lib	Sco	Sag	Cap	Aqu	Pis	1928 1947 1966 1985 2004
Vir	Lib	Sco	Sag	Cap	Aqu	Pis	Ari	Tau	Gem	Can	Leo	1929 1948 1967 1986 2005
Cap	Aqu	Pis	Ari	Tau	Gem	Can	Leo	Vir	Lib	Sco	Sag	1930 1949 1968 1987 2006
Gem	Can	Leo	Vir	Lib	Sco	Sag	Cap	Aqu	Pis	Ari	Tau	1931 1950 1969 1988 2007
Lib	Sco	Sag	Cap	Aqu	Pis	Ari	Tau	Gem	Can	Leo	Vir	1932 1951 1970 1989 2008
Pis	Ari	Tau	Gem	Can	Leo	Vir	Lib	Sco	Sag	Cap	Aqu	1933 1952 1971 1990 2009
Can	Leo	Vir	Lib	Sco	Sag	Cap	Aqu	Pis	Ari	Tau	Gem	1934 1953 1972 1991 2010
Sco	Sag	Cap	Aqu	Pis	Ari	Tau	Gem	Can	Leo	Vir	Lib	1935 1954 1973 1992 2011
Ari	Tau	Gem	Can	Leo	Vir	Lib	Sco	Sag	Cap	Aqu	Pis	1936 1955 1974 1993 2012
Leo	Vir	Lib	Sco	Sag	Cap	Aqu	Pis	Ari	Tau	Gem	Can	1937 1956 1975 1994 2013

3) How to find your VENUS Sign P.96

Stage 1
Check for your Year of Birth on the table below to find your Venus Zone

LOVE ZONE   YEAR OF BIRTH

	1908	1916	1924	1932	1940	1948	1956	1964	1972	1980	1988	1996
	1915	1923	1931	1939	1947	1955	1963	1971	1919	1987	1995	1997
Venus Zone 1	1908	1916	1924	1932	1940	1948	1956	1964	1972	1980	1988	1998
Venus Zone 2	1909	1917	1925	1933	1941	1949	1957	1965	1973	1981	1989	1999
Venus Zone 3	1910	1918	1926	1934	1942	1950	1958	1966	1974	1982	1990	2000
Venus Zone 4	1911	1919	1927	1935	1943	1951	1959	1967	1975	1983	1991	2001
Venus Zone 5	1912	1920	1928	1936	1944	1952	1960	1968	1976	1984	1992	2002
Venus Zone 6	1913	1921	1929	1937	1945	1953	1961	1969	1977	1985	1993	2003
Venus Zone 7	1914	1922	1930	1938	1946	1954	1962	1970	1978	1986	1994	2004
Venus Zone 8	1915	1923	1931	1939	1947	1955	1963	1971	1979	1987	1995	2005

Now on the Tables below find your VENUS LOVE ZONE.

Check the abbreviated Star Sign to see where Venus resided in the heavens at the time of your birth. (Your Venus Sign may be the same as your Sun Sign, but equally, it may not.)

Abbreviations

Ari = Aries, Tau = Taurus, Gem = Gemini, Can = Cancer, Leo = Leo, Vir = Virgo, Lib = Libra, Sco = Scorpio, Sag = Sagittarius, Cap = Capricorn, Aqu = Aquarius, Pis = Pisces

VENUS Love Zone 1

Jan 1 – Jan 17	AQU
Jan 18 – Feb 10	PIS
Feb 11 – Mar 7	ARI
Mar 8 – Apr 3	TAU
Apr 4 – May 7	GEM
May 8 – Jun 23	CAN
Jun 24 – Aug 3	GEM
Aug 4 – Sept 7	CAN
Sept 8 – Oct 5	LEO
Oct 6 – Oct 31	VIR
Nov 1 – Nov 25	LIB
Nov 26 – Dec 19	SCO
Dec 20 – Dec 31	SAG

VENUS Love Zone 2

Jan 1 - Jan 12	SAG
Jan 13 – Feb 5	CAP
Feb 6 – Mar 1	AQU
Mar 2 – Mar 25	PIS
Mar 26 - Apr 18	ARI
Apr 19 – May 12	TAU
May 13 – Jun 6	GEM
Jun 7 - Jun 30	CAN
Jul 1 – Jul 25	LEO
Jul 26 – Aug 19	VIR
Aug 20 – Sept 13	LIB
Sept 14 – Oct 9	SCO
Oct 10 – Nov 5	SAG
Nov 6 – Dec 6	CAP
Dec 7 – Dec 31	AQU

VENUS Love Zone 3

Jan 1 – Apr 6	AQU
Apr 7 – May 4	PIS
May 5 – May 31	ARI
Jun 1 – Jun 26	TAU
Jun 27 – Jul 21	GEM
Jul 22 – Aug 15	CAN

Aug 16 – Sept 9	LEO
Sept 10 – Oct 3	VIR
Oct 4 - Oct 27	LIB
Oct 28 – Nov 20	SCO
Nov 21 – Dec 13	SAG
Dec 14 – Dec 31	CAP

VENUS Love Zone 4

Jan 1 – Jan 7	CAP
Jan 8 – Jan 31	AQU
Feb 1 – Feb 24	PIS
Feb 25 – Mar 20	ARI
Mar 21 – Apr 14	TAU
Apr 15 – May 10	GEM
May 11 – Jun 6	CAN
Jun 7 – Jul 7	LEO
Jul 8 – Nov 9	VIR
Nov 10 – Dec 7	LIB
Dec 8 – Dec 31	SCO

VENUS Love Zone 5

Jan 1 – Jan 2	SCO
Jan 3 – Jan 27	SAG
Jan 28 – Feb 20	CAP
Feb 21 - Mar 16	AQU
Mar 17 – Apr 9	PIS
Apr 10 – May 3	ARI
May 4 – May 28	TAU
May 29 – Jun 21	GEM
Jun 22 – Jul 16	CAN
Jul 17 – Aug 9	LEO
Aug 10 – Sept 2	VIR
Sept 3 - Sept 27	LIB
Sept 28 – Oct 21	SCO
Oct 22 – Nov 15	SAG
Nov 16 – Dec 10	CAP
Dec 11 – Dec 31	AQU

VENUS Love Zone 6

Jan 1 – Jan 4   AQU
Jan 5 – Feb 1   PIS
Feb 2 – Mar 14   ARI
Mar 15 – Mar 30   TAU
Mar 31 – Jun 4   ARI
Jun 5 – Jul 6   TAU
Jul 7 – Aug 3   GEM
Aug 4 – Aug 29   CAN
Aug 30 – Sept 23   LEO
Sept 24 – Oct 18   VIR
Oct 19 – Nov 11   LIB
Nov 12 – Dec 5   SCO
Dec 6 – Dec 29   SAG
Dec 30 – Dec 31   CAP

VENUS Love Zone 7

Jan 1 – Jan 21   CAP
Jan 22 – Feb 14   AQU
Feb 15 – Mar 10   PIS
Mar 11 – Apr 3   ARI
Apr 4 – Apr 28   TAU
Apr 29 – May 23   GEM
May 24 – Jun 17   CAN
Jun 18 – Jul 12   LEO
Jul 13 – Aug 8   VIR
Aug 9 – Sept 6   LIB
Sept 7 – Oct 15   SCO
Oct 16 – Nov 7   SAG
Nov 8 – Dec 31   SCO

VENUS Love Zone 8

Jan 1 – Jan 5   SCO
Jan 6 – Feb 5   SAG
Feb 6 – Mar 4   CAP
Mar 5 – Mar 29   AQU
Mar 30 – Apr 24   PIS
Apr 25 – May 19   ARI
May 20 – Jun 12   TAU
Jun 13 – Jul 7   GEM
Jul 8 – Jul 31   CAN

Aug 1 – Aug 25   LEO
Aug 26 – Sept 18   VIR
Sept 19 - Oct 12   LIB
Oct 13 – Nov 5   SCO
Nov 6 – Nov 29   SAG
Nov 30 – Dec 23   CAP
Dec 24 – Dec 31   AQU

4) MARS SIGNS P. 105

To find where MARS was at the Time of your Birth, find first the year of your birth below; then read across to the abbreviated Star Sign next to the relevant date.

The abbreviated Star Sign you find reveals where MARS was in the heavens at the time of your birth. (Your MARS Sign may be the same as your Sun Sign, but equally, it may not)

Abbreviations

Ari = Aries, Tau = Taurus, Gem = Gemini, Can = Cancer, Leo = Leo, Vir = Virgo, Lib = Libra, Sco = Scorpio, Sag = Sagittarius, Cap = Capricorn, Aqu = Aquarius, Pis = Pisces

1930

Jan 1 – Feb 5	CAP
Feb 6 – Mar 16	AQU
Mar 17 – Apr 23	PIS
Apr 24 - Jun 2	ARI
Jun 3 – Jul 13	TAU
Jul 14 – Aug 27	GEM
Aug 28 – Oct 19	CAN
Oct 20 – Dec 31	LEO

1931

Jan 1 – Jan 17	LEO
Jan 18 – Mar 29	CAN
Mar 30 – Jun 9	LEO
Jun 10 – Jul 31	VIR
Aug 1 - Sept 16	LIB
Sept 17 – Oct 29	SCO
Oct 30 – Dec 9	SAG
Dec 10 – Dec 31	CAP

1932

Jan 1 – Jan 17	CAP
Jan 18 – Feb 24	AQU
Feb 25 – Apr 2	PIS
Apr 3 – May 11	ARI

May 12 – Jun 21	TAU
Jun 22 – Aug 3	GEM
Aug 4 – Sept 19	CAN
Sept 20 – Nov 12	LEO
Nov 13 – Dec 31	VIR

1933

Jan 1 – Jul 5	VIR
Jul 6 – Aug 25	LIB
Aug 26 – Oct 8	SCO
Oct 9 – Nov 18	SAG
Nov 19 – Dec 27	CAP
Dec 28 – Dec 31	AQU

1934

Jan 1 – Feb 3	AQU
Feb 4 – Mar 13	PIS
Mar 14 – Apr 21	ARI
Apr 22 – Jun 1	TAU
Jun 2 – Jul 14	GEM
Jul 15 – Aug 29	CAN
Aug 30 – Oct 17	LEO
Oct 18 – Dec 10	VIR
Dec 11 – Dec 31	LIB

1935

Jan 1 – Jul 28	LIB
Jul 29 – Sept 15	SCO
Sept 16 – Oct 27	SAG
Oct 28 – Dec 6	CAP
Dec 7 – Dec 31	AQU

1936

Jan 1 – Jan 13	AQU
Jan 14 – Feb 21	PIS
Feb 22 – Mar 31	ARI
Apr 1 - May 12	TAU
May 13 – Jun 24	GEM
Jun 25 – Aug 9	CAN
Aug 10 – Sept 25	LEO
Sept 26 – Nov 13	VIR
Nov 14 – Dec 31	LIB

1937

Jan 1 – Jan 4	LIB
Jan 5 – Mar 12	SCO
Mar 13 – May 13	SAG
May 14 – Aug 7	CAP
Aug 8 – Sept 29	SAG
Sept 30 – Nov 10	CAP
Nov 11 – Dec 20	AQU
Dec 21 0 Dec 31	PIS

1938

Jan 1 – Jan 29	PIS
Jan 30 – Mar 11	ARI
Mar 12 – Apr 22	TAU
Apr 23 - Jun 6	GEM
Jun 7 – Jul 21	CAN
Jul 22 – Sept 6	LEO
Sept 7 – Oct 2	VIR
Oct 25 – Dec 10	LIB
Dec 11 – Dec 31	SCO

1939

Jan 1 – Jan 28	SCO
Jan 29 – Mar 20	SAG
Mar 21 – May 24	CAP
May 25 – Jul 20	AQU
Jul 21 - Sept 23	CAP
Sept 24 – Nov 18	AQU
Nov 19 – Dec 31	PIS

1940

Jan 1 – Jan 3	PIS
Jan 4 – Feb 16	ARI
Feb 17 – Mar 31	TAU
Apr 1 – May 16	GEM
May 17 – Jul 2	CAN
Jul 3 – Aug 18	LEO
Aug 19 – Oct 4	VIR
Oct 5 – Nov 18	LIB
Nov 19 – Dec 31	SCO

1941

Jan 1 – Jan 3	SCO

Jan 4 – Feb 16	SAG
Feb 17 – Apr 1	CAP
Apr 2 – May 15	AQU
May 16 – Jul 1	PIS
Jul 2 – Dec 31	ARI

1942

Jan 1 – Jan 10	ARI
Jan 11 – Mar 6	TAU
Mar 7 – Apr 25	GEM
Apr 26 – Jun 13	CAN
Jun 14 – Jul 31	LEO
Aug 1 – Sept 16	VIR
Sept 17 – Oct 31	LIB
Nov 1 – Dec 14	SCO
Dec 15 – Dec 31	SAG

1943

Jan 1 – Jan 25	SAG
Jan 26 – Mar 7	CAP
Mar 8 – Apr 16	AQU
Apr 17 – May 26	PIS
May 27 – Jul 6	ARI
Jul 7 – Aug 22	TAU
Aug 23 – Dec 31	GEM

1944

Jan 1 – Mar 27	GEM
Mar 28 – May 21	CAN
May 22 – Jul 11	LEO
Jul 12 – Aug 28	VIR
Aug 29 – Oct 12	LIB
Oct 13 - Nov 24	SCO
Nov 25 – Dec 31	SAG

1945

Jan 1 – Jan 4	SAG
Jan 5 – Feb 13	CAP
Feb 14 – Mar 24	AQU
Mar 25 – May 1	PIS
May 2 – Jun 10	ARI
Jun 11 – Jul 22	TAU
Jul 23 – Sept 6	GEM

Sept 7 – Nov 10	CAN
Nov 11 - Dec 25	LEO
Dec 26 – Dec 31	CAN

1946

Jan 1 – Apr 21	CAN
Apr 22 – Jun 19	LEO
Jun 20 - Aug 8	VIR
Aug 9 – Sept 23	LIB
Sept 24 – Nov 5	SCO
Nov 6 – Dec 16	SAG
Dec 17 – Dec 31	CAP

1947

Jan 1 – Jan 24	CAP
Jan 25 – Mar 3	AQU
Mar 4 - Apr 10	PIS
Apr 11 – May 20	ARI
May 21 – Jun 30	TAU
Jul 1 – Aug 12	GEM
Aug 13 – Sept 29	CAN
Sept 30 - Nov 31	LEO
Dec 1 – Dec 31	VIR

1948

Jan 1 – Feb 11	VIR
Feb 12 – May 17	LEO
May 18 – Jul 16	VIR
Jul 17 – Sept 2	LIB
Sept 3 – Oct 16	SCO
Oct 17 – Nov 25	SAG
Nov 26 – Dec 31	CAP

1949

Jan 1 – Jan 3	CAP
Jan 4 – Feb 10	AQU
Feb 11 – Mar 20	PIS
Mar 21 – Apr 29	ARI
Apr 30 – Jun 9	TAU
Jun 10 – Jul 22	GEM
Jul 23 – Sept 6	CAN
Sept 7 – Oct 26	LEO

Oct 27 – Dec 25	VIR
Dec 26 – Dec 31	LIB

1950

Jan 1 – Mar 27	LIB
Mar 28 - June 10	VIR
June 11 – Aug 9	LIB
Aug 10 – Sept 24	SCO
Sept 25 – Nov 5	,SAG
Nov 6 – Dec 15	CAP
Dec 16 – Dec 31	AQU

1951

Jan 1 – Jan 21	AQU
Jan 22 – Feb 28	PIS
Mar 1 – Apr 9	ARI
Apr 10 – May 20	TAU
May 21 – Jul 2	GEM
Jul 3 – Aug 17	CAN
Aug 18 – Oct 4	LEO
Oct 5 – Nov 23	VIR
Nov 24 – Dec 31	LIB

1952

Jan 1 – Jan 19	LIB
Jan 20 – Aug 26	SCO
Aug 27 – Oct 11	SAG
Oct 12 - Nov 20	CAP
Nov 21 – Dec 29	AQU
Dec 30 – Dec 31	PIS

1953

Jan 1 – Feb 7	PIS
Feb 8 – Mar 19	ARI
Mar 20 – Apr 31	TAU
May 1 – Jun 13	GEM
Jun 14 – Jul 28	CAN
Jul 29 – Sept 13	LEO
Sept 14 – Oct 31	VIR
Nov 1 – Dec 19	LIB
Dec 20 – Dec 31	SCO

1954

Jan 1 – Feb 8	SCO
Feb 9 – Apr 11	SAG
Apr 12 – Jul 2	CAP
Jul 3 – Aug 23	SAG
Aug 24 – Oct 20	CAP
Oct 21 – Dec 3	AQU
Dec 4 – Dec 31	PIS

1955

Jan 1 – Jan 14	PIS
Jan 15 – Feb 25	ARI
Feb 26 – Apr 9	TAU
Apr 10 - May 25	GEM
May 26 – Jul 10	CAN
Jul 11 – Aug 26	LEO
Aug 27 – Oct 12	VIR
Oct 13 – Nov 28	LIB
Nov 29 – Dec 31	SCO

1956

Jan 1 – Jan 13	SCO
Jan 14 – Feb 27	SAG
Feb 28 – Apr 13	CAP
Apr 14 – Jun 2	AQU
Jun 3 – Dec 5	PIS
Dec 6 – Dec 31	ARI

1957

Jan 1 – Jan 27	ARI
Jan 28 – Mar 16	TAU
Mar 17 – May 3	GEM
May 4 – Jun 20	CAN
Jun 21 – Aug 7	LEO
Aug 8 – Sept 23	VIR
Sept 24 – Nov 7	LIB
Nov 8 - Dec 22	SCO
Dec 23 – Dec 31	SAG

1958

Jan 1 – Feb 2	SAG
Feb 3 – Mar 16	CAP
Mar 17 – Apr 26	AQU
Apr 27 – Jun 6	PIS

Jun 7 - Jul 20	ARI
Jul 21 – Sept 20	TAU
Sept 21 – Oct 27	GEM
Oct 28 – Dec 31	TAU

1959

Jan 1 – Feb 9	TAU
Feb 10 – Apr 9	GEM
Apr 10 – May 30	CAN
May 31 – Jul 19	LEO
Jul 20 – Sept 4	VIR
Sept 5 – Oct 20	LIB
Oct 21 – Dec 2	SCO
Dec 3 – Dec 31	SAG

1960

Jan 1 – Jan 13	SAG
Jan 14 – Feb 22	CAP
Feb 23 – Apr 1	AQU
Apr 2 – May 10	PIS
May 11 – Jun 19	ARI
Jun 20 – Aug 1	TAU
Aug 2 – Sept 20	GEM
Sept 21 – Dec 31	CAN

1961

Jan 1 – May 5	CAN
May 6 – Jun 27	LEO
Jun 28 – Aug 16	VIR
Aug 17 – Sept 30	LIB
Oct 1 – Nov 12	SCO
Nov 13 – Dec 23	SAG
Dec 24 – Dec 31	CAP

1962

Jan 1 – Jan 31	CAP
Feb 1 - Mar 11	AQU
Mar 12 – Apr 18	PIS
Apr 19 – May 27	ARI
May 28 – Jul 8	TAU
Jul 9 – Aug 21	GEM
Aug 22 – Oct 10	CAN

Oct 11 – Dec 31   LEO

1963
Jan 1 – Jun 2   LEO
Jun 3 – Jul 26   VIR
Jul 27 – Sept 11   LIB
Sept 12 – Oct 24   SCO
Oct 25 - Dec 4   SAG
Dec 5 – Dec 31   CAP

1964
Jan 1- Jan 12   CAP
Jan 13 – Feb 19   AQU
Feb 20 – Mar 28   PIS
Mar 29 – May 6   ARI
May 7 – Jun 16   TAU
Jun 17 – Jul 29   GEM
Jul 30 – Sept 14   CAN
Sept 15 – Nov 5   LEO
Nov 6 – Dec 31   VIR

1965
Jan 1 – Jun 28   VIR
Jun 29 – Aug 19   LIB
Aug 20 – Oct 3   SCO
Oct 4 – Nov 13   SAG
Nov 14 – Dec 22   CAP
Dec 23 – Dec 31   AQU

1966
Jan 1 – Jan 29   AQU
Jan 30 – Mar 8   PIS
Mar 9 – Apr 16   ARI
Apr 17 – May 27   TAU
May 28 – Jul 10   GEM
Jul 11 - Aug 24   CAN
Aug 25 – Oct 11   LEO
Oct 12 – Dec 3   VIR
Dec 4 – Dec 31   LIB

1967
Jan 1 – Feb 11   LIB
Feb 12 – Mar 30   SCO

Mar 31 – Jul 18	LIB
Jul 19 – Sept 9	SCO
Sept 10 – Oct 22	SAG
Oct 23 – Nov 31	CAP
Dec 1 – Dec 31	AQU

1968

Jan 1 – Jan 8	AQU
Jan 9 – Feb 16	PIS
Feb 17 – Mar 26	ARI
May 27 – May 7	TAU
May 8 – Jun 20	GEM
Jun 21 – Aug 4	CAN
Aug 5 – Sept 20	LEO
Sept 21 – Nov 8	VIR
Nov 9 – Dec 28	LIB
Dec 29 – Dec 31	SCO

1969

Jan 1 – Feb 24	SCO
Feb 25 – Sept 20	SAG
Sept 21 – Nov 3	CAP
Nov 4 - Dec 14	AQU
Dec 15 – Dec 31	PIS

1970

Jan 1 – Jan 23	PIS
Jan 24 – Mar 6	ARI
Mar 7 – Apr 17	TAU
Apr 18 – Jun 1	GEM
Jun 2 – Jul 17	CAN
Jul 18 – Sept 2	LEO
Sept 3 – Oct 19	VIR
Oct 20 – Dec 5	LIB
Dec 6 – Dec 31	SCO

1971

Jan 1 – Jan 22	SCO
Jan 23 – Mar 11	SAG
Mar 12 – May 2	CAP
May 3 – Nov 5	AQU
Nov 6 – Dec 25	PIS
Dec 26 – Dec 31	ARI

1972

Jan 1 – Feb 9	ARI
Feb 10 – Mar 26	TAU
Mar 27 – May 11	GEM
May 12 – Jun 27	CAN
Jun 28 – Aug 14	LEO
Aug 15 – Sept 29	VIR
Sept 30 – Nov 14	LIB
Nov 15 – Dec 29	SCO
Dec 30 – Dec 31	SAG

1973

Jan 1 – Feb 11	SAG
Feb 12 – Mar 25	CAP
Mar 26 – May 7	AQU
May 8 – Jun 19	PIS
Jun 20 – Aug 11	ARI
Aug 12 – Oct 28	TAU
Oct 29 – Dec 23	ARI
Dec 24 – Dec 31	TAU

1974

Jan 1 – Feb 26	TAU
Feb 27 – Apr 19	GEM
Apr 20 – Jun 8	CAN
Jun 9 – Jul 26	LEO
Jul 27 – Sept 11	VIR
Sept 12 – Oct 27	LIB
Oct 28 – Dec 9	SCO
Dec 10 – Dec 31	SAG

1975

Jan 1 – Jan 20	SAG
Jan 21 – Mar 2	CAP
Mar 3 – Apr 10	AQU
Apr 11 – May 20	PIS
May 21 – Jun 30	ARI
Jul 1 – Aug 13	TAU
Aug 14 – Oct 16	GEM
Oct 17 – Nov 24	CAN
Nov 25 - Dec 31	GEM

1976

Jan 1 – Mar 17	GEM
Mar 18 – May 15	CAN
May 16 – Jul 5	LEO
Jul 6 – Aug 23	VIR
Aug 24 – Oct 7	LIB
Oct 8 – Nov 19	SCO
Nov 20 – Dec 31	SAG

1977

Jan 1 – Feb 8	CAP
Feb 9 – Mar 19	AQU
Mar 20 – Apr 26	PIS
Apr 27 – Jun 5	ARI
Jun 6 – Jul 16	TAU
Jul 17 – Aug 31	GEM
Sept 1 – Oct 25	CAN
Oct 26 – Dec 31	LEO

1978

Jan 1 – Jan 25	LEO
Jan 26 – Apr 9	CAN
Apr 10 – Jun 13	LEO
Jun 14 – Aug 3	VIR
Aug 4 – Sept 18	LIB
Sept 19 – Nov 1	SCO
Nov 2 – Dec 11	SAG
Dec 12 – Dec 31	CAP

1979

Jan 1 – Jan 19	CAP
Jan 20 – Feb 26	AQU
Feb 27 – Apr 6	PIS
Apr 7 – May 15	ARI
May 16 – Jun 25	TAU
Jun 26 – Aug 7	GEM
Aug 8 – Sept 23	CAN
Sept 24 – Nov 18	LEO
Nov 19 – Dec 31	VIR

1980

Jan 1 – Mar 10	VIR
Mar 11 – May 3	LEO
May 4 – Jul 9	VIR

Jul 10 – Aug 28	LIB
Aug 29 – Oct 11	SCO
Oct 12 – Nov 21	SAG
Nov 22 – Dec 29	CAP
Dec 30 – Dec 31	AQU

1981

Jan 1 – Feb 5	AQU
Feb 6 – Mar 16	PIS
Mar 17 – Apr 24	ARI
Apr 25 – Jun 4	TAU
Jun 5 – Jul 17	GEM
Jul 18 – Sept 1	CAN
Sept 2 – Oct 20	LEO
Oct 21 – Dec 15	VIR
Dec 16 – Dec 31	LIB

1982

Jan 1 – Aug 2	LIB
Aug 3 – Sept 19	SCO
Sept 20 – Oct 30	SAG
Oct 31 – Dec 9	CAP
Dec 10 – Dec 31	AQU

1983

Jan 1 – Jan 17	AQU
Jan 18 – Feb 24	PIS
Feb 25 – Apr 4	ARI
Apr 5 – May 15	TAU
May 16 – Jun 28	GEM
Jun 29 – Aug 12	CAN
Aug 13 – Sept 29	LEO
Sept 30 – Nov 17	VIR
Nov 18 – Dec 31	LIB

1984

Jan 1 – Jan 10	LIB
Jan 11 – Aug 16	SCO
Aug 17 – Oct 4	SAG
Oct 5 – Nov 14	CAP
Nov 15 – Dec 24	AQU
Dec 25 – Dec 31	PIS

1985

Jan 1 – Feb 1	PIS
Feb 2 – Mar 14	ARI
Mar 15 – Apr 25	TAU
Apr 26 – Jun 8	GEM
Jun 9 – Jul 24	CAN
Jul 25 – Sept 9	LEO
Sept 10 – Oct 26	VIR
Oct 27 – Dec 13	LIB
Dec 14 – Dec 31	SCO

1986

Jan 1 – Feb 1	SCO
Feb 2 – Mar 27	SAG
Mar 28 – Oct 8	CAP
Oct 9 – Nov 25	AQU
Nov 26 – Dec 31	PIS

1987

Jan 1 – Jan 7	PIS
Jan 8 – Feb 19	ARI
Feb 20 – Apr 4	TAU
Apr 5 – May 20	GEM
May 21 – Jul 5	CAN
Jul 6 – Aug 20	LEO
Aug 21 – Oct 7	VIR
Oct 8 – Nov 23	LIB
Nov 24 – Dec 31	SCO

1988

Jan 1 – Jan 7	SCO
Jan 8 – Feb 21	SAG
Feb 22 – Apr 5	CAP
Apr 6 – May 21	AQU
May 22 – Jul 12	PIS
Jul 13 – Oct 22	ARI
Oct 23 – Oct 31	PIS
Nov 1 – Dec 31	ARI

1989

Jan 1 – Jan 18	ARI
Jan 19 – Mar 10	TAU

Mar 11 - Apr 28	GEM
Apr 29 – Jun 15	CAN
Jun 16 – Aug 2	LEO
Aug 3 – Sept 18	VIR
Sept 19 – Nov 3	LIB
Nov 4 – Dec 17	SCO
Dec 18 – Dec 31	SAG

1990

Jan 1 – Jan 28	SAG
Jan 29 – Mar 10	CAP
Mar 11 – Apr 19	AQU
Apr 20 – May 30	PIS
May 31 – Jul 11	ARI
Jul 12 – Aug 30	TAU
Aug 31 – Dec 13	GEM
Dec 14 – Dec 31	TAU

1991

Jan 1 – Jan 19	TAU
Jan 20 – Apr 1	GEM
Apr 2 – May 25	CAN
May 26 – Jul 14	LEO
Jul 15 – Aug 31	VIR
Sept 1 –Oct 15	LIB
Oct 16 – Nov 27	SCO
Nov 28 – Dec 31	SAG

1992

Jan 1 – Jan 8	SAG
Jan 9 – Feb 17	CAP
Feb 18 – Mar 26	AQU
Mar 27 – May 4	PIS
May 5 – Jun 13	ARI
Jun 14 – Jul 25	TAU
Jul 26 – Sept 11	GEM
Sept 12 – Dec 31	CAN

1993

Jan 1 – Apr 26	CAN
Apr 27 – Jun 22	LEO
Jun 23 – Aug	VIR

Aug 11 – Sept 25	LIB
Sept 26 – Nov 8	SCO
Nov 9 – Dec 18	SAG
Dec 19 – Dec 31	CAP

1994

Jan 1 – Jan 27	CAP
Jan 28 – Mar 6	AQU
Mar 7 – Apr 13	PIS
Apr 15 – May 22	ARI
May 23 – Jul 2	TAU
Jul 3 - Aug 15	GEM
Aug 16 – Oct 3	CAN
Oct 4 – Dec 11	LEO
Dec 12 – Dec 31	VIR

1995

Jan 1 – Jan 21	VIR
Jan 22 – May 24	LEO
May 25 – Jul 20	VIR
Jul 21 – Sept 6	LIB
Sept 7 – Oct 19	SCO
Oct 20 – Nov 29	SAG
Nov 30 – Dec 31	CAP

1996

Jan 1 – Jan 7	CAP
Jan 8 – Feb 14	AQU
Feb 15 – Mar 23	PIS
Mar 24 – May 1	ARI
May 2 - Jun 11	TAU
Jun 12 – Jul 24	GEM
Jul 25 – Sept 8	CAN
Sept 9 – Oct 29	LEO
Oct 30 – Dec 31	VIR

1997

Jan 1 – Jan 2	VIR
Jan 3 – Mar 7	LIB
Mar 8 – Jun 18	VIR
Jun 19 - Aug 13	LIB
Aug 14 – Sept 27	SCO

Sept 28 – Nov 8	SAG
Nov 9 – Dec 17	CAP
Dec 18 – Dec 31	AQU

1998

Jan 1 – Jan 24	AQU
Jan 25 – Mar 3	PIS
Mar 4 – Apr 11	ARI
Apr 12 - May 22	TAU
May 23 – Jul 5	GEM
Jul 6 – Aug 19	CAN
Aug 20 – Oct 6	LEO
Oct 7 – Nov 26	VIR
Nov 27 – Dec 31	LIB

1999

Jan 1 – Jan 25	LIB
Jan 26 – May 4	SCO
May 5 – Jul 3	LIB
Jul 4 – Sept 1	SCO
Sept 2 – Oct 15	SAG
Oct 16 – Nov 25	CAP
Nov 26 – Dec 31	AQU

2000

Jan 1 – Jan 2	AQU
Jan 3 – Feb 10	PIS
Feb 11 – Mar 21	ARI
Mar 22 – May 2	TAU
May 3 – Jun 15	GEM
Jun 16 – Jul 30	CAN
July 31 – Sept 15	LEO
Sept 16 – Nov 2	VIR
Nov 3 – Dec 27	LIB
Dec 28 – Dec 31	SCO

5) JUPITER SIGNS P. 114

Now find your Jupiter Sign and read how this optimistic, expansive planet influences your Luck in life and read your Fortune for the year ahead.

Jupiter in ARIES:

6th June 1927 - 11th September 1927
24th January 1928 - 4th June 1928
11th May 1939 – 20th October 1939
21st Dec 1939 – 15 May 1940
22nd April 1951 – 28th April 1952
4th April 1963 – 11th April 1964
19th March 1975 – 25th March 1976
3rd March 1987 – 8th March 1988
13th February 1999 – 20th June 1999
23rd October 1999 – 14th February 2000

Jupiter in TAURUS:

4th June 1928 - 12th June 1929
16th May 1940 – 26th May 1941
29th April 1952 – 9th May 1953
12th April 1964 – 22nd April 1965
26th March 1976 – 22nd August 1976
17th October 1976 – 3rd April 1977
9th March 1988 – 21st July 1988
1st December 1988 – 10th March 1989
21st June 1999 – 23rd October 1999
15th February 2000 – 30th June 2000

Jupiter in GEMINI:

12th June 1929 - 27th June 1930
27th May 1941 – 9th June 1942
10th May 1953 – 23rd May 1954
23rd April 1965 – 20th Sept 1965
17th Nov 1965 – 5th May 1966

23rd August 1976 – 16th October 1976
4th April 1977 – 20th August 1977
31st December 1977 – 11th April 1978
22nd July 1988 – 30th November 1988
11th March 1989 – 30th July 1989
30th June 2000 - 13th July 2001

Jupiter in CANCER:

12th July 1918 - 2nd August 1919
27th June 1930 – 17th July 1931
10th June 1942 – 30th June 1943
24th May 1954 – 12th June 1955
21st Sept 1965 – 16th November 1965
6th May 1966 – 27th Sept 1966
16th January 1967 – 22nd May 1967
21st August 1977 – 30th December 1977
12th April 1978 – 4th September 1978
1st March 1979 – 19th April 1979
31st July 1989 – 17th August 1990

Jupiter in LEO:

2nd August 1919 - 27th August 1920
17th July 1931 - 11th August 1932
1st July 1943 – 25th July 1944
13th June 1955 – 16th November 1955
18th January 1956 – 7th July 1956
28th September 196 – 15th January 1967
23rd May 1967 – 18th October 1967
27th February 1968 – 15th June 1968
5th September 1978 – 28th February 1979
20th April 1979 – 28th September 1979
18th August 1990 – 11th September 1991

Jupiter in VIRGO:

27th August 1920 - 26th September 1921
11th August 1932 - 10th September 1933

26th July 1944 – 24th August 1945
17th November 1955 – 17th January 1956
8th July 1956 – 12th December 1956
20th February 1957 – 6th August 1957
19th October 1967 – 26th February 1968
16th June 1968 – 15th November 1968
31st March 1969 – 15th July 1969
29th September 1979 – 26th October 1980
12th September 1991 – 10th October 1992

Jupiter in LIBRA:

26th September 1921 - 27th October 1922
10th September 1933 - 11th October 1934
25th August 1945 – 24th September 1946
13th December 1956 – 19th February 1957
7th August 1957 – 13th January 1958
21st March 1958 – 6th September 1958
16th November 1968 – 30th March 1969
16th July 1969 – 16th December 1969
30th April 1970 – 15th August 1970
27th October 1980 – 26th November 1981
10th October 1992 – 10th November 1993

Jupiter in SCORPIO:

27th October 1922 - 25th November 1923
11th October 1934 - 9th November 1935
25th September 1946 – 23rd October 1947
14th January 1958 – 20th March 1958
7th September 1958 – 10th February 1959
25th April 1959 – 5th October 1959
17th December 1969 – 29th April 1970
16th August 1970 – 13th January 1971
5th June 1971 – 11th September 1971
27th November – 25th December 1982
10th November 1993 – 9th December 1994

Jupiter in SAGITTARIUS:

25th November 1923 - 18th December 1924
9th November 1935 – 2nd December 1936
24th October 1947 – 14th November 1948
11th February – 24th April 1959
6th October 1959 – 1st March 1960
10th June 1960 – 25th October 1960
14th January 1971 – 4th June 1971
12th September 1971 - 6th February 1972
25th July 1972 – 25th September 1972
26th December 1982 – 19th January 1984
9th December 1994 – 1st January 1996

Jupiter in CAPRICORN:

18th December 1924 - 6th January 1926
2nd December 1936 – 20th December 1937
15th November 1948 – 12th April 1949
28th June 1949 – 30th November 1949
2nd March 1960 – 9th June 1960
26th October 1960 – 14th March 1961
12th August 1961 – 3rd November 1961
7th February 1972 – 24th July 1972
26th September 1972 – 22nd February 1973
20th January 1982 – 6th February 1985
2nd January 1996 – 20th January 1997

Jupiter in AQUARIUS

18th January 1927 – 6th January 1926
20th December 1937 – 14th May 1938
5th August 1938 – 30th December 1938
13th April 1949 – 27th June 1949
1st December 1949 – 14th April 1950
15th September 1950 – 1st December 1950
15th March 1961 – 11th August 1961
4th November 1961 – 25th March 1962
23rd February 1973 – 7th April 1974
7th February 1985 – 20th February 1986
21st January 1997 – 4th February 1998

Jupiter in PISCES:

18th January 1927 - 6th June 1927
11th September 1927 - 24th January 1928
1st June 1938 – 30th July 1938
30th October 1939 – 21st December 1939
5th January 1939 – 11th May 1939
15th April 1950 – 14th September 1950
2nd December – 21st April 1951
26th March 1962 – 3rd April 1963
8th April 1974 – 18th March 1975
21st February – 2nd March 1987
5th February 1998 – 13th February 1999

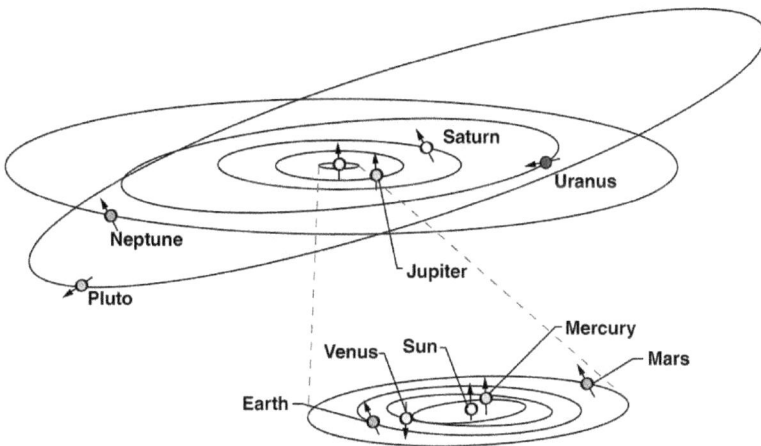

6) AZTEC Love Style Oracle. P331

Could Ancient America hold the clue to your destiny?

The Aztec Zodiac is based on an ancient astrological system which uses 13 day cycles to yield 20 signs.

The Aztec symbols are Crocodile, Wind, House, Lizard, Serpent, Owl, Deer, Rabbit, Water, Flower, Monkey, Grass, Reed, Ocelot, Eagle, Vulture, Earthquake, Flint, Rain, and Dog...

Find out which symbol will reveal your Aztec personality and Soul Mate by following the five simple steps below.

Stage 1: To begin the process, find the month of your birth below, which will give you a figure to carry over to the next stage.

January, begin with	0
February, begin with	31
March, begin with	59
April, begin with	90
May, begin with	120
June, begin with	151
July, begin with	181
August, begin with	212
September, begin with	243
October, begin with	273
November, begin with	304
December, begin with	334

For example, if you were born in July, jot down the number 181, and if you were born in January, you actually do not have a number to begin with yet.

Stage 2: Add the number of the day you were born to your number from stage 1. For example, if you were born on 11th July, add 11 to 181 to give you 192. For those born in January, you now have your day of birth as your starting point.

Stage 3: Now add the number which corresponds with your year of birth on the table below. For example if you were born on 11th July 1974, add 5 to 192, giving you 197.

1900	17
1901	2
1902	7
1903	12
1904	18
1905	3
1906	8
1907	13
1908	19
1909	4
1910	9
1911	14
1912	0
1913	5
1914	10
1915	15
1916	1
1917	6
1918	11
1919	16
1920	1
1921	7
1922	12
1923	17
1924	2
1925	8
1926	13
1927	18
1928	3
1929	9
1930	14
1931	19

1932	4
1933	10
1934	15
1935	0
1936	5
1937	11
1938	16
1939	1
1940	6
1941	12
1942	17
1943	2
1944	7
1945	13
1946	18
1947	3
1948	8
1949	14
1950	19
1951	4
1952	9
1953	15
1954	0
1955	5
1956	10
1957	16
1958	1
1959	6
1960	11
1961	17
1962	2
1963	7
1964	12
1965	18
1966	3
1967	8
1968	13
1969	19
1970	4
1971	9
1972	14
1973	0
1974	5
1975	10
1976	15
1977	1
1978	6

1979	11
1980	16
1981	2
1982	7
1983	12
1984	17
1985	3
1986	8
1987	13
1988	18
1989	4
1990	9
1991	14
1992	19
1993	5
1994	10
1995	15
1996	0
1997	5
1998	16
1999	1

Stage 4: If you were born in a leap year, ON or AFTER 29th February in the following years, add 1 to your current result. 1948, 1952, 1956, 1960, 1964, 1968, 1972, 1976, 1980, 1984

Stage 5: You should now have your final number, which for the example we are using is 197.

Find the last digit of your number in the ONES DIGIT column below. Number 7 is the last digit of our example, which reveals Deer or Earthquake as the possible symbols for this date of birth.

To find which sign is yours look at your second to last digit and match it to the TENS DIGIT BOX below.

So for our example, the number 9 is the second to last digit, which reveals the sample symbol to be Earthquake....Earth shattering!

ONES DIGIT	TENS DIGIT	
	0 2 4 6 8	1 3 5 7 9
1	Crocodile	Monkey
2	Wind	Grass
3	House	Reed
4	Lizard	Ocelot
5	Serpent	Eagle
6	OWL	Vulture
7	Deer	Earthquake
8	Rabbit	Flint
9	Water	Rain
0	Flower	Dog

ABOUT THE AUTHOR

SARAH DELAMERE HURDING IS ONE OF IRELAND'S AND
AMERICA'S BEST KNOWN MYSTICS. A SEER, HEALER,
LIFE COACH, WRITER, AUTHOR, ACADEMIC, FORMER CBS
RADIO HOST AND WORLD PUJA NETWORK PRESENTER,
OM TIMES FEATURED WRITER AND CONSCIOUSNESS
FACILITATOR, SARAH BRINGS A FULL RANGE OF TAL-
ENTS TO THE TABLE.

Sarah is known for her accuracy, healing and
manifesting abilities. Louis Walsh and Simon Cowell were stunned
into silence when Sarah predicted the full line up of Irish Popstars
SIX. She read for 32 talented kids and accurately named the final six.
Sarah has also have been publically recognised as an effective healer.
She can lift pain with her hands pretty much instantly, and has helped
clients with all kinds of issues and
conditions. Her specialities are lifting pain and
depression, as well as energy boosts, major clearings and resets using
distance healing techniques. Once you sign up with Sarah, her commitment to you is relentless and strong. She works with you 24/7
with advice, guidance, energy, prayer and mutually agreed intentions
for days, weeks and months depending on your needs. Find Sarah at
www.sarahdelamer.com

#mermaidmagic

www.ingramcontent.com/pod-product-compliance
Lightning Source LLC
Chambersburg PA
CBHW060234100426
42742CB00011B/1527